Handbook of Research on Catholic Education

Recent Titles in
The Greenwood Educators' Reference Collection

Planning and Managing Death Issues in the Schools: A Handbook
Robert L. Deaton and William A. Berkan

Handbook for the College Admissions Profession
Claire C. Swann and Stanley E. Henderson, editors

Student Records Management
M. Therese Ruzicka and Beth Lee Weckmueller, editors

Supportive Supervision in Schools
Raymond C. Garubo and Stanley William Rothstein

Substance Abuse on Campus: A Handbook for College and University Personnel
P. Clayton Rivers and Elsie R. Shore, editors

Working with Lesbian, Gay, Bisexual, and Transgender College Students: A Handbook
for Faculty and Administrators
Ronni L. Sanlo, editor

Practical Pedagogy for the Jewish Classrooom: Classroom Management, Instruction,
and Curriculum Development
Daniel B. Kohn

Students in Discord: Adolescents with Emotional and Behavioral Disorders
C. Robin Boucher

Higher Education Administration: A Guide to Legal, Ethical, and Practical Issues
Norma M. Goonen and Rachel S. Blechman

Issues in Web-Based Pedagogy: A Critical Primer
Robert A. Cole, editor

Succeeding in an Academic Career: A Guide for Faculty of Color
Mildred García, editor

Developing Non-Hierarchical Leadership on Campus: Case Studies and Best Practices
in Higher Education
Charles L. Outcalt, Shannon K. Faris, and Kathleen M. McMahon, editors

Handbook of Research on Catholic Education

Edited by
Thomas C. Hunt, Ellis A. Joseph,
and Ronald J. Nuzzi

The Greenwood Educators' Reference Collection

GREENWOOD PRESS
Westport, Connecticut • London

Library of Congress Cataloging-in-Publication Data

Handbook of research on Catholic education / edited by Thomas C. Hunt, Ellis A. Joseph,
 and Ronald J. Nuzzi.
    p. cm.—(The Greenwood educators' reference collection, ISSN 1056–2192)
    Includes index.
    ISBN 0–313–31341–5 (alk. paper)
    1. Catholic Church—Education—United States.   2. Catholic schools—United States.
 I. Hunt, Thomas C., 1930–   II. Joseph, Ellis A.   III. Nuzzi, Ronald James, 1958–   IV. Series.
 LC501.H34 2001
 371.071'2'73—dc21   00–069133

British Library Cataloguing in Publication Data is available.

Library of Congress Catalog Card Number: 00–069133
ISBN: 0–313–31341–5
ISSN: 1056–2192

First published in 2001

Greenwood Press, 88 Post Road West, Westport, CT 06881
An imprint of Greenwood Publishing Group, Inc.
www.greenwood.com

Printed in the United States of America

The paper used in this book complies with the
Permanent Paper Standard issued by the National
Information Standards Organization (Z39.48–1984).

10 9 8 7 6 5 4 3 2 1

Contents

Tables and Figures

TABLES

FIGURES

Preface

Research in Catholic education has been accomplished with very few outlets of high quality. For years the Catholic University of America provided an admirable service by publishing doctoral dissertations treating historical, philosophical, and timely practical topics in depth. Recently, the University of Dayton, the University of San Francisco, Saint Louis University, and Fordham University have launched a scholarly publication, *Catholic Education: A Journal of Inquiry and Practice*. It represents the major organ for research in Catholic education.

In the 1960s, the *National Catholic Guidance Conference Journal* succeeded the *Catholic Counselor*. Both no longer exist. *The Catholic Educational Review, The Catholic School Journal, Notre Dame Journal of Education*, and *The Catholic Educator* also no longer exist. The National Catholic Educational Association (NCEA) currently supports *Momentum*, and this journal and *Today's Catholic Teacher* constitute the principal publications for practitioners. The NCEA has also provided a comprehensive summary of research in Catholic education by publishing 10-year updates. Over the years, doctoral-granting Catholic colleges and universities have been sources of research on Catholic education even though none can be classified as research universities. Summaries of recent doctoral dissertations in Catholic education have been published by the NCEA.

The editors have sought to compile a handbook of research on Catholic education in areas such as philosophy, law, curriculum, Church documents, and so on. While handbooks on research have proliferated in recent years in public education, none have been attempted for Catholic education. The impetus for handbooks of research has been to acknowledge the existence of a knowledge base undergirding educational practice. The editors feel Catholic education deserves the same impetus.

Acknowledgments

The editors are greatly indebted to the authors for their contributions to the *Handbook* and for their adherence to the policies that guided the preparation of this volume.

We are grateful to Mrs. Colleen Wildenhaus for her assistance in preparing this volume. Ms. Barbara Day contributed to the development of two sections of the *Handbook*.

The Greenwood Publishing Group has been most cooperative in confirming the vision to produce this volume.

Special gratitude is expressed to Thomas Lasley II, Dean of the School of Education and Allied Professions at the University of Dayton, for his support of serious scholarship and for his personal commitment to scholarly activity.

The editors dedicate this volume to Karen Hunt, Guitta Joseph, and Paul and Ann Nuzzi.

Handbook of Research on Catholic Education

Chapter 1

Selected Church Documents: The Organization of Centralized Authority in Catholic Educational Administration

Ronald J. Nuzzi

This chapter focuses on the centralization of authority in Rome for all Catholic educational institutions. By tracing the ever-increasing involvement of Rome in matters of education, we can appreciate the intricacies of the historical process and gain a vantage point from which to understand current church structures. While there are certainly other avenues available to see this process at work in history, official church documents on educational administration dating back to the sixteenth century establish a solid foundation on which to begin.

The current delineation of the hierarchical structure of the Roman Catholic Church can be found in the annual publication *Annuario Pontificio*. Published every year in Rome, the *Annuario Pontificio* lists the offices as well as the names of the current office holders for all Vatican departments. Although the Italian title roughly translates as "Pontifical Annual" or "Pontifical Yearbook," it is known simply as the *Annuario*. It describes the up-to-date structure of all curial offices, including the congregation or Vatican office with authority for Catholic education. Vatican offices are commonly referred to as "curial" offices and the members as belonging to the "Curia." The Latin cognate suggests that curial officials are charged to care for a particular area of administration. Vatican departments are known as congregations. The text of the *Annuario* is by custom written in Italian. The Italian title for the congregation responsible for education translates as the "Congregation for Catholic Education and for Seminaries and Other Institutions of Study." The Latin title, often used in official congregational documents, is *Congregatio de Institutione Catholica de Seminariis atque Studiorum Institutis* (*Annuario Pontificio*, 1993). While introducing the Congregazione Per L'Educazione Cattolica (Dei Seminari e Degli Instituti Di Studi), the *Annuario* refers readers to a lengthy footnote that contains the history of the congregation. The historical note is a veritable treasure, tracing in broad strokes the past 400 years of the congregation's work.

> Con la Cost. *Immensa* (22 gen. 1588) Sisto V eresse la *Congregatio pro universitate studii romani* per presiedere agli studi della Universita di Roma e di altre insigni Universita (Bologna, Parigi, Salamanca, ecc.). Leone XII, con la Cost. *Quod divina sapientia*(28 ag. 1824), creo la *Congregatio studiorum* per le scuole dello Stato Pontificio. Dal 1870 questa cominicio ad esercitare la sua autorita sulle universita cattoliche. La riforma di San Pio X (Cost. Apost. *Sapienti consilio*, 29 giu. 1908) le confermo tale compito. Benedetto XV, con Motu Proprio del 4 nov. 1915, eresse in Congregazione la sezione dei Seminari esistenti presso la Congr. Concistoriale e vi uni la *Congregatio Studiorum* dandole il titolo di *Congrega tio de Seminariis et Studiorum Universitatibus*. Con la Cost. Ap. *Regimini Ecclesiae Universae*, del 15 ag. 1967, Paolo VI le conferi il titolo di *S. Congregatio pro Institutione Catholica* aggiungendo un terzo Ufficio per le Scuole cattoliche.
> Presso la medesima Congregazione e stata eretta la Pontificia Opera per le Vocazioni Sacerdotali (Motu Proprio di Pio XI *Cum Nobis*, del 4 nov. 1941), la cui azione ha ricevuto maggior impulso e illustrazione dal Decreto Conciliare *Optatam totius*, n. 2 (28 ott. 1965).
> La competenza della Congregazione per l'Educazione Cattolica si esplica in tre settori diversi: a) su tutti i Seminari—eccettuati quelli dipendenti dalle Congregazioni per le Chiese Orientali e per l'Evangelizzazione dei Popoli—e su tutte le Case di formazione degli Istituti Religiosi o Secolari per quanto attiene alla formazaione scientifica dei loro alunni; b) su tutte le Universita, Facolta, Istituti e Scuole Superiori di studi ecclesiastici o civili dipendenti da persone fisiche o morali ecclesiastiche, nonche sulle Istituzioni e Associazioni aventi scopo scientifico; c) su tutte le Scuole e Istituti di istruzione e di educazione di qualsiasi ordine e grado pre-universitario dipendenti dall'Autorita Ecclesiastica, diretti alla formazione della gioventu laica, esclusi quelli dipendenti dalle Congregazione per le Chiese Orientali e per l'Evangelizzazione dei Popoli. La Costituzione Apostolica *Pastor Bonus*, del 28 giu. 1988, ha cambiato il nome della Congregazione in Congregazione per l'Educazione Cattolica (dei Seminari e degli Istutiti di Studi), confermando sostanzialmente la competenza che le era stata affidata dalla *Regimini Ecclesiae Universae*. (1993, pp. 1732–1733)

With the Constitution *Immensa* (Jan. 22, 1558) Sixtus V established the *Congregation pro universitate studii romani* to preside over the studies of the University of Rome and other notable universities (Bologna, Paris, Salamanca, etc.). Leo XII, with the Constitution *Quod divina sapientia* (Aug. 28, 1824), created the *Congregatio studiorum* for the schools of the Papal State. From the year 1870 this congregation began to exert its authority over the Catholic universities. The reform of St. Pius X (Apostolic Constitution *Sapienti consilio*, June 29, 1908) confirmed such a duty. Benedict XV, with a Motu Proprio of November 4, 1915, established in the congregation the section of existing seminaries beside the consistorial congregation and united them with the *Congregatio Studiorum*, giving them the title *Congregatio de Seminariis et Studiorum Universitatibus*. With the Apostolic Constitution *Regimini Ecclesiae Universae* of Aug. 15, 1967, Paul VI conferred upon them the title of *Sacra Congregation pro Institutione Catholica*, adding a third office for Catholic schools.

Along with this same congregation was established the Pontifical Work for Priestly Vocations (Motu Proprio of Pius XII *Cum Nobis*, of November 4, 1941), an action which received a major impetus and further explanation by the conciliar decree of Vatican II, *Optatam totius*, n. 2 (October 28, 1965).

The sphere of jurisdiction of the Congregation for Catholic Education consists of three distinct areas: a) over all Seminaries—excluding those dependent on the Congregation for Eastern Churches and the Congregation for the Evangelization of the People—and over all of the houses of formation for Religious or Secular Institutes regarding the academic formation of their students; b) over all universities, faculties, institutes, and schools of higher education for ecclesiastical studies or civil dependents of persons with a moral or physical ecclesiastical affiliation, not only over the institutions and associations whose aims are academic; c) over all the schools and institutes of instruction and education of whatever level and pre-university grade which are dependents of an ecclesiastical authority, directed to the formation of non-clerical youth, not including those dependents of the Congregation for the Eastern Churches and the Congregation for the Evangelization of the People.

The Apostolic Constitution *Pastor Bonus*, of June 28, 1988 changed the name of the congregation to the Congregation for Catholic Education (Of Seminaries and Institutes of Study), confirming fundamentally the jurisdiction that was already put forth in *Regimini Ecclesiae Universae* (*Annuario Pontificio* 1993, pp. 1732–1733). [Unpublished translation provided by James M. Frabutt, The University of North Carolina, Greensboro.]

We have here in abbreviated form the documentary history of the Congregation for Catholic Education as well as the official delineation of the current three spheres of jurisdiction it enjoys. Before examining the precise nature of its spheres of jurisdiction, a summary and analysis of the documents cited is in order.

In the historical note from the *Annuario Pontificio* (1993) cited, a total of eight church documents are listed as playing a part in the historical formation and development of the congregation. Table 1.1 summarizes the historical development by indicating the document, its date of publication, and the pope under whom it was issued. While all of the documents are important in terms of establishing a direction for the congregation, it is especially important to distinguish among them the type of document that each one is. In short, while all eight are official church documents, the eight represent a total of three different types of documents, each with a different purpose and force. The three types of documents represented in the list include: (1) five apostolic constitutions; (2) two documents issued *motu proprio*; and (3) one conciliar decree.

Apostolic constitutions are formal papal decrees concerning matters of faith and the affairs of the universal church. It is a "most solemn document issued by a pope in his own name" (*New Catholic Encyclopedia*, 1967b, p. 946). While the subject being addressed may be doctrinal, disciplinary, or administrative, the apostolic constitution is usually reserved for matters of great importance. As such, apostolic constitutions are written according to a formal style, usually beginning with the words *Constitutio Apostolica*, followed by a statement of the subject matter (*New Catholic Encyclopedia*, 1967a). The name of the pope in whose name it is promulgated is then inscribed.

Table 1.1
Historical Development of Documents

Document	Date of Publication	Pope
Immensa	January 22, 1588	Sixtus V
Quod divina sapientia	August 28, 1824	Leo XII
Sapienti consilio	June 29, 1908	St. Pius X
Seminaria clericorum[1]	November 4, 1915	Benedict XV
Cum Nobis	November 4, 1941	Pius XII
Optatam totius	October 28, 1965	Paul VI
Regimini Ecclesiae Universae	August 15, 1967	Paul VI
Pastor Bonus	June 28, 1988	John Paul II

[1]The document issued *motu proprio* by Benedict XV, *Seminaria clericorum*, is not mentioned by name in the historical note from the *Annuario Pontifico*. The *Annuario* simply makes mention of the fact that Benedict XV published a document *motu proprio* on November 4, 1915, without making reference to its title. The name of the document is supplied here for consistency in the table. A discussion of the content of the document will follow.

A document issued *motu proprio* is a papal pronouncement as well, but is a less solemn document drawn up and issued by the pope in his own name and on his own initiative (*New Catholic Encyclopedia*, 1967b) The Latin phrase *motu proprio* means "by his own force or will." A document issued *motu proprio* is understood to be an executive act of the pope and therefore concerns only disciplinary matters of a less than urgent nature (*Code of Canon Law*, 1983).

Conciliar decrees are, by nature, acts of ecumenical councils and are directed to the universal church. They are produced by the worldwide body of bishops in union with the pope and address issues of importance to the entire church. The most recent ecumenical council, Vatican II, produced 16 such decrees of which *Optatam totius* (Paul VI, 1965) is one.

The various documents that constitute the history of the Congregation for Catholic Education are categorized as follows:

Apostolic Constitution	Motu Proprio	Conciliar Decree
Immensa	*Seminaria clericorum*	*Optatam totius*
Quod divina sapientia	*Cum Nobis*	
Sapienti consilio		
Regimini Ecclesiae Universae		
Pastor Bonus		

Proceeding in chronological order according to date of publication, an analysis and commentary on each document will provide an understanding of the centralization of authority in Rome for all Catholic educational institutions.

The official history of this congregation begins with the publication of the Apostolic Constitution *Immensa* by Sixtus V on January 22, 1588. The official Latin version of *Immensa* can be found in *Bullarium Romanum A Pio Quarto Usque Ad Innocentium IX*, 9th edition, vol. II, pp. 615–622. The Latin title translates "Papal Bulls from Pius IV to Innocent IX." *Immensa* (Sixtus V, 1588) structured the Vatican offices into 15 departments. *Immensa* was the foundational document for the Roman Curia as it divided papal advisors into separate departments or congregations, each headed by a cardinal. What *Immensa* termed *Congregatio decima*, or the tenth congregation, was the congregation *pro Universitate Studii Romani*, the congregation to preside over the studies of the University of Rome (Sixtus V, 1588). In establishing this official structure for oversight of university education, *Immensa* makes clear the jurisdiction that the congregation will enjoy and why it is necessary. The full citation from *Immensa* concerning the purpose of the congregation reads:

Illud etiam cogitantes, quod literarum cognitio, liberalesque doctrinae et disciplinae, quibus iuuentus in publicis Gymnasiis instruitur et eruditur magnam Christianae Reip.si cum pietate coniungantur, afferunt utilitatem: tunc enim Ciuitates et Regna optime administrantur, cum sapientes atque intelligentes gubernacula possident, ob eam sane causam Romani Gymnasii eiusque Universitatis ornandae et amplificandae curam merito gerimus, unde et ipsam universitatem ab aere alieno vigintiduorum millium scutorum et aliis pluribus oneribus sublevavimus, ac plane liberavimus.

Itaque ut illius rationibus quamoptime prospiciamus, Cardinales quinque eidem Gymnasio, et universitati, illiusque reformationi praeficimus, quibus facultatem concedimus, ut cum opus fuerit, praeclaros Theologiae Magistros, Iurisconsultos egregios, et liberalium artium professores eximios undecumque ad iuuentutem erudiendam euocent, qui morum integritate, eruditione, atque elegantia literatum non minus praestent, quam peritia, usque docendi, assiduisque praeletionibus iuuentes instruant, utque singulis scientiarum Magistris pro meritorum ratione, re tamen nobiscum, aut cum successoribus nostris participata, stipendum constituant. Insuper, cum in hac Alma Urbe nostra, singulari Dei beneficio iner alias discentium scholas Graecorum, Maronitarum, Neophytotum, ingeneri Pontificum liberalitate, atque munificentia, erecta sint Collegia, congruisque redditibus dotata, in quibus sacra Theolgia, liberalesque artes Hebraice, Graece, Arabice, et Chaldaice edocentur, eisdem Cardinalibus iniungimus, ut horum Collegiorum Alumnos ad literatum studia ardentior animo complectenda, quod ad fidei Catholicae propagationem, et literarum ornamentum, et ingenia excolenda maxime pertinet, opportune pro eorum pietate et prudentia omni adhibito studio, excitari curent. Denique cum in praecipius Christiani Orbis partibus sancta haec Apostolica Sedes, ut pia mater, in signes quasdam Universitates, in quibus sacrarum literarum, legum, et attium praestantissima studia florent, olim in tutelam, et clientelam receperit suam, nimirum Parisiensem, Oxoniensem, Bononiensem, Salamantinam, ut in eis scilicet ex Apostolicae Sedis protectione bonarum artium studia, tanto maiori cum fructu excolerentur, nos et illas ipsas, et caetetas Catholicas Universitates paterna benevolentia complectentes, nec ipsam Oxoniensem, quantum in nobis est, deferentes, sed exintimo animi affectu ad mattis gremium, et ad viam salutis revocantes, omnesque intimo cordis affectu, et summa benevolentia prosequentes, ac sub nostra et beati Petri Apostolorum Principis protectione iterum suscipientes eidem Congregationi imponimus, ut earundem Universitatum, atque ad eas pertinentium nego- tiorum apud Sedem Apostolicam curam gerat, illarumque necessitates, nobis successo- ribusque notris ordine exponat, ut eis ex paterna charitate opem et auxilium affere valeamus, easque interdum per literas, visitet, nostroque nomine Catholicis viris Apos- tolicam benedictionem impertiatur, illisque ut prospera cuncta eueniant, aliis vero spiri- tum consilii sanioris, a Deo Optimo Maximo deprecetur. (Sixtus V, 1588, pp. 619–620)

In order to advance the learning of arts and sciences so that the students in public schools, combining knowledge and Christian integrity, may be better prepared to become good administrators and intelligent governors of cities and kingdoms, we allocate twenty- two thousand monetary units to expand and improve the schools and the University of Rome; moreover, we exempt and free them from all fiscal duties.

For the reasons mentioned we appoint five cardinals to oversee these reforms of the Gymnasium (secondary school) and of the University. We give them authority to select, as needed by the students, eleven prominent Masters of Theology, famous lawyers, and notable professors of the liberal arts. They should be righteous, learned, well-versed in letters, experienced teachers, and dedicated to the education of children. They should be remunerated for their services according to their expertise; we and our successors shall allocate a fund for this purpose. Moreover, in this Great City, which accommodates different schools such as those of the Greeks, the Maronites, and the Neophites, we should be able, by the grace of God, to establish colleges for the study of Greek, Hebrew, Arabic, and the Chaldean languages, as well as for the learning of Holy Theology and the liberal arts. These schools shall be endowed with adequate income by the great liberality and munificence of the Supreme Pontiff. We demand that the same cardinals use all their efforts to stimulate the students of these colleges to eagerly embrace the study of letters, for the development of their intelligence, virtue and righteousness, for the propagation of the Catholic faith and to eradicate illiteracy. Finally, we shall enact the same plan used by the Apostolic See in the past, when it sponsored famous univer- sities in strategic parts of the Christian World, such as the Universities of Paris, Oxford, Bologna and Salamanca, which excel greatly in the studies of the Holy Letters, the Law and the Fine Arts. In order to improve the sponsorship of the Apostolic See for the propagation of the fine arts, we shall take fatherly care of all Catholic universities; we will do everything we can not only for the University of Oxford, which we esteem greatly, but for every university, which we will heed with the love of the heart of a mother. Impelled by our benevolence, we invoke the protection of Peter, Prince of the Apostles, and we appoint this Congregation to be a liaison between the Apostolic See and the universities for all needs and concerns. It shall advise our successors how to continue this endeavor and it shall visit and impart in our name the Apostolic blessing on all Catholic men, and pray to our great God to prosper us and give wisdom to all. (Sixtus V, 1588, pp. 619–620) [Translation is original.]

As the first document to define and describe the role of the central admin- stration of the Catholic Church in relation to university education, *Immensa* (Sixtus V, 1588) has broad goals. Caring for the development, maturation, and education of future religious and political leaders is foremost among these goals. As we have already seen, universities provided a fertile ground for the nurturing of young talent and a gathering place for the children of nobility.

We have mentioned here for the first time a concern for the qualifications of those who would teach in the university. *Immensa* (Sixtus V, 1588) demands not only that they be extremely well qualified professionally, but also that they be righteous and dedicated to children. Their compensation is to be fixed according to their level of expertise.

In promising financial support for its mandates, the Apostolic See portrays itself as a kind parent figure in its solicitude for universities. The document states that the Apostolic See will "take fatherly care" of all Catholic universities and that this care will show itself as "the love of the heart of a mother." Clearly, the Apostolic See views itself in a nurturing and supportive role and expresses it through the use of the parent-child image. Children, however, often need the protection of their parents. As the children of the Apostolic See, the universities are the object of the financial support and benevolence of the pope. The congregation is established to be a liaison, a surrogate parent, in order to make known to the parent the needs of the children. In this regard, the congregation is to communicate the needs and concerns of universities to the Apostolic See.

The next official papal action regarding this congregation and its involvement with educational concerns comes centuries later in the Apostolic Constitution *Quod divina sapienta* of Pope Leo XII. Published August 28, 1824, the document had a general concern for education and a particular interest in the schools within the Papal State.

Titulus I.
De congregatione Studiorum

1.

#2. Congregatio extabit, quae tum Romae tum in Pontificia studiis praeerit.

2.

Constabit S.E.R. cardinalibus secretario status, S.E.R. camerario, urbis vicario, praefecto Indicis, praefecto Boni Regiminis, aliisque cardinalibus quos summus pontifex delegerit: e quibus Sanctitas sua congregationis praefectum nominabit.

3.

Huic erit a secretis dignus, et idoneus vir ecclesiasticus vel familiaris summi pontificis, vel curiae Romanae praelatus. Ipsa in comitiis ac deliberationibus caeterarum congregationum leges servabit. Secretarius diligenter in tabulas acta referet, tabulari curam geret, aliaque a s. congregatione, eiusque praefecto sibi commissa perficiet.

4.

Sacrae huiusmodi congregationi universitates omnes, publicae, ac privatae scholae urbis ac totius Pontificiae ditionis, quodvis etiam collegium, caeterique erudiendis adolescentibus addicti parento in iis omnibus, quae ad institutionem pertinent.

5.

Hasce consitutiones, ac ceteras, quae in posterum in lucem prodierint, sacra congregatio diligentissime servandas curabit.

6.

Si quando s. congregationi placuerit universitatem aliquam, seu scholam publicam, vel aliud tradendae doctrinae institutum publicum invisere, per legatum aliquem id praestet, qui aut sacram congregationem de rerum statu certiorem reddat, aut ex eiusdem auctoritate provideat in iis, quorum sibi cura demandata fuerit.

7.

Si quis a superioribus locorum in rebus ad universitates, publicas scholas, aliave tradendae doctrinae instituta spectantibus, aliquid gravaminis sibi illatum judicet, ad sacram congregationem preces deferat.

8.

Quodvis rescriptum aut summi pontificis, aut ex eius audientia datum in rebus ad studia pertinentibus executionem non hebeat, nisi postquam s. congregationis secretariae exhibitum, ut in tabulas referatur.

Titulus II
De universitatibus

9.

#3. Duae sunto universitates primariae, universitas Romana, quae dicitur archigymnasium Romanum, et universitas Bononiensis.

10.

In unaquaque ipsarum cathedrae extabunt non minus quam triginta octo praeter musea, atque alia instituta doctrinarum, ad hoc, ut adolescentes possint proficere in omni disciplinarum varietate; quique studiorum cursum expleverint, opportunitatem habeant, atque excitentur, ut doctrinarum, quibus iam se excoluerint, uberrimam cognitionem acquirant.

11.

Quinque sunto universitates secundariae, Ferrariensis, Perusina, Camerinensis, Macaeratensis, et Firmana. In hisce universitatibus extabunt cathedrae non minus quam decem, et septem, praeter musea, atque alia opportuna instituta.

12.

Antequam universitates secundariae valeant uti privilegio conferendarum laurearum, aliorumque graduum, a s. congregatione per viros ab ipsa delectos, et instructos monitis necessariis, et opportunis perlustrentur.

13.

S. congregatio iubeat typis imprimi et cathedrarum elenchum vulgari, quas universitates habebunt: nec minui, nec augeri earum numerum fas erit, quae cuique universitatum assignatae sint, necque res tradendae mutari possint sine eiusdem congregationis facultate; secus privilegium conferendi laureas aliosque gradus amitatur. (pp. 86–87)

Chapter One
The Congregation of Studies

1.

#2. A congregation shall be established which should be in charge of all schools in Rome and in the Pontifical lands.

2.

It shall include His Most Reverend Eminence, the Cardinal Secretary of State, His Most Reverend Eminence, the Cardinal Chamberlain, the Vicar of Rome, the Superintendent of the Index, the Superintendent of the Good Regimen, and all other cardinals chosen by the Pontiff, from whom His Holiness shall select a President.

3.

A worthy, competent Secretary should be selected from the clergymen, from the friends of the Pontiff, or from the prelates of the Roman Curia. He shall diligently keep in the registry all the records of the assemblies and deliberations of the other congregations. He shall also take care of the archives and all the documents concerning the Holy Congregation and its President.

4.

He should keep all the records related to all the Universities of this Holy Congregation, to all the public and private schools of Rome and the Pontifical lands, to all the students attending our schools and to everything else pertaining to our institutions.

5.

He should save all the new rules and regulations that this Holy Congregation will issue in the future.

6.

A legate should be appointed who, when the Holy Congregation deems it necessary, shall inspect a university, a public school, or a public trade institute. He should give account to the Holy Congregation of the status of that institution or, by his own authority, take the necessary measures for the care of the matters assigned to him.

7.

If any of the superintendents of the local universities, public schools, or other trade institutes feels burdened by matters pertaining to studies, he should appeal to the Holy Congregation.

8.

No transcript relative to the Pontiff or one of his audiences regarding school matters should be issued without a previous consent of the Secretary of this Holy Congregation, so that it be registered in the archives.

Chapter Two
On Universities

9.

#3. The primary schools are two, the University of Rome, otherwise called the Roman Archgymnasium, and the University of Bologna.

10.

In each of these schools should be present not less than thirty-eight classes and curricula. Our students should be eager and able to choose among a variety of disciplines, should be encouraged to complete their studies, and should be allowed to gain great knowledge and understanding.

11.

The secondary universities are five: the Universities of Ferrara, Perugia, Camerino, Macerata, and Fermo. In each of these universities, there should be no less than seventeen chairs, besides the other classes and suitable curricula.

12.

These secondary universities may grant degrees and diplomas only after a committee of teachers, chosen by this Holy Congregation, have thoroughly tested the candidates.

13.

The superintendents should publicly keep a list of all those appointed to the chairs of the universities. The number of the chairs assigned to each university should not be increased nor decreased without a prior permission of the Congregation. The same applies to all other matters pertaining to study, since the Congregation reserves to itself alone the privilege of granting degrees and diplomas. (Leo, XII, 1824, pp. 86–87) [Translation is original.]

Although centuries have passed between the publication of this document and *Immensa* (Sixtus V, 1588), both constitutions are clearly addressed to similar issues. In the case of *Quod divinia sapientia* (Leo XII, 1824), the concerns of the congregation have expanded, and along with them, the language used to express that concern. Whereas *Immensa* focused primarily on the University of Rome and a few selected other universities, this document shows a broader interest in all the schools of the papal states. Furthermore, *Quod divina sapientia* moves away from the poetic, familial images of *Immensa* and makes its claim for oversight in far more juridical language.

Rules and regulations have become a concern. Preserving them for posterity is judged important. An individual is chosen to perform this task. Another individual is appointed to enforce the rules and to serve as a type of visitor or inspector of the universities and schools. This person, which the document calls a legate, is obligated to report his findings to the Congregation or may even be empowered to correct any inadequacies that he finds. Thus, the Congregation asserts at this stage a supervisory jurisdiction over schools and universities in the papal states and reserves to itself the right to intervene as necessary. In a new but clear assertion of its authority, the Congregation directs that all information pertaining to school matters in the papal states, whether going to or coming from the Pontiff, will first pass through the Secretary of the Holy Congregation.

The administrative interests of the Congregation are, at this point, highly juridical in nature. They are concerned about the granting of degrees, the competence of candidates, the structure of the curriculum, and the number of professors. Even the number of classrooms is of concern. The focus of the concern of the Congregation has widened to the schools and universities of the papal states, but the concern itself has gone beyond the previous parental solicitude. Practical and legal matters are explicitly addressed.

Pius X issued the Apostolic Constitution *Sapienti consilio* on June 29, 1908, in an effort to restructure and reform the Roman Curia. While this document goes on at length in its discussion of other curial offices and practices, it has but two sentences on the *Congregatio Studiorum* which constitute its paragraph #11:

Est huic sacrae Congregationi commissa moderatio studiorum in quibus versari debeant maiora athenaea, seu quas vocant Universitates, seu Facultates, quae ab Ecclesiae auctoritate dependent, comprehensis iis quae religiosae alicuius familiae sodalibus administrantur. Novas institutiones perpendit approbatque; facultatem concedit academicos gradus conferendi, et, ubi agatur de viro singulari doctrina commendato, potest eos ipsa conferre. (p. 14)

To this Holy Congregation should be given the authority to supervise all of the major institutes of education, whether Universities or Colleges, subject to the jurisdiction of the Church, including those directed by a religious order. The same Congregation may approve and suggest the creation of new institutes, may grant the authority of conferring degrees and diplomas, and may directly confer honorary degrees to individuals with a remarkable character and talent. (p. 14) [Translation is original.]

Sapienti consilio (Pius X, 1908) thus confirmed the activity and jurisdiction first annunciated in *Quod divina sapientia* (Leo XII, 1824), and ordered few modifications. The one expansion of authority indicated is the inclusion of universities directed by religious communities.

A few years later in 1915, Benedict XV made a structural change in the congregation by legislating his personal concern for seminary education. In the document issued *motu proprio* entitled *Seminaria clericorum*, published November 4, Benedict voiced his solicitude for both seminaries and universities:

Verum cum apud hanc Sacram Congregationem negotiorum moles praeter modum excreverit, et Seminariorum cura maiorem in dies operam postulet, visum est Nobis as omnem eorum disciplinam moderandam novum aliquod consilium inire.

Alias quidem, cum Romane Curiae nova pararetur ordinatio, de peculiari S. Congregatione instituenda cogitatum est, quae Seminariis praeesset; quod consilium cum temporum adiuncta prohibuerint quominus efficeretur, Nos revocandum censemus, non ita tamen ut tractatio rerum quae de Seminariis sunt, detracta ac omnino seiuncta a Sacra Congregatione Consistoriali habenda sit, cum unam et alteram Congregationem aliquo nexu velimus inter se coniungi.

Re igitur mature considerata, exploratisque aliquot Cardinalium sententiis, haec apostolica auctoritate decernimus ac statuimus quae infra scripta sunt.

I. De Seminariis propria iam esto Sacra Congregatio, ad formam ceterarum Romane Curiae, ad eamque omnia pertineant quae usque adhunc de Seminariorum rebus apud Congregationem Consistorialem agebantur, ita ut eius posthac sit clericorum tum mentes tum animos fingere.

II. Huius Sacra Congregationis muneribus munera accedant Congregationis Studiorum; itaque haec eadem Congregatio "De Seminariis et de studiorum Universitatibus" appeletur. (pp. 494–495)

However, since the amount of work assigned to this Holy Congregation has greatly increased, and while the modern seminaries still demand a great deal of attention, we have decided that a new policy should be enacted.

Therefore, in the new ordinance about the Roman Curia should be included the creation of this unique Holy Congregation which shall oversee the seminaries. Meanwhile, since the present circumstances are preventing the new assembly to unite and deliberate, we ourselves establish that this new congregation be completely separated from the Holy Consistorial Congregation regarding matters pertaining to seminaries.

All things considered, after listening to the advice of several Cardinals, by the authority given me by the Apostles, we decide and establish the following statutes:

I. This Holy Congregation of the seminaries should be organized like the other congregations of the Roman Curia. It should itself assume all responsibilities and matters pertaining to seminaries, which once belonged to the Consistorial Congregation, to properly provide from now on for the well-being of the minds and souls of the clergy.

II. Since this Holy Congregation inherits all the burdens and responsibilities pertaining to a congregation for study, the name of the congregation should now be the "Congregation of Seminaries and of University Studies." (pp. 494–495) [Translation is original.]

In effect, Benedict XV added a new division to the *Congregatio Studiorum*, one dealing explicitly with seminary concerns. It appears from the text of the document that seminaries had been previously governed by another congregation, the Consistorial Congregation. The document removes that affiliation and places seminary concerns as a special and unique entity in the *Congregation Studiorum*. Hence, the Congregation receives a new name that more clearly reflects its interests and jurisdiction: the Congregation of Seminaries and University Studies.

The document *Cum Nobis*, issued *motu proprio* by Pius XII, was published on November 4, 1941, and effectively expanded the sphere of influence of the congregation. Specifically, *Cum Nobis* is directed to establishing what amounts to an additional office or interest in the congregation, that of the promotion of vocations to the priesthood.

Cum Nobis Sacra Congregatio Seminariis et Studiorum Universitatibus praeposita per-opportunum fore renuntiaverit Opus primarium Sacerdotalium Vocationum condere, quod sibi proponat in Christifidelibus—omni sane consilio, sed potissimum per diversa in singulis Diocesibus constituta id genus Opera—voluntatem excitare fovendi, tuendi iuvandique Ecclesiaticas Vocationes, rectam de dignitate ac necessitate Catholici Sacerdotii notitiam pervulgare, itemque fideles ex omnibus orbis partibus in communionem precum ac piorum exercitiorum vocare; Nos, motu proprio ac de Apostolicae plenitudine potestatis, *Opus*, quod *Pontificium* nominamus, *Vocationum Sacerdotalium* apud eamdem Sacram Congregationem constitutum volumnus ac decernimus, addita facultate aggregandi Opera ac personas, quae id postulaverit, simulque omnes Indulgentias et favores spirituales, concessos vel concedendos, ad universos adscriptos extendendi.

Quod quidem ratum firmumque sic ac permaneat, contrariis quibus libet non obstantibus.

Datum Romae, apud Sanctum Petrum, die IV mensis Novembris, in festo S. Caroli Borromaei, anno MCMXXXXI, Pontificatus Nostri tertio. (p. 479)

The Sacred Congregation of Seminaries and Universities has presented to us the opportunity to establish a central Work for Vocations to the Priesthood which proposes: to increase among the faithful by all means possible, but particularly through groups of laity already in many dioceses, the desire of promoting, protecting, and assisting priestly vocations; to distribute correct knowledge of the dignity and necessity of the Catholic priesthood; to unite the faithful of the entire world in communion with prayers and holy practices.

We, therefore, of our own authority and with the fullness of our apostolic authority, will and decree established in the Sacred Congregation of Seminaries and Universities a Work for Priestly Vocations, to which we give the title "Pontifical," with the task of coordinating the work of societies and individuals, and at the same time, of extending the indulgences and spiritual benefits granted or to be granted to all of its members.

May this decision have full force and effect, notwithstanding anything to the contrary.

Given at Rome, from the See of Peter, on the fourth day of November, the feast of St. Charles Borromeo, 1941, the third year of our Pontificate. (p. 479) [Translation is original.]

Cum Nobis (Pius XII, 1941) had the effect of establishing a type of vocations office within the congregation, and one with universal jurisdiction at that. The

office, or "work" as the document calls it, had the responsibility to bring vocation awareness into the faith experience of Catholics around the world.

While it is not inconsistent to find this vocation theme in a congregation
overseeing seminaries, we should recall that the congregation also had involvement with Catholic universities and institutions of higher learning. In terms of
administrative organization, *Cum Nobis* (Pius XII, 1941) placed responsibility
for the promotion of priestly vocations in the hands of those already dealing
with higher education. This is to suggest that the work of promoting vocations
to the priesthood and ministry of education are somehow related. In what
amounted to an addendum to the *motu proprio Cum Nobis*, Pius XII had distributed and promoted along with the document a prayer he personally composed
for priestly vocations. In addition to praying for generous hearts in young men,
it also prayed for teachers: "Bestow upon their teachers the essential light for
cultivating in their young hearts the delicate plant of a vocation until the day
when, ardent and pure, they shall mount to Thy holy altar" (Pius XII, 1942,
pp. 148–149).

The Pontifical Work for Priestly Vocations remains to this day as a division
of the same congregation and is still charged with the same responsibilites (*Annuario Pontificio*, 1999). It is one of only two subdivisions of the congregation
not explicitly linked to educational institutions. The other body that falls under
the jurisdiction of this congregation, but is without a concrete relationship to an
educational institution, is the Permanent Interdicasterial Commission for a more
Equitable Distribution of Priests in the World, what the *Annuario Pontificio*
(1993) calls the Commissioni Interdicasteriali Permanenti Per una Distrubuzione
Piu Equa dei Sacerdoti nel Mondo. The commission was established on June
13, 1991, at the direction of Pope John Paul II. See *Letter of Cardinal Angelo
Sodano to Cardinal Pio Laghi*, Vatican Archives, N.290.198/G.N., as recorded
in the acts of the Sacra Congregatio Pro Institutione Catholica, Rome, February
18, 1994, Prot. N. 439/93/1.

As mentioned in the *Annuario Pontificio*, (1993), the work of *Cum Nobis*
(Pius XII, 1941) was affirmed and given more explicit direction in the Vatican
II document *Optatum Totius*, (Paul VI) published on October 28, 1965. Calling
for a more intensive fostering of priestly vocations, *Optatam Totius* said:

The duty of fostering vocations falls on the whole Christian community, and they should
discharge it principally by living full Christian lives. The greatest contribution is made
by families which are animated by a spirit of faith, charity and piety and which provide,
as it were, a first seminary. . . . Teachers and all who are in any way involved in the
education of boys and young men—and this applies especially to Catholic societies—
should endeavor to train the young entrusted to them to recognize a divine vocation and
to follow it willingly. (p. 708)

Again emphasizing the role of educators in fostering vocations, *Optatam Totius*
goes on to refer to *Cum Nobis*:

The Council also directs that the organizations for promoting vocations which have been—or are about to be—set up in the various dioceses, regions, or countries, in accordance with the relevant pontifical documents, should coordinate and systematize all pastoral work for vocations and develop them with as much discretion as zeal, making full use of the aids provided by modern psychological and sociological teaching. (p. 709)

Paul VI initiated a reform of the Roman Curia following upon the conclusion of Vatican II. The Apostolic Constitution *Regimini Ecclesiae Universae*, published on August 15, 1967, reorganized curial structure and scope, including the Congregation for Seminaries and Universities. In Chapter 8 of *Regimini Ecclesiae Universae*, the changes in the congregation are made clear:

Sacra Congregatio pro Institutione catholica

75.   Quae hactenus Sacra Congregatio de Seminariis et Studiorum Universitatibus nuncupata est, nomen sumit Sacrae Congregationis pro Institutione catholica.

76.   1. Congregatio, cui praeest Cardinalis Praefectus, iuvantibus Secretario et Subsecretario, competentiam habet circa ea quae respiciunt promovendam clericorum formationem et scientificam institutionem catholicam sive clericorum sive laicorum, firma competentia tum Congregationis pro Religiosis et Institutis saecularibus in iis quae ad religiosos qua tales formandos pertinent, tum Congregationis pro Gentium Evangelizatione.

2. Congregatio in triplex dispescitur officium.

77.   PER PRIMUM OFFICIUM videt:

1. —omnia quae spectant ad regimen, disciplinam, temporalem administrationem seminariorum, salva competentia Congregationis pro Gentium Evangelizatione, quacum concordi consilio et debita rerum coordinatione agendum est;

2. —ea quae attingunt promovendam educationem cleri diocesani atque scientificam institutionem religiosorum et institutorum saecularium; peculiariter vero perpendit et approbat seminariorum regionalium vel interregionalium statuta, ab Episcopis quorum interest parata.

78.   PER SECUNDUM OFFICIUM moderatur Universitates vel Facultates, Athenaea, necnon quaevis instituta seu coetus superiororum, quae catholico nomine rite ornentur, quatenus ab Ecclesiae auctoritate quomodocumque dependeant, haud exclusis iis quae a religiosis reguntur vel a laicis; institutiones et associationes ad studia provehenda fovet et approbat; adnititur ut in Universitatibus catholicis habeantur tum instituta quae primariae investigationi scientificae vel artisticae promovendae inserviunt, tum saltem cathedra sacrae theologiae, in qua lectiones tradantur laicis quoque alumnis accommodatae; normas praebet qouad academias et bibliothecas, praeter Vaticanam catholicarum atque consociationes earum sive nationales sive internationales; adlaborat ut apud Universitates non catholicas erigantur convictus et centra universitaria catholica.

79.   PER TERTIUM OFFICIUM curat erectionem scholarum paroecialium et dioecesanarum, invigilat omnibus scholis catholicis, cuiusque generis et gradus, infra tamen Universitates et Facultates, itemque institutis instructionis seu educationis ab auctoritate Ecclesiae dependentibus, nisi agatur de scholis quae dumtaxat praeparent ad vitam religiosam, firmo tamen praescripto n. 77, #2; idcirco ad universum orbem catholicum extenditur eius competentia ad scholas quod attinet, nisi agatur de locis dependentibus a

Congregatione pro Ecclesiis Orientalibus vel a Congregatione pro Gentium Evangelizatione.

80.   Praeterea Congregatio quaestiones generales perscrutatur educationem et studia respicientes; cooperationem curat cum Conferentiis Episcopalibus, itemque cum auctoritatibus civilibus coetibusque nationalibus et internationalibus, servata debita coordinatione cum S. (pp. 885–928)

The Sacred Congregation for Catholic Education

75.   What has until now been known as the Sacred Congregation for Seminaries and Universities will now become the Sacred Congregation for Catholic Education.

76.   1. Presiding over the congregation will be a Cardinal Prefect, assisted by a Secretary and an Undersecretary. The competence of the congregation includes all that pertains to the formation of clergy and Catholic education, in the arts and in the sciences, both of the clergy and of the laity, and without affecting the jurisdiction of the Congregation for Religious and Secular Institutes in matters which concern them, nor the Congregation for the Evangelization of People.

2. The congregation is divided into three offices.

77.   The First Office oversees:

1. —all that pertains to the direction, discipline, and temporal administration of seminaries, without effecting the jurisdiction of the Congregation for the Evangelization of People, with which this congregation should work cooperatively;

2. —those matters which concern the education of diocesan clergy and education in the arts and sciences of Religious and Secular Institutes; it takes a special interest in and approves the statutes of regional and inter-regional seminaries.

78.   The Second Office oversees universities and faculties of study, athenea, and any other institutions of higher learning which have the name Catholic, in as much as they depend in some fashion on the authority of the Church, and not excluding those which are operated by Religious and laity. The congregation must also advance and approve institutions and associations that foster study. It encourages Catholic universities to include related institutes of primary studies in the arts and sciences in addition to chairs of sacred theology where lectures are presented in a way intelligible to laity.

79.   The Third Office cares for the erection of parochial and diocesan schools; it oversees all Catholic schools of whatever kind or level below universities, as well as all institutions of instruction or education dependent on the authority of the Church, unless they are schools whose only object is preparation for religious life, and without affecting the prescriptions of 77, #2. The competence of the congregation includes schools all over the world, with the exception of those dependent on the Congregation for Oriental Churches and the Congregation for the Evangelization of People.

80.   In addition, the congregation considers general questions regarding education and study. It aims for cooperation with episcopal conferences and national and international civil authorities, with due respect for the necessity of coordinating with the Sacred Council for the Public Affairs of the Church. It coordinates the resources and the means to protect the rights and freedom of schools, and it makes recommendations to national and international congresses during which it debates such questions. (Paul VI, 1967, pp. 885–928) [Translation is original.]

That the first order of business is the changing of the name of this congregation to a title more directly associated with its work is significant. Heretofore, the congregation was principally focused on seminary education and the formation of clergy. With a growing interest in and jurisdiction over Catholic universities, the congregation gradually widened its sphere of control. While seminary education has been its constant focus over several centuries, the congregation's influence has experienced a progression toward more and more centralization of authority. This progression reaches its zenith as *Regimini Ecclesiae Universae* (Paul VI, 1967) introduces a new third office to the congregation, one which is concerned with all Catholic schools below the university level. This is a new and striking development; for the first time in its 400-year history, the Vatican congregation with jurisdiction over the educational institutions in the Church asserted control over Catholic schools at the pre-university level.

We have here the fully realized centralization of authority in Rome for all Catholic educational institutions. Begun four centuries previously with the Apostolic Constitution *Immensa* of Sixtus V (1588), full authority rests with the Vatican congregation now known as the Congregation for Catholic Education. Thus, in the period from 1588 to 1967, we see the interests, control, and jurisdiction of the Vatican congregation initially devoted to seminary education steadily expanding to encompass all Catholic schools at every level.

Two distinctions are of interest here concerning the universality of the congregation's jurisdiction. The first concerns the other congregations named in the document. In the delineation of the duties of both the First Office and the Third Office of the congregation, exceptions are stated to the absolute competence of the congregation to deal with matters proper to it. The exceptions are in matters related to Oriental churches and those concerning the Congregation for the Evangelization of People. In short, the congregation does not assert a universal jurisdiction over every seminary, university, and Catholic school in the entire world. There are such institutions of Catholic learning that are excluded from its purview. These can be found in churches still considered to be mission territories, and throughout Oriental churches. Developing countries, still considered mission fields, fall completely under the jurisdiction of the Congregation for the Evangelization of People, known commonly as *Propaganda Fide*, or the promotion of the faith. All relations with Rome in such countries are routinely handled through *Propaganda Fide*, including the selection of bishops, the erection of dioceses, and the establishment of seminaries, universities, and schools. Because developing nations are perceived to have special needs, they are freed from the constraints of dealing with a wide variety of curial offices, and have all of their business conducted through *Propaganda Fide* (Congregation for Catholic Education, 1990).

Oriental churches, because of their unique status, have an entirely separate congregation for their concerns, the Congregation for Oriental Churches. As in the case of developing nations, Oriental churches deal exclusively with their own congregation for all matters of importance to the Holy See and do not relate directly with other individual congregations. This allowance was made in particular to address cultural differences of Oriental churches and because of the predominance of Western views in much of official church policy and law (Congregation for Catholic Education, 1990).

While institutions that come under *Propaganda Fide* and the Congregation for Oriental Churches are similar in that they are somewhat independent of all other Vatican administrators, there is one significant difference. Membership in the Congregation for Oriental Churches is constant and permanent; a local church is a member by virtue of its historical connection to an Oriental rite. *Propaganda Fide*, on the other hand, regularly "advances" a national church to fuller status when it becomes mature and self-directed. When this occurs, the national church begins relations with other curial departments and moves out of *Propaganda Fide*. This is clearly seen in Rome, where seminary students from such countries no longer attend the seminary operated by *Propaganda Fide* but join another nationally erected seminary or even establish their own. The movement out of *Propaganda Fide* and into independent existence is a significant one in terms of curial administration. For example, the United States was under the jurisdiction of *Propaganda Fide* until 1905, and American seminarians did not move to the Pontifical University of Gregorianum until 1930. Thus, in the view of the Vatican, the United States was mission territory until quite recently and, despite its economic dominance and worldwide leadership role, is nevertheless a recent arrival to the world's religious stage. This, perhaps, explains why some believe that the self-importance of the American church is a trait that needs to be challenged in light of history (Ellis, 1994). The development of the American church and its ongoing relationship with the Vatican is addressed by Gerald P. Fogarty in *The Vatican and the American Hierarchy from 1870–1965* (1985).

A second distinction of importance concerns the difference between Catholic universities and ecclesiastical faculties. The Second Office of the congregation asserts oversight of "any . . . institutions of higher learning which have the name Catholic, *in as much as they depend in some fashion on the authority of the Church*" [italics added] (see The Second Office). Catholic universities are the more common phenomenonon, having been established as institutions of higher learning with a special interest in the Catholic intellectual tradition and the teaching mission of the church. There are over 900 such universities and colleges in the world, 240 of them in the United States (Congregation for Catholic Education, 1990). Their Catholic identity is supported by Canon Law and comes under the supervision of a local ordinary, even if the larger institution is governed by civil law. A debate on the relationship of the local bishop to the faculty of a Catholic university within his diocese has been ongoing since the publication of the revised *Code of Canon Law* in 1983. The issues relate to canons 807–814, and particularly focus on canon 812 involving the canonical mandate to teach theology. While beyond the scope of this chapter, the dialogue highlights the importance of the distinction between Catholic universities and ecclesiastical faculties (*Code of Canon Law*, 1983; Gallin, 1992).

Ecclesiastical faculties, on the other hand, are operated under the authority of the Holy See and have a direct, canonical relationship to the Vatican. While very often housed at universities, ecclesiastical faculties grant pontifical degrees from the Holy See and are governed exclusively by church law. There are over 100 of these faculties in existence today, including in the United States, programs at Berkeley, California; Weston, Massachusetts; Mundelein, Illinois; St. Mary's, Baltimore; the Josephinum, Columbus, Ohio; and the Marianum, Dayton, Ohio. The Catholic University of America in Washington, DC is also an ecclesiastical faculty. (For a complete national and international listing, see *Annuaire des Universities Catholiques et des Autre Instituts Catholiques d'Etudes Superieures*, Congregation for Catholic Education, 1990.)

The distinction between Catholic universities and ecclesiastical faculties is important because ecclesiastical faculties have a much closer link to the Holy See than do Catholic universities. While this congregation would still claim jurisdiction over Catholic matters at all Catholic institutions of learning, it bears a special responsibility to ecclesiastical faculties; and since intervention into the internal affairs of institutions recognized in civil law is likely to generate prolonged public litigation, Vatican actions are more likely within ecclesiastical faculties (Gallin, 1992).

The final document cited in the *Annuario Pontificio* (1993) as being a part of the history of the congregation is *Pastor Bonus*, an Apostolic Constitution of John Paul II. *Pastor Bonus* was published on June 28, 1988, in commemoration of the four-hundredth anniversary of *Immensa*, the Apostolic Constitution of Sixtus V (1588). While *Immensa* signaled the beginning of official church involvement in education, *Pastor Bonus* represents a *terminus ad quem* as the most recent definitive statement concerning official church responsibility for Catholic educational efforts.

Divided into sections known as articles, *Pastor Bonus* (John Paul II, 1988) addresses the issue of educational institutions in articles 112 through 116. Entitled *Congregatio De Seminariis Atque Studiorum Institutis* (Congregation for Seminaries and Institutes of Study), it reads:

Art. 112

Congregatio exprimit atque exercet Sedis Apostolicae solicitudinem circa eorum formationem, qui ad sacros ordines vocantur, necnon circa promotionem et ordinationem institutionis catholicae.

Art. 113

#1. Episcopis adest, ut in eorum Ecclesiis vocationes ad sacra ministeria quam maxime colantur atque in Seminariis, ad normam iuris constituendis ac gerendis, alumni solida formatione tum humana ac spirituali, tum doctrinali et pastorali apte edoceantur.

#2. Sedulo invigilat ut seminariorum convictus regimenque rationi institutionis sacerdotalis plene respondeant atque superiores ac magistri exemplo vitae ac recta doctrina ad formandas personas sacrorum ministrorum quam maxime conferant.

#3. Eius praeterea est seminaria interdiocesana erigere eorumque statuta appro-
bare.

Art. 114

Congregatio adnititur, ut fundamentalia principia de catholica educatione prout ab Ecclesiae Magisterio proponuntur altius usque investigentur, vindicentur atque a Populo Dei
cognoscantur.

Ea pariter curat, ut in hac materia Christifideles sua officia implere possint ac dent
operam et nitantur ut etiam civilis societas ipsorum iura agnoscat atque tueatur.

Art. 115

Congregatio normas statuit, quibus schola catholica regatur; Episcopis diocesanis adest,
ut scholae catholicae ubi fieri potest, constituantur, et summa sollicitudine foveantur
utque in omnibus scholis educatio catechetica et pastoralis cura alumnis Christifidelibus
per opportuna incepta praebeantur.

Art. 116

#1. Congregatio vires impendit, ut Universitatum ecclesiasticarum et catholicarum cet-
erorumque studiorum Institutorum sufficiens copia in Ecclesia habeatur, in quibus
sacrae disciplinae altius investigentur necnon humanitatis scientiaeque cultus, habita
christianae veritatis ratione, promoveatur et Christifideles ad propria munera im-
plenda apte formentur.

#2. Universitates et Instituta ecclesiastica erigit aut approbat, eorum statuta rata habet,
supremam moderationem in eis exercet atque invigilat, ut catholicae fidei integritas
in tradendis doctrinis servetur.

#3. Ad Universitates Catholicas quod attinet, ea agit quae Sanctae Sedis competunt.

#4. Cooperationem mutuumque adiutorium inter Studiorum Universitates earumque con-
sociationes fovet iisdemque praesidio est. (pp. 888–889)

THE CONGREGATION FOR SEMINARIES AND EDUCATIONAL INSTITUTIONS

The congregation never formally adopted this name and title as given in
Pastor Bonus (John Paul II, 1988). On February 26, 1989, a few days before
the coming into force of *Pastor Bonus* (March 1, 1989), the soon-to-be-
published title was changed to "Congregation for Catholic Education (for Seminaries and Educational Institutions)." See letter of the Secretariat of State, prot.
no. 236.026, Vatican archives. The letter refers to canon 360 of the *Code of
Canon Law* granting the pope powers to make special laws with regard to the
structuring of the Curia.

Art. 112

The Congregation for Seminaries and Educational Institutions gives practical expression
to the concern of the Apostolic See for the training of those who are called to holy
orders, and for the promotion and organization of Catholic education.

Art. 113

#1. It is available to the bishops so that in their churches vocations to the sacred ministry may be cultivated to the highest degree, and seminaries may be established and conducted in accordance with the law, where students may be suitably trained, receiving a solid formation that is human and spiritual, doctrinal and pastoral.

#2. It carefully gives great attention that the way of life and program of the seminaries is in full harmony with the idea of priestly education, and that the superiors and teachers, by the example of their life and sound doctrine, contribute their utmost to the formation of the personality of the sacred ministers.

#3. It is also to erect interdiocesan seminaries and to approve their statutes.

Art. 114

The Congregation makes every effort to see that the fundamental principles of Catholic education as set out by the magisterium of the Church be ever more deeply researched, championed, and known by the people of God.

It also takes care that in this matter the Christian faithful may be able to fulfill their duties by striving to bring civil society to recognize and protect their rights.

Art. 115

The Congregation sets the norms by which Catholic schools are governed. It is available to diocesan bishops so that, wherever possible, Catholic schools be established and fostered with the utmost care, and that in every school appropriate undertakings bring catechetical instruction and pastoral care to the Christian students.

Art. 116

#1. The Congregation works to ensure that there be in the Church a sufficient number of ecclesiastical and Catholic universities as well as other educational institutions in which the sacred disciplines may be pursued in depth, studies in the humanities and the sciences may be promoted, with due regard for Christian truth, so that the Christian faithful may be suitably trained to fulfill their own functions.

#2. It erects or approves ecclesiastical universities and institutions, ratifies their statutes, exercises higher supervision on them and exercises great attention so that the integrity of the Catholic faith is preserved in teaching doctrine.

#3. With regard to Catholic universities, it deals with those matters that are within the competence of the Holy See.

#4. It fosters cooperation and mutual help between universities and their associations and serves as a resource for them. (John Paul II, 1988, pp. 888–889) [Translation is original.]

While the text of the document affirms the existence of an office for Catholic schools, a development first expressed in *Regimini Ecclesiae Universae* (Paul VI, 1967), it has been noted that in practice the school division has exercised more of a promotional authority than a juridical one. Recent documents that have been published on the nature of the Catholic school, the unique dimensions of Catholic education, and the place of Catholic schools in the overall mission of the church have their origin in the school division of this congregation. These documents would include *The Catholic School* (Congregation for Catholic Education, 1977); *Lay Catholics in Schools: Witnesses to Faith* (Congregation for Catholic Education, 1982); and *The Religious Dimension of Education in a Catholic School* (Congregation for Catholic Education, 1988). All of these documents were published in Rome by this congregation. The school division has also played the role of advisor or consultant to struggling schools and has attempted to be a sort of clearinghouse for information and statistics relative to primary and secondary Catholic schools. For the most part, the school division limits its contact within the church to local bishops; it does not normally open communication or establish dialogue with individual schools or persons. An exception to this rule would be the purely promotional practice of sending pontifical greetings to a particular school or Catholic educator on the occasion of a special celebration or anniversary, upon request by the proper authorities.

The increased frequency of school closings and mergers in the United States during the past several decades has provoked a marked increase in correspondence to the school division from individual Catholics in recent years. While the majority of these communications take the form of requesting an appeal of the decision of a local bishop, the congregation does not entertain appeals from individuals or groups who seek to overturn the decision of a diocesan bishop to close, move, or merge a school. The faithful do possess rights in this regard (*Code of Canon Law*, 1983), but appeals of episcopal decisions are made formally to the Apostolic Signatura, not to specific congregations. The Apostolic Signatura is the highest church court and the last venue of appeal for internal juridical matters of the church. Whereas supervisory intervention is common in the other two offices of the congregation, the school division is not inclined to such direct action. Confining official business to private communication with bishops, the school division functions in a supportive role of local ordinaries, not a confrontational one. Thus, while a concern at a seminary or a Catholic university might be of such magnitude that a Vatican intervention would be warranted, it is unlikely that this congregation would impose its will on any primary or secondary Catholic school. In fact, even the most recent attempts of Vatican officials to exercise a supervisory jurisdiction over universities and seminaries have not emanated from the Congregation for Catholic Education. The Vatican has customarily defined the problems as theological and doctrinal and has confined discussion of the issues to another congregation, namely the Congregation for the Doctrine of the Faith.

From the point of view of diocesan bishops, it can be asserted that seminaries and Catholic universities have a special relationship to the universal church, and therefore fall particularly under the jurisdiction of this congregation. With the special case of ecclesiastical faculties, this relationship is even stronger and explicit in law. Individual Catholic schools at the pre-university level have their primary relationship with the local church of which they are a part. Hence, they fall almost totally under the jurisdiction of the local bishop. Stated another way, seminaries and Catholic universities are responsible to both Rome and the local ordinary, and can reasonably expect to be in dialogue with both. Individual Catholic schools at the pre-university level need only relate formally to the local bishop.

A modicum of supervisory jurisdiction is seen from the school office in its collection of school-related data for the required *Ad Limina* visits of bishops. Every five years, bishops must file extensive reports on the status of their dioceses and then personally report to the Holy Father and curial officials on the content of that report. Chapter Ten of the *Ad Limina* summary deals with all aspects of Catholic education within a diocese, including priestly formation in seminaries, Catholic universities and colleges; Catholic schools; the teaching of religion in public schools or to Catholic children not enrolled in Catholic schools; and the status of religious vocations. *Ad Limina* summaries and even the blank forms themselves are normally considered private communication and are not published.

Thus, while seminaries, Catholic universities, and ecclesiastical faculties have stronger ties to the international church and more direct and frequent communication with this congregation as a result, Catholic schools below the university level tend to enjoy a relative autonomy in relationship to a local bishop. For the most part, they are able to govern themselves. While they are clearly Catholic institutions and in relationship to church authorities, their administration is carried out with little external interference. In paraphrasing the *Annuario Pontificio*'s (1993) official delineation of the role of this congregation, P. J. Kenedy's *The Official Catholic Directory* (1994) summarizes the responsibilities of the Congregation for Catholic Education in these words:

> It is competent for all that pertains to the formation of clerics and the Catholic education both of clerics and of the laity. The first office is charged with the direction, discipline and temporal administration of seminaries and whatever touches the education of the diocesan clergy and the scientific formation of religious and secular institutes. The second office oversees universities, faculties, athenaea and any institute of higher learning which has the name "Catholic" insofar as they depend on the authority of the Church, not excluding those directed by religious or the laity. The third office cares for the establishment of parochial and diocesan schools below the level of a university and faculty, as well as all institutes of instruction or education dependent on the authority of the Church.
>
> Also within the Congregation is located the Pontifical Work for Vocations, which is charged with coordinating and promoting the work of fostering all ecclesiastical vocations. (p. xxxiv)

Having seen the historical development of this congregation as well as the various offices or responsibilities mentioned, we can understand the gradual ways in which different areas of concern came into the congregation's purview. The gradual centralization of authority, and the growing sphere of influence to include all levels of Catholic education are clearly seen in the documents that are foundational to the congregation's existence. Seminaries were the original concern of church officials, followed by universities. Only recently did Catholic schools below the university level receive any solicitude. How that jurisdiction came to be exercised and the contemporary operation of the Congregation for Catholic Education differ from division to division. We have also seen that the congregation, while enjoying a broad competence, does not have unfettered universal jurisdiction. These issues are significant for the abiding presence of collegiality in Catholic school administration as they point to some areas of autonomy and freedom that were preserved even in the midst of centralization in Rome.

NOTE

Permission to reproduce the original Latin versions of church documents, including *Annuarii Pontificii, Immensa, Quod divina sapientia, Sapienti consilio, Seminaria clericorum, Cum Nobis, Regimini Ecclesiae Universae*, and *Patsor Bonus*, obtained from Libreria Editrice Vaticana, Vatican City.

REFERENCES

Annuario pontificio. (1993). Rome: Libreria Editrice Vaticana.
Annuario pontificio. (1994). Rome: Libreria Editrice Vaticana.
Annuario pontificio. (1999). Rome: Libreria Editrice Vaticana.
Benedict XV. (1915). Seminaria clericorum. [On seminary education]. In *Acta apostolicae sedis* (Vol. VII, No. 18, pp. 494–495). Rome: The Vatican.
Code of canon law: Text and commentary. (1983). Mahwah, NJ: Paulist Press.
Congregation for Catholic Education. (1977). *The Catholic school.* Washington, DC: United States Catholic Conference.
Congregation for Catholic Education. (1982). *Lay Catholics in schools: Witnesses to faith.* Boston: Author.
Congregation for Catholic Education. (1988). *The religious dimension of education in a Catholic school.* Washington, DC: United States Catholic Conference.
Congregation for Catholic Education. (1990). *Annuaire des universites Catholiques et des autre instituts Catholiques d'etudes superieures.* [A directory of Catholic universities and other Catholic institutions of higher learning]. Vatican City.
Ellis, A. T. (1994). *Serpent on the rock.* London: Hoder & Stoughton.
Flannery, A. (Ed.). (1987). *Vatican council II: The conciliar and post-conciliar documents.* Northport, NY: Costello Publishing.
Fogarty, G. P. (1985). *The Vatican and the American hierarchy from 1870–1965.* Wilmington, DE: Michael Glazier.
Gallin, A. (1992). *American Catholic higher education.* Notre Dame, IN: University of Notre Dame Press.
John Paul II. (1988). *Pastor bonus.* [Good shepherd]. In *Acta apostolicae sedis* (LXXX, No. 7, pp. 831–934). Rome: The Vatican.
Kenedy, P. J. (1994). *The official Catholic directory* (XXXIV). Wilmette, IL: P. J. Kenedy & Sons.

Leo XII. (1824). *Quod divina sapientia.* [On education in the papal states]. In R. Segreti (Ed.), *Bullarii romani summorum pontificum* [Roman bulls of the holy father] (Vol. XVI, pp. 86–87). Rome: The Vatican.

New Catholic encyclopedia. (1967a). (Vol. 4). Washington, DC: The Catholic University of America.

New Catholic encyclopedia. (1967b). (Vol. 10). Washington, DC: The Catholic University of America.

Paul VI. (1965). *Optatam totius.* [Decree on priestly formation]. Rome: The Vatican.

Paul VI. (1967). Regimini ecclesiae universae. [On reforming the Roman curia]. In *Acta apostolicae sedis* (Vol. LIX, pp. 885–928). Rome: The Vatican.

Pius X. (1908). *Sapienti consilio.* [On seminary education]. Rome: The Vatican.

Pius XII. (1941). *Cum nobis.* [On vocation awareness]. In *Acta apostolicae sedis* (Vol. XXXIII, No. 13, p. 479). Rome: The Vatican.

Pius XII. (1942). *Emmanuel.* Rome: The Vatican.

Sixtus V. (1588). *Immensa.* [On the Roman curia]. In *Bullarium Romanum a Pio quarto usque ad Innocentium IX* [Papal bulls from Pius IV to Innocent IX] (9th ed., Vol. 11, pp. 615–622). Rome: The Vatican.

Chapter 2

The Philosophy of Catholic Education

Ellis A. Joseph

The many conceptions of philosophy in general and of philosophy of education in particular contribute to confusion in these fields of study. The notion of Catholic philosophy of education presents its own set of difficulties. Consequently, research in these three areas (philosophy, philosophy of education, and Catholic philosophy of education) will be elaborated in order to map complexities and clarity of focus when the latter is possible.

VARIOUS CONCEPTIONS OF PHILOSOPHY

Philosophy is a subject with many branches; thus it has many objects of study. Ayer (1973), in his classic work *The Central Questions of Philosophy*, treats the traditional topics in philosophy: logic, metaphysics, epistemology, and so on. He stresses the thread which emerges in these topics that has to do with criteria, that is, the standards which govern the use of concepts, assessments of conduct, methods of reasoning, and evaluations of evidence. Beauchamp, Blackstone, and Feinberg (1980) chose, in an introductory text, to focus upon moral and social philosophy instead of "certain abstruse theories from the heartland of traditional philosophy that have commonly populated introductory textbooks in philosophy" (p. iv).

Abstruse theories perhaps are perceived as such because, as Boyer (1949) acknowledges, philosophers "are inclined to use a vocabulary which is both complicated and confusing" (p. 3). Perhaps this vocabulary is what it is "for the simple reason that philosophy has no specific type of subject matter which differentiates it from all other fields of investigation" (p. 10). Boyer contributes little to specifying philosophy's subject matter when he avers philosophy may be a guide to life and citizenship. While he acknowledges that one cannot master all the sciences, he assigns philosophy the role of assisting in mastering the principles of every science, of being a direct aid in thinking about thinking. For Joad (1936) abstruseness and obscurity are not necessary. He makes a distinction between two kinds of obscurity: obscurity of expression and expression of obscurity. The former is bad craftsmanship. Joad's philosopher would attempt to make the discipline understandable. The expression of obscurity is pardonable and inevitable because there is no necessary reason why "persons of average capacity should be enabled easily to grasp the thoughts of the profoundest intelligences that life has yet succeeded in evolving" (p. 11). For Joad the attraction of philosophy consists in its seeking to comprehend the universe as a whole instead of treating a special department of the whole, as is the case of the physicist or the biologist. He concludes that understanding philosophy entails some knowledge of other subjects such as physics, theology, history, biology, aesthetics, and literature. He reflects on the boundlessness of philosophy by stating, "I have judged a general disquisition upon the nature, scope and methods of philosophy to be superfluous" (p. 9).

There is evidence that many philosophers conceive of philosophy as satisfying a longing for meaning and thus define philosophy as the interpretation of life (Honer & Hunt, 1973; Nagel, 1987; Patrick, 1924). Honer and Hunt (1973) see the philosopher's quest as identified by the following questions: "Who or what am I? What, if anything, can I firmly believe? Is the universe friendly or indifferent to man and his purposes? Are some things clearly good and right, or do values differ from time to time and place to place? Does man have an obligation to his fellow men? How can one best proceed to find the truth? Is there some ultimate meaning in life?" (p. 2). The "meaning" emphasis is treated by Nagel (1987) when he urges students of philosophy to reflect on what the human mind finds puzzling and to think about these conundrums directly. Nagel provides some examples of his thinking directly. While the historian may focus upon determining what happened at some time in the past, the philosopher asks, "What is time?" Mathematicians deal with relations between numbers; the philosopher asks, "What is a number?" For a psychologist, a concern could be "how children learn a language, but a philosopher will ask, 'What makes a word mean anything?' " (Nagel, 1987, p. 5). Like Nagel, Fiebleman (1973) focuses upon starting points, namely, the innocence which characterizes the childhood stage: "If philosophy has any native home, it is in the questions of children. Their state of innocence is not after all so innocent" (p. 11).

Fiebleman (1973) cautioned that philosophy has technical terms which are difficult and which require arduous work by those who wish to understand them. Others seem to despair at the possibility that precision and distinctiveness might characterize how philosophy is understood. Danto (1968) (see also Hall, 1955) acknowledges that philosophy books seem always to have to say what philosophy is. He seems unconvinced that the ever-present "guides to philosophy" will make matters more precise: "So guides to philosophy seem curiously useless. When one needs them most, they are not understandable; and when they are understandable, they are not needed at all. A guide to philosophy, unless it is understood *philosophically*, is not rightly understood. But how, then, are we to understand a guide philosophically if we do not first know what philosophy is?" (pp. xiii–xiv). Sprague (1961) wrestles with the question of what philosophy is. He likens this question to the question, "What is furniture? Both 'philosophy' and 'furniture' are words that can be applied to many things" (pp. 3, 4). Rosenberg (1978), like Sprague and Danto (1968), sees ambiguity and a certain amount of imprecision as inevitable in learning philosophical techniques. He says he learned his philosophical techniques "the way quaint villagers learned their native folk dances, by joining in and stumbling until I got the hang of it" (p. xi). For years he has been inviting his students to join the dance. He advises, if you want to know what philosophy is about, then stumble along with me and after a while you will get the hang of it. He admits this doesn't work very well.

THE BROADER CONTEXT OF PHILOSOPHY OF EDUCATION

It is generally acknowledged that courses in the philosophy of education are taken grudgingly by students preparing for teaching and other professions in education (Beyer, 1997). In addition to this situation, the field of philosophy of education continually has been the subject of scholars who are wrestling with just what is philosophy of education.

In 1956, no less than 25 scholars participated in a Harvard symposium devoted to the aims and content of philosophy of education (*Harvard Educational Review*, 1956). In the symposium, Frankena referred to the three-parts theory, that is, philosophy of education could be normative, speculative, and analytical in approach. Frankena would like to see "either of two states prevail, (a) one in which each philosopher of education is engaged in all three kinds of inquiry, or (b) one in which some philosophers of education are engaged in one kind of inquiry, some in another, and some in the third" (p. 95). Flower averred "the philosophic enterprise does not prescribe ultimate norms, but examines them" (p. 100). Others deal with the issue of "philosophy" and "philosophy of" and as to whether the distinction (if any) clarifies the utility and nature of philosophy and philosophy of education. Symposium participant C. J. Ducasse considers this distinction by examining Broudy's (1955) treatment of the issue. Broudy wondered how philosophical philosophy of education can be. Ducasse states the distinction is artificial. For him, all philosophy is philosophy of something: for example, logic is philosophy of inference; epistemology, the philosophy of knowledge, and so on. The 25 scholars participating in the symposium elaborate, in one way or another, upon the positions of Frankena, Flower, Broudy, and Ducasse.

In 1969, Christopher J. Lucas edited a book of readings entitled *What Is Philosophy of Education?* Forty-five authors (many of them were participants in the Harvard symposium 13 years earlier) contributed articles, some of which

were identical to their symposium presentations, leaving the observer to conclude that the multiplicity of views on the nature of the philosophy of education
had not congealed any more than was the case in 1956. Lucas' book, however,
did make an attempt to devote some attention to the relevance of educational
philosophy for the teacher. It is suggested that philosophy, while a poor source
for instructional tools and methodologies, could contribute in terms of raising
questions instead of providing answers.

Also, in 1969, Van Cleve Morris (1969) edited a compilation of articles treating modern movements in educational philosophy. Morris acknowledges the
tenuousness of various articles exploring one or the other sphere of educational
philosophy. He doubts that all the various ideas can be presented in such a
manner that a coherent line of argument amidst several points of view can be
sustained. Many textbooks by a simple author may accomplish some form of
coherence at the cost of presenting a work from his or her private base of
understanding. Morris, however, hopes that an anthological potpourri may
achieve some coherence by considering contemporary philosophical thinking
instead of the traditional "isms" of an earlier epoch (i.e., Thomism, realism,
idealism, etc.). Certain aspects of contemporary thinking such as philosophical
anthropology in educational thought, analytical philosophy, and existential philosophy are regarded as tendencies or movements which have not coalesced into
schools of thought.

One school of thought (Dewey, 1982), pragmatism, has coalesced into a philosophical formulation in which philosophy is regarded as an intellectualized
wish; it is an aspiration subject to tests and rational discriminations; it is a social
hope leading to a working program of action; and it is a prophecy of the future
disciplined by serious thought and knowledge.

In addition to the Harvard symposium and Lucas' book of readings, Phenix
(1961) edited still another book of readings by 14 authors; many of them were
the same ones who contributed to the symposium and to Lucas' publication.
The period from 1956 to 1963 was particularly noted for speculations on the
nature of philosophy of education. Phenix quite rightly summarized the positions
of many thinkers of this period when he stated, "The question of what is philosophy of education opens a Pandora's box of other questions" (p. iii). Price
(1955) even questioned whether a philosophy of education is necessary. Most
scholars, of course, would answer that question in the affirmative. They (Beyer,
1997) demand, however, that care be taken to reconnect philosophy of education
with ethical and moral questions, and with an emphasis upon social and political
domains, as well as with school life.

T. W. Johnson's book *Discipleship or Pilgrimage? The Educator's Quest for
Philosophy* (1995) is a lengthy, serious study of the nature of philosophy of
education. It serves as an excellent transition to the treatment of the nature of
Catholic philosophy of education. Johnson's distinction between discipleship
and pilgrimage is particularly useful. Disciples are those who have essentially
ceased their philosophical quest. They have adopted a single system of philos-

ophy as the final answer and thus have found their dogma. Johnson suggests the quest must never be fulfilled if the philosopher's spirit of inquiry is to survive. The philosopher's quest, then, should be a pilgrimage that can never be consummated.

PHILOSOPHY OF CATHOLIC EDUCATION AND THE CATHOLIC PHILOSOPHY OF EDUCATION

The terms "philosophy of Catholic education" and the "Catholic philosophy of education" are used perhaps to distinguish, as Maritain (1937) does, between philosophy and theology. Theology is the science of God. One can attain the science or knowledge of God "naturally by the unassisted powers of reason" (p. 124). For Maritain, "The premises of theology are the truths formally revealed by God (*dogmas* or articles of faith), and its primary criterion of truth the authority of God who reveals it" (p. 125). Conversely, "The premises of philosophy are independent of theology, being those primary truths which are self-evident to the understanding, whereas the premises of theology are the truths revealed by God" (p. 126). Philosophy is a science which studies the highest principles and first causes of all things through the *natural* light of reason. The light in theology is supernatural. Thus, "as a superior science, theology judges philosophy and exercises guidance or government over it . . . which consists in rejecting as false any philosophic affirmation which contradicts a theological truth" (Maritain, 1937, p. 126; see also Elders, 1999). Consequently, the term "Catholic philosophy of education" may lead to much confusion, especially in determining what makes a Catholic school Catholic. Judging by the seemingly continual flow of writings (Pilarczyk, 1982; Trafford, 1993; Veverka, 1993) over the years about Catholic school identity, what makes a Catholic school Catholic may not be clearly understood because philosophy has been identified with theology.

There are many issues in the philosophy of curriculum which theology cannot resolve. For example, should facts or broad concepts prevail? Should the curriculum be organized with the child as the starting point, or should the nature of the disciplines dictate their sequence? Should there be liberal education for all? These are issues associated with pilgrimage. Questions surrounding them will be (as they have been) continually debated philosophically. Attempting to make disciples by ending the debate with some philosophic dogma would be unphilosophical.

What makes Catholic schools Catholic are the theological truths which govern and give guidance to both philosophy and to persons of Catholic faith. These truths have made the Catholic Church a countercultural church. It is a church which stands in resistance to birth control, to violence and death, to premarital sex, to abortion and euthanasia, to divorce, and so on. The failure on the part of Catholic schools to understand that their guidance emanates from theology, and not solely from philosophy, may account for their problems with identity and distinctiveness.

McLaughlin (1996), stressing the need for clarity in relation to the distinctiveness of Catholic education, claims, "no distinctively Catholic systematic account of the nature and role of education has yet emerged" (p. 139). Thus, he concludes, there is a need for a distinctively Catholic philosophy of education. Haldane (1995, 1998) agrees with McLaughlin, and, in a broader context, states he does not know what future Catholic philosophy has. He acknowledges, however, that it would be interesting to view the contributions that philosophers who are Catholic may make. McLaughlin and Haldane use the term "Catholic philosophy of education" and then speak of philosophers who are Catholic, thereby suggesting the confusion surrounding the issue of whether it is philosophy or theology which is equipped to provide systematic direction to the distinctiveness of Catholic schools.

Evidence for this confusion and the recent concern over the future of Catholic philosophy and the Catholic philosophy of education may be found by examining a relatively current encyclopedia on the philosophy of education (Chambliss, 1996). A total of 184 authors contributed selections. Not one contributor addressed either the Catholic philosophy of education or philosophy as it relates to Catholic schooling. Eleven of the contributors resided in Catholic institutions of higher learning. None discussed philosophy as it relates to Catholic education. They chose instead to write about Heidegger, Milton, pragmatism, and so on. Elias (1999) describes the eclipse of a distinctive philosophy of education in an article entitled "Whatever Happened to Catholic Philosophy of Education?" The article title seems appropriate given the non-appearance of Catholic philosophy of education just three years earlier in the major encyclopedia devoted to the field.

Several authors, many of them professional philosophers of education writing for school practitioners, reflect both an imprecise use of language and confusion over the juxtaposition of "Catholic" and "philosophy." Ward's (1963) text does not address the issue; his book is entitled *Philosophy of Education*. Johnston (1963) (see also Fitzpatrick, 1950) admits there is an issue of terminology, and he refers to Donlon (1952), who early on decisively stated, "Theology, as the wisdom of Christian life and thought, must have an essential relation to Christian education" (p. 10). One may observe Johnston's book is entitled *A Philosophy of Education* and Donlon's employs the title *Theology and Education*. Dupuis and Nordberg (1964) were most emphatic about the issue when they stated, the "notion of *a* Catholic philosophy of education is very false" (p. 31). For them a system of philosophy can be Catholic insofar that it has arisen within the Church and is compatible with revealed truths of theology. Their book uses the title *Philosophy and Education*. Dupuis' other work (1966) treated the philosophy of education in historical perspective. Again, no mention was made of the Catholic philosophy of education. McGucken (1962) entitled his book *The Catholic Way in Education*. He avoids the terminology issue by referring to "a complete workable scheme of Catholic education" (p. x). The supernatural, for McGucken, is the key of the Catholic system (i.e., there can be no true education that is not directed to human beings' last end).

In the 1930s, three influential books appeared. Franz De Hovre (1930, 1934) authored two of them, which were used in Europe and in the United States. They were entitled *Catholicism in Education* and *Philosophy and Education*. The first was subtitled "A Positive Exposition of the Catholic Principles of Education with a Study of the Philosophical Theories of Some Leading Catholic Educators." Internally, he employed the term Catholic "manner" (1934, p. 358). The second book mentioned (1930) used the title *Philosophy and Education*, not Catholic philosophy of education. Its subtitle clearly indicates that it is a textbook for normal schools and teachers colleges. De Hovre was a professor of pedagogy in the Higher Institute of Antwerp, Ghent, and Brussels. He took the position that education by nature is a function of philosophy, of metaphysics. He stated, "the great battles of education are being waged today beyond the frontiers of education properly so-called; in other words, in the domain of philosophy" (1930, p. viii). A third work which appeared in the 1930s (Fitzpatrick, 1936), was most respected as a reference work. It contained 738 topics for its various readings, and Catholic philosophy of education was not used as terminology.

In 1961, Phenix edited a respected book on "contemporary philosophies" of education which contained selections representative of different perspectives. Rev. Robert J. Henle (1961), a noted leader in Catholic education, was chosen to treat the Catholic perspective. His selection was entitled "A Roman Catholic View of Education." He did not put forth a claim to a Catholic philosophy of education.

Maritain contributed a selection to *Modern Philosophies and Education: The Fifty-fourth Yearbook of the National Society of Education, Part I* (Henry, 1955), entitled "Thomist Views on Education." In the article, Maritain observed the distinction between Thomistic philosophy and Thomistic theology. He never used the terminology "Catholic philosophy of education." In *Philosophies of Education: The Forty-first Yearbook of the National Society for the Study of Education* (Henry, 1942), McGucken entitled his contribution "The Philosophy of Catholic Education." Again, in representing the Catholic position, he never used the term "Catholic philosophy of education." He acknowledges there could be theological bases of what he called the "Catholic theory of education." He also states the "supernatural" is the basis of the Catholic system. It is interesting to note that McGucken (1962), in his own book, used the title *The Catholic Way in Education*. Perhaps that confusion of imprecise terminology resolved itself by the time the eightieth yearbook of the National Society for the Study of Education was published in 1981 (J. Soltis, Ed.). The Catholic view was not represented at all. The respected Catholic educational leader Malcom Carron (Carron & Cavanaugh, 1963), Jacques Maritain (1955), and many other Catholic thinkers felt an intellectual closeness to Mortimer Adler. They regularly cited him and, in some instances, included his writings in publications intended for a Catholic audience. Adler (1963) stated, in a selection in Carron and Cavanaugh's book: "No part of what is strictly the philosophy of education is either a matter of faith or of opinion" (p. 9).

Francis (1979) and Hull (1976) indicate there can be connections between theology and educational theory. While they make appropriate distinctions between theology and education, they sometimes revert to using the term "Christian philosophy" which reflects imprecision and confusion (McCluskey, 1962). Redden and Ryan (1956) hold with the position that there is a Catholic philosophy of education. The title of their book, greatly influential and widely used and quoted in its time, is *A Catholic Philosophy of Education*. They make the bold assertion: "Catholic philosophy offers principles and norms that govern the entire scope of education" (p. viii). Their purpose is to present a Catholic philosophy of education flowing from a Catholic philosophy of life in three ways: (1) setting forth fundamental educational principles in light of scholastic philosophy, (2) by applying that philosophy in a critical evaluation of false philosophies, and (3) presenting evidence to show Catholic education takes into account the "whole man" (p. vii).

Etienne Gilson (1962), one of the most famous philosophers in Catholic intellectual life, takes a more balanced approach than Redden and Ryan. While Gilson defends the notion of Christian philosophy, he writes: "For it is of the essence of philosophy to pursue the knowledge of causes in the light of natural reason, and if, on the contrary, it is of the essence of theology to pursue the same quest in the light of supernatural revelation, then it is clearly impossible that one single discipline would share in the nature of both" (pp. 192–193). Gilson believes there is a certain way to apply philosophical methods to the investigation of faith. He, nevertheless, acknowledges that even though the subtitle of Pope Leo XIII's (1879) encyclical, *Aeterni Patris*, reads: "On the Restoration in Catholic Schools of Christian Philosophy According to the Mind of the Angelic Doctor Saint Thomas Aquinas," the Pope does not use the term "Christian philosophy."

Maritain (1948b) adds to the discussion of the connection between philosophy and theology when he writes that philosophy, "while remaining absolutely distinct from, is still in vital communication with, the superior wisdom of theology and contemplation" (p. xiii). There are several authors, however, who take a more direct approach in relation to the influence of theology as directing the Catholic educational system. Jones (1934) unambiguously writes, "The core of the Catholic system is theology" (pp. 29–31). Kelly (1999) and Ramsey (1976), 23 years apart, both entitle their articles "Towards a Theology of Catholic Education" and "Towards a Theology of Education," respectively. Kelly (1999) sees four themes converging as an emerging theology of education: "the nature of the person, the function of knowledge, human destiny within history, and the individual's stance toward society" (p. 6). Theology's influence upon these themes contributes to "the transformation of students and their engagement in secular society as the primary educational aim" (p. 6). Ramsey (1976), in reflecting upon what is a theology of education, does not see theology as prescribing what education should be. He sees theology as seeking "informal links" (p. 137) with education; he does not see theology as prescriptive and authoritarian. Hull's (1977) answer to the question: What is theology of education? "is that there are almost as many theologies of education as there are theologies" (p. 3). He avers that there are Jewish, Islamic, Catholic, Lutheran and other theologies of education. As complicated as these theologies are, they are further complicated when mediated by the term "education." For traditional Catholic teaching, theology has an essential relation to education. Donlon (1952), in his book *Theology and Education*, is unambiguous about the relationship. He wonders "why there are no texts in Catholic educational theory that bear the title of theology" (p. 18). He is emphatic when he totally agrees with the statement that "Catholic educators can claim no complete philosophy of education because no such thing exists. There is only a theology of Catholic education" (p. 18).

The apparent confusion over what makes Catholic schools Catholic may indeed be due to the failure to realize there can only be a theology of Catholic education leading to the integration of the tenets of Catholic faith in the school's curriculum and academic life in general. There is little scholarly evidence this integration has been accomplished. When it is even partially accomplished, perhaps major spokesmen for the nature of Catholic education will no longer write: "I am in no sense an expositor of the Catholic viewpoint on education. For one thing, I am not sure that such a viewpoint, except in the vaguest and most general terms, exists" (Graham, 1961, p. 400). This expression of uncertainty appeared in the prestigious *Harvard Educational Review*, when a prominent Catholic clergyman and thinker was invited to contribute.

NATURE OF THE CATHOLIC PHILOSOPHY OF EDUCATION

Despite the treatment of Catholic philosophy of education in the previous section and the confusion attached to utilizing that terminology, it is that very terminology which will be employed during the rest of this review, because most thinkers employ it.

The problem of deciding how to proceed concerning alternative ends confounds the great secular philosophers of education. Sidney Hook (1969), for example, states, "If we have only one end, we have no moral problem. It is only a question of means" (p. 56). While means are vigorously debated in Catholic education circles (O'Brien, 1987), there is no ambiguity as to the end of education. The most authoritative document on the end of Catholic education is Pope Pius XI's encyclical, *The Christian Education of Youth* (1939). The encyclical states: "that there can be no true education which is not wholly directed to man's last end" (p. 5). The "whole work of education is intimately and necessarily connected . . . in pursuit of the last end" (p. 5). Elsewhere in the encyclical, Pius XI reiterates: "The proper and immediate end of Christian education is to cooperate with divine grace in forming the true and perfect Christian, that is, to form Christ Himself in those regenerated by baptism, according to the emphatic expression of the Apostle: 'My little children, of whom I am in labor again, until Christ be formed in you'" (p. 35). For Shields (1917), Christian education "aims at bringing the flesh under control of the spirit. . . . In one word, it aims at transforming a child of the flesh into a Child of God" (p. 180). Spalding's (1905) views are congruent with Pius XI and Shields. He writes, "Education is the soul's response to God's appeal to make itself like unto Him,— self-active, knowing, wise, strong, loving, and fair; and the most permanent example of the most complete hearkening to this appeal is the life and teaching of Christ" (p. 105). Fitzpatrick (1930) sees the end as spiritual, other-worldly, supernatural, life everlasting, life eternal, the life of Christ, and the life of grace. These are primary. He is not unmindful of social welfare, social transformation, wealth, power, prestige, position, notoriety, scholarship, research, vocational skill, and so on. All of these aims are not primary; indeed they are incidental results of Catholic education, not ends at all. The Sacred Congregation for Catholic Education (1977), in its publication *The Catholic School*, is clear about what is the primary end of Catholic education: "It is precisely in the Gospel of Christ, taking root in the minds and lives of the faithful, that the Catholic school finds its definition as it comes to terms with the cultural conditions of the times" (p. 7).

Since when one speaks of ends, one speaks philosophically, an examination of the philosophy which undergirds the end of Catholic education is in order. The Church has indicated that scholastic philosophy (the philosophy of St. Thomas Aquinas) is its official philosophical teaching (Lumbreras, 1944). Scholastic philosophy is understood to mean "exclusively" (p. 31) the philosophy of St. Thomas Aquinas. This philosophy stands for 24 theses approved by the Sacred Congregation of Studies:

General Metaphysics

Thesis I. Potency and Act so divide being that whatsoever exists either is Pure Act, or is necessarily composed of Potency and Act, as to its primordial and intrinsic principles.

Thesis II. Act, because it is perfection, is not limited except by Potency, which is capacity for perfection. Therefore, in the order in which the Act is pure, it is unlimited and unique; but in that in which it is finite and manifold, it comes into a true composition with Potency.

Thesis III. Wherefore, in the exclusive domain of existence itself God alone subsists, He alone is the most simple. Everything else, which participates in existence, has a nature whereby existence is restricted, and is composed of essence and existence as if two really distinct principles.

Thesis IV. Being, which derives its name from existence, is not predicated univocally of God and creatures; nor yet merely equivocally, but analogically by the analogy both of attribution and proportionality.

Thesis V. There is, moreover, in every creature a real composition of subsisting subject with forms secondarily added—that is, accidents; but such a composition could not be understood unless the existence were received into a distinct essence.

Thesis VI. Besides the absolute accidents there is also a relative accident, or "toward something." For although "toward something" does not mean, by its own nature, anything inhering in something, frequently, however, it has a cause in things, and therefore, a real entity distinct from the subject.

Thesis VII. The spiritual creature is as to its essence altogether simple. Yet there remains a twofold composition in it: that, namely, of essence with existence and that of substance with accidents.

Cosmology

Thesis VIII. The corporeal creature, on the contrary, is in its very essence composed of Potency and Act. Such a Potency and Act of the essential order are designated by the names of matter and form.

Thesis IX. Neither of those parts has existence properly speaking; nor is produced or destroyed; nor is placed in a category except by way of reduction, as a substantial principle.

Thesis X. Although extension into integral parts follows corporeal nature, it is not, however, the same for a body to be a substance and to be extended. For substance of itself is indivisible; not certainly after the manner of a point, but after the manner of that which is outside the order of dimension. On the other hand, Quantity, which makes substance to be extended, really differs from substance, and is a veritable accident.

Thesis XI. Matter as subjected to quantity is the principle of individuation or numerical distinction—impossible among pure spirits—whereby individuals of the same species are distinct from each other.

Thesis XII. It is also quantity that makes a body to be circumscriptively in one place and to be incapable, by any means, of such a presence in any other place.

Psychology

Thesis XIII. Bodies are divided into two classes: some are living, others without life. In living bodies, in order to have intrinsically a moving part and a moved part in the same subject, the substantial form, called the soul, requires an organic disposition, or heterogeneous parts.

Thesis XIV. Souls of the vegetative and sensitive order, properly speaking, do not subsist and are not produced, but merely exist and are produced as a principle whereby the living thing exists and lives. Since they depend entirely on matter, at the dissolution of the compound, they are indirectly destroyed.

Thesis XV. On the contrary, the human soul subsists by itself, and is created by God when it can be infused into a sufficiently disposed subject, and is incorruptible and immortal by nature.

Thesis XVI. This same rational soul is so united to the body as to be its single substantial form. By it man is man, and animal, and living, and body, and substance, and being.

Soul, therefore, gives man every essential degree of perfection. It communicates to the body, furthermore, the act of existence whereby itself exists.

Thesis XVII. Faculties of a twofold order, organic and inorganic, naturally spring from the human soul. The subject of the organic, to which sense belongs, is the compound. The subject of the inorganic is the soul alone. The intellect, then, is a faculty intrinsically independent of any organ.

Thesis XVIII. Intellectuality follows immateriality, and in such a manner that the degree of intellectuality is in proportion to the remoteness from matter. The adequate object of intellection is being as such; but the proper object of the human intellect, in the present state of union, is restricted to the essences abstracted from material conditions.

Thesis XIX. We, therefore, receive our knowledge from sensible things. But since no sensible thing is actually intelligible, besides the intellect which is properly intelligent we must admit in the soul an active power which abstracts the intelligible forms from the phantasms.

Thesis XX. Through these species we directly know the universal; the singular we know by the senses, and also by the intellect through a conversion to the phantasms; we rise by analogy to the knowledge of the spiritual.

Thesis XXI. The will follows, does not precede, the intellect; it necessarily desires that which is offered to it as a good which entirely satisfies the appetite; it freely chooses among several good things that are proposed as desirable by the wavering judgment. Election, then, follows the last practical judgment; still, it is the will which determines it to be the last.

Natural Theology

Thesis XXII. That God exists we do not know by immediate intuition, nor do we demonstrate it a priori; but certainly a posteriori, that is, by things which are made, arguing from effect to cause. Namely, from things which are in movement and cannot be the adequate principle of the motion, to the first mover immovable; from the procession of worldly things from causes, which are subordinated to each other, to the first uncaused cause; from corruptible things, which are indifferent alike to being and non-being, to the absolutely necessary being; from things, which, according to their limited perfection of existence, life, intelligence, are more or less perfect in their being, their life, their intelligence, to Him who is intelligent, living, and being in the highest degree; finally, from the order, which exists in the universe, to the existence of a separate intelligence which ordained, disposed, and directs things to their end.

Thesis XXIII. The Divine Essence is well proposed to us as constituted in its metaphysical concept by its identity with the exercised actuality of its existence, or, in other terms, as the very subsisting being; and by the same token it exhibits to us the reason of its infinity in perfection.

Thesis XXIV. By the very purity of His being God is, therefore, distinguished from all finite beings. Hence, in the first place, it is inferred that the world could not have proceeded from God except through creation; secondly, that the creative power, which directly affects being as being, cannot be communicated, even miraculously, to any finite nature; and, finally that no created agent exercises any influence on the being of any effect but on account of a motion received from the first cause. (Lumbreras, 1944, pp. 13–29)

These theses and Thomism, or scholasticism, date from the thirteenth century. Many Catholic thinkers in the modern era who have attempted to apply these theses to the Catholic philosophy of education have been called neo-scholastics or neo-Thomists. Even though Maritain has been identified with neo-scholasticism, he disdains the label when he states, "There is a Thomist philosophy, there is no neo-Thomist philosophy. We make no claim to include anything of the past in the present, but to maintain in the present the 'actuality' of the eternal" (Maritain, 1948b, p. ix). Maritain (1948a) acknowledges modern philosophers have a nobility in that they are genuinely elevated to the mind even when on occasion they ruin it. He feels their devotion to the mind has been greater than their love of God. Aquinas, he avers, loves God more than the mind, yet his devotion "to the mind is greater than the devotion of all the other philosophers" (p. 69). Cunningham (1928) reinforces the importance of the proper relationship between body and mind and the connection between them and the "nature of God in relation to man working out his eternal salvation in a social environment" (p. 278). Maritain (1931) feels Aquinas is the only thinker who has a correct idea of human nature, an idea which he regards as the central factor in education. Maritain boldly claims Aquinas' theory of human nature

is the only theory that draws a clear distinction between the natural and supernatural order while pointing out their essential accord. It is the only theory that provides a rational basis for the spiritual order in which mankind is raised to kinship with God through the action of God. It is the only theory that maintains the primacy of will, of love, in the practical order, that is, in the field of human acts, in the formation of character and in the conduct of life. In brief, it is to St. Thomas we must go for enlightenment with regard to the factors without a complete understanding of which a sound theory of education is impossible. (p. x)

Many scholars find it incomprehensible that the Church would adopt Thomism as its official philosophy. De Hovre (1934) (see also McCluskey, 1966), however, maintains authority is essential to the notion of Catholicism. Power in the Church is centralized, organization is hierarchical, and doctrine is infallible. These elements of Catholicism are aristocratic, yet the Church is said to have created an atmosphere in which the spirit of democracy has thrived. Graham (1961) recounts that "Catholicism claims to be, in certain respects, the lineal descendant of Old Testament theocracy. The Church's official rulers have an authority which is not dependent on the consent of the ruled" (p. 400). Pius XI (1930) explains the proper mission of the Church is faith and morals and it shares in the Divine Magisterium through God Himself. Through special privilege the Church has been granted immunity from error, and it has an inherent, inviolable right to freedom in teaching. As a consequence, it is independent of any earthly power in exercising its educational mission. Kerr (1999) wonders why the pope is so dogmatic about the truth of Catholic faith, since it is truly reasonable. He gives several reasons. He maintains there is no thought without dogma. Even the empiricists are said to have their dogmas. The philosophical errors of relativism and scientism are cited as rationales for dogma. The former denies access to ultimate truths and values. The latter claims that everything can be known by the empirical sciences. Kerr also defends dogma in that Catholics, even though they may regard their faith as reasonable, there is no guarantee that believers will be. Sin, disordered use of freedom, temptations, and so on may lead believers to culturally more acceptable and easier routes.

The conflict between faith and reason for the Catholic intellectual has arisen frequently, and Catholic scholars are still widely held suspect (O'Dea, 1958). In fact, John Tracy Ellis (1955), in his famous and often quoted article on "American Catholics and the Intellectual Life," chastised Catholic scholars for their weak showing and for their ghetto mentality. His work, no doubt, added to the view that Catholic intellectuals were suspect. O'Dea (1958) asks the question, "Are the explicit teachings of the Catholic Church hostile to the life of the intellect?" (p. 52). For Catholic scholars, of course, the answer lies "in the conviction that truth is one and indivisible, and that reason and revelation cannot at their most profound levels be in contradiction with each other" (p. 53) (see also Newman, 1960). O'Dea maintains this has remained the dominant characteristic of the Catholic view. Critics frequently cite the rejection by churchmen of Galileo, Darwin, and others. O'Dea calls these cases historical accidents. He calls the Church's attitude intransigent and shortsighted. He admits such an attitude alienated many the Church should have embraced, for the "clergy should have understood that all attacks on freedom of thought, when neither morals nor dogmas were concerned, made enemies of the very people it most needed" (O'Dea, 1958, p. 57).

Some see Vatican II as having stimulated changes in the Church's teaching, thus contributing to less clarity. In addition, differences between conservatives and liberals in areas such as the Magisterium (the teaching authority of the Church), theological dissent, and the issue of ecclesiastical authority surfaced (Elias, 1999; Gleason, 1994). While Vatican II is seen to have set forth the concepts of collegiality and shared authority, the "Declaration on Christian Education" is described as not having a philosophical base and as being a document which breaks little new ground (Abbott, 1966; Malone, 1967). There is little doubt that past conciliar thinkers are wondering whatever happened to Catholic philosophy of education (Elias, 1999; Carr, Haldane, & McLaughlin, 1995; Langan, 1978). Langan states: "The fact must be faced: there is no dominant Catholic philosophical tradition today. The reason for that is neither institutional, sociological, nor conspiratorial. Rather it is purely *philosophical*" (p. 12). Reasons for this situation lie in the emergence of contending camps within neo-Thomism; the inability of Thomism, with some exceptions, to exploit its strength against empiricism and positivism by employing descriptive analyses of basic cognitive processes; and so on.

Carr et al. (1995) maintain that little if any progress has been made in identifying a distinctively Catholic philosophy of education since Maritain published

Education at the Crossroads in 1943. While it is obvious Catholic philosophers no longer take an oath to Thomism, Carr et al. stress it is perhaps hardly possible to even think of developing a Catholic philosophy of education without thinking of Thomism. Of course, Maritain, whom they respect, is, as was stated previously, identified with Thomism. Analysts of the current scene in Catholic philosophy of education seem not to realize Maritain's educational thought is theocentric (Joseph, 1966). It is inspired by theology. Indeed, Aquinas' *Summa Theologica* (1947) is a work in theology. Given these points, it seems misplaced to fret over the notion that absolutism in philosophy is untenable for philosophic investigation. As mentioned previously, however, absolutism in theology, which undergirds education, is not untenable.

The "Professional" Philosophers of Education. Prior to 1943, the date of Maritain's Terry Lectures at Yale, which culminated in the publication of his *Education at the Crossroads*, many authors wrote works in philosophy of education intended primarily for education students in Catholic colleges and universities. Selected for review here are three major works in the 1930s, two in the 1950s, four in the 1960s, and three in the 1970s.

In 1930, Rev. Franz De Hovre published *Philosophy and Education*, which was intended as a textbook for normal schools and teachers' colleges. It was read by students in Europe and America. De Hovre received a favorable reaction from students in America; they were said to find discussion of education from a philosophical viewpoint to be practical. De Hovre's work aimed to equip students to engage in critical analyses of other schools of thought, using scholastic philosophy as a base. His work was devoted to examining naturalism, socialism, and rationalism with critical analyses of each. His other volume, *Catholicism in Education*, appeared in 1934. In this book De Hovre puts forth the thesis that not only psychology, but philosophy should undergird the knowledge base of education. He avers that if one digs deeper, one "will find the bed-rock of Catholicism" (p. v). As in his 1930 book, he intends to equip the Catholic teacher to reach educational conclusions that flow naturally from *philosophia perennis* (perennial philosophy). He wishes to have students gain a knowledge of the principles which form the bases of the Church's system of education. The contributions of Catholic educators to formulation of a "universal" philosophy are emphasized. For example, he introduces students to Spalding, covering such topics as contemporary psychology, training of the intellect, character education, and the education of women. Also, Newman is covered extensively.

McGucken's often cited book, *The Catholic Way in Education*, appeared in 1962. It was bold in connecting educational theory to one's view of the dogma of original sin. McGucken strongly agrees with Pius XI's contention that there could be no true education which is not wholly directed to the educand's last end. Like De Hovre, McGucken rejected pedagogic naturalism in the teaching of youth because of its denial or forgetfulness of original sin and grace, relying solely on the powers of human nature. He was one of the earliest Catholic thinkers to be open to the contributions educational psychology could make to philosophy, but he cautioned that experimental psychology could not lay claim to being a philosophy itself. Tracing an unbroken line of thought from Aristotle through Aquinas to the present, McGucken maintains allegiance to the notion that every substantial unit in nature, man or tree or whatever, is composed of two consubstantial principles—matter and entelechy:

> Matter is the principle of divisibility and quantification, the determinable element. *Entelechy* is the principle of unification and specification, the determining element, that which makes of a given unit a single and determinable whole, makes it to be that which it is. The entelechy of human beings is called a soul and its material complement is called an organism. The human being, therefore, is a physical organism living by and informed by a spiritual soul. (McGucken, 1962, p. 90)

It is this notion of entelechy which prompted McGucken (1962) to reject John Dewey's philosophy, which "has spread like a plague through American normal schools and schools of education" (p. 19). McGucken even cites by page number one of Dewey's books in which the concept of soul is rejected. He chides Dewey for his unwise fear of other-worldliness.

In the 1930s, when the Catholic reaction to Dewey (1982) and other pragmatists, naturalists, positivists, and so on was so great, Fitzpatrick (1936) produced an unusual volume, 809 pages in length, entitled *Readings in the Philosophy of Education*. It contained selections representing a wide variety of philosophic positions by many of the greatest thinkers of that time. Selections were included by Dewey, Kilpatrick, Spencer, Locke, Thorndike, Gates, and many others not in the scholastic tradition. Fitzpatrick, who was dean of the School of Education at Marquette University, truly believed in exposure to other philosophic traditions. Approximately 30 years later, also at Marquette University, Dupuis (1966) and Dupuis and Nordberg (1964) continued the practice of presenting many viewpoints along with a variety of traditions within Catholic scholarship. Along with philosophies of Catholic education, Dupuis and Nordberg (1964) considered materialism, progressivism, scientific realism, Marxism, atheistic existentialism, and idealism. Dupuis (1966), in taking a historical perspective to the philosophy of education, chose to treat issues within the context of educational conservatism and liberalism. In treating different traditions and topics, Dupuis sought to accomplish in a systematic way what few philosophers of education have attempted. In connection with each major topic, he elaborated how advocates of that topic would consider several questions; for example, What is man? How do we know? How do we teach? What is truth? What is good? What is the purpose of school? What should be taught? How should pupils be evaluated? How are freedom and discipline to be harmonized? and so on.

Redden and Ryan's (1956) often cited work, *A Catholic Philosophy of Education*, is characterized by a strictly apologetic treatment of the child, curriculum, educational aims, moral education, methods, physical education, and so on. In addition they provide a systematic scholastic critique of experimentalism's position on such topics as the soul, the origin of ideas, truth, knowledge, the will, morality, democracy, the individual and society, and God. The method of critique is to first explain experimentalism's position on each topic as they conceive of it, elaborate the view of scholasticism, and then proceed to indicate what they refer to as the fallacies of experimentalism.

Ward (1958, 1963) authored two books on the philosophy of Catholic education which were not as widely known as those mentioned previously. In them he adopted a typical Catholic position. He acknowledged Dewey's contributions more than some authors. One unique feature of his writings is his insight on a whole school system, which was begun and maintained by Catholics in America. Ward feels Catholics are too close to their school system to see that it is a major achievement of American life. He eloquently describes the system as consecrated, dedicated, and built on sacrifice: "just when almost everything else has long been given to lush profit, here is something given through poverty and penury to the service of man and God" (1958, p. 90).

Johnston's (1963) *A Philosophy of Education* is self-described as intended for graduate and undergraduate students. It is not unlike the typical text of this kind except in its relatively extended (more so than in similar works) treatment of habits and virtues, and in its mention of the role of philosophy in educational administration.

Natural Law. As mentioned in a previous section, the Catholic Church is counter to culture. Students in Catholic schools for whom the Catholic philosophy of education is intended are in the full bloom of life, particularly adolescents. The Church asks them, particularly in sexual matters, to exercise a kind of discipline and self-control foreign to many of their peers and indeed to the culture at large. The Church ultimately justifies its stand by citing natural law doctrine, and it intends that "the Catholic school by no manner of means escapes the natural law governing the operation of the school community" (McCluskey, 1969, p. 340). Historically, the Church has taught that natural law is based on human nature and is immutable and universally valid. Some argue, of course, that natural law precepts do not hold across cultures, are not immutable, and are subject to relativism of time and place (Hall, 1981). The Church, however, has not allowed arguments for relativism to influence its insistence that human beings have certain innate inclinations which are grounded in human nature (Fremantle, 1963). Catholics believe the natural law is derived from God at creation, and that it is present in human existence and is the source of discerning what is forbidden and not in conformity with rational and social nature. It is inherent in human beings by nature and through it we perceive what we ought to do and avoid. The natural law is thus the eternal law (Rommen, 1998). The Church is regarded as competent to interpret the natural moral law, and it teaches that "Jesus Christ, when communicating to Peter and to the Apostles His divine authority and sending them to teach all nations His commandments, constituted them as guardians and authentic interpreters of . . . the natural law, which is also an expression of the will of God, the faithful fulfillment of which is . . . necessary for salvation" (Paul VI, 1968, p. 3).

It is not difficult for Catholics to understand the notion that human beings have certain innate inclinations which are grounded in human nature. The *precepts* of natural law which flow from these innate inclinations are a source of great difficulty. For example, adolescents have little difficulty in understanding that a desire to propagate the species and to care for the upbringing of children is an innate inclination. They have great difficulty, however, in understanding the precepts which flow from that fundamental inclination (Joseph, 1984).

Despite such difficulty, students and their teachers are reminded that "Catholic theology teaches—rightly teaches—that human reason is in itself capable of coming to the knowledge of natural law" (Fuchs, 1965, p. 191). It teaches that natural law is valid for every salvation situation and always has an actual validity and a possibility of being applied. It is related to absolute elements and is not conditioned by the particular situation. The natural law itself is divine: "the Church in her own Code emphatically refuses to recognize any legislation that contradicts the natural law" (Fuchs, 1965, p. 8).

Most general principles are basic forms of human good and are in the human heart. Sane and reasonable people are capable of seeing that life, knowledge, fellowship, offspring, and a few other basic aspects of human existence are, as such, good and worth having. Moral implications of first principles, however, are capable of being obscured or distorted by prejudice, oversight, convention, and the sway of desire for particular gratifications (Finnins, 1980). The great failure is how to explain "just how the specific moral rules which we need to guide our conduct can be shown to be connected with allegedly self-evident principles" (Finnins, 1980, p. 34).

There is little evidence that Catholic schools admit to and address this failure by developing instructional materials and teaching strategies which the young can understand and which are developmentally appropriate. There is evidence for being alarmed. In 1982, surveys were administered to 8,000 young adolescents and 10,000 of their parents. These surveys constituted a study entitled *Early Adolescents and Their Parents* (Benson, Wood, & Johnson, 1984). The study included respondents from many religious denominations, including 1,130 Catholic school youth and 965 parents. While Catholic youth are more likely to see abortion as morally wrong, "an index of traditional moral beliefs shows them to be slightly less affirming of traditional moral positions than the other youth and more interested and active in the area of sexuality" (Manno, 1984, p. 13). The percentage of youth who claim they have engaged in intercourse was surprisingly high given the Church's teaching.

In this entire fourth section and in section three, it is obvious that the failure to understand the distinction between philosophy and theology has been motivated by convenience and a reluctance to grapple with the difficulties in integrating elements of Catholic theology in the school curriculum. McGucken (n.d.), in his *Catholic Education: Its Philosophy, Its Fundamentals, Its Objec-*

tives, explains that in his formulation "Catholic" or "Christian" philosophy is used "for convenience to designate all the philosophical-theological bases of the Catholic outlook on life" (p. 1). It seems, from what has been examined thus far, that those who would deal with the philosophy of Catholic education have considered philosophical and theological bases as one. This melting has contributed to the arduousness of the task to discover the distinctiveness of the Catholic school. The permeation of philosophical issues in the curriculum will not contribute to distinctiveness. These issues are also germane to public schools. If Catholic theology, on the other hand, successfully, and with intellectual sophistication, permeates the school curriculum, then it may very well lead to distinctiveness.

JACQUES MARITAIN

Perhaps a few words by Daniel Sargent (1934) will give us the central intuition of Maritain's influence in educational circles during the past six decades: "Maritain, Maritain—We are beginning to be beset by his name. At first it approached us from footnotes, then from quotations of him by others, then from title pages of his own books which have been translated into English. Beset we are, and glad we are beset" (p. 567).

Sargent's passage reveals what any serious student of educational philosophy already comprehends; namely, that Maritain's voice has become a prominent one. Maritain dares to philosophize about education during a time of flux, crisis, and ambivalence. He dares to use the imperative when recommending a practical course of action. He dares, as a philosopher, to descend to the level of practical educational considerations at a time when such a descent is perhaps most discouraging.

It is reported that, for several years, Maritain "concerned himself only with metaphysics and pure ideas; he passed among men without paying a great deal of attention to them" (R. Maritain, 1945, p. 216). Many times he refused to make his more abstruse studies clearer, "out of respect for the dignity of the queen of sciences" (p. 216). The presence of social and ethical problems of the greatest magnitude is the factor which has made Maritain the philosopher and his philosophy more humanized and attuned to the practical. He has entered "into the thick of human affairs" and has proclaimed the necessity of wrestling successfully with the problems of our time (p. 216). He has realized that to win victories one must get from behind fortresses (Maritain, 1952); that Thomism in our time has to live outside the schools as well as in the schools if it is to animate contemporary researchers (Maritain, 1941).

In this brief treatment we shall not discuss the usual well-known dates of Maritain's birth, marriage, conversion to Catholicism, and other biographical data, for this work has already been done very well by many writers. Rather, the primary intent is to establish the fact that there exists a sensitivity and a state of readiness in the mind of Maritain to grasp the importance of practical matters and to propose courses of action in the domain of the practical.

Maritain is convinced that the philosopher has the right and duty, if he is needed, to enter the practical domain and to judge various practical questions as a philosopher, to take a stand on problems of immediate practical concern. Maritain is also convinced that the philosopher's vocation is not hindered or fruitlessly interrupted by incursions into the practical order. On the contrary, he sees such incursions, especially when the need arises, as part of the very vocation of philosophy, and as doing honor to philosophy rather than as detracting from its dignity (Gallagher, 1950). Maritain, speaking of Thomism, has forcefully and eloquently stated:

I even think that the time has come for it to spread into every kind of profane speculative activity, to quit the confines of the school, seminary or college and to assume throughout the whole world of culture the role appropriate to a wisdom of the natural order: its place is among its sister sciences and it must exchange ideas with politics and ethnology, history and poetry; bred in the open air, in the free discussions of peripateticism, its desire is, while holding aloof from the active business of mankind, to take an interest in everything that concerns human life. (Maritain, 1948b, p. 82)

Maritain (1933) is continually incensed at those who term an ancient philosophy a static one. He counters with his well-known expression, "The philosophy that is not ancient is very soon old" (p. 58). He (1948a) has bluntly stated that "Thomism is not a museum piece" (p. 1), that the *Philosophia perennis* has both continuity and traditional wisdom, and that it cannot be fixed in a particular stage of its development; for it has an essentially progressive nature. Maritain strongly feels that Thomism "is relevant to every epoch. It answers modern problems, both theoretical and practical. In face of contemporary aspirations and perplexities, it displays a power to fashion and emancipate the mind. We therefore look to Thomism at the present day to save in the speculative order, intellectual values, in the practical order, so far as they can be saved by philosophy, human values" (p. 1).

Maritain sees his philosophical principles living "in the market place of today's world" and sees Thomism bringing "to the problems of today an understanding nourished in the permanent principles of St. Thomas" (Pegis, 1955, p. 1).

It has been said that those who think with St. Thomas are of necessity *antimoderne* because Thomas is *ultramoderne*. Maritain feels St. Thomas wrote not for the thirteenth century but for our own times; for "His own time is the time of the spirit, which dominates the ages" (Maritain, 1948b, p. 69). Maritain (1948b) thinks of him as a contemporary writer and the most modern of all philosophers.

Maritain has successfully fulfilled his vocation to carry the light of his philosophy and thought to the problems of our times (R. Maritain, 1945). His practical attitude has been demonstrated in his thinking on certain very real educational problems which exist currently.

The French edition of *Education at the Crossroads* (*L'education a lacroisée des chemins*), for example, contains an annex devoted exclusively to the practical problems of the public school in France (Maritain, 1947). In one of Maritain's (1955) most extensive articles on the subject of education, "Thomist Views of Education," he continually devotes as much attention to the application of principles to practical problems as he does to the stating of the principles. In this article Maritain states: "So I shall . . . divide into two parts the considerations that I should like to submit, one dealing with philosophical principles, the other with practical application" (p. 57). In the same article Maritain explains that, in his estimation, progressive education is the education which is predominantly in practice, and he feels it is an education which often makes appeal for support from many philosophical systems, but most notably from pragmatism. Maritain importantly claims his outlook on education agrees "in many respects with the practical ways and methods of progressive education" (1995, p. 57), when such an education is not led astray by prejudice or ideological intemperance. Far from displaying intemperance, Maritain is very much in favor of the concern progressivists have "with the inner resources and vital spontaneity of the pupil," and feels others could profitably demonstrate such an interest (p. 57).

Maritain (1931) feels much real progress has been made in modern education by those who appeal to philosophical systems other than his own. While he doesn't sanction all of the changes and experiments which have been taking place, he feels it is necessary to understand the problems of modern education so that what is important in the methodology of the traditional can be maintained "on a level with all the real progress that the newer education has been able to register" (p. vi). Maritain seems to imply that the "older" education has not been able to register progress with the rapidity or the effectiveness of the newer. If it had, there would be little need for him to admire in glowing terms the strides of the latter. This is not to say, however, that the treasure of Thomistic thought has not the sources of guidance within it to deal with the practical problems of modern education.

Maritain (1930b) has said that, whether we treat the problem of children's education or any other problem, "we have at our command a vast and continually augmenting treasure of instructions from which . . . to draw a speculative and practical guidance of the highest value, thoroughly adapted to the needs of modern civilization" (p. 538). It is clear, then, that there is nothing inherent in the "treasure of instructions" which prohibits rapid progress in practical matters. Progress is hindered, however, by good principles badly applied (Maritain, 1944, p. 63), by undue confidence in novelty for novelty's sake, by mistaken conceptions of progress (Phelan, 1937), by certain pretexts of fidelity to fragments of the past (Maritain, 1930b), and by those who stand for what has been forcefully called an "archaeological" and not a "living" Thomism (Phelan, 1937).

It has been said that "Maritain stands for a living, not an archaeological

Thomism (Phelan, 1937, p. 31). Even those not in agreement with Maritain in the area of educational thought have paid him tribute by stating that he has done much to widen the scope of perennialism: "It is probable that no perennialism of our time compares with Maritain in the success with which ancient-medieval ideas in this sphere have been restated and applied to the arts of today and tomorrow" (Brameld, 1950, p. 312). Maritain does not mind being called a perennialist; in fact, he desires to be called a perennialist—not a mediaevalist—whose philosophy is actual (Maritain, 1948b). He feels that if something is actual it is up to the minute. There are really two ways of being actual he says: "What is by its very essence in time, is actual only by, and for, the instant . . . it is actual—of the moment—only because it can suffer change. But that which is above time is actual without suffering change" (Maritain, 1933, p. 58).

Maritain (1933) has no intention of repeating the failure of what he calls the "decadent scholastics" of the sixteenth and seventeenth centuries to fulfill their duty of temporal actuality in the use of their wisdom, and of also failing to grasp the eternal actuality of that wisdom.

In these few introductory comments we have not attempted to prove that Jacques Maritain *is* a man who has successfully dealt with practical problems; we have attempted to demonstrate that there exists an *attitude*, a state of readiness, in Maritain's mind to grasp the importance of practical problems. Having demonstrated the existence of such an attitude, we can now turn to an allied consideration which is, generally speaking, concerned with certain imperatives Maritain feels should pertain to the institution of the school if it is to educate for what he calls a new humanism.

The belief that most, if not all, of humans' existence is to take place on this earth, the belief in a natural order of things without supernatural influence, and the belief in humans' full perfectability on this earth, are largely responsible for what Maritain calls a state of anthropocentric humanism.

In this humanism only the operational is real, only the demonstrable is certain, and only the quantifiable is worthy of our veneration. Consequently, this humanism has seen methodological principles elevated to philosophical positions. If one were pressed to describe the central intuition of anthropocentric humanism, one would have to say it is the belief that the mind of the individual, by itself alone, is capable of achieving the greatest good for the individual. It is little wonder, then, that the disease afflicting the modern world is foremost of all a disease of the mind; "it began in the mind, it has now attacked the roots of the mind" (Maritain, 1948b, p. 56). Maritain (1943b) is aware that the word "humanism" as a general term lends itself to many different interpretations. With regard to a general definition, he says: "let us say simply that humanism tends essentially to render man more truly human and to manifest his original greatness by enabling him to partake of everything in nature and in history capable of enriching him. It requires both that man develop the latent tendencies he possesses, his creative powers, and the life of reason; and that he work to transform into instruments of his liberty the forces of the physical universe" (p. 3).

Maritain's (1959) idea of humanism, however, goes much further than the one previously given; for he continually warns against defining humanism "by excluding all reference to the superhuman and by foreswearing all transcendence" (pp. 5–6). Thus, we have what has been called a dispute between two conceptions of humanism—a theocentric or Christian conception and an anthropocentric conception. It has been said that the distinction between theocentric and anthropocentric humanism is analogous to the distinction between an open and a closed reason. Closed reason is not aware of the beyond. Open reason is aware that an individual's experience includes much which his or her intellect must acknowledge without mastering. Open reason is said to work in a God-made universe where God, not individuals, is the measure of all things (Allen, 1951).

Maritain (1943b) feels that anthropocentric humanism "walls the creature up in the abyss of animal vitality" (p. 10). Such a humanism for him means that individuals alone, and by themselves alone, work out their salvation. According to this humanism, then, individuals' salvation and destiny are merely and exclusively temporal and are to be achieved without God. An anthropocentric humanism suffers from the anachronism of styling itself as "humanistic" while at the same time ignoring the Author of all humanity. Maritain feels such an anachronism allows the atheistic to destroy a humanism which is only professed in theory. Maritain's (1939) concept of an integral, progressive, and Christian humanism—theocentric humanism, if you will—is one "which considers man in the wholeness of his natural and supernatural being, and which sets no a priori limit to the descent of the divine into man" (p. 8). Maritain has often called such a humanism the "humanism of the Incarnation" (p. 8). In the integral, progressive, or Christian humanism mentioned there is no choice between the vertical movement toward eternal life, which is present and initiated here below, and the horizontal movement whereby the creative forces of humans are progressively revealed in history. The horizontal movement has its own proper temporal finalities, and while it tends to better an individual's condition here below, it prepares for eternal life. The two movements are not separate. They must be pursued simultaneously, and there can be no mutual exclusion of one by the other.

Also, the horizontal movement of historical progression cannot be effectively achieved and cannot be prevented from being an instrument in the destruction of humans unless it is vitally joined to the vertical movement toward eternal life. This horizontal movement has laudable and proper temporal aims and tends to—but does not completely achieve—better the condition of individuals. It provides for human beings within human history the chance to earn that which is beyond human history—the Kingdom of God (Maritain, 1943b).

The task of the new humanism, then, demands a sanctification of the profane and the temporal. It demands that the human person be viewed with a more profound sense of dignity than ever before; consequently, persons must rediscover God and at the same time rediscover themselves in God. It demands,

Whalen (1965) is one of the few authors who even begins to address with some specificity the kinds of issues which would assist those developing a course of studies characterized by integration. He sees social science and the Church's teaching coming together, since both have human beings as their object, human beings as members of society, families, and so on. Connections between languages and religion are possible, depending upon the literature selected. He acknowledges that the challenge to achieve integration with chemistry, physics, biology, and mathematics is greater than for other disciplines. What he calls the science-theology conflict is a formidable obstacle. For the most part, scientists have little patience with theologians, and theologians have little patience with scientists. Whalen observes that the heart of the problem may be "a basic misunderstanding of the theological approach to truth by scientists and of the scientific approach to truth by theologians" (p. 474). Whalen cautions that the following intellectual behaviors are unsatisfactory: repudiate theology; repudiate science; see science as subordinate to theology; make theology subordinate to science. It is interesting to note that scholars not associated with the Catholic tradition may be in the forefront of dealing with these basic misunderstandings (see: Swinburne, 1996; Feynman, 1998).

McGucken (1962) and Maritain (1963) are concerned that synthesis and integration may be hindered for two reasons. One is the great mass of material (facts, dates, etc.) forced upon students. Another is the failure to develop the habit of contemplation in students and teachers. Consider, for example, the contemplation required if one is to gain meaning from Pieper's (1954) contention that history is extra-temporal, beyond time; and if viewed in this manner, then the events within time should be considered in terms of salvation and disaster. Theology and history come together deeply and beautifully in Pieper's book *The End of Time*, and contemplation is a must if qualitative linkages are to be made.

A Failure of Pedagogical Means. During the last 30 years, especially, there has been an intense interest manifested in the architecture or structure of knowledge. Difficult questions have been asked as to what should be the scope of the curriculum, the sequence of studies, and so on. The serious architects of knowledge haven't resolved these difficult questions—they have, however, almost always agreed that students should be exposed to symbolics, empirics, aesthetics, and the synthetic disciplines.

Absent from their deliberations has been any serious consideration of the role of theology (and to a lesser extent, philosophy) in the structure of knowledge. The architects of knowledge in Catholic education have recognized that theology and philosophy are legitimate realms of meaning and must exist if a school is truly to be a school. This recognition constitutes one of the strongest rationales for the Catholic school. Seeking unity in the realms of meaning is essentially seeking to view ways of knowing, seeking the study of human nature. It is because Catholic educators do not wish to affirm a human nature as closed in upon itself or absolutely self-sufficient that there is a desire to study the educand in a Catholic school.

The architects of knowledge in Catholic education have dared to assign a hierarchy of values to the realms of meaning. Atop this hierarchy stands theology, and philosophy as it borders upon theology. Furthermore, these two disciplines are to permeate and vivify all the other realms of meaning. The failure lies in a Catholic education which has been unfaithful to the meaningful implementation of a curriculum genuinely inspired by theology and philosophy. Such a failure is analogous to those disheartened by the failure of Christianity to abide by its principles (Ryan, 1964). The most generous alternative such a disillusionment produces, both in and out of education, may be observed in institutions and individuals which adopt an anthropocentric orientation state in their sometimes heroic battle to fulfill the promise of Christian principles minus the authority who originated them.

The failure of theology and philosophy to meaningfully serve as a unifying force in the curriculum occurred with hardly a serious effort to accomplish such a unity. Many a high school principal has seen that there may be some merit for teachers of literature and history to collaborate on teaching the Renaissance period. The fusion does not occur automatically or accidentally. The teachers involved painstakingly create a syllabus with appropriate materials in order to accomplish such a unifying experience. This is the practical pedagogical endeavor which has been so repulsive to us in Catholic education. Perhaps Catholic schools are too independent (O'Gorman, 1987). Perhaps they are too sophisticated for such massive, practical pedagogical activities.

At any rate, on the level of practice, one is hard-pressed to find research specifically dealing with the *means of how* the realms of meaning may be unified by theology and philosophy. Efforts dealing with the *means* of implementing that unity, not with a verbal or philosophical model which, de jure, merely affirms that such a unity is logical and proper, are lacking. Until such efforts are made, students in a given discipline are not likely to isolate a significant aspect of a given discipline and ask: What does this significant aspect mean to me in terms of salvation and disaster?

Clerics for most of the history of Catholic education have constituted a reference group which has had the responsibility for defining the nomothetic dimension of their institutions—this is the dimension of the institution and its role expectations. In recent years the idiographic dimension of Catholic educational institutions—the dimension of the individual faculty member and his or her need dispositions—has been populated predominantly by laymen.

Several quite normal incongruities have existed between the two dimensions in Catholic institutions; quite normal because these incongruities also exist in non-Catholic institutions. These incongruities need not cause the dissolution of Catholic schooling; nor need they cause both clerics and laymen on the idiographic dimension to flee. These things will not happen if the following efforts are made by those who find themselves in their respective dimension: first, the nomothetic dimension, previously dominated by clerics, must be increasingly populated by laymen; second, and this logically follows the first point, laymen who ascend to the nomothetic dimension must assume an increasing role in defining that dimension by cooperating with those on the idiographic level; third, the major disagreements within the reference groups defining institutional role expectations will be somewhat lessened as a result of the two measures referred to previously; and fourth, one has to hope that individuals in the idiographic dimension will experience fewer contradictions between roles. Also, one has to hope that such individuals will experience fewer contradictions between the expectations of two or more roles which they are called upon to occupy at the same time.

Perhaps these efforts will create an ethos conclusive to attention to the kind of pedagogical means which give allegiance to metaphysics long advocated by Catholic thinkers; that is, seeking unity in diversity with God at the center.

LEARNING AND TEACHING

Historically, the study of the psychology of learning by Catholic scholars and educators has been the study of philosophical psychology. Brennan's (1941) book, *Thomistic Psychology*, was used in many Catholic colleges and universities in the 1940s and 1950s. It is typical in that it covers the psychology of Aristotle and St. Thomas: perfection of the will, the role of habit in human life, sense and intellect, laws of association, and so on. No empirical studies are employed or cited. In treating laws of association, for example, nothing is included beyond Aristotle, Plato, Socrates, and Aquinas.

Much of the psychology associated with Catholic education emphasizes the strength and perfection of the will (Cunningham, 1940; Lindworsky, 1929). Lindworsky, significantly, entitled his book *The Training of the Will*, reflecting much of the pedagogy which characterized and, to some extent, still characterizes Catholic schools. Lindworsky uses a few studies to undergird his work; his major contribution is affirming that there is a relationship between pedagogy and implementing with training.

It is of great historical significance to note the publication of Maher's book, *Psychology*, in 1915. While Maher's treatment is primarily philosophical, he acknowledges experimental methods. He does little more than describe them. He also treats the relationships between psychology and physiology. In general, psychology for Maher remains "that branch of philosophy which studies the human mind or soul . . . the thinking principle" (p. 1).

Psychology, and ultimately educational psychology, steadily developed; and in 1956 Kelly, acknowledging his debt to Maher, developed a text, *Educational Psychology*, which had wide exposure through the early 1960s. Kelly's text is comprehensive in including the fundamental equipment of the learner: sensation, perception, imagination, memory, association, attention, transfer, feelings and emotions, motivation, growth and development, measurement, guidance, intellect, will, and so on. He cited empirical studies and documented philosophical roots.

Texts of educational psychology currently used in Catholic colleges and universities preparing teachers are virtually indistinguishable from those used in secular institutions of higher learning. Vatican II, however, created an ethos for the presentation of a balanced educational psychology when it stated, "with the help of advances in psychology and in the art and science of teaching, children and young people should be assisted in the harmonious development of their physical, moral, and intellectual endowments" (Abbott, 1966, p. 639). This statement by the Council established two major trends: (1) that the advances in psychology are relevant to pedagogy, and (2) that teaching is an art informed by science.

Perhaps Pius XII (1963) created a climate for the Council's balanced educational psychology in his 1958 address to the Congress of the International Association of Applied Psychology, in Rome. The pope delineated a concept of human personality from the psychological and moral point of view. He reaffirmed a definition of personality which affects the psychosomatic unity of the human person, a unity governed and determined by the soul. Pius XII indicated that psychologists could not disregard the eschatological aspect of personality, that is, he stressed, "once the soul has been separated from the body by death, it remains fixed in the dispositions acquired during life" (p. 197). He reminded psychologists that regardless of the clever methods and skills they employ, these "do not succeed in penetrating the area of the psyche . . . which constitutes the center of the personality and which always remains a mystery" (p. 199).

Pope John XXIII also emphasized a consciousness of the eschatological when, in 1959, he addressed members of the Italian Association of Teachers and reminded them that nothing could be greater than to direct the soul and mold the habits of adolescents.

Habits and Virtues. Molding habits has always been central to character education in Catholic schools. In the strongest terms, Lindworsky (1929) stated that moral training and character formation are at the "very heart of the educational problem" (p. 7). Mayer (1929) contends, equally strongly, the very criterion of educability is the ability to form a habit.

The notion of habit is regarded as that which inclines an individual to act with facility in a certain way. Aquinas (1953), in his *De Magistro (The Teacher)*, sees a stage in which habits are not completely formed; they exist in the persons as natural inclinations. Afterwards, through much practice, they are actualized and formed. Thus, the role of the teacher is to make explicit what is implicit in the learner.

The intellectual habits or virtues in Thomistic philosophy are speculative and practical (Maritain, 1930a). The speculative virtues are concerned with de facto what as a matter of fact is. They are concerned with things in being which the human person finds and does not make. The speculative virtues are science, wisdom, and understanding. Science is a mental habitus oriented toward proximate causes. Wisdom is knowledge of things in their ultimate causes. Understanding is a knowledge of the first principles of humans and the universe. The practical habits or virtues are art and prudence. Art involves the right way to make things. Prudence involves the right reasons about things to be done. While the speculative virtues are concerned with finding things in being, the practical virtues are concerned with making things from what is found. The moral virtues are prudence, fortitude, justice, and temperance. It is important to note that prudence is both a moral and an intellectual virtue.

The Teacher. Teachers in Catholic schools are expected to have become competent in these virtues (Aquinas, 1953). They also are expected to know the psychology of the child and adolescent and to have a genuine love of youth. The teacher's calling is regarded as second only to that of the priest, for those in pedagogical professions should see all things in the light of eternity and of the omnipresence of God (De Hovre, 1934; Pius XI, 1939). Indeed, the Sacred Congregation (1977) indicates the crucial role of teachers in transmitting the Christian message. According to the Sacred Congregation, teachers transmit that message by word, and by every gesture of their behavior. This constitutes the distinction between a school where religion is an academic subject like any other and a school whose curriculum and extra-curriculum is permeated by the Christian spirit.

Teachers involved in transmitting the Christian spirit and in teaching subjects in the curriculum are encouraged to keep abreast of recent methods, teaching aids, and questioning skills which lead to searching inquiries (Abbott, 1966). They are directed to develop listening skills, to not look upon achievement of pupils with condescension, and to not issue orders, rules, and restrictions without giving reasons. They are reminded that the dignity of the student demands respect for free choice and the responsibility associated with it, for authentic freedom is an exceptional sign of the divine image within the human person. All of these pedagogical inclinations should be manifested with the realization that students operate in a culture which is described as new and different from the old (Barta, 1967). Christian teachers are cautioned to avoid a narrow, detailed system of surveillance, "a mechanical restriction of the pupils' freedom which threatens to destroy the very foundation of a strong and virile piety" (De Hovre, 1930, pp. 418–419). The passive quality of plasticity is encouraged. This quality involves the capacity to make modifications to one's existing modes of activity "and to establish entirely new modes of activity to meet new and changed conditions" (Shields, 1917, p. 17). Education presupposes plasticity, should increase and prolong it, and the very value of methods and schooling should be measured by the increase and prolongation of plasticity (Shields, 1917). In modern terminology, plasticity involves one's ability to change oneself and the surrounding environment.

Contrary to old stereotypes of teaching in Catholic schools, Maritain (1943a) eloquently calls for liberating what he calls the preconscious spiritual dynamism of the student. This freeing for the flowering of the creative imagination would not be sacrificed for the excessive pressure (some, he acknowledges, is necessary) of cramming memorization drill, and "mechanical and hopeless cultivation of overspecialized fields of learning" (pp. 42–43). What matters most for Maritain's notion of what the teacher should foster in the intellectual life of the student is insight or intuition. There is little evidence that the literature on pedagogy in modern Catholic education reflects serious research in specific methodologies resulting in freeing students' life of the mind for intuition and insight.

Historically, there are two sources in Catholic scholarship which are regarded as classics on the philosophy of teaching. They are the *De Magistro* of Aquinas and the *De Magistro* of Augustine. With the exception of Mayer (1929), there is little evidence of a systematic and comprehensive philosophy of teaching for Catholic education. Both Aquinas (1953) and Augustine (1938) are preoccupied with the nature of signs. Aquinas takes the position that one does not gain a knowledge of things through a sign. The knowledge of things is more genuine than the knowledge of signs, since the knowledge of signs is a means to the end of achieving a knowledge of things. Such language is difficult and probably not too familiar to the modern elementary or high school teacher. It is dangerous to draw practical implications from the positions taken by Aquinas and Augustine. Perhaps they mean to emphasize the importance of experiencing things and not merely the signs of things.

Augustine (1938) considers many topics related to signs and words and things: for example, seeing the meaning of words only through words, whether anything can be shown without a sign, whether signs are shown by signs, reciprocal signs, signs which signify themselves, whether certain things can be taught without signs, that the sign is learned after the thing is cognized is more the case than the thing itself is learned after the sign is given; and he avers that a student learns when the interior truth makes known to him or her that true things have been said by the teacher.

Aquinas (1953) contends that knowledge pre-exists in the learner potentially, and, therefore, reason by itself may reach knowledge of unknown things, and this is called *discovery*; when someone else assists the learner, this is called *learning by instruction*.

Traditionally, the philosophers of Catholic education have been far more concerned with liberal education than with teaching methods. The assumption has been that teachers should have a liberal education if they are to impart such to students. This implies that the speculative intellectual virtues are their own reward, that professional or commercial education comes after liberal education (Newman, 1960). Despite the value placed upon liberal education by Catholic thinkers (Fitzpatrick, 1927; Newman, 1960; Ryan, 1950; Spalding, 1909), the curriculum of Catholic schools is perhaps characterized by educational atomism as much as public schools (Fitzpatrick, 1927). Newman's (1960) notion that knowledge is its own end and is pursued for its own sake has never been clearly understood, nor has it elicited a structural commitment by most Catholic schools.

Teachers in Catholic schools, given the history of the Church's teachings, are, at least implicitly, expected to stimulate an orientation toward social reform and a concern for social justice by students (Barta, 1967; John XXIII, 1961; Leo

XIII, 1939; Pius XII, 1953; Ryan, 1950). Six social documents have been attributed to Pope Pius XII. Leo XIII was concerned about the condition of labor in general, with oppression, child labor, just wages, and so on. John XXIII built upon the themes of his predecessors in the papacy and addressed reconstruction, social progress, disinterested aid, and so on. Barta (1967), in discussing post-conciliar students, indicated that "over sixty per cent have the care of other people as an influential factor in their vocational choice" (p. 24).

Oldenski (1997) acknowledges that movements such as critical pedagogy and liberation theology have as their starting point the Scriptures and the teachings of Jesus. Oldenski sees an integrative model of liberation theology and critical pedagogy. He avers that "a sense of community inheres in the discourse of liberation theology and critical pedagogy as well as in the practices and culture of Catholic schools" (p. 99). Oldenski, in reflecting upon Church documents since Vatican II, sees a sense of community as not being *"per se* the Kingdom of God, but rather a means to the Kingdom" (p. 99). His view is that there has been a paradigm shift in which "The Catholic Church now finds the Kingdom of God wherever there is peace, justice, freedom, and love" (p. 99). This sense of community, he says, must become a part of the climate and identity of Catholic schools.

Despite much literature on the subject of critical pedagogy as it is related to theology, no systematic philosophy of education encompassing the integrative model has been developed.

REFERENCES

Abbott, W. (Ed.). (1966). *The documents of Vatican II.* New York: Guild Press.
Adler, M. (1963). In defense of the philosophy of education. In M. Carron & A. Cavanaugh (Eds.), *Readings in the philosophy of education* (pp. 6–38). Detroit: University of Detroit Press.
Allen, E. (1951). *Christian humanism: A guide to the thought of Jacques Maritain.* New York: Philosophical Library.
Aquinas, T. (1947). *Summa theologica.* New York: Benziger Brothers.
Aquinas, T. (1953). *The teacher.* Chicago: Henry Regnery Co.
Augustine. (1938). *Concerning the teacher and on the immortality of the soul* (G. Leckie, Trans.). New York: Appleton-Century.
Ayer, A. J. (1973). *The central questions of philosophy.* New York: Holt, Rinehart and Winston.
Barta, J. (1967). Understanding the post-conciliar student. In G. Donovan (Ed.), *Vatican Council II: Its challenge to education* (pp. 15–32). Washington, DC: The Catholic University of America Press.
Beauchamp, T. L., Blackstone, W. T., & Feinberg, J. (Eds.). (1980). *Philosophy and the human condition.* Englewood Cliffs, NJ: Prentice-Hall.
Benson, P., Wood, P., & Johnson, A. (1984). Findings of early adolescents and their parents study. *Momentum, XV (1),* 9–11.
Beyer, L. E. (1997). The relevance of philosophy of education. *Curriculum Inquiry, 27 (1),* 82–94.

Boyer, M. W. (1949). *Highways of philosophy.* Philadelphia: Muhlenberg Press.

Brameld, T. (1950). *Patterns of educational philosophy.* Yonkers-on-Hudson, NY: World Book Co.

Brennan, R. (1941). *Thomistic psychology: A philosophic analysis of the nature of man.* New York: The Macmillan Co.

Broudy, H. (1955). How philosophical can philosophy of education be? *The Journal of Philosophy, LII,* 612–622.

Bryk, A., Holland, P., Lee, V., & Carriedo, R. (1984). *Effective Catholic schools: An exploration.* Washington, DC: National Catholic Educational Association.

Buetow, H. (1985). *A history of United States Catholic schooling.* Washington, DC: National Catholic Educational Association.

Buetow, H. (1988). *The Catholic school.* New York: Crossroad Publishing.

Carr, D., Haldane, J., & McLaughlin, T. (1995). Return to the crossroads: Maritain fifty years on. *British Journal of Educational Studies, XXXIII (2),* 64–78.

Carron, M., & Cavanaugh, A. (Eds.). (1963). *Readings in the philosophy of education.* Detroit: University of Detroit Press.

Chambliss, J. (Ed.). (1996). *Philosophy of education: An encylopedia.* New York: Garland Publishing.

Cunningham, W. (1928). The function of a school of education. *America, 39,* 278.

Cunningham, W. (1940). *The pivotal problems of education.* New York: The Macmillan Co.

Danto, A. C. (1968). *What philosphy is.* New York: Harper & Row.

De Hovre, F. (1930). *Philosophy and education* (E. B. Jordan, Trans.). New York: Benziger Brothers.

De Hovre, F. (1934). *Catholicism in education* (E. B. Jordan, Trans.). New York: Benziger Brothers.

Dewey, J. (1982). *The middle works, 1899–1924* (Vol. II). Cardondale, IL: Southern Illinois University Press.

Donlon, T. (1952). *Theology and education.* Dubuque, IA: William C. Brown Co.

Dupuis, A., & Nordberg, R. (1964). *Philosophy and education.* Milwaukee, WI: Bruce Publishing Co.

Dupuis, A. (1966). *Philosophy of education in historical perspective.* Chicago: Rand-McNally.

Elders, L. (1999). Catholic theology at the threshold of the third millennium. *Fellowship of Catholic Scholars Quarterly, 22 (1),* 17–27.

Elias, J. (1999, Winter). Whatever happened to Catholic philosophy of education? *Religious Education, 94 (1),* 92–109.

Ellis, J. (1955). American Catholics and the intellectual life. *Thought, 30,* 351–388.

Feynman, R. (1998). *The meaning of it all: Thoughts of a citizen scientist.* Reading, MA: Helix Books/Addison-Wesley.

Fiebleman, J. K. (1973). *Understanding philosophy.* New York: Dell Publishing Co.

Finnins, J. (1980). *Natural law and natural rights.* Oxford: Clarendon Press.

Fitzpatrick, E. (1927). *The scholarship of teachers in secondary schools.* New York: The Macmillan Co.

Fitzpatrick, E. (1930). *The foundation of Christian education.* Milwaukee, WI: Bruce Publishing Co.

Fitzpatrick, E. (1950). *Exploring a theology of education.* Milwaukee, WI: Bruce Publishing Co.

Fitzpatrick, E. (Ed.). (1936). *Readings in the philosophy of education.* New York: D. Appelton-Century.

Francis, L. (1979). Theology and education: A research perspective. *Scottish Journal of Theology, 32,* 61–70.

Fremantle, A. (Ed.). (1963). *The social teachings of the church.* New York: The New American Library.

Fuchs, J. (1965). *Natural law, a theological investigation.* New York: Sheed and Ward.

Gallagher, D. (1950). Contemporary Thomism. In V. Ferm (Ed.), *A history of philosophical systems* (p. 462). New York: Philosophical Library.

Gilson, E. (1962). *The philosopher and theology.* New York: Random House.

Gleason, P. (1994). *What made Catholic identity a problem?* Dayton, OH: University of Dayton Press.

Graham, A. (1961). Towards a Catholic concept of education in a democracy. *Harvard Educational Review, 31 (4),* 399–412.

Haldane, J. (1995). Philosophy and Catholic education. *The Sower, 16 (3),* 30–31.

Haldane, J. (1998). What future has Catholic philosophy? In M. Baur (Ed.), *Values and virtue theories* (Vol. LXX, pp. 79–89). Washington, DC: American Catholic Philosophic Association.

Hall, C. (1955). Sources of a philosophy of education. *Peabody Journal of Education, 32 (6),* 351–356.

Hall, R. (1981). The alterability of natural law. *New Scholasticism, LV (4),* 474. *Harvard Educational Review, 26 (2)* (1956).

Henle, R. (1961). A Roman Catholic view of education. In P. Phenix (Ed.), *Philosophies of education* (pp. 75–83). New York: John Wiley and Sons.

Henry, N. (Ed.). (1942). *Philosophies of education: The forty-first yearbook of the National Society of Education, Part I.* Chicago: University of Chicago Press.

Henry, N. (Ed.). (1955). *Modern philosophies and education: The fifty-fourth yearbook of the National Society for the Study of Education, Part I.* Chicago: University of Chicago Press.

Honer, S. M., & Hunt, T. C. (1973). *Invitation to philosophy.* Belmont, CA: Wadsworth Publishing.

Hook, S. (1969). Does philosophy have a future? In C. J. Lucas (Ed.), *What is philosophy of education?* (pp. 136–139). London: The Macmillan Co.

Hull, J. (1976). Christian theology and educational theory: Can there be connections? *British Journal of Educational Studies, XXIV (2),* 127–143.

Hull, J. (1977). What is theology of education? *Scottish Journal of Theology, 30,* 3–29.

Joad, C.E.M. (1936). *Guide to philosophy.* New York: Dover Publications.

John XXIII. (1959). *The holy father speaks to teachers.* Washington, DC: National Catholic Welfare Conference.

John XXIII. (1961). *Mater et magistra.* New York: Paulist Press.

Johnson, T. W. (1995). *Discipleship or pilgrimage? The educator's quest for philosophy.* Albany: State University of New York Press.

Johnston, H. (1963). *A philosophy of education.* New York: McGraw-Hill.

Jones, H. (1934). The relation of the humanities to general education. *Proceedings of the Institute for Administrative Officers of Higher Education Institutions, VI,* 29–31.

Joseph, E. (1966). *Jacques Maritain on humanism and education.* Fresno, CA: Academy Guild Press.

Joseph, E. (1984). It's time to make the natural law understandable to the young. *Momentum, XV (1)*, 56–57.

Kelly, B. (1999). Toward a theology of Catholic education. *Religious Education, 94 (1)*, 6–23.

Kelly, W. (1956). *Educational psychology*. Milwaukee, WI: Bruce Publishing Co.

Kerr, G. (1999). On Pope John Paul II's fides et ratio. *Fellowship of Catholic Scholars Quarterly, 22 (2)*, 13–14.

Langan, T. (1978). Is a Catholic philosophy department possible? *Occasional Papers on Catholic Higher Education*. Washington, DC: Association of Catholic Colleges and Universities.

Leo XIII. (1879). *Aeterni patris*. [Scholastic philosophy]. New York: Paulist Press.

Leo XIII. (1939). *Rerum novarum*. [On the condition of labor]. New York: Paulist Press.

Lindworsky, J. (1929). *The training of the will*. Milwaukee, WI: Bruce Publishing Co.

Lucas, C. J. (Ed.). (1969). *What is philosophy of education?* London: The Macmillan Co.

Lumbreras, P. (1944). *The twenty-four fundamental theses of official Catholic philosophy*. Notre Dame, IN: University of Notre Dame Press.

Maher, M. (1915). *Psychology*. New York: Longmans, Green.

Malone, J. (1967). Vatican Council II: Its challenge to education. In G. Donovan (Ed.), *Vatican Council II: Its challenge to education* (pp. 107–118). Washington, DC: The Catholic University of America Press.

Manno, B. (1984). A look at the Catholic components of the study. *Momentum, XV (1)*, 12–14.

Maritain, J. (1930a). *Art and scholasticism* (J. Scanlon, Trans.). New York: Charles Scribner's Sons.

Maritain, J. (1930b). Catholic thought and its mission. *Thought, IV*, 538.

Maritain, J. (1931). Preface. In F. De Hovre (Ed.), *Philosophy of education* (pp. v–xi) (E. B. Jordan, Trans.). New York: Benziger Brothers.

Maritain, J. (1933). *Theonas, conversations with a sage* (F. Sheed, Trans.). New York: Sheed and Ward.

Maritain, J. (1937). *An introduction to philosophy* (E. J. Watkin, Trans.). New York: Sheed and Ward.

Maritain, J. (1939). Integrated behaviors and the crises of modern times. *Review of Politics, I*, 8.

Maritain, J. (1941). Concerning a critical review. *Thomist, III*, 45–53.

Maritain, J. (1943a). *Education at the crossroads*. New Haven, CT: Yale University Press.

Maritain, J. (1943b). *The twilight of civilization* (L. Landry, Trans.). New York: Sheed and Ward.

Maritain, J. (1944). *Christianity and democracy* (D. Anton, Trans.). New York: Charles Scribner's Sons.

Maritain, J. (1947). Annexe, Le probleme de lécole publique en France. In *Léducation a la croisée des chemins*. Paris: Edloff.

Maritain, J. (1948a). *A preface to metaphysics*. New York: Sheed and Ward.

Maritain, J. (1948b). *St. Thomas Aquinas, angel of the schools*. London: Sheed and Ward.

Maritain, J. (1952). *The range of reason*. New York: Charles Scribner's Sons.

Maritain, J. (1955). Thomist views on education. In N. Henry (Ed.), *The fifty-fourth yearbook of the National Society for the Study of Education, part one* (pp. 57–90). Chicago: University of Chicago Press.

Maritain, J. (1959). Integrated humanism and the crisis of modern times. In M. A. Fitzsimons, T. T. McAvoy, & F. O'Malley (Eds.), *The image of man* (pp. 5–6). Notre Dame, IN: University of Notre Dame Press.

Maritain, J. (1963). On some typical aspects of Christian education. In M. Carron & A. Cavanaugh (Eds.), *Readings in the philosophy of education* (pp. 239–257). Detroit, MI: University of Detroit Press.

Maritain, R. (1945). *Adventures in grace* (J. Kernan, Trans.). New York: Longmans, Green.

Mayer, M. (1929). *The philosophy of teaching of St. Thomas Aquinas*. Milwaukee, WI: Bruce Publishing Co.

McCluskey, N. (1962). *Catholic viewpoint on education*. Garden City, NY: Doubleday.

McCluskey, N. (1966). Catholic schools after Vatican II. In C. A. Koob (Ed.), *What is happening to Catholic education* (pp. 1–12). Washington, DC: National Catholic Educational Association.

McCluskey, N. (1969). Catholic schools after Vatican II. In R. Shaw & R. Hurley (Eds.), *Trends and issues in Catholic education* (pp. 335–347). New York: Citation Press.

McGucken, W. (1962). *The Catholic way in education*. Chicago: Loyola University Press.

McGucken, W. (n.d.). *Catholic education: Its philosophy, its fundamentals, its objectives*. New York: The America Press.

McLaughlin, T. (1996). The distinctiveness of Catholic education. In T. McLaughlin, J. O'Keefe, & B. O'Keeffe (Eds.), *The contemporary Catholic school: Context, identity and diversity* (pp. 136–154). London: The Falmer Press.

Morris, V. C. (Ed.). (1969). *Modern movements in educational philosophy*. Boston: Houghton Mifflin Co.

Nagel, T. (1987). *What does it all mean?* New York: Oxford University Press.

Newman, J. (1960). *The idea of a university*. New York: Holt, Rinehart and Winston.

O'Brien, S. (1987). *Mixed messages*. Washington, DC: National Catholic Educational Association.

O'Dea, T. (1958). *American Catholic dilemma*. New York: Sheed and Ward.

O'Gorman, R. (1987). *The church that was a school: Catholic identity and Catholic education in the United States since 1790*. The Catholic Futures Project.

Oldenski, T. (1997). *Liberation theology and critical pedagogy in today's Catholic schools*. New York: Garland Publishing.

Patrick, G. (1924). *Introduction to philosophy*. Boston: Houghton Mifflin Co.

Paul VI. (1968). *On the regulation of birth*. Washington, DC: United States Catholic Conference.

Pegis, A. (1955). Preface. In N. Michener (Ed.), *Maritain on the nature of man in a Christian democracy*. Hull, Canada: Editions L'éclair.

Phelan, G. (1937). *Jacques Maritain*. New York: Sheed and Ward.

Phenix, P. (Ed.). (1961). *Philosophies of education*. New York: John Wiley and Sons.

Pieper, J. (1954). *The end of time* (M. Bullick, Trans.). New York: Pantheon Books.

Pilarczyk, D. (1982). What makes a Catholic school Catholic? In National Catholic Educational Association (Eds.), *Catholic secondary education: Now and in the future* (pp. 16–22). Dayton, OH: University of Dayton Press.

Pius XI. (1930). The Christian education of youth. *The Catholic Educational Review, 28*, 133–134.

Pius XI. (1939). *The Christian education of youth in five great encyclicals*. New York: Paulist Press.

Pius XII. (1953). *Six social documents of His Holiness Pope Pius XII*. Huntington, IN: Our Sunday Visitor Press.

Pius XII. (1963). Morality and applied psychology. In A. Fremantle (Ed.), *The social teachings of the church* (pp. 192–207). New York: The New American Library.

Price, K. (1955). Is a philosophy of education necessary? *Journal of Philosophy, 52*, 622–633.

Ramsey, I. (1976). Towards a theology of education. *Learning for Living, 15 (4)*, 137–147.

Redden, J., & Ryan, F. (1956). *A Catholic philosophy of education*. Milwaukee, WI: Bruce Publishing Co.

Rommen, H. (1998). *The natural law* (T. Hanley, Trans.). Indianapolis, IN: Liberty.

Rosenberg, J. F. (1978). *The practice of philosophy*. Englewood Cliffs, NJ: Prentice-Hall.

Ryan, J. (1950). *Beyond humanism*. New York: Sheed and Ward.

Ryan, M. (1964). *Are parochial schools the answer?* New York: Holt, Rinehart and Winston.

Sacred Congregation for Catholic Education. (1977). *The Catholic school*. Rome: Vatican Press.

Sargent, D. (1934). A word about Maritain. *Commonweal, XIX*, 567.

Shields, T. (1917). *Philosophy of education*. Washington, DC: The Catholic Education Press.

Soltis, J. (Ed.). (1981). *Philosophy of education: The eightieth yearbook of the National Society for the Study of Education, Part I*. Chicago: University of Chicago Press.

Spalding, J. (1905). *Religion and art and other essays*. Chicago: A. C. McClurg.

Spalding, J. (1909). *Means and ends of education*. Chicago: A. C. McClurg.

Sprague, E. (1961). *What is philosophy?* New York: Oxford University Press.

Swinburne, R. (1996). *Is there a God?* New York: Oxford University Press.

Trafford, L. (1993). What makes Catholic schools Catholic? *Grail, 9*, 27–49.

Veverka, F. (1993, Spring). Re-imagining Catholic identity: Toward an analogical paradigm of religious education. *Religious Education, 88*, 238–254.

Ward, L. (1958). *New life in Catholic schools*. St. Louis: Herden Book Co.

Ward, L. (1963). *Philosophy of education*. Chicago: Henry Regnery Co.

Whalen, J. (1965). The integration of theology, science and mathematics. In W. Kolesnik & E. Power (Eds.), *Catholic education* (pp. 472–484). New York: McGraw-Hill.

Chapter 3

Spirituality and Religious Education

Ronald J. Nuzzi

> Go, therefore, and make disciples of all the nations . . . Teach them to carry
> out everything I have commanded you.
>
> —Matthew 28:19, 20

Education is a ministry close to the heart of the Church. John Paul II's Apostolic Constitution *Ex Corde Ecclesiae* (1990) affirms that Catholic institutions of higher learning participate in the overall educational mission of the Church. More recent Vatican documents on Catholic schools make the claim more explicitly: "The ecclesial nature of the Catholic school . . . is written in the very heart of its identity as a teaching institution" (Congregation for Catholic Education, 1999, #11). From the time of Jesus and the very first disciples, believers have insisted on sharing their faith, experience, and life with others. Personal commitment was just a beginning. Early Christian communities were characterized by a missionary spirit; they continually reached out to others in an effort to share the good news of Jesus Christ.

In today's Church, wonderful programs and structures have developed to meet the religious education needs of God's people. Most parishes and dioceses have a variety of formal and informal ways in which people can seek to learn more about the Catholic faith while fostering a deeper and more meaningful relationship with God. Catholic schools participate in the great heritage of the Church's evangelical mission, becoming in the 1900s the most effective catechetical tool the Church has ever witnessed (Greeley, 1982). No matter what the shape of the process, the purpose remains the same: life in Christ. All religious education, all sacramental celebrations, all parish programs, and Catholic schools share this in common; they seek to help the people of God to discern and interpret the ongoing revelation of God in their lives.

While no area in Church life has been exempt from the spirit of the Second Vatican Council (Vatican II), development and change in the teaching of religion and in religious education programs have been gradual and steady. Perhaps it was because of the private, classroom-based nature of catechetical efforts, or the teachers' and catechists' own needs to prepare adequately for shifts in the content and style of teaching. Whatever the cause, developments were ongoing and incremental. Hence, there is arguably no singular event or text that precipitated changes in the way religious instruction was delivered beyond the Council itself.

However, there were forces at work, pulling on the leadership and making demands of curricula, programs, and instruction. Although a comprehensive overview and historical analysis of this period of Church history and its relationship to religious education are beyond the scope of these pages, we offer here a look at several of the important questions that have surfaced since the Second Vatican Council about religious education in general, and provide a summary of the thinking of seven scholars who have made significant contributions to the field.

Topics discussed below include: the understanding of religious education as catechesis; a growing emphasis on spirituality; a summary of the work of Thomas Merton, Parker Palmer, Timothy Arthur Lines, Francoise Darcy-Berube, Gabriel Moran, Maria Harris, and Thomas Groome; and recent research in multicultural religious education.

RELIGIOUS EDUCATION AS CATECHESIS

A profound and fundamental shift in religious education since Vatican II concerns the very purpose and goal of education in the faith. Boys (1989) stated that this shift involved the articulation of new questions by religious educators. The question for many years was, "How do I convey God's revelation?" Today's question has become, "What does it mean to educate in faith?" (Boys, 1989, p. 4). Boys argued that the earlier question initiated a propositional approach to the faith, whereby one could be said to know the faith when one knew and could repeat the formulae and credal statements that expressed it accurately. The later question invited a more personal reflection, opened religious education to social science research, and placed religious educators on a path that was more emotional, holistic, and personalized.

The traditional, propositional approach to religious education might be faulted by modern educators for many reasons, but clarity would not be among them. With an emphasis on God's transcendence, the goal of religious education was faithful transmission about the truths of the faith. The deposit of faith needed to be handed on intact, and it was the singular job of religious educators to pass on that deposit unchanged. Truths were eternal, and the faith, unchanging. Religious education came into being as the vehicle by which this transfer could take place.

So conceived, the educational tasks became highly concentrated on proclamation and transmission. Doctrine was the curriculum and it was an essential curriculum, for salvation depended on mastering it.

In the Catholic Church of the third millennium, religious education has taken on a new approach that alters both the curriculum and instructional methodologies that are used. Based on more personalist categories adopted from a growing appreciation of the social sciences, religious education efforts are now highly adaptive to the particular psychological and pedagogical needs of various groups. Developmental factors such as family history, age, socioeconomic status, and ethnic origin are all concerns for today's religious educators. Accurate proclamation of the faith is still a priority, but educators now have the additional challenge of teaching the faith in a way that is specially crafted to meet the needs and touch the hearts of an increasingly diverse Church.

This respect for and reliance upon the social sciences received affirmation in the national catechetical directory for Catholics in the United States, *Sharing the Light of Faith* (United States Catholic Conference), published in 1979. Emphasizing the role of what it terms the behavioral sciences, *Sharing the Light* stated: "The Church encourages the use of the biological, social, and psychological sciences in pastoral care. The catechetical movement will in no way be able to advance without scientific study. Manuals for catechists should take into account psychological and pedagogical insights, as well as suggestions about methods" (#175). This explicit affirmation of the value of the social sciences has many implications for religious education. One of the most important is the understanding that because people grow, change, and progress through various stages throughout the course of life, their relationship with God can be properly understood as ongoing and changing as well. "As the quality of a friendship between human beings is affected by such things as their maturity and freedom, their knowledge of each other, and the manner and frequency of their communication, so the quality of a friendship with God is affected by the characteristics of the human party. Because people are capable of continual development, so are their relationships with God" (United States Catholic Conference, 1979, #173).

An important distinction has been drawn by some theorists between religious education and catechesis. Understood in terms of the processes of schooling, especially in the public sector, religious education can easily be understood as education about religion or even religions. As Arthur and Gaine (1996) stated, "religious education is aimed equally at pupils of whatever religious conviction or none; faith is presupposed neither in teacher nor in pupil" (p. 340). Thus, religious education is primarily an education structured around learning about and from various religions. While the result of such a program of instruction may be to foster the deepening of an individual student's personal faith life, it does not aim at such. Understood in these broad terms, religious education is not concerned with developing practicing believers of any denomination.

Catechesis, on the other hand, is generally agreed to describe an education in the faith by those who themselves are already committed to the practice of that faith. It aims at conversion, and while it necessarily involves some religious instruction, encompasses much more. Rossiter (1982) suggested that Catholic religious education needed to be re-conceptualized, and advocated for what he called a "creative divorce" between catechesis and religious education in Catholic schools. Catechesis, conceived as a process fostering ongoing conversion, was difficult to deliver in compulsory, school-based classroom lessons.

Most educators tend to use the terms "religious education" and "catechesis" interchangeably. This is regrettable, for the distinction highlights what may be the difference between the experience one receives through a Catholic school education and the experience of a parish-based program. *The Religious Dimension of Education in a Catholic School* (Congregation for Catholic Education, 1988) seemed to acknowledge this distinction. Catechesis was described as the manifold handing on of the Gospel to be received as a "salvific reality." Religious instruction, on the other hand, has knowledge as its goal, and is very much an academic discipline. Religious education or instruction was part of the time and space of the school day, whereas catechesis is a lifelong project that is rooted in a faith community.

Given this distinction between religious instruction and catechesis, it should also be noted that there exists a close connection between them. Catechesis is always founded on doctrine and involves the transmission of knowledge. Religious instruction can lead to the deepening of faith among believers as well as the evangelization of non-believers.

With the great influence in modern society on religious experience and personal commitment, the need for both effective religious education and catechesis is paramount. A general hunger for spirituality exists, a hunger that is often unrelated to organized religion (O'Murchu, 1998). This spiritual hunger is seen across denominations and national borders and is very much a characteristic of our post-modern age (Chandler, 1992). As individuals yearn to make sense of an ever-increasing complexity in their lives, clarity of thought and conviction in religious education and catechesis become even more important. Thus, the spiritual quest of many young adults can properly be understood as a search for more instruction and more catechesis, for more information and for more personal relevance.

LEADING THEORISTS

Thomas Merton

Thomas Merton, one of the great spiritual writers of this century, believed that all education was in some sense religious. Although he was a cloistered monk at a Cistercian monastery in Kentucky, Merton remained in contact with the world and its struggles. He realized through his own spiritual journey that knowledge was insufficient, even large amounts of knowledge. In fact, Merton maintained that any renewal or transformation of society needed to begin first and foremost in a personal transformation of the heart. He wrote: "Our real journey in life is interior: It is a matter of growth, deepening, and of an even greater surrender to the action of love and grace in our hearts" (1973, p. 296). Merton was one of the first religious educators to speak of a holistic approach to education and to acknowledge the need for a pastoral focus in our educational efforts.

Because of his focus on the interior life, Merton maintained that self-discovery was the true purpose of education (DelPrete, 1990). The true self, Merton held, remained shrouded in mystery and buried beneath the many masks and facades of the false self. While the false self is, in some sense, psychologically necessary for survival, Merton called the false self an illusion: an illusion that we are in control of our own lives and destiny, an illusion that the ultimate purpose of our lives can be found in our own work and self-realization. Lost in the pursuits of the false self, the true self recedes and can easily be lost.

The true self, far from being a psychological self-realization, involves a deep, inner discovery of the person that one is called to be by God. Indeed, the journey to the true self is a journey that approaches the divine, for Merton believed that all of our lives are somehow caught up in the mystery of God. In *Conjectures of a Guilty Bystander* (1966), he wrote: "at the center of our being is a nothingness which is untouched by sin and illusion, a point or spark which belongs entirely to God, which is never at our disposal, from which God disposes of our lives, which is inaccessible to the fantasies of our own minds or the brutalities of our own will. This little point of nothingness and of absolute poverty is the pure glory of God in us" (p. 142). For Merton, the best education is one that encouraged and supported the individual in making the journey from the false self to the true self so as to encounter this core of our being.

Merton labored throughout his life balancing his monastic vocation with the call to be involved in the issues outside of his monastery. Although a cloistered, contemplative monk, his writings often reveal sharp and pointed analyses of many of the political and religious dilemmas of his day. Thus, while he was physically apart from the pace of the everyday world, he was very much involved in its struggles. The sheer volume of his books, letters, and diaries displays his willingness to share the fruits of his contemplative life with his brothers and sisters.

Merton's solidarity with so many people and causes is an endearing quality even until this day. His taking up various battles for social justice, peace, and disarmament, as well as so many individual and personal concerns, is a trait that has made him attractive to many. In fact, his example as a monk has made his witness all the more striking. If one Christian so physically removed and geographically isolated from the world can be so caught up and engaged by faith in the issues of the day, how much more so are those who live and work in the everyday world called to bring their faith into the marketplace. In what is perhaps the most often-quoted passage from Merton's collected works, we learn about a moment that fostered his intense solidarity with others:

> In Louisville, at the corner of Fourth and Walnut, in the center of the shopping district, I was suddenly overwhelmed with the realization that I loved all those people, that they were mine and I theirs, that we could not be alien to one another even though we were total strangers. It was like waking from a dream of separateness, of spurious self-isolation in a special world, the world of renunciation and supposed holiness. The whole illusion of a separate holy existence is a dream. (Merton, 1966, p. 140)

Merton reveled in his participation in the human family, in the fact that he was indeed a man among and for others, and a member of the race, as he put it, "in which God Himself had become incarnate" (Merton, 1966, p. 141). So over-powering was the vision of this oneness with others, Merton concluded: "There is no way of telling people that they are all walking around shining like the sun. . . . There are no strangers!" (pp. 141–142).

As a spiritual mentor and guide, Merton is easily one of the most read masters of the modern age. His own spiritual autobiography, *The Seven Storey Mountain* (1948), has been published in dozens of languages and is still in print more than 50 years after its original publication. A special fiftieth anniversary edition was recently completed (Merton, 1998). Bellarmine College in Louisville, Kentucky, a short drive from the Bardstown, Kentucky monastery of Gethsemani where Merton lived, houses the Merton Library and Archives. Books, articles, disser-tations, and speeches about Merton continue to be written. His ability to name and give voice to religious experience was a shaping force in the post–Vatican II era of aggiornamento.

Parker Palmer

A Quaker author and sociologist, Parker Palmer has written extensively about spirituality (Palmer, 1980, 1990; Yanni, 1992), especially as it applies to edu-cation (Palmer, 1983, 1998, 1999). In his seminal work on the spirituality of education, *To Know as We Are Known* (1983), Palmer described a set in interior dispositions that assists teachers in their struggle to be present to their students in helpful ways. Calling education a form of spiritual formation, Palmer believed that formal educational programs had much to learn from some very traditional practices rooted in Christian history. Among the sources for wisdom in educa-tional theory, Palmer named the monastic tradition.

In Palmer's view, the monastic tradition contained at least three items that would help us to recover the notion of education as spiritual formation: (1) a studying of sacred texts; (2) the practice of prayer and contemplation; and (3) the gathered life of the community itself (Palmer, 1983).

Palmer offered a strident critique of the traditional classroom. While his analysis was focused on all educational endeavors, they have particular relevancy for religious education and catechesis, as they are concerned directly and explicitly with deeper questions of religious faith. Some of the challenges facing conventional classroom education are: (1) the hidden curriculum, wherein students learn first and foremost about the power relationships in the classroom, and learning can become an increasingly spectator sport; (2) the tendency to neglect the inner realities of the teacher and students and to focus on seemingly objective reality "out there"; (3) the tendency to isolate the knowing self. Palmer lamented the fact that despite advances in pedagogical techniques and technology, conventional pedagogy is decidedly anticommunal and competitive. We become manipulators of each other and the world rather than mutually responsible participants and co-creators (Palmer, 1983).

Palmer fully developed several spiritual principles to guide the formation and training of teachers, for if education is spiritual formation, teachers are in some sense spiritual directors. In his book *The Courage to Teach: Exploring the Inner Landscape of a Teacher's Life* (1998), Palmer delineated the educational paradoxes that good teachers must hold in balance. Defining teaching as "to create a space in which obedience to truth is practiced" (1983, p. 69), Palmer maintained that good teaching managed to hold several tensions together, balanced opposing forces, and in so doing created a spark that kept the learning environment positively charged. The paradoxes are: (1) the (learning) space should be bounded and open; (2) the space should be hospitable and charged; (3) the space should invite the voice of the individual and the voice of the group; (4) the space should honor the little stories of the students and the big stories of the disciplines and tradition; (5) the space should support solitude and surround it with the resources of the community; and (6) the space should welcome both silence and speech (Palmer, 1998).

Palmer's work has been instrumental in educational renewal at every level, for his insights have helped to move the role of the teacher back into prominence. Many renewal efforts in schools have been focused exclusively on materials and facilities, technologies and strategies, curriculum revisions, and Internet capabilities. Palmer reminded leaders that renewal in education begins and ends in the heart of teachers.

In our rush to reform education, we have forgotten a simple truth: reform will never be achieved by renewing appropriations, restructuring schools, rewriting curricula, and revising texts if we continue to demean and dishearten the human resources called the teacher on whom so much depends. Teachers must be better compensated, freed from bureaucratic harassment, given a role in academic governance, and provided with the best possible methods and materials. But none of that will transform education if we fail to cherish—and challenge—the human heart that is the source of good teaching. (Palmer, 1998, p. 3)

Following the conviction that educational reform must begin with the teacher, Palmer has established a spiritual renewal for teachers, especially veteran teachers (Palmer, 1999). Sponsored by the Fetzer Institute, the program has the structure of a religious retreat experience and calls teachers to reflect on their own personal identity as a teacher as a way to foster growth in their integrity as teachers. Adopting Merton's notion of the true self, Palmer challenges teachers to move beyond the preoccupation with technique and to consider what it means to teach from one's heart as an expression of identity and integrity. "We teach who we are" (Palmer, 1999, p. 1), and not just by what we do. Recently, Palmer has been involved in renewal efforts in higher education and in taking the message of the need for a spirituality in education to continuing education programs and job training efforts in business and industry.

Timothy Arthur Lines

Lines, a Southern Baptist religious educator, has authored a comprehensive synthesis of religious education theory, applying insights from various fields and disciplines to the concrete needs of religious educators. Beginning with the application of systems theory to religious education processes, Lines (1987) developed a collection of taxonomies for religious educators that serves as a model or paradigm for classroom teachers, catechists, ministers, and clergy. Using an analytical method similar to Avery Dulles in his *Models of the Church* (Dulles, 1974), Lines articulated what he called "functional images" of the religious educator, a series of 10 models or descriptors of various aspects of the ministry of religious education (Lines, 1992). While not intended as an exhaustive treatment of pedagogical theory, the 10 models offer both descriptive and prescriptive information regarding the nature of religious education and its overall mission in the context of modern Christianity.

Building on the work of previous scholars, Lines demonstrated that typologies for understanding religious educators have been limited to historical and professional constructs. Historical typologies treated the place of religious instruction in Church history, whereas professional typologies came to understand the religious educator as a professional and religious education as a professional field, requiring a certain set of demonstrable skills. Lines offered metaphorical typologies, preferring instead the language of symbolism and poetry in order to highlight the complexity of the role of a modern-day religious educator. In Lines' view, the religious educator functions in the following roles: parent, coach, scientist, critic, storyteller, artist, visionary, revolutionary, therapist, and minister (Lines, 1992).

Lines developed each functional image rather extensively, following an outline to create a thorough and well-articulated understanding of each functional image that could be operationalized by religious educators. For each functional image, the following characteristics were explained: dimensions of the role, aim, function, primary virtues, activities, shadow role, a faith tradition resource, a historical personage, a contemporary example, a representative teaching procedure, and an experiential simulation (Lines, 1992). Lines' work offers a truly comprehensive vision of religious education and provides educators with a plethora of examples, provocative models, and an effort at establishing a plan for the systemic integration of religious education. As such, it is one of the most holistic approaches to religious education available.

Francoise Darcy-Berube

Called one of the great mothers of contemporary catechetics by her former student Thomas Groome, Francoise Darcy-Berube (1995) has been a leading scholar at the international level in religious education and catechesis. Born in Paris and educated at both the Sorbonne and L'Institut Catholique, Darcy-Berube's work has impacted religious education practices in Europe, Canada, and the United States for several decades. Thrust into the limelight by an article on curriculum design for a catechetical journal (International Centre, 1961), she was the principal author for the landmark religion series *Come to the Father* (Canadian Catholic Conference, 1967), one of the first efforts at designing curriculum material to reflect the spirit of renewal fostered at Vatican II.

Darcy-Berube advocated for a holistic approach to catechesis and named conversion as the primary goal. Concerned that the uncertainty of modern times might precipitate a return to a more content-oriented approach to religious education, she delineated the essential aspects of a holistic religious education. Such an education aims at:

- facilitating ongoing conversion
- moving toward discipleship
- reaching down to the core of the being
- teaching for the heart, mind, and soul
- educating for wisdom
- facilitating belonging and not only believing
- educating for personal and social transformation (Darcy-Berube, 1995, p. 18).

This description helps to point out that religious education includes both information and formation. Information involves new knowledge about Scripture, history, the sacraments, and theology. Formation calls the believer to appropriate this new knowledge in service of a life of faith, beginning a process of interior conversion that will ultimately manifest itself in the life of community.

Darcy-Berube believed that structural changes were needed in the Church to support such a holistic vision. Pointing to obstacles that stood in the way of such a vision (1995), she enumerated two basic problems: (1) the very generosity and zeal of catechists themselves, serving as a kind of negative enabling of the wider parish community to be inactive; and (2) a compartmentalized mentality, most evident in the competition between Catholic schools and parish-based religious education programs. In the first case, energetic catechists take on too much responsibility for the holistic vision, attempting to provide teaching, prayer opportunities, community involvement, family catechesis, and everything else one could imagine as part of a comprehensive program. Darcy-Berube maintained that such an overly generous response on the part of many catechists actually had the negative effect of permitting the wider parish community to be dormant and fail to take on the responsibilities that are properly theirs, such as welcoming, fellowship, affective support, and mission and service to others (Darcy-Berube, 1995). In the second instance, the competition and lack of communication between Catholic school personnel and religious education staff does little to foster parish or diocesan unity. Darcy-Berube recounted several instances of being invited to speak in dioceses and parishes in different parts of the United States and Canada, where the invitation to attend the presentation was not even extended broadly enough to include parents and educators from both groups (Darcy-Berube, 1995).

Darcy-Berube was sympathetic to the analysis of Richard Reichert (1992), which stated that a major cause of religious education's problem in the post–Vatican II Church is a type of "ecclesiological schizophrenia" (p. 167). This situation occurs when catechists and teachers function with, incarnate, and teach with a renewed understanding of the Church and of Christian education, while at the same time the clerical leadership of the parish and some professional staff function in a pre–Vatican II mode and make every effort, especially liturgically, to propound their views. Such situations are regrettable, highly dysfunctional, and typically result in frustration both at the personal and professional levels.

Darcy-Berube (1995) was a strong advocate for the place of parents as the primary religious educators of their children and worked to help parents become true spiritual guides for their families. She proposed that the central emphasis of early childhood catechesis should be "enhancing the contemplative potential of the child" (p. 138).

Gabriel Moran

Known better for his foundation work in fundamental theology and revelation (Moran, 1966a, 1966b), Gabriel Moran has nonetheless been a major contributor to the fields of teaching, religious education, and catechesis. Focusing on the philosophical underpinnings of the educational process and the meaning of teaching, Moran has attempted to construct a religious understanding of teaching and to situate teaching as a moral vocation (Moran, 1997).

For Moran, teaching creates a moral dilemma. Unequal power relationships in the classroom, adult-child conflicts, ever-changing subject areas, economic limitations, and unequal access to resources are just a few of the factors at work in the emotionally and morally charged educational environments of the modern world.

The language of teaching and learning was most troublesome for Moran. He felt that it assumed that teaching was talking and learning was listening, with the implicit agreement that all involved parties would begin and end at the same time. Often, teaching assumed that an adult was in the front of the room talking to children. Moran desired to create a new language for teaching through which the dynamism of human interactions in the classroom could be more fully expressed. Moran named desirable techniques for achieving this goal, including: (1) teaching with the end in view; (2) teaching to remove obstacles; and (3) teaching the conversation (Moran, 1997).

In a strong critique of the most popular simile used to describe Catholic parishes and schools, Moran maintained that it was not pedagogically helpful to characterize institutions as "like a family." A family is by definition singular and one's own. Applying the notion to one's school runs the risk of devaluing one's true family and changes the educational environment into something that it was never intended to be. Moran wrote:

A school need not be one big happy family; it does need some minimum conditions of physical comfort, efficient organization and a nonhostile body of people. Both the teachers and the students deserve some respect for their personal dignity. The school ought to teach decency in being a school. The metaphor of family should be used sparingly in reference to schools. The school should be a partial embodiment of community, that is, a communal expression that complements the family. Schools need not have father and mother figures, nor obedient children (including grown ups who are treated like children). (Moran, 1997, p. 176)

Moran was influential in creating a bridge between the work of developmental psychology and religious education, demonstrating how the insights of Erikson, Piaget, Levinson, Kohlberg, and others could be beneficial to the practice of catechesis (Moran, 1983). Proposing what he termed a "grammar of religious education" and a "grammar of educational development," Moran constructed a theory of religious education development firmly rooted in contemporary theories of human development (1971, 1981, 1983).

Maria Harris

Maria Harris' interests in and contributions to an ongoing development of religious education are very similar to Moran's. In fact, they have authored several books together (Harris & Moran, 1968, 1998). Harris helped conceptualize an integrated theology of parish ministry which supported a variety of emerging ministries, including youth ministry and directors of religious education (DREs) (Harris, 1976, 1981).

In a 1987 book, *Teaching and Religious Imagination*, Harris turned her attention to the spirituality of teachers and to the need to foster an ever-deepening spirituality, especially in veteran teachers. Harris characterized teaching as a work of religious imagination and invited teachers to be contemplative about their classroom experiences and to look for meaning in their vocation through the lenses of that experience. Harris employed a highly metaphorical language to describe the nature of teaching and to relate it to religious imagination. Four ideas provided the interpretive key in her analysis: (1) incarnation, (2) revelation, (3) power, and (4) re-creation. Harris believed that the religiously imaginative teachers were able to incarnate their subject matter and make it present to their students in new and life-giving ways. Such incarnations could be powerful revelations for students. With such knowledge of subjects and self-knowledge, new and graced power becomes present in the classroom, inviting both teacher and students to reconceptualize their worldviews, fashion new opinions, and thereby re-create a part of the universe. Harris stated her thesis thus: "Teaching, when seen as an activity of religious imagination, is the incarnation of subject matter in ways that lead to the revelation of subject matter. At the heart of this revelation is the discovery that human beings are the primary subjects of all teaching, subjects who discover themselves as possessing the grace of power, especially the power of re-creation, not only of themselves, but of the world in which they live" (1987, p. xv). Understood as an explicit deployment of imagination, teaching and especially religious education can be seen as redemptive enterprises (Harris, 1987).

Thomas Groome

Acknowledged as the leading religious education theorist in the United States, Thomas Groome has been integrating the disciplines of theology, education, and philosophy for several decades. A prolific author, university professor, and international lecturer, Groome's understanding of Christian religious education has been at the heart of many renewal efforts since Vatican II.

Three of Groome's books stand out as landmark contributions: *Christian Religious Education: Sharing Our Story and Vision* (1980); *Sharing Faith: A Comprehensive Approach to Religious Education and Pastoral Ministry* (1991); and *Educating for Life: A Spiritual Vision for Every Teacher and Parent* (1998). Groome's strength has been in the ability to synthesize insights from divergent disciplines and to place that collected wisdom at the service of religious education. Delving often into educational philosophy, social theory, biblical scholarship, liberation theology, and critical pedagogy, Groome articulated foundational principles for religious education that incorporated findings from these various fields.

The result of this synthesis is Groome's unique contribution, the shared praxis method, a pedagogical approach that has been a creative force in the development of religious education curriculum materials, ministering training programs, and formation processes. Groome (1980) defined this approach as "a group of Christians sharing in dialogue their critical reflection on present action in light of the Christian Story and its Vision toward the end of lived Christian faith" (p. 184). So conceived, Groome (1980) enumerated five main components to Christian education via shared praxis: (1) present action; (2) critical reflection; (3) dialogue; (4) the Story; and (5) the Vision that arises from the story.

Present action involves much more than simply the ever-fleeting now. It concerns all human projects and endeavors and is inclusive of the physical, psychological, spiritual, emotional, and intellectual aspects of the person. It offers a holistic view of the person, rooted in a particular time and place, but is more expansive than what is happening to me today. The critical reflection Groome invited is based in the work of Paulo Freire (1970, 1973, 1978), and is an analysis wherein assumptions are uncovered, ideologies unmasked, and a deeper level of engagement with the present moment is sought. Crucial to this reflective exercise are the powers of memory and imagination. Groome (1980) maintained that critical memory is necessary to uncover how the past has made itself felt in the present moment, and that critical imagination is the power that helps us envision how the future is already an active force in the present.

Dialogue is the central component to the process. While this goal can be accomplished by many means, Groome believed that it is absolutely crucial for learners to name, as much as possible, their own understandings, apprehensions, ideas, feelings, questions, and concerns as a way of coming in touch with the Christian Story. Groome dodged the traditional dichotomy of Scripture and tradition by the use of the concept "Story," though much of what he advocates for in the dialogue about the Story is essentially helping others to name salient features of their life story so that the links between one's personal story and the Christian story are brought into the light. Although there is no singular expression of the Christian Story that suffices for all time and all people, Groome's dynamic, dialogical process allows for an ongoing revelation of the Story and a critical, dialogical, and ongoing discernment of that revelation.

The process reaches its zenith in the embrace of the Vision, understood as God's vision for creation. "It invites a lived response that is faithful to the reign of God" (Groome, 1980, p. 193). The Vision is our response to the Story, and it finds expression in a community of faith.

Groome's more recent work (1998) offered a comprehensive look at the concept of spirituality as it applies to the vocations of teaching and parenting. Sympathetic to the struggles in the contemporary Church between religious education personnel and Catholic school teachers, Groome aimed at an inclusive understanding of spirituality for adults that offers hospitality to all.

MULTICULTURAL RELIGIOUS EDUCATION

Multicultural concerns are a growing area of interest for society at large. Cultural change is upon us as demographics shift like in no other period in recent memory. Non-White population groups represent the fastest growing segment of the population. While analysis of the descriptive statistics is beyond our current purposes here, it should be noted that students of color were already a majority in 25 of the largest school districts in the United States in the early 1990s. By the middle of the twenty-first century, it is estimated that half of the nation's population will be people of color (Banks, 1992).

Multicultural religious education involves the efforts of teachers, catechists, pastors, clergy, and other educational leaders to meet the spiritual needs of this diverse population. It promotes the view that "religious education which is authentically Christian should be as wide as the arms of Christ and embrace with equal warmth persons of every ethnic and cultural group" (Wilkerson, 1997, p. 4).

Multicultural religious education faces several important challenges. Among them are: appreciating the sociological and psychological forces at work in any culturally diverse settings; designing pastorally and educationally appropriate learning experiences for different cultural groups; curriculum design; and theological foundations (Wilkerson, 1997). In general, scholarly efforts in these areas have attempted to move thinking beyond the "different strokes for different folks" mentality, into a fuller appreciation of the God-given goodness inherent in all (Jenkins & Kratt, 1997, p. 56). Psychological research has demonstrated the existence of a variety of learning styles, with important differences found between the typical Eurocentric learner and the preferred learning style of people of color (Ratcliff, 1997). Culturally specific pedagogical texts, once rare, are now common, with authors designing curricula and lessons with a specific cultural or ethnic group in mind, tailoring the learning experiences to the psychological research cited above (Banks, 1994, 1997; Matczynski & Lasley, 1997; Sawchuck & Taylor, 1997; Shade, Kelly, & Oberg, 1997).

Successful multicultural education has been interpreted as a politically, theologically, and psychologically viable approach. The Scriptures have been read with a multicultural worldview and Jesus found to be an inclusive Messiah (Crump Miller, 1997). Multicultural learning experiences promote social and emotional adjustment and healthy family relations in ethnic minority families (Taylor & Wang, 1997). Catholic school personnel and religious educators have been encouraged to be more attentive and responsive to the changing needs of their students and families (Frabutt, 1999). Some have even argued for a type of "cultural therapy" with teachers and students as a way to build cognitive bridges for understanding (Spindler & Spindler, 1994). Preferred techniques for religious education in culturally diverse situations have been identified, as well as pedagogical strategies for inclusive religious education (Nuzzi, 1996, 1999).

While every aspect of society is being touched in some way by the increasing cultural diversity of the U.S. population, multicultural sensitivity will be a special challenge for religious educators in the beginning of the third millennium of Christianity.

CONCLUSION

Pope John Paul II spoke about the renewal of religious education programs at the beginning of his pontificate. In 1979 he wrote: "Catechesis needs to be continually renewed by a certain broadening of its concept, by the revision of its methods, by the search for suitable language, and by the utilization of new means of transmitting the message" (#17).

What becomes clear throughout this renewal of religious education is that we are describing a lifelong process. There is no safe harbor in the spiritual life, no point at which we can assume that our learning is over. As long as we live, we continue to grow in our knowledge and understanding of God's will for our lives. Our personal experiences enrich this understanding, as we come to see our lives and our world more and more through the eyes of faith.

The life of Jesus provides us with some insight. While Jesus was certainly one who led a deeply reflective, spiritual life, his prayerfulness had a human face. His convictions manifested themselves in the community and were experienced by others as loving gifts. While the Gospels frequently report that Jesus is off by himself to pray, he is even more often engaged in caring for others, teaching about God, reaching out to the marginalized, and ministering to those who come to him. Jesus is clearly prayerful and his inner journey leads him to be involved in the community and present to others in helpful and giving ways.

Jesus' example must be the paradigm for all we strive to learn, both in the Catholic school and in religious education programs. Personal prayer is an essential component of the Christian life. Ongoing efforts to learn more about our world and our faith are healthy signs of growth; but unless our learning and our prayerfulness show themselves as gifts to the community, our goals may become self-serving. The example of Jesus calls us to be prayerful, learned, and oriented to life in community.

The importance of following Jesus' example in balancing personal holiness and life in community is difficult to overemphasize. Parker J. Palmer has observed that Christians have often spoken of knowing Jesus in a way that tends toward one of two extremes. Palmer (1983) wrote: "Either the believer 'knows' Jesus in a way that excuses him or her from knowing anything else (like physics or psychology or English literature), or the believer contains the 'knowledge' of Jesus in a compartment labeled 'religious' and engages in other forms of knowing as if there were no connection" (p. 49).

Far from excusing us from worldly concerns, a deep and healthy prayer life leads us into caring relationships with others. Rather than isolating our religious convictions from interaction with the rest of our lives, religious education aims to point out that all learning and all knowledge have their origin and destiny in God. Such integration of contemplation and action, of religion and knowledge, would be an appropriate focus for parish religious education programs, Catholic schools, youth ministry, and adult education programs, as the entire ecclesial community journeys forward in the third millennium of Christianity.

REFERENCES

Arthur, J., & Gaine, S. (1996). Catechesis and religious education in Catholic theory and practice. In L. J. Francis, W. K. Kay, & W. S. Campbell (Eds.), *Research in religious education* (pp. 335–355). Macon, GA: Smith & Helwys.

Banks, J. (1992, September). National council on social studies curriculum guidelines for multicultural education. *Social Education, 274.*

Banks, J. (1994). *Multiethnic education: Theory and practice* (3rd ed.). Needham Heights, MA: Allyn & Bacon.

Banks, J. (1997). *Educating citizens in a multicultural society.* New York: Teachers College Press.

Boys, M. C. (1989). *Educating in faith: Maps and visions.* San Francisco: Harper & Row.

Canadian Catholic Conference. National Office of Religious Education. (1967). *Come to the Father.* New York: Paulist Press.

Chandler, R. (1992). *Racing toward 2001: The forces shaping America's religious future.* San Francisco: HarperSanFrancisco.

Congregation for Catholic Education. (1988). *The religious dimension of education in a Catholic school.* Washington, DC: Author.

Congregation for Catholic Education. (1999). The Catholic school on the threshold of the third millennium. *Catholic Education: A Journal of Inquiry and Practice, 2 (1),* 4–14.

Crump Miller, R. (1997). Bible, theology, and multicultural religious education. In B. Wilkerson, (Ed.), *Multicultural religious education* (pp. 129–157). Birmingham, AL: Religious Education Press.

Darcy-Berube, F. (1995). *Religious education at a crossroads: Moving on in the freedom of the spirit.* Mahwah, NJ: Paulist Press.

DelPrete, T. (1990). *Thomas Merton and the education of the whole person.* Birmingham, AL: Religious Education Press.

Dulles, A. (1974). *Models of the church.* Garden City, NY: Doubleday.

Frabutt, J. (1999). Parenting in ethnic minority families. *Catholic Education: A Journal of Inquiry and Practice, 3 (2),* 245–254.

Freire, P. (1970). *Pedagogy of the oppressed.* New York: Seabury Press.

Freire, P. (1973). *Education for critical consciousness.* New York: Seabury Press.

Freire, P. (1978). *Pedagogy in process.* New York: Seabury Press.

Greeley, A. (1982). *Catholic high schools and minority students.* New Brunswick, NJ: Transaction Books.

Groome, T. (1980). *Christian religious education: Sharing our story and vision.* San Francisco: Harper & Row.

Groome, T. (1991). *Sharing faith: A comprehensive approach to religious education and pastoral ministry.* San Francisco: Harper.

Groome, T. (1998). *Educating for life: A spiritual vision for every teacher and parent.* Allen, TX: Thomas More.

Harris, M. (1976). *The D.R.E. book: Questions and strategies for parish personnel.* New York: Paulist Press.

Harris, M. (1981). *Portrait of youth ministry.* New York: Paulist Press.

Harris, M. (1987). *Teaching and religious imagination.* New York: Harper & Row.

Harris, M., & Moran, G. (1968). *Experiences in community: Should religious life survive?* New York: Herder & Herder.

Harris, M., & Moran. G. (1998). *Reshaping religious education: Conversations on contemporary practice.* Louisville, KY: Westminster John Knox Press.

International Centre for Studies in Religious Education. (1961). *Lumen vitae.*

Jenkins, C., & Kratt, D. (1997). Sociological foundations of multicultural religious education. In B. Wilkerson (Ed.), *Multicultural religious education* (pp. 56–92). Birmingham, AL: Religious Education Press.

John Paul II. (1979). *Catechesi tradendae: Apostolic exhortations of His Holiness Pope John Paul II to the episcopate, the clergy and the faithful of the entire Catholic church on catechesis in our time.* Washington, DC: United States Catholic Conference.

John Paul II. (1990). *Ex corde ecclesiae.* Washington, DC: National Conference of Catholic Bishops.

Lines, T. A. (1987). *Systemic religious education.* Birmingham, AL: Religious Education Press.

Lines, T. A. (1992). *Functional images of the religious educator.* Birmingham, AL: Religious Education Press.

Matczynski, T., & Lasley, T. (1997). *Strategies for teaching in a diverse society: Instructional models.* Belmont, CA: Wadsworth.

Merton, T. (1948). *The seven storey mountain.* New York: Harcourt Brace.

Merton, T. (1966). *Conjectures of a guilty bystander.* Garden City, NY: Doubleday.

Merton, T. (1973). *The Asian journal of Thomas Merton.* N. M. Stone, P. Hart, & J. Laughlin, Eds. New York: New Directons.

Merton, T. (1998). *The seven storey mountain* (50th anniv. ed.). New York: Harcourt Brace.

Moran, G. (1966a). *Catechesis of revelation.* New York: Herder & Herder.

Moran, G. (1966b). *Theology of revelation.* New York: Herder & Herder.

Moran, G. (1971). *Design for religion: Toward ecumenical education.* New York: Herder & Herder.

Moran, G. (1981). *Interplay: A theory of religion and education.* Winona, MN: Saint Mary's Press.

Moran, G. (1983). *Religious education development: Images for the future.* Minneapolis, MN: Winston Press.

Moran, G. (1997). *Showing how: The act of teaching.* Valley Forge, PA: Trinity Press International.

Nuzzi, R. (1996). *Gifts of the spirit: Multiple intelligence in religious education.* Washington, DC: National Catholic Educational Association.

Nuzzi, R. (1999). *Gifts of the spirit: Multiple intelligence in religious education* (2nd ed.). Washington, DC: National Catholic Educational Association.

O'Murchu, D. (1998). *Reclaiming spirituality.* New York: Crossroad Publishing.

Palmer, P. (1980). *The promise of paradox: A celebration of contradictions in the Christian life.* Notre Dame, IN: Ave Maria Press.

Palmer, P. (1983). *To know as we are known: A spirituality of education.* San Francisco: Harper.

Palmer, P. (1990). *The active life: A spirituality of work, creativity, and caring.* New York: Harper & Row.

Palmer, P. (1998). *The courage to teach: Exploring the inner landscape of a teacher's life*. San Francisco: Jossey-Bass.

Palmer, P. (1999). *Teaching from the heart: Seasons of renewal in a teacher's life*. [Video]. San Francisco: Jossey-Bass.

Ratcliff, D. (1997). Psychological foundations of multicultural religious education. In B. Wilkerson (Ed.), *Multicultural religious education* (pp. 93–128). Birmingham, AL: Religious Education Press.

Reichert, R. (1992). Catholics confront ecclesiological schizophrenia. *The Living Light, 28 (2)*, 166–175.

Rossiter, G. (1982). The need for a "creative divorce" between catechesis and religious education in Catholic schools. *Religious Education, 77*, 21–40.

Sawchuck, M., & Taylor, N. (1997). *Teaching for cultural fluency*. Los Angeles: Prism Publishing.

Shade, B., Kelly, C., & Oberg, M. (1997). *Creating culturally responsive classrooms*. Washington, DC: American Psychological Association.

Spindler, G., & Spindler, L. (Eds.). (1994). *Pathways to cultural awareness: Cultural therapy with teachers and students*. Thousand Oaks, CA: Corwin Press.

Taylor, R., & Wang, M. (Eds.). (1997). *Social and emotional adjustment and family relations in ethnic minority families*. Mahwah, NJ: Lawrence Erlbaum.

United States Catholic Conference. (1979). *Sharing the light of faith: National catechetical directory for Catholics of the U.S.* Washington, DC: Author.

Wilkerson, B. (Ed.). (1997). *Multicultural religious education*. Birmingham, AL: Religious Education Press.

Yanni, K. (1992). *The active life: Leader's guide/Parker Palmer*. San Francisco: HarperSanFrancisco.

Chapter 4

Curriculum and Instruction in Catholic Schools

Robert B. Williams

The directors of Catholic schools, under the vigilance of the local ordinary, are to see to it that the instruction given in them is at least as academically distinguished as that given in the other schools of the region.

—Canon 806-§2

INTRODUCTION

Canon 806-§2 seems to encourage, if not mandate, research on the academic instruction in Catholic schools. The canon provides explicit guidance as to what is of interest to the Church about instruction in Catholic schools. It states that the Church is interested in knowing whether the academic instruction in Catholic schools is as good as instruction in other schools of a locality. Inquiry into this question will also generate data for the accountability that Catholic schools have to parents about the education that is being provided (Canon Law Society of America, 1983). Throughout this chapter, curriculum is defined primarily from the narrow, traditional, or academic perspective (Miller, 1967). Curriculum in this context refers to academic subjects such as English and reading, mathematics, history and social studies, and science.

This chapter reviews several approaches to research on curriculum and instruction in Catholic schools: (1) administration of standardized measures of achievement, (2) the study of students' responses to curriculum and instruction, (3) evaluation of curricular content against recognized curricular prototypes, and (4) practical issues regarding curriculum. These approaches to research allow the examination of curricula in Catholic schools from the perspectives of achievement, the processes of instruction, concordance with recognized curricular prototypes, practical issues related to curricula, or a combination of these approaches. The chapter includes the citation of Catholic, government, and private resources related to curricula, instruction, and educational research that readers may find useful for making further investigations into the feasibility of undertaking research on curricula.

Measures of Achievement

Currently, one of the most popular approaches to investigating the quality of academic instruction is by assessing the level of students' mastery of the curricular content, or what is commonly referred to as "academic achievement with multiple-skill tests" (Salvia & Ysseldyke, 1991). One acceptable way to obtain data to respond to the question of whether instruction or curricula in Catholic schools are comparable to those in other schools is by administering standardized achievement tests. Standardized achievement tests "are probably the most valid, reliable, and useful measures available to the educational researcher" (Borg & Gall, 1983, p. 332). Yet there are issues that administrators and educational researchers need to be mindful of as they select standardized measures of achievement: (1) Assess the content *validity* of the achievement measures by comparing the test and curricular content being taught (Borg & Gall, 1983). (2) The *norms* provided ought to adequately describe an appropriate comparative population. Investigate the reputation of the tests among educational and measurement professionals. (3) Check the *reliability* or stable reproducibility of the achievement measures in different contexts. (4) Be sure the test can be *easily administered* by classroom teachers. (5) Be sure that the achievement test and the *results* are reported in a manner that can be understood by parents and the public. It is also important to keep in mind and to let parents know that the term "standardized" in the label standardized achievement tests has nothing to do with educational standards per se (Bennett, Finn, & Cribb, 1999). (6) If financial resources are limited, it is best to commit to assessing from among the basic skill areas of the curriculum such as reading, language, or arithmetic. Thus, for example, reading may be the most important of the skill areas because first, students learn to read, and then they read to learn.

A useful resource for information about many of the issues referred to in this discussion of standardized achievement tests is the staff and publications of the Buros Institute of Mental Measurement at the University of Nebraska (Murphy, Conoley, & Impara, 1994). Diligent research on the part of test-users into the adequacy of standardized measures of achievement intended to assess students' mastery of the curriculum can help to avoid the embarrassment of using inadequate and less-than-respectable measures. Some Catholic schools advertise their use of standardized achievement measures as a way of verifying the adequacy of their curriculum and instruction in the information they provide about their academic program. An example is St. John's School in Bangor, Maine, whose web page reports that "Each year the Metropolitan Achievement Test (MAT) is administered to the children in grades 1–8. Approximately 80% of our student body score above grade level. Of these students, many perform at significantly higher grade levels" (Saint John's School Curriculum, 1999). Parents and the public can have confidence in the positive results reported by St. John's School because historically, Catholic school children have had the reputation of performing better than public school children on standardized tests of achievement (Convey, 1992).

The yearly administration of achievement tests to the same group of children as they matriculate from the first through eighth grade is a longitudinal approach to tracking the students' academic achievement. Convey (1992) notes that "No important study of Catholic schools under Catholic auspices has used longitudinal methodology. . . . A longitudinal study permits a microscopic view of development and growth. In such a study, the individual studied becomes his or her own control" (p. 183). It is likely that there are other Catholic schools across the country, like St. John's, that administer achievement tests every year, but are unaware that they are generating longitudinal data that are useful for understanding the influence of their curriculum and instructional practices.

Curriculum Research Resources. If an administrator does not have the resources to learn more from the achievement test results than the scores, it may be helpful to investigate the possibility of collaborative research with the faculty and students of a Catholic college or university. There are many ways that faculty and students may be helpful, especially if they are involved in a teacher-training program. Some examples of research on curriculum and academics that might be undertaken include: (1) evaluation of the compatibility between the curriculum and the achievement test questions for one or more of the subject areas tested; (2) a comparison of prior and current achievement test results to identify where students are strong, maintaining, or weak; (3) an examination of student-earned grades and achievement test results for one or more subjects; (4) investigation into the curriculum content of one or more schools whose students are successful in achievement, to develop a prototype curriculum. An example of a recent prototype curriculum developed in this manner is the "Core Knowledge Sequence" (Bennett, Finn & Cribb, 1999; Core Knowledge Foundation, 1999).

Regardless of how the collaboration between a school, a diocesan department of education, and a college or university comes about, it is important for the Catholic school administrator(s) to have access to a written policy on collaborative research. An administrator must be certain that the research consultants are competent to carry out an analysis that will result in a meaningful study. The question to be answered is whether the consultants have a track record, examples of prior studies, and references to vouch for their competence. Before any research is applied even to aggregate achievement scores, there are important issues that need to be resolved, such as (1) the limits of confidentiality, (2) who is vested with ownership and control of the data and the resulting study, and (3) whether the findings and recommendations will be presented in a format that can be acted upon in a practical way for the benefit of the students, teachers, and school. It is also essential to be guided by a plan with a full description of the research that indicates: (1) who is doing it, (2) what question(s) it will answer, (3) where it will be done, (4) how the research is to be carried out, (5) when the research will begin and end, (6) consideration of potential psychological, social, legal, or other risks and evaluation of the likelihood of their occurrence, and (7) how informed consent will be obtained if it is needed.

Many colleges and universities have institutional review boards that provide guidelines and review and approve all research undertaken by faculty and staff for the protection of potential research subjects. Some informative resources on issues that arise regarding research within a Catholic educational perspective will be found in the policies of the Catholic Education Office Melbourne (1991, 1996, 1999a, 1999b) and Catholic Education Commission of Victoria (1992) in Australia, that can be accessed via the World Wide Web. It would be helpful to Catholic college and university programs if there were a nationwide compendium of the curricular areas, issues, problems, or circumstances where research in Catholic schools would be helpful. Such a compendium ought to include a list of the schools where there is longitudinal tracking of students' academic achievement by yearly administration of achievement tests to the same children from kindergarten through twelfth grade.

State and National Measures of Achievement. The participation of Catholic schools in national and state assessment efforts during the past 25 years has brought them some prominence due to the positive results noted when comparisons with public schools are made (Bryk, Lee, & Holland, 1993; Convey, 1992; Doyle, 1996; Sebring & Camburn, 1992; Shokraii, 1997). Currently, the Archdiocese of Chicago mandates the Archdiocesan Testing/Assessment Program, TERRA NOVA, because it is based on national standards for student achievement, and 22 states are using some components of this program (Schuster, 2000). Schuster (2000) reports that the TERRA NOVA results are used to "strengthen the curriculum, to plan teaching strategies and to develop learning objectives." This testing program is related to the recent development of the academic accountability movement among the states that legislate minimum standards, linking promotions and high school graduation to examination results. Concern about inappropriate use and overuse of achievement test results to the exclusion of other data in making educational decisions has influenced Senator Paul Wellstone of Minnesota to introduce a bill to provide for fairness and accuracy in student testing. Whether or not the bill becomes the law, it is well worth reading since it proposes standards of fairness be applied when tests are used to influence "high-stakes" decisions such as promotion or graduation (American Educational Research Association, American Psychological Association, & National Council on Measurement in Education, 1999; Wellstone, 2000).

The participation of Catholic schools in state-mandated testing is not a recent development. In the 1970s, for example, parochial high school seniors in Florida took a state examination whose results were used to support applications to the state's universities. In some contexts, the state mandates are not regarded with much sympathy by Catholic educators. This was the case when the Louisiana State Superintendent of Education proposed that non–public school seniors be required to participate in the state exit examination. Gary (1989) testified before the Louisiana State Board of Elementary and Secondary Education that 71% of the 1988 graduating classes of 52 Louisiana Catholic high schools scored above the state's average composite score of 17.1 on the American College Test, indicating that a state exit examination would be unwarranted. The positive aspect of this response is in the fact that the parochial schools had data to demonstrate that the academic instruction in Catholic schools was as good as the instruction in Louisiana's public schools. As Convey (1992) has observed, Catholic school students have usually fared quite well on commercially developed tests of achievement. As long as there continues to be a good match between the curricula of Catholic schools and the state tests, Catholic schools will not need to be concerned about demonstrating the outstanding quality of their curricula and instruction.

Study of Students' Responses to Curricula

This section of the chapter describes a program of the direct study of students' responses to curricula and instruction. The primary reason for proposing the study is that discovering the issues and problems firsthand has a much greater impact on the understanding and solution-seeking of school personnel than just reading about them. Classrooms are the great laboratories for the study of teachers' implementation of curricula and students' responses to it. Often, the decision about where the focus of the study will be is influenced by what administrators and teachers have learned from achievement test results, and comparison of their curricula with other curricular materials (Benton & Wasko, 2000).

The activities for the study of students' responses to curricula are adapted from a program developed by Daniel A. Prescott, Fritz Redl, Caroline Zachry, and others at the Universities of Chicago and Maryland in the 1940s (Brandt & Perkins, 1956; Commission on Teacher Education, 1945; *Direct Study*, 1989– 1990; Eliot & Gardner, 1985; Morgan, 1989; Prescott, 1957, 1962). In Prescott's (1957) words, the "program is not a course of instruction which participants receive. Rather, it is a program of guided experiences that participants undergo and through which they gradually learn to see school situations through the eyes of individual children" (p. 467). It is noteworthy that "At its apogee, 150,000 teachers received a year or its equivalent of child study in 35 states and 8 foreign nations. Put differently, at least 3 million children were attending classes under participating teachers during the years when the teachers were enrolled" (Eliot & Gardner, 1985). There is little evidence in the literature that Catholic school personnel have had the opportunity to participate in this form of child and curriculum study.

Since 1985, under the leadership of Dr. James E. Gay, the School of Education of the University of Dayton has sponsored a program whose focus has included the study of students' responses to curricula (Gay & Williams, 1993a, 1993b; Sudzina & Gay, 1993; Williams & Gay, 1998a, 1998b). Participating school personnel have included teachers, supervisors, principals, counselors, and school psychologists in elementary, middle, and high schools. A problem-based learning example will be presented later in this section to introduce some of the most important processes involved in the study of students' responses to curricula and instruction.

To carry out the study, school personnel organize themselves into voluntary inservice study groups moderated by a participant-leader who has received leadership training. The leadership training is required even if an individual has previously participated as a group member in the study of students' responses to curricula.

Ethics and Confidentiality. At the initial meeting, the group develops a code of ethics to ensure the protection and confidentiality of the students whose responses are being studied. The code states that all information in the written curriculum study records is kept confidential and inaccessible to non-group members. All information presented during group meetings must be treated as confidential by all members of the group. Only information and data written in the curriculum study record are communicated (read) to the group. This ensures that the information given to group members about the curriculum responses of students being studied will be documented and available for use during all of the curriculum study activities.

Writing the Curriculum Study Record. After the code of ethics has been established and agreed to, the group members choose students to study. Information for the curriculum study record is gathered by school personnel during daily observation of students' responses to one or more curricular subjects, including the teaching of lessons, homework, testing, review of the cumulative records, and consultations with other staff, professionals, and parents. The results of the observations and collected information are entered in a bound composition notebook in the form of written anecdotes and summaries. A good written anecdote or summary includes (1) the date it was entered in the curriculum study record, (2) source of the data (e.g., test results, parents, etc.), (3) the original date of the data, and (4) behavioral anecdotes that report contexts, behaviors, verbalizations, responses of others, and " 'mood cues'—postures, gestures, voice qualities, and facial expressions that give cues to how the child felt" (Prescott, 1957, p. 154). Group members confidentially share the information about students' responses to curriculum and work together analyzing, coding, and interpreting it during their meetings. Curricular study record development occupies the group for about the first six meetings, during which they learn to differentiate objective from subjective anecdotal information. As a method for maintaining sensitivity to the subjective aspects of information, parentheses are placed around information that is identified as subjective.

Analysis of the Curriculum Study Record. There are several analytical or interpretive activities that participants apply to the curriculum study record during the first year. These activities provide the experiences through which participants deepen their understanding and insights about learning and the students' responses to curricula. At about the seventh or eighth meeting, the group is oriented to identifying and listing recurring behaviors. When a behavior is documented twice in the curriculum record, it is a recurring behavior. Subsequent recurrences of the behavior are noted by listing the dates (e.g., month and day) of recurrence. It is very likely that at least a dozen patterns of recurring behaviors will be documented in a record, particularly if participants list the behaviors in discrete terms.

An even better understanding of the influences on a student's recurring behaviors and responses to the school curriculum and developmental tasks can be gained by applying the multiple hypotheses method. From the list of recurring behaviors any pattern of behavior that is of interest or challenge to the teacher may be selected for analysis by the multiple hypotheses method. This type of analysis involves two steps: (1) listing as many reasons as possible for a behavior (multiple hypotheses) stated in as specific and testable forms as possible; and (2) identifying facts contained in the curriculum study record that support or refute the hypotheses. The curriculum study record is read anecdote by anecdote, to identify and record the facts that support or refute the hypotheses. Anecdotal facts supporting a hypothesis are listed with a plus sign (+) before the date of the anecdotal source of the fact, and facts refuting the hypothesis are listed with a minus sign (−) before the date. Teachers gain confidence about the hypotheses refuted or supported by this activity and the results can then be summarized (see examples in Gay & Williams, 1993b; Williams & Gay, 1998b).

Direct Examination of Curricula

An alternative to researching achievement test results or the study of students' responses to curricula is to examine curricula against a recognized curricular standard. In this section of the chapter, selected examples from among the extensive resources on curriculum and standards are cited. Educational researchers observed some time ago that "Curriculum development is often guided by a curriculum philosophy or academic discipline rather than . . . empirical research. . . . Studies by the Educational Products Information Exchange revealed that less than 1 percent of the half million or so curriculum materials sold by the publishing industry have ever been field-tested with students and revised prior to publication" (Borg & Gall, 1983, p. 773). Readers of *The Educated Child: A Parent's Guide from Preschool through Eighth Grade* learn that "One main purpose of this book is to help . . . appraise the job your school does in teaching English, history, geography, math, science, and the arts" (Bennett, Finn & Cribb, 1999, p. 95). Curriculum guides are provided for the subjects of English, history and geography, art and music, and mathematics and science. The curriculum for each subject covers the content sequentially from the primary years of kindergarten to third grade, the intermediate years of fourth to sixth grade, and grades seven and eight. The authors indicate that the curriculum guides are drawn from *The Core Knowledge Sequence: Content Guidelines for K–8* developed by the Core Knowledge Foundation at Charlottesville, Virginia. Bennett, Finn, and Cribb (1999) make the observation that "The Core Knowledge Sequence is the best content guide for the elementary grades that we have seen. It is meant by its authors to occupy at least 50 percent of the whole school curriculum" (p. 100). In the instructions to parents, the authors of *The Educated Child* (Bennett et al.) warn that the curriculum guides do not include everything that is studied in elementary school, nor are they intended to preclude other important areas of study. It is not necessary that a school's curriculum line up exactly with the core curriculum proposed. On the other hand, there are some indicators that parents are encouraged to look for. Among these indicators are: (1) an academic mission statement that identifies the knowledge and skills that students are to master, (2) communication of expectations for students, teachers, and the school, and (3) the practice of continuous assessment and feedback to parents and students.

These indicators are included in the guidelines and policies of Catholic education systems. For example, the Catholic Education Commission of Victoria (1994a, 1994b, 1994c, 1994d) in Australia addresses the issue of how Catholic schools should develop policies defining curriculum, assessment, and reporting in a series of policies. Utilizing these documents as a framework, the individual school is expected to develop its own policies. In one of the documents, curriculum is defined as "all the arrangements the school makes for students' learning and development. It includes the content of courses, student activities, teaching approaches, and the ways in which teachers and classes are organized" (Catholic Education Commission of Victoria, 1994a). This definition of curriculum is the one provided by the Ministry of Education of the Australian State of Victoria. It is clearly a definition of curriculum from a very broad perspective (Miller, 1967).

The South Australian Commission for Catholic Schools (1998) mandates that all Catholic schools have "an articulated curriculum map document (or scope and sequence document, or student learning document) for each learning area, that will provide the basis for teachers' programming" (p. 3). In the United States, the National Catholic Educational Association has published *Creating a Curriculum That Works: A Guide to Outcomes-Centered Curriculum Decision-Making* (Ozar, 1994). Durante and Haney (1994) state, in their Foreword to the text, that it "challenges Catholic educators to readjust their curriculum lenses to focus on results rather than tabulating time spent and lessons taught. As a result of implementing this guide of outcomes-centered curriculum, the focus shifts to the knowledge and skills students should accrue before graduating" (p. iii). In this text, researchers will also find other sources of curricular standards developed by organizations dedicated to particular content areas such as the arts, English, mathematics, science, civics, history, geography, and social sciences.

Another resource for curricula to make comparisons are the many high-quality and comprehensive curricula being made available on the web sites of state and provincial departments of education. One outstanding example is the Oregon Department of Education's web site material, under the title "Teaching and Learning to Standards: Teacher Resources" (Oregon Department of Education, 1999). This site offers extensive curricular materials on science, social studies, the arts, second languages, reading, writing, speaking, and mathematics that can be downloaded and printed. Another example is the Canadian Province of Ontario's Ministry of Education's web site that offers standards and guidance regarding elementary and secondary curricula. The Canadian Province of Alberta prepares and distributes Catholic versions of elementary curricula handbooks for parents, and these can be accessed via the Alberta Learning web site.

Finally, a recent doctoral dissertation by Dennehy-White (1999) finds that the greatest influences on the lessons taught in Catholic schools "were textbook scope and sequence charts and State Curriculum Frameworks. . . . It is the conclusion of the researcher that one would be in error to say that the observed success of the Catholic schools in California is due mainly to Catholic Schools' curriculum" (p. 3332). Researching into what really constitutes curricula in Catholic schools offers a continuous opportunity for investigation. The preferred curricular resources for comparison are those that produce the most outstanding academic achievement results. It is also noteworthy that this is one way that parents can evaluate curricular content and exercise their responsibility regarding their children's education (Congregation for Catholic Education, 1988; Pius XI, 1929; Sacred Congregation for Catholic Education, 1982; Second Vatican Council, 1975).

Practical Issues Regarding Curricula

Much of the current research literature on curricula focuses primarily on the innumerable practical or "how or why to" issues. Practical issues regarding curricula include such topics as affective influences and outcomes, attitudes, congruence of mission and practice, discipline content, diversity, economics, innovations, licensure or certification requirements, methods, personnel, philosophy, resources, social influences, standards, technology, and values. Often, research on practical issues and curricula involves dealing with one or more of these topics in the same project. Many studies result in what Convey (1992) refers to as "snapshots of a group of students at a particular time" (p. 183).

Doctoral dissertations are one of the most useful resources for current and past research on practical issues related to curricula in Catholic schools. There are several published sources on dissertations completed on Catholic schools from 1976 to 1997 (Hunt, 1998; Traviss, 1989). The most complete listing of Catholic school dissertations will be found at the University of San Francisco's School of Education web site. Two aspects of this site that make it uniquely useful are the list of Catholic school dissertations prior to 1976, which is no longer available from the National Catholic Educational Association (NCEA), and the listing of the most recent dissertations. These citations give the author, title, university, and year of the dissertation. With this information, a researcher can access the abstracts in the *Dissertation Abstracts International* that are available at many college and university libraries. Among the 302 dissertations cited in *Doctoral Dissertations on Catholic Schools in the United States 1988–1997* (Hunt, 1998), only 18 or about 6% were listed under the rubric of curriculum and academic programs. It would seem that this is a quite limited number in light of the total number of dissertations completed during the 10-year period. One speculation about this small number is that curriculum may not be recognized as an issue of concern for Catholic schools.

The most extensive resource for the educational researcher is the ERIC database. This database of more than a million abstracts of research on education is updated monthly and is available at a web site designated: AskERIC (http://www.askeric.org/About/). Among the items are those on Catholic schools in other countries where English is spoken, such as Australia, Canada, New Zealand, and the United Kingdom. The U.S. Department of Education is also a worthwhile source of statistical data on private schools that includes Catholic schools (Broughman & Colaciello, 1999). Researchers will also find that the National Catholic Educational Association publishes research studies on Catholic schools and has established a section dedicated to generic educational research in its journal *Momentum*. Several of the recent articles have covered topics related to curricula.

A survey of dissertations and articles published from 1994 through 1999 researching curricula in Catholic schools reveals the variety of the general and practical topics covered. Below are selected examples of dissertations and articles on practical issues related to curricula.

Attitudes toward Curriculum. Brehm (1997) reports that Catholic leadership personnel from a Midwestern diocese ranked instructional programs in fifth place among priorities for school improvement, whereas nearly "50% ranked physical plant as the highest priority" (p. 1509).

Curricular Innovations. Davis' (1996) research was intended to promote a middle school's (grades 6–8) structure and program to meet the social, physical, psychological, and academic needs of preadolescents within the context of the traditional K–8 Catholic school setting. Litton (1998) explicates the processes undertaken by Catholic educators at the elementary level to integrate the perspectives of students of differing cultural backgrounds into the curricula.

Heltsley (1998) identified computer software used in Catholic elementary schools and evaluated it to determine if its content was in accord with a Catholic philosophy of education. The issue is that educators need to be vigilant about the possibility of introducing computer software whose content might be in conflict with the values of a Catholic curriculum.

Nuzzi (1998) advocates for the adoption of cooperative learning strategies by Catholic schools because it has positively impacted achievement, social behavior, and attitudes, and is congruent with values of charity and personal responsibility.

Schinzel (1996) investigated the kind of planning that is necessary to offer advanced placement science programs in Catholic high schools. The result was the following guidelines: (1) take a survey of the demand for the courses, (2) assess financial resources to support the project, (3) form a team of teachers, administrators, and outside experts to implement the project, (4) provide for collaboration of teachers and administrators in scheduling, (5) provide adequate laboratory time for each course, (6) appoint a coordinator of the advanced placement science program, (7) have the project team identified in #3 participate in selection of the faculty, (8) have faculty qualifications include a graduate degree, teaching experience, and content competence, (9) fill this faculty position with the best possible candidate, (10) offer professional development opportunities, (11) offer the advanced placement teacher additional planning time, (12) delineate the use of examination results in teacher evaluation process, and (13) establish a policy about the role of examinations in the advanced placement science course.

Methods. Grogan (1994) completed a data analysis of mathematics instruction of 8th graders in Catholic and public schools and found no differences in efficiency between the schools, or for high, middle, and low achievement subgroups.

Personnel. O'Keefe (1999) reviews data on the national teacher shortage and proposes some economical remedial approaches for Catholic schools to respond to the developing shortages.

Social and Affective Influences. Brahier (1995) investigated the beliefs and aspirations of 8th graders electing a first-year algebra course. The most common reasons given for taking algebra were course acceleration, high school preparation, and desire for a challenge. Choosing to take algebra was influenced by parents and it was noted that girls were twice as likely as boys to be influenced by peers.

Behrends (1996) learns from students that caring is realized via "caring educators, a caring curriculum, and a caring environment, placing . . . emphasis on caring educators. Students viewed caring educators as those who create and maintain family-like relationships . . . , help . . . with personal or academic problems, challenge students, expect a lot from them, and encourage them. . . . Catholic school students and students in small public choice schools perceive caring similarly" (p. 2428).

Brutsaert (1998) reports that the academic achievement among Belgian elementary school children of low socioeconomic origins was better in Catholic than in public schools.

Sander (1996) found that for average students, a Catholic elementary education is linked to the attainment of higher vocabulary, math, and reading scores, but not higher scores in science.

These examples reveal the diversity of topics one is likely to encounter in

research on practical issues related to curricula and academics. Many are prototypes for educational practice and future research in Catholic educational settings.

SUMMARY

This chapter proposes approaches for researching curricula and academics that
will result in data for (1) determining whether the academic instruction in Catholic schools is as good as that in other schools, and (2) being accountable to
parents about the education that is being provided (Canon Law Society of America, 1983). The approaches for researching curricula and academics in Catholic
schools that are the resources for data regarding instruction and accountability
to parents are (1) the administration of standardized measures of achievement,
and (2) evaluation of curricular content against recognized curricular prototypes.
These approaches to research allow the examination of curricula in Catholic
schools from the perspectives of achievement, the processes of instruction, concordance with recognized curricular prototypes, or combinations of these approaches. A third approach, research into practical issues relating to curricula,
is the one most encountered in the literature. Research on practical issues relating
to curricula is useful in that it often supports maintaining, developing, and improving curricula. The chapter liberally cites selected resources from Catholic,
government, and private organizations that produce information related to curricula, instruction, and educational research that readers may find useful for
making further investigation into the feasibility of researching curricula and
academics in Catholic schools.

Finally, this chapter concludes with comments on education that are as relevant today as they were when they were written 70 years ago by Pius XI (1929):
"At no time has education been so much discussed as at the present day; there
has consequently been a great increase in the number of pedagogical theorists,
who claim, by the new methods and maxims which they advocate and propound,
to be able to provide an easier and more effective education" (#4).

REFERENCES

American Educational Research Association, American Psychological Association, &
    National Center on Measurement in Education. (1999). *Standards for educational
    and psychological testing.* Washington, DC: American Educational Research As-
    sociation.
Behrends, M.K.P. (1996). Categories of caring in urban minority schools of choice: High
    school seniors' perspectives. *Dissertation Abstracts International, 57*(6A), 2428.
Bennett, W. J., Finn, C. E., Jr., & Cribb, J.T.E., Jr. (1999). *The educated child: A parent's
    guide from preschool through eighth grade.* New York: The Free Press.
Benton, J., & Wasko, J. (2000). "Anything worthwhile takes time": Eight schools discuss
    impacts and impressions of doing action research. *Networks: An On-line Journal*

for Teacher Research, 3 (1). Retrieved June 7, 2000 from the World Wide Web: http: //www.oise.utoronto.ca/~ctd/networks/journal/Vol%203(1).2000april/Article 3.html.

Borg, W. R., & Gall, M. D. (1983). *Educational research: An introduction* (4th ed.). New York: Longman.

Brahier, D. J. (1995). Eighth graders in first-year algebra from selected Catholic schools in northwest Ohio: Influences, aspirations, and dispositions toward mathematics. *Dissertation Abstracts International, 56*(5A), 1696.

Brandt, R. M., & Perkins, H. V. (1956). Research evaluating a child study program. *Monographs of the Society for Research in Child Development, 21* (1, Serial No. 62).

Brehm, M. S. (1997). A comparative study of kindergarten through eighth-grade Catholic school effectiveness and priorities for improvement as perceived by leadership personnel in a diverse midwestern diocese. *Dissertation Abstracts International, 58*(5A, 1509).

Broughman, S. P., & Colaciello, L. A. (1999). *Private school universe survey, 1997–98.* Washington, DC: U.S. Department of Education, National Center for Educational Statistics. Retrieved February 25, 2000 from the NCES World Wide Web Home Page: http://NCES.ed.gov.

Brutsaert, H. (1998). Home and school influences on academic performance: State and Catholic elementary schools in Belgium compared. *Educational Review, 50*, 37–43.

Bryk, A. S., Lee, V. E., & Holland, P. B. (1993). *Catholic schools and the common good.* Cambridge, MA: Harvard University Press.

Canon Law Society of America. (1983). *Code of canon law: Latin-English edition.* Washington, DC: Author.

Catholic Education Commission of Victoria. (1992). Confidentiality in Catholic education, CECV Policy 1.12. In *Catholic schools Victoria: Education policy manual.* Author. Retrieved December 29, 1999 from the World Wide Web: http:// www.cecv.melb.catholic.edu.au/ policies/pol112.htm.

Catholic Education Commission of Victoria. (1994a). Curriculum, assessment and reporting for Catholic schools P-12, CECV Policy 1.15. In *Catholic schools Victoria: Education policy manual.* Author. Retrieved December 29, 1999 from the World Wide Web: http://www.cecv.melb.catholic.edu.au/policies/pol115.htm.

Catholic Education Commission of Victoria. (1994b). Guidelines for curriculum in the Catholic school P-12, CECV Policy 1.15A. In *Catholic schools Victoria: Education policy manual.* Author. Retrieved December 29, 1999 from the World Wide Web: http://www.cecv.melb.catholic.edu.au/policies/pol115a.htm.

Catholic Education Commission of Victoria. (1994c). Guidelines for assessment in the Catholic school P-12, CECV Policy 1.15B. In *Catholic schools Victoria: Education policy manual.* Author. Retrieved December 29, 1999 from the World Wide Web: http://www.cecv.melb.catholic.edu.au/policies/pol115b.htm.

Catholic Education Commission of Victoria. (1994d). Guidelines for reporting student outcomes in the Catholic school P-12, CECV Policy 1.15C. In *Catholic schools Victoria: Education policy manual.* Author. Retrieved December 29, 1999 from the World Wide Web: http://www.cecv.melb.catholic.edu.au/policies/pol115c.htm.

Catholic Education Office Melbourne. (1991). *CEOM Policy 2.10. Ad hoc research pro-*

jects carried out or underwritten by the Catholic Education Office. Retrieved December 29, 1999 from the World Wide Web: http://web.ceo.melb. catholic.edu.au/policydoc/pol210.htm.

Catholic Education Office Melbourne. (1996). *CEOM Policy 2.7. Access to CEOM official records for purposes of research.* Retrieved December 29, 1999 from the World Wide Web: http://web.ceo.melb.catholic.edu.au/policydoc/pol27.htm.

Catholic Education Office Melbourne. (1999a). *CEOM Policy 2.8. Access to schools for purposes of research: Guidelines for intending researchers.* Retrieved December 29, 1999 from the World Wide Web: http://web.ceo.melb.catholic.edu.au/policydoc/pol28.htm.

Catholic Education Office Melbourne. (1999b). *CEOM Policy 2.9. Access to schools for purposes of research: Guidelines for principals and Catholic education office personnel.* Retrieved December 29, 1999 from the World Wide Web: http:// web.ceo.melb.catholic.edu.au/ policydoc/pol29.htm.

Commission on Teacher Education. (1945). *Helping teachers understand children.* Washington, DC: American Council on Education.

Congregation for Catholic Education. (1988). *The religious dimension of education in a Catholic school: Guidelines for reflection and renewal.* Washington, DC: United States Catholic Conference.

Convey, J. J. (1992). *Catholic schools make a difference: Twenty-five years of research.* Washington, DC: National Catholic Educational Association.

Core Knowledge Foundation. (1999). *Who decided what's in the sequence.* Retrieved January 31, 2000 from the World Wide Web: http://www.coreknowledge.org/ CKproto2/about/index.htm#WHO.

Davis, A. M. (1996). Middle schools: A non-traditional program for traditional K–8 Catholic schools. *Dissertation Abstracts International, 56*(9A), 3448.

Dennehy-White, M. C. (1999). A comparison of perceptions regarding curriculum among Catholic school principals and teachers in California. *Dissertation Abstracts International, 59*(9A), 3332.

Direct study of academic behavior: Garrett County. (1989–90). Unpublished manuscript. University of Maryland, Institute for Child Study/Department of Human Development, College Park, MD.

Doyle, D. P. (1996). *The social consequences of choice: Why it matters where poor children go to school* [On-line]. Available: http://www.heritage.org/.

Durante, S., & Haney, R. (1994). Foreword. In L. A. Ozar (Ed.), *Creating a curriculum that works: A guide to outcomes-centered curriculum decision-making* (p. iii). Washington, DC: National Catholic Educational Association.

Eliot, J., & Gardner, A. (1985). *Update 1985: Institute for Child Study/Department of Human Development* [Pamphlet]. College Park, MD: College of Education, University of Maryland.

Gary, L. P., Jr. (1989, April). *The threat of a state graduation examination for non-public schools in Louisiana.* Paper presented to the Louisiana State Board of Elementary and Secondary Education at a public meeting, Baton Rouge, LA. (ERIC Document Reproduction Service No. ED 328 566.)

Gay, J., & Williams, R. (1993a). *Activities for seeing school through the eyes of children from differing sociocultural backgrounds.* Paper presented at the 48th Annual Conference of Association for Supervision and Curriculum Development, Washington, DC.

Gay, J. E., & Williams, R. B. (1993b). Case study training for seeing school through adolescents' eyes. *Adolescence, 28*, 13–19.

Grogan, T. J. (1994). A data envelopment analysis of eighth grade mathematics instruction with a comparison of Catholic and public schools. *Dissertation Abstracts International, 55*(1A), 59.

Heltsley, C. (1998). Opening the classroom door to a stranger and leaving the room: The importance of scrutinizing values implanted in computer software. *Momentum, 29 (4)*, 53–61.

Hunt, T. C. (1998). *Doctoral dissertations on Catholic schools in the United States 1988–1997*. Washington, DC: National Catholic Educational Association.

Litton, E. F. (1998). Voices from the vineyard: Gifts of diversity from Catholic elementary school educators. *Momentum, 29 (2)*, 54–59.

Miller, M. J. (1967). Curriculum, philosophy of. In Editorial Staff at The Catholic University of America, *New Catholic encyclopedia, Vol. IV, Com to Dys* (pp. 542–544). New York: McGraw-Hill.

Morgan, H. G. (1989). *Roots: Needs of the time—beginning of Institute for Child Study/ Department of Human Development*. Paper presented at the Institute for Child Study/Department of Human Development Spring Alumni Meeting, University of Maryland, College Park, MD.

Murphy, L. L., Conoley, J. C., & Impara, J. C. (Eds.). (1994). *Tests in print IV*. Lincoln, NE: Buros Institute of Mental Measurements, University of Nebraska Press.

Nuzzi, R. J. (1998). Cooperative learning and Catholic schools: A natural partnership. *Momentum, 29 (1)*, 70–75.

O'Keefe, J. H. (1999). Creative resourcing for Catholic schools: The critical issue of hiring and retaining high-quality teachers. *Momentum, 30 (4)*, 54–58.

Oregon Department of Education. (1999). *Teaching and learning to standards teacher resources for use during the 1999–2000 school year*. Retrieved February 1, 2000 from the World Wide Web: http://www.ode.state.or.us/cifs/Standards/index.htm.

Ozar, L. A. (1994). *Creating a curriculum that works: A guide to outcomes-centered curriculum decision-making*. Washington, DC: National Catholic Educational Association.

Pius XI. (1929). *Divini illius magistri* [The Christian education of youth]. London: Catholic Truth Society.

Prescott, D. A. (1957). *The child in the educative process*. New York: McGraw-Hill.

Prescott, D. A. (1962). *The impact of child study on education*. Columbus: Ohio Department of Education.

Sacred Congregation for Catholic Education. (1982). Catholic schools. In A. Flannery (Ed.), *Vatican II: More post-conciliar documents* (pp. 606–629). Collegeville, MN: The Liturgical Press.

Saint John's school curriculum. (1999). Retrieved October 25, 1999 from the World Wide Web: http://www.saintjohn-bangor.pvt.k12.me.us/curriculum.html.

Salvia, J., & Ysseldyke, J. E. (1991). *Assessment* (5th ed.). Boston: Houghton Mifflin Co.

Sander, W. (1996). Catholic grade schools and academic achievement. *Journal of Human Resources, 31*, 540–548.

Schinzel, D. D. (1996). Advanced placement science programs in Catholic high schools. *Dissertation Abstracts International, 57*(3A), 1084.

Schuster, E. (2000). *Superintendent Elaine Schuster reports on the state of Catholic schools in the Archdiocese of Chicago.* Retrieved January 31, 2000 from the World Wide Web: http://www.archdiocese-chgo.org/newsreleases/new-school 0128.html.

Sebring, P. A., & Camburn, E. M. (1992). *A profile of eighth graders in Catholic schools.* Washington, DC: National Catholic Educational Association.

Second Vatican Council. (1975). Gravissimum educationis. In A. Flannery (Ed.), *Vatican Council II, Volume 1: The conciliar and post-conciliar documents* (pp. 725–737). Northport, NY: Costello Publishing.

Shokraii, N. H. (1997). *Why Catholic schools spell success for America's inner-city children.* [On-line]. Available: http://www.heritage.org/.

South Australian Commission for Catholic Schools. (1998). *A curriculum policy for Catholic schools.* Thebarton, SA: Catholic Education Office.

Sudzina, M. R., & Gay, J. E. (1993). Child study: A process for teachers' personal and professional growth. *Journal of Humanistic Education and Development, 31,* 171–180.

Traviss, M. P. (1989). *Doctoral dissertations on Catholic schools, K–12, 1976–1987.* Washington, DC: National Catholic Educational Association.

Wellstone, P. (2000). A bill to provide for fairness and accuracy in student testing. Retrieved April 7, 2000 from the World Wide Web: http://wellstone.senate.gov/.

Williams, R. B., & Gay, J. E. (1998a). Understanding our students: A case study method. *The Clearing House, 72 (1),* 44–46.

Williams, R. B., & Gay, J. E. (1998b). Church through the eyes of Sunday school children. *Education, 119,* 77, 78–81.

Chapter 5

Research on Administration, Leadership, and Governance

Mary Peter Traviss

INTRODUCTION TO THE RESEARCH

Scholars, particularly those who investigate Catholic schools, maintain that the principal, or the academic administrator, is the key to a school's success (Bryk, Lee, & Holland, 1993; Buetow, 1970, 1988; Lamb, 1997; Moriarty, 1989; O'Donnell, 1983; Petersen, 1991; Sergiovanni, 1987). The researchers who have directed the major studies of the past 40 years have spent little time, however, examining the role or the function of the principal. In fact, in his excellent review of 25 years of Catholic school research, *Catholic Schools Make a Difference*, John Convey (1992) devoted only one short section of four paragraphs to administration and leadership and little to governance. In contrast, he has a full chapter dedicated to the topic of the "Teacher," which includes the following subsections: "Demographic Characteristics," "Preparation and Experience," "Goal Consensus," "Work Conditions, Commitment and Satisfaction," and "Perceived Teacher Quality," all areas of the school's life for which the principal is ultimately responsible.

The all-pervasive role of the principal may be one of the reasons we find so little research on leadership and administration in the major studies. The researchers may have assumed that in an investigation of the numerous aspects of the school—quality of instruction, academic organization and curriculum, the role of the faculty, health of student life, place and contribution of extracurricular activities, spiritual and moral climate, and morale—the reliance on the principal and his or her support staff is understood. All school studies could, in one sense, be reduced to an investigation of the principal. This is especially true when reviewing research on inner-city schools (Cibulka, O'Brien, & Zewe, 1982; Vitullo-Martin, 1977).

Lipsitz's (1984) widely quoted research on effective schools challenged the prevailing practice of measuring successful schools by student achievement. She elaborated on the definition of "effective" in her study to include climate, community, and the roles of faculty and administrators. In her summary on effective schools, she mentioned the principal in 9 of her 17 conclusions, and associated the contribution of the principal with several other characteristics of effective schools, items such as "level of caring" (p. 181), "staff and students made to feel like chosen people" (p. 172), and "the schools made powerful statements . . . about their purposes" (p. 172).

This chapter will review the topics of administration and governance treated by the major studies of the past 40 years, beginning with the first significant piece of research on a Catholic school, Fichter's (1958) classic case study of a "typical" Catholic parochial school. Citations of relevant doctoral studies by categories will follow it.

MAJOR RESEARCH STUDIES, 1958–2000

Fichter's (1958) *Parochial School: A Sociological Study*, a year-long observational study underwritten by the University of Notre Dame, did not treat the construct of leadership or governance by itself, but included the description of the principal with other variables under study (e.g., discipline, homework, lay teachers, the pastor, and registration). In fact, the terms "leader," "administration," "governance," and "vision" are not listed in an unusually exhaustive index, but the term "principal" is connected to 23 other concepts. As a result of his descriptive analysis, Fichter concluded that although Weber's definition of the term "bureaucrat" could be applied to the local public school principal in 1958, it did not accurately describe the Catholic school principal, who had social esteem, and was appointed, but did not have tenure or pecuniary compensation; nor was the administrator, at least in the mid-twentieth century, a career person.

For the first time there was a scientific piece of research that concluded that the principal of a Catholic school has a different kind of role from that of the public school principal (Fichter, 1958). This differentiation has been explored again and again in subsequent studies (Bryk, 1996; Carr, 1995; Helm, 1989; Holland, 1985; Howe, 1995; Puglisi, 1983). One of the most widely quoted pieces of research making this distinction was the Manno (1985) research, which organized the values, competencies, and qualities of the principalship into a portrait of a Catholic school principal. This research served Catholic schools well during the transition from lay to religious personnel, and continues to be used by scholars writing about the Catholic school principalship. Manno introduced three types of competencies needed by a Catholic school principal: pastoral, professional educational, and professional managerial; and three kinds of qualities: spiritual, professional, and personal.

Reading Fichter's (1958) study in 2000 gives a historical depiction of how hundreds of Catholic schools across the United States formed Catholic youngsters in the 1940s and 1950s and into the mid-1960s. It is particularly strong in detailing the practices and policies that delineate the building of school culture and identity. It is the building of a very definable culture chronicled by this study that subsequent researchers claim is closely connected to both the role and function of the principal (Buetow, 1988; McLaughlin, O'Keefe, & O'Keeffe, 1996; Sergiovanni, 1987).

After the publication of Fichter's (1958) study, Lieberman made his watershed address at the National Catholic Educational Association meeting in Atlantic City, New Jersey. He chided the Catholic educational community for not producing more research on its schools, research that could answer such burning questions as "How divisive are the Catholic schools?" "Do Catholic schools actually preserve the faith life of the student?" "How do Catholic schools compare to public schools?" "Should the Catholic Church concentrate on educating the adult or the child?" After the unanticipated reaction to the Leiberman address had subsided, there was a nationwide call for research. Unfortunately, the major studies that followed did not address the leadership or governance of Catholic schools in any great depth.

There is always the assumption that it was the leadership of the Catholic schools that was responsible for the so-called "Catholic school effect," but it was not singled out for study by a Catholic school researcher. Coleman and Hoffer (1987) contributed significantly to understanding this phenomenon with their introduction of the "functional community" and the construct of "social capital." The Coleman and Hoffer study has a brilliant chapter on how various leadership units associated with the school, including the principal, should use social capital.

The 1960s witnessed a major research work by Greeley and Rossi (1966), which did not explore leadership, governance, or administration per se, but offered one intriguing personal suggestion in a conversation by the authors with Gerhard Lenski. Lenski suggested that the impressive shift away from racial intolerance and anti-Semitism among young Catholic school students reported on by Greeley and Rossi may have been due in part to the fact that the same young people were "more effectively plugged into the Catholic 'communication network' " (1966, p. 135), which informed them about the teachings of Vatican II. The communication network was, of course, the religious women, of whom the greater number were teaching in the schools. It has been suggested that the Sisters at that time were the avant-garde of the Church and were passing along the liberal ideas of the post–Vatican II period to their students. This sort of communicative mentorship has always been at the heart of the Catholic school community, including its leadership and governance. It is unfortunate that this particular influence of religious women has not been more carefully documented. As we begin the twenty-first century and experience their dramatic diminishment, it may be too late for such documentation to take place.

Catholic Schools in Action (CSIA), edited by Neuwien in 1966 and financed by the University of Notre Dame and the Carnegie Foundation (sometimes referred to as "The Notre Dame Study" or "The Carnegie Study"), was published the same year as the Greeley and Rossi study. The researchers gathered a variety of data for the year 1962 from 92% of the Catholic elementary schools and 84% of secondary schools operating in the nation. Like the previous studies, CSIA did not give direct attention to the investigation of administration, leadership, or governance, but it did present some demographics of interest. In the section on "Staff of Catholic School" are reported statistical data about full-time, part-time, and lay principals, including their preparation, salaries, and support systems.

More such statistical snapshots concerning the administration of Catholic schools became available after the National Catholic Educational Association (NCEA) established a national data bank in 1969. Annual reports were compiled and published and became available to researchers through the NCEA offices. Broad, detailed data for the year 1983 were gathered in two NCEA studies, *The Catholic High School: A National Portrait* (Yeager, Benson, Guerra, & Manno, 1985) and its spin-off, *Catholic Schools: Their Impact on Low-Income Students* (Yeager et al., 1986). The advantage of the studies over the data bank reports was the insightful interpretation of the data and the helpful conclusions drawn to inform future decision makers. The studies served as models of how local administrators might examine the findings generated by the data bank reports.

A National Portrait posed 91 questions to its respondents about administration and 71 questions about boards and governance. Administration was mentioned in three of the major findings. The first finding specified that the administrators of Catholic schools did not reflect the ethnic make-up of the students. For example, 18% of students in the schools nationwide were minority, and only 3% of the administrators and 4% of board members were minority. The second finding addressed turnover of administrators. Between 1974 and 1984, 51% of Catholic high schools had at least three principals; 11% had just one principal, 38% had two, 32% had three, and 19% had four or more principals. The authors called for more research in order to assess the impact of high turnover, but not to investigate the cause. The latter topic remains a research need.

The third finding reported that the principals themselves confirmed a common perception among the teachers that the principal of a Catholic school has far greater powers than those given to public school principals. Bryk (1996) confirmed this conclusion, although teachers "did not have much decision making authority, even on matters of curriculum and graduation requirements" (p. 123). The author also suggested that this "relatively small role the teachers play in governance may also contribute to the turnover rates" (p. 180) among the teachers, and recommended a re-examination of the governance structures and a larger role for teachers in decision making. Muccigrosso (1983) made the same recommendation a year earlier, and Bryk, Lee, and Holland (1993), a decade later. Some researchers associated involvement in decision making with a faculty's self-perception and morale (Kushner, 1982). Weaver's (1997) data confirmed Helm's (1989) idea that providing opportunities for decision making on the part of teachers by the principal developed collegiality and helped establish a common vision.

A National Portrait also reported that in 1982, 72% of the Catholic high schools had school boards and that 67% of the board membership was lay. The authors compiled an index of overall decision-making authority based on 11 issues and concluded that the principal or other school administrators make "the final decision in 80% of the cases, the school board in 21%, and teachers in 14% of the decision making opportunities" (Yeager et al., 1985, p. 88).

In 1985, Yeager et al. re-analyzed the data collected for *A National Portrait* in order to focus on schools with low-income students. They conducted an additional in-depth study of minority students and teachers, and published their findings and recommendations in *Catholic High Schools: Their Impact on Low-Income Students* (1986). The results compared the Catholic schools at the national level with the low-income schools (schools that had 10% or more students below the federal poverty level). Since the stated purpose was to study teachers and students, there are little data on administration, leadership, and governance. One finding worthy of note was that while in the suburban and rural Catholic schools, 38% of the principals of Catholic high schools were religious women (23% were Catholic laymen, 3% were Catholic laywomen, 1.1% were non-Catholic laymen, 21% were priests, and 14% were male religious), 46% of the principals of the low-income Catholic high schools were religious women (20% were Catholic laymen, 3% were Catholic laywomen, .6% were non-Catholic laywomen, 21% were priests, and 9% were male religious). Religious women, who by that time were part of the decision-making process about where they would minister, were choosing to work among the low-income families.

A related aspect of governance not receiving the attention it deserved from the Catholic school community is found in Andrew Greeley's *Catholic High Schools and Minority Students* (1982). The research conclusively put to rest the misconception that any so-called "Catholic school effect" can be attributed to Catholic schools enrolling only the brightest students. In fact, one of the most important contributions of this study was that Catholic schools were the true "common schools," and worked best among the "triple disadvantaged" students. The study provided data showing a consistent relation between high-quality instruction, disciplinary control, and ownership by a religious order. The impact of religious order ownership needs to be studied further if it is to be replicated by current high school governance teams; and so does leadership contributions of religious women in diocesan offices of education (Boland & Watkins, 2000).

Because of the dearth of information on elementary school principals, Harkins (1993) designed a study in 1992 consisting of a four-part survey and sent it to 1,000 elementary Catholic school principals in the United States. The results make up, in the comparative words of the author, a family picture album. Included are self-taken pictures with the help of a timer, composite photographs, group portraits, and many different snapshots of a long list of variables. The small volume is a fascinating look into the thinking of the nation's Catholic

Table 5.1
Summary of Responses

Statement: "Two teachers of equal experience and generosity apply for a 6th grade teaching position. One is a good, but not exceptional, teacher and a very committed Catholic. The second is an exceptional and creative teacher but is not Catholic and is not involved in religion. The principal should hire the committed Catholic." N = 783

Part III, #13	TA	SA	A	D	SD	TD
Total	62%	16.1%	45.8%	31.9%	6.2%	38%
Religious	68%	18.4%	49.7%	26.3%	5.5%	32%
Lay	56%	14.0%	42.2%	39.6%	6.9%	44%

Legend: TA = *totally agree*; SA = *strongly agree*; A = *agree*; D = *disagree*; SD = *strongly disagree*; TD = *totally disagree*.
Statistically significant difference between groups: p = .002

Source: Adapted from Harkins (1993), p. 55.

elementary school principals (N = 783; 49.8% = religious; 49.7% = lay; and .5% = priests). It is greatly hoped that this survey will be replicated at least every 20 years. The survey items are insightful and address many of the concerns the Catholic community has about its elementary school principals. To illustrate, one of the questions (see Table 5.1) is reproduced with the data from the research.

Three open-ended items of the Harkins Survey (1993) included, "What one personal characteristic is most essential in a good Catholic school principal?" "The single most important thing a good Catholic elementary principal must do is ———." and "One thing a good Catholic school principal does not do is ———." While some of the agree and disagree statements were taken from the O'Brien (1987) study *Mixed Messages*, the Harkins study is not a duplication, but a fine example of dovetailing one study with another to add thickness to the research.

One of the few studies to contain an entire chapter on governance is the powerful volume *Catholic Schools and the Common Good*, by Bryk, Lee, and Holland (1993). The authors described the Catholic schools of the 1980s and 1990s as continuing to be autonomous, administratively structured in almost as many ways as there are schools, informal and varied in decision making, and on the brink of changing drastically because of the increasing number of lay administrators.

The authors wrote of the "central role of the Catholic school principal" (p. 163), yet noted a "curious paradox" (p. 163) in principals' behaviors and aspirations. Their data showed that principals uniformly identify the need to exercise leadership in building up the faith community of the schools, and yet mundane managerial tasks claim the major portion of their time, leaving them little time to lead.

One of the most interesting common variables researchers have uncovered is the respect and deference paid to members of religious orders, and thus to the school administrators. The question which researchers raised, as the principle of subsidiary promises to enjoy a wider practice, is how this climate of respect and deference will or will not influence the future decision-making structure of the Catholic schools. This phenomenon, especially exercised in girls' schools operated by religious orders of women, has not been adequately studied (Greeley, 1982). A desire by every group in the school community to share in decision making has been reported often in the research, especially during the 1980s and 1990s (Bryk et al., 1993; Dias, 1994; Melton, 1981; Weaver, 1997; Yeager et al., 1985). The research indicates that teachers are still, as we approach the new century, not satisfied with their amount of involvement in decision making. It will be interesting to observe how faculty will enlarge their role to include decision making.

Governance

Questions of governance are best understood against the backdrop of historical research (Buetow, 1970, 1988; Burns, 1912; Fichter, 1958; McCluskey, 1964; Walch, 1996). After two years of inquiry into the effectiveness of Catholic schools, Bryk, Holland, Lee, and Carriedo (1984) concluded that there are two major problems facing Catholic education: finance and governance; and of the two concerns, perhaps governance is the more severe (see Figures 5.1, 5.2, and 5.3).

Bryk (1996) described the Catholic schools as a "very loose federation" (p. 31). Most studies on governance are, by necessity, quasi–case studies, or studies with a tightly focused and limited population.

DOCTORAL RESEARCH STUDIES, 1960–2000

The dissertations on administration over the years have provided a steady output of research. Olsen (1975) reported that between the years 1968 and 1975, 47 dissertations were written on the areas of administration, leadership, and supervision, while 50 were completed in the years between 1976 and 1987, with an additional six devoted to the topic of boards (Traviss, 1989). Between 1988 and 1997, 40 dissertations on the subject of administration, four on the topic of boards, and 3 on the issue of governance were completed (Hunt, 1998).

Leadership

In the general area of administration and governance, leadership is, by far, the single most studied topic among doctoral students. The majority of the recent

Figure 5.1
A Simplified Organizational View of the Governance Structure for a Parish School

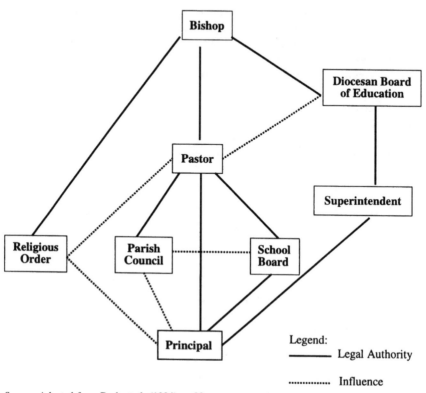

Source: Adapted from Bryk et al. (1984), p. 93.

researchers reported on the increasing expressions of inability on the part of principals to exercise their talents for leadership and at the same time perform the daily and varied administrative tasks that they are required to do. The Holland (1985) study observed this tension, which seems to be exacerbated by the Catholic school principal having to wear so many different hats. Bryk et al. (1984) commented: "In talking about their roles, principals conveyed many images: community builder, instructional leader, financial and personal manager, recruiter, reconciler, promoter, enforcer, and general morale builder" (p. 96).

Clearly, principals see the need to devote more time to leadership, but the urgent very often takes precedence over the important. Leithwood and Jantzi (1992) wrote that "our administrators have a preoccupation with instructional leadership," and that this absorption "threatens to underestimate the challenge of school leaders in post-bureaucratic schools by a shocking amount" (p. 32). The authors maintained that school leaders want to lead, but they do not know

Figure 5.2
Simplified Orientational View of the Governance Structure for a Diocesan School

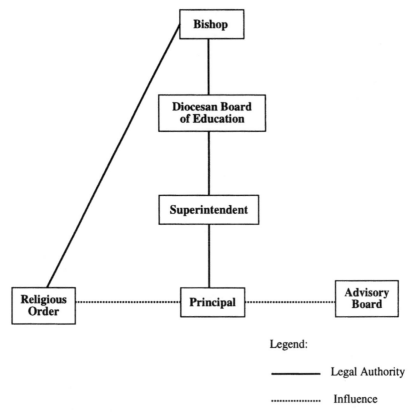

Legend:

———— Legal Authority

················ Influence

Source: Adapted from Bryk et al. (1984), p. 94.

how to get out from under the administrative burden. Of particular interest are those studies indicating that, given the time, Catholic school principals could be effective leaders (Moriarty, 1989), even transformational ones (Coley, 1993; Hocevar, 1989; Lamb, 1997). The tension is a problem that the public school community experiences as well, even though the Catholic school principal is called to leadership in more areas.

Many of the studies used the Ohio State Leader Behavior Description Questionnaire (LBDQ-XII) to measure leadership styles. Other studies, however, utilized the LBAII Self and Other instrument, developed by Hersey and Blanchard (1988) to assist leaders in identifying their leadership style. Four styles are identified: S1–High Directive, Low Supportive Behavior; S2–High Directive, High Supportive Behavior; S3–High Supportive, Low Directive Behavior; and S4–Low Supportive, Low Directive Behavior. Matan (1999) reported that the

Figure 5.3
Simplified Orientational View of the Governance Structure for a Religious Order School

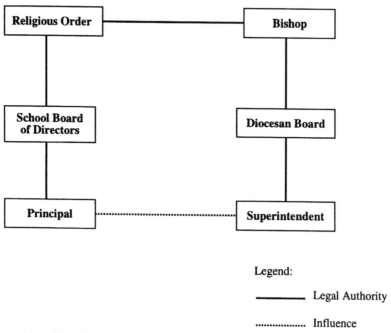

Legend:

—————— Legal Authority

················ Influence

Source: Adapted from Bryk et al. (1984), p. 94.

primary leadership style among effective Catholic secondary school principals was S3. Also, the INTJ (inwardly focused, energized by inner thoughts, future and globally oriented, objective, planned, and organized) was the highest reported personality type, as defined by the Myers-Briggs Type Indicator. Again, Matan found a significant difference in the self-reported perceptions of principals and staffs, a recurring finding in the doctoral research. Lamb (1997) reported that effective Catholic school principals are becoming more transformational in style, a trend that Keane (1983), Hocevar (1989), and Coley (1993) had uncovered earlier in their research, and which Matan would seem to confirm in her work.

Carr (1995) reported a reciprocal relationship between a principal's sense of efficacy and satisfaction. She found that religiosity consistently predicted efficacy and mission motivation. Lay principals reported higher levels of educational efficacy while lay and religious principals reported similar levels of spiritual efficacy. Religious principals had higher levels of spiritual satisfaction while lay principals had higher levels of managerial efficacy, and educational satisfaction. Her research indicated that leadership efficacy and satisfaction among Catholic school principals increased when the religious mission of the school influenced the religiosity of principals.

The research revealed a mixed bag regarding the differences in perception of leadership styles between the principals and the teachers. Johnson (1995) and Seymour (1990) found a significant difference between the two groups; Higgins (1993) and O'Donnell (1982) did not, although the latter's study was done only with women. According to McIlmurray (1980), faculty members at high schools of fewer than 500 students had higher expectations, closer to the ideal role of the principal than did faculty at schools with more students. This finding was supported by Bryk (1996).

Buckley's (1984) data revealed a relationship between the perceived qualities of principals and the readiness for change in schools. Other data on variables and leadership have concluded that leadership was correlated with student achievement (Brennan, 1983; Haymon, 1990; Politz, 1991).

Catholic School Principalship

A study by Holland (1985) focused on the basic tasks and function of Catholic high school principals. The major differences between the responsibilities of Catholic school principals and their public school counterparts were items which appear again and again in the research literature: extended financial and personal responsibilities, the articulation of a spiritual and academic vision, and community relations. Holland's data reinforced the popular notion that the role of norms and standards, organizational value systems, and the principal's vision were salient in building consensus within Catholic high schools. He found a tendency for Catholic school principals to delegate curriculum and supervision tasks to assistants. However, as mentioned, the tension between managerial and leadership functions continues to grow for Catholic school administrators.

Helm (1989), in her research on cultural symbols and leadership, found that the school culture can be attributed to the principal, confirming Sergiovanni's (1987) assertion that the principal provides leadership by establishing a discernible culture. Her data revealed that the strategies employed by the principal to establish such a culture were frequent and informal supervision, feedback, contact, varied efforts to give recognition and express gratitude, and treating parents as valued partners. According to Helm, a leader modeled values and carefully selected teachers who fit the vision of the school. Climate-setting behaviors included protecting teachers' time and providing them with necessary materials.

Recruitment and Preparation

Because of the current shortage of Catholic school principals, data on and strategies for the recruitment and preparation of Catholic elementary school principals is a research priority. Anastasio (1996) found that "slightly more than half of the dioceses in the United States have recruitment programs, and slightly more than two-thirds of the dioceses have selection and preparation programs" (p. 114). The dioceses rely on the Catholic colleges and universities to offer academic programs, while the dioceses do apprentice-like activities to help with the practical preparation. These activities ranged from an annual meeting to frequent structured opportunities for growth. The data suggested that programs are strengthened when dioceses collaborate with other dioceses, with the colleges and universities, and with the local pastors. The research revealed that the programs are uneven in both quality and in Catholicity.

Peters (1984) looked at those factors that lead teachers in Catholic schools to consider careers in administration and found that each diocese is different, and that what attracts a potential principal in one area does not in another. It appears from the findings that knowing what factors have priority in a given area would be helpful for recruitment. Petro (1982), on the other hand, conducted a study to ascertain if Catholic colleges and universities had more of an influence in motivating underclassmen to seek ministry in Catholic schools. The three areas in which the young people were tested were community involvement, support for Catholic schools, and level of social consciousness. There was no difference in perceived impact between Catholic and non-Catholic institutions of higher learning. In light of *Ex Corde Eccelesia*, it would be interesting to pursue this research and explore the reasons for lack of differences.

Rocchio (1993) studied the mentoring process as a means for preparing future principals and found that the participants identified a future role for religious as mentors in this area. Especially needed was preparation in the spiritual leadership role about which the laypersons in the study were noticeably ambiguous. The role, suggested the prospective principals, should also include recruitment and vigilance with regard to assuring that the charisms of the religious congregations be shared with successive generations. There are many doctoral dissertations researching the preservation of individual religious charisms, Jesuit, Dominican, Salesian, and Marianist (Hunt, 1998; Traviss, 1989), but the question "why" must be asked. If the laity are taking responsibility for the school, why not develop a lay charism?

According to Diamond's (1997) study, participation in professional activities is the largest single influence on the principal's leadership. Frequency of participation in workshops is the chief contributor to the principal's leadership behavior. He also found that almost one-third of his population had previous professional experience in a school setting other than a Catholic school. Diamond indicated that there was a strong likelihood that this trend would not only continue, but increase, depending on the kind of experience. This could be a troublesome development, depending on the length of the "other" service, the internalization of its philosophy, and the absence of a working knowledge of Catholic schools.

In his study of lay principals of secondary schools, Wallace (1995) reported that 70% of his sample of 324 lay principals (with 14% formerly vowed religious) said that their faith preparation was "inadequate." Unlike Wallace, Hines'

(1999) data indicated that the elementary school principals perceived their faith formation to be very good (24.5%) or good (25.5%). Only 14.9% felt it was weak or very weak. Principals reported that they were currently receiving support chiefly from diocesan programs. Hines asked "What should be included in the preparation of principals for faith leaders?" Ninety-three principals (84.5%) responded that "spirituality" and "mentorship with a faith leader" should be included, followed by "theology" chosen by 81 (73.6%), "church documents" identified by 56 (50.9%), and "other" by 10 (11%) respondents.

Puglisi (1983) designed a study of the effectiveness of a university leadership program, the Fordham University Nonpublic School Administrators Program (NSAP), and reported that those who participated in this program were more involved with religious leadership in their schools, more involved in formal supervision, and needed central office guidance and training less. There were no differences between the NSAP principals who did not participate in NSAP in the area of formal supervision. Research on the many Catholic school administration programs nationwide would be helpful in order to demonstrate their value to Catholic schools. Use of the evaluation instruments from either of the dissertations would be useful for program comparisons.

Lay Catholic School Administrators

With the dramatic increase of lay administrators toward the middle of the 40-year period under study (Guerra, 2000; Kealey, 1999; McDonald, 1999), it is understandable that researchers sought to investigate their performance and their comparison with the religious administrators, as well as a relationship to a number of other variables. Most of the studies concluded that there was little difference between the lay and religious administrators in leadership style, professional competence (Anastasio, 1996; Antoniswami, 1983; Hood, 1991; John, 1984; McCormick, 1985; Rocchio, 1993), role expectations (Convey, 1987), or spirituality (Diamond, 1997). Lay teachers, however, perceived a difference in leadership style between the religious and lay principals, and found the lay principals "more careful" in transmitting communication than their religious principal colleagues (Hood, 1991).

Antoniswami's (1983) study showed a significant difference between lay principals and lay teachers in regard to perception of climate. Quinn (1985) studied the commitment of the lay administrator based on Becker's side bar theory and found the lay administrators "deeply committed," as did Cusack's study (1983). According to Dias (1994), religious principals perceived more faculty involvement than did lay principals. She also found that the faculty perception of their own involvement correlated significantly with their perception of morale. This latter finding supports the research of Donovan (1980), who found that both the lay and religious teachers wanted greater shared decision-making participation in the area of curricula and instructional programs. It also supports Kushner (1982), whose research discovered that significant relationships indicated that teachers' perceptions of principals' leadership influenced perceptions of themselves as a staff; and that of Bryk, Lee and Holland, (1993), in which they reported that faculty felt disengaged from the decision making of the school, especially in the areas of budget and staffing. These findings seem in contradiction to the reported trend (Muccigrosso, 1996) of Catholic school administrators moving toward transformational leadership.

The studies also found widespread support for lay administrators among the younger clergy. The religious principals expressed confidence in the lay principals while the evidence of parent support was contradictory. Parents felt that religious principals did a better job in religion and discipline. Cusack (1983) noted that a pastor may terminate a lay principal, without reason, at the end of a school year, and suggested that forums for appeal be established throughout the Catholic school community. A study of Jesuit lay administrators found that lay administrators have a "less than adequate understanding" of the principles of Ignatian education, but the Jesuit administrators themselves had only a "slightly better understanding" (Carey, 1987).

COMPARISON OF CATHOLIC AND PUBLIC SCHOOL ADMINISTRATORS

The few studies (McGraw, 1981; Mignacca, 1988; Petty, 1992) that have been written comparing public and Catholic school principals conclude that there are more differences than similarities in both the role and the function of the principalship; hence it is difficult to compare the administrators of the two kinds of schools. Petty (1992) cited the differences in terms of the lack of autonomy of the public school principals in decision making, the little influence they exert on day-to-day decisions, and the challenges they face in contrast to Catholic school principals. Bryk (1996) reported that "a striking feature of their [the Catholic school principals'] responses is that principals see themselves as having primary influence on all matters except for hiring their replacements" (p. 180). The author's field observations corroborated this perception.

In a study conducted at Stanford University, Howe (1995) reported the inability of principals to exercise instructional leadership in a political environment. His study frames the problem in a larger context, the bureaucratic governance system of American schools. His research showed that Catholic schools do not share this particular problem of leadership, and that the environment created in these schools offers the most powerful explanation for the variance in perceived instructional leadership. Other contributing factors to the variance are organizational factors related to teachers, and personal and institutional environmental factors. While the data suggested that public schools look to these environmental factors and attempt to incorporate them into their schools, Catholic school policymakers and practitioners would do well to identify the factors and make sure that they are not sacrificed for other priorities. Although he did not study public schools, Moriarty (1989) also found that bureaucratic control had a dysfunctional consequence for integrated leadership and instrumental effectiveness in Catholic schools.

Both Mignacca (1988) and Byrd (1997) found a relationship between job satisfaction of public school principals and job factor variables, notably the support of the superintendent and organizational effectiveness. There was no relationship for the Catholic school principals. Data gathered by Camarena (1987) suggested that the organizational structures, including legal and financial restrictions, allowed Catholic school administrators to reward or sanction teachers more frequently. There was more emphasis on academic goals in Catholic schools, resulting in greater effectiveness. Principals encouraged high expectations of low-ability students, a finding repeated in many studies of Catholic schools (Bryk, Lee, & Holland, 1993; Coleman & Hoffer, 1987; Coleman, Hoffer, & Kilgore, 1982; Greeley, 1982).

Using the Leader Behavior Description Questionnaire (LBDQ), Ubokudom (1981) found a significant difference between the self-perceived leadership behavior of public and Catholic school principals, with the public school principals scoring higher in consideration. Catholic school department heads were more oriented toward initiating structure than either Catholic school principals or vice-principals.

Stress Level in Principals

An increasing number of dissertations are being written on the stress level of principals. Poupard (1982) identified experiences and actions that have been stressful for Catholic school principals. She organized the data in three major dimensions—external influences, nomothetic, and ideographic. She found that no one category yielded distress in itself, but when there was interplay among the three categories, there was severe distress, and principals were unable to use their typical coping strategies. One coping strategy found to be highly effective was the principals' association.

Variables negatively associated with stress in the Jones-Stewart (1986) study were fewer hours worked per week, younger administrators, and shorter terms as principal. On the other hand, those variables positively associated with stress were large school populations, longer terms as principal, high social and economical status of the parent population, and interestingly, a higher number of workshops attended on stress.

While administrators reported significantly more incidents of burnout than teachers, according to Costello (1981), they also felt a deeper sense of personal involvement. Her data showed that principals had significantly more absenteeism than teachers. It also indicated that those who devote themselves to meeting the needs of others are the ones who are most likely to experience frustration and disillusionment, and find their energy exhausted. Costello gave several suggestions for fighting stress, chief among which is enlarging one's work by developing close relationships with others, especially family.

Using the current principals of the Archdiocese of Chicago as her population, Mastalerz (2000) compared her data with that of Jones-Stewart, who had studied the stress level of the principals of the Archdiocese of Chicago 14 years earlier. Both employed the Maslach Burnout Inventory. Mastalerz found higher emotional exhaustion scores, a slightly lower depersonalization score, and a higher personal accomplishment score among participants.

Mastalerz introduced the construct of hardiness to determine if the findings would differ. The concept of hardiness (Kobasa, 1979; Maddi, 1997, 1998; Kobasa & Maddi, 1976; Maddi & Kobasa, 1984) places its emphasis on how people construct the meaning in their lives through the decisions they make and the importance, therefore, of their accepting responsibility for what they become. Hardy people are characterized as: "possessing the belief that they can control or influence the events of their experience; an ability to feel deeply involved in or committed to the activities of their lives; and an anticipation of change as a challenge to further development" (Kobasa, 1979, p. 2). Interestingly, by incorporating hardiness as an investigative tool, Mastalerz determined that her findings had the following implications for leadership in the reduction of stress: less stress-filled principals used a holistic approach to preventing and treating stress. They worked smarter, not harder, and changed harmful practices. They were better at using coping strategies and support mechanisms, and they increased their self-perception through hardiness training.

Studies on Evaluation of Principals

Based on the transcendental method of Lonergan, doctoral study research by O'Donnell (1983) developed a theory of insightful evaluation of Catholic school administrators. Iaffaldano's (1985) study also developed an instrument after investigation of the educational evaluation process in the Archdiocese of Omaha. The data suggested that the procedure should be in the hands of the diocesan office; the instrument should be based on the philosophy of education of a given diocese; that the purpose for principal evaluation be explicated for everyone involved; and that an annual conference with the principal be scheduled to discuss results and establish future goals.

SUPERINTENDENTS OF SCHOOLS

As a delegate of the bishop, the superintendent of schools is a factor in the governance of Catholic schools. The office evolved from a board of school inspectors, which mainly consisted of pastors appointed by their bishops (Augenstein, 1996). Burns (1912) also provided a concise description of the role of the early superintendent. In his research on the position, De Walt (1965) claimed that the position lacked a common definition and that the bishops adapted the office to meet their individual leadership styles and needs. The situation remains the same today, according to Vanders (2000).

Table 5.2
Canonical Status of Superintendents in 1999 (N = 153)

Status	f	%
Priest	7	5
Brother	8	5
Deacon	2	1
Sister	55	36
Layman	52	34
Laywoman	29	19

Source: Adapted from Vanders (2000), p. 42.

While the role of the superintendent varied substantially across dioceses nationwide, the single goal of the office seems largely unchanged since Voelker (1935) asserted it was "to promote the educational life of the parish school, while at the same time . . . to coordinate and direct the pre-eminent work of the Church according to the Bishop" (p. 37).

In the first empirical study of superintendents, Voelker (1935) reported that the majority of superintendents were priests, usually a pastor, and often not able to work full-time as superintendent. Voelker even entitled his research dissertation *The Diocesan Superintendent of Schools: A Study of the Historical Development and Functional Status of His [sic] Office.* By 1987, Dixon (1987) reported that, of her respondents (N = 105), 56 were men (27 priests, 9 religious community members, 120 laymen) and 49 were women (43 religious community members, 6 laywomen). Vanders (2000) updated the canonical status of the superintendents 12 years after Dixon. He had a sample of 153 superintendents and his data are depicted in Table 5.2.

Vanders (2000) also collected data on age, education, experience, and salary of superintendents. His primary focus was on motivation and job satisfaction of those serving as Catholic school superintendents. He found that ministry, the work itself, and achievement were the primary motivators. The two chief satisfiers were achievement and ministry. Job dissatisfiers were salary, working conditions, and status. The satisfiers far outweighed the dissatisfiers.

Another study conducted on the superintendent was that done by Ford (1989), who found that the evaluation of the person occupying the office of superintendent differed, depending on who it was. Both summative and formative evaluation models were used for the lay superintendents, while the formative process was not often used for clergy who are superintendents. In the same year, Ouellette (1989) researched the administrative tasks being performed by diocesan offices and concluded that these tasks were overlapping with those of individual schools. Cababe's (1997) study focused on women and the way women superintendents perceived and used the power associated with the office. Recently, there has been a call for more research about the leadership role of the assistant superintendent (Boland & Watkins, 2000).

Governance and Boards

As mentioned, the dissertation research on governance tends to be focused on parish schools. One exception is a study of school boards by Lourdes Sheehan (1981), which investigates boards in the aftermath of Vatican II. A helpful study to read in conjunction with the Sheehan study is that of Hocevar (1989), whose data showed that the governance of Catholic schools is moving, and will continue to move, in the direction of transformational leadership. The Kettenbach (1994) study also showed the increasing practice of transformational leadership by Catholic school principals.

Puma (1994) found the make-up of the boards of the Catholic schools and public schools similar in respect to age, gender, race, and occupation. The notable exception was religion. Almost 50% of public school and other private school board members were Jewish, 40% were Protestant, and only 9% Catholic. Catholic school board members were 90% Catholic. In her summary statement, Puma had a comment that is true of all doctoral research and points to its value: "While the report is essentially a picture of what is in the world of organizational boards, to the discerning reader it offers clues as to what ought to be" (p. 184).

One of the ought-to-be recommendations emerging from Carroll's (1984) study related to the data on perceptions about the involvement of the board in the decision-making process. Carroll found that there were significant differences in the pastors' perceptions, the boards' perceptions, and the principals' perceptions, and he suggested that there be regularized training programs for the three groups, which would not only present common expectations of the boards, but also establish means for mediating role conflicts on boards.

Personnel in the schools have been all too aware of what has been happening to Catholic hospitals in regard to Catholic identity. The concern seems evident in the investigation of school boards. Cody (1980) researched the contradictory trends he found still existed among Catholic school boards: the boards whose members have the control, and those which make sure through the bylaws that the sponsoring religious bodies have the control.

New Models of Governance

Because of the increasing complexity of secondary school leadership, the demands of an individual in terms of time and skills, and the enormous overload, about 5% of Catholic secondary schools have adopted various styles of the principal/president model. It is a model that the Jesuits have used for several years, and as it is being adapted for use in other schools, it has exhibited several variations. Mullen (1998) investigated the roles and responsibilities of each administrator and how they dovetailed. He reported that the level of success was higher the longer the model was used, and the degree of individual satisfaction was greater the longer the term of service by those holding the two positions. Mullen concluded that it was the quality of the relationship between the two administrators that determined its viability.

Dygert's (1998) investigation of the model found that it provided for the practice of expertise and the time for concentration of leadership in the dual area of academic instruction and institutional advancement, although in some cases the model involved more than the two individuals. He also reported that the majority of those using the model would also recommend the model to others. His qualitative and quantitative study includes a history of the model, the perceived advantages and disadvantages, and variations of the model.

Hocevar (1989) proposed a similar model in her dissertation, but with important differences, namely, that the two administrators are both principals, and they are equal in their exercise of authority. There is a principal for educational programs and a principal for institutional advancement. Often in the president/principal model, the president is the chief operating officer and the one ultimately responsible to the school's board.

FUTURE RESEARCH

The Catholic school community's research agenda for the next 20 years, as it concerns leadership, administration, and models of governance, should include a study of ways to resolve the tension between exercising a transformational style of leadership and attending to daily, administrative tasks. Acquiring skills of delegation is not the complete answer, as vision is communicated in the details. This will be important research for the many university and diocesan-based leadership programs to have, in order to build their program offerings around felt needs. Each of the two roles, academic instruction and institutional advancement, requires leadership in its own area, and each needs a competent administrator. Exploring additional models would be useful.

Another area of investigation should include involvement of teachers in decision making about finances, including budgets, curriculum, hiring; and the connection between involvement in decision making and teacher morale should also be investigated.

Perhaps now that Gardner (1999) has raised the question of a moral intelligence at the very time that we have witnessed such a display of violence in our schools, we can expect some investigation of moral leadership in our educational institutions. It is often assumed that moral leadership is part and parcel of the Catholic school principalship. Others expect Catholic school principals as moral persons to play a central role in the moral life of the school. If this expectation is a reality, how is that leadership practiced? Is moral leadership part of the preparation of Catholic school principals, or is it learned from the environment? Does moral leadership have an impact on students directly, or does it filter through the teachers? This research has value both in its importance and immediacy.

What about the role of the lay principal and other governance roles in formulating and promoting a lay charism in a Catholic school? While it is widely believed that lay principals, particularly lay principals educated in a charism, can effectively continue leadership according to the spirit of that charism, there is a question about lay principals and faculty who "inherit" charisms. What kind of leadership is needed in developing a lay charism? This study would be well suited to one similar to the remarkable *Growing Up American*, researched by Peshkin (1978).

What new differences exist between Catholic school principals and public school principals? We need research to again clarify the distinctive role of the Catholic school principal, to examine the relationships between Catholic school leadership models and the need for change.

REFERENCES

Anastasio, P. (1996). *The recruitment, selection, and preparation of Catholic school principals in six dioceses in the United States.* Unpublished doctoral dissertation, Fordham University.

Antoniswami, A. (1983). *Analysis of lay and religious principals' and teachers' perceptions of leadership behavior styles and organizational climate in Catholic schools.* Unpublished doctoral dissertation, The Catholic University of America.

Augenstein, J. (1996). *Lighting the way: The early years of Catholic school superintendency.* Washington, DC: National Catholic Educational Association.

Boland, M., & Watkins, M. R. (2000) Like the mustard seed: An unfolding leadership role for assistant superintendents. *Momentum, 31 (1),* 19–23.

Brennan, J. (1983). *The relationship of principals' leader behavior and student achievement in Catholic elementary schools.* Unpublished doctoral dissertation, University of San Francisco.

Bryk, A. (1996). Lessons from Catholic high schools on renewing our educational institutions. In T. McLaughlin, J. O'Keefe, & B. O'Keeffe (Eds.), *The contemporary Catholic school: Context, identity and diversity* (pp. 25–41). Washington, DC: Falmer Press.

Bryk, A., Holland, P., Lee, V., & Carriedo, R. (1984). *Effective Catholic schools: An exploration.* Washington, DC: National Catholic Educational Association.

Bryk, A., Lee, V., & Holland, P. (1993). *Catholic schools and the common good.* Cambridge, MA: Harvard Educational Press.

Buckley, M. L. (1984). *The relationship between readiness to change in elementary Catholic schools and the faculty's perception of the leader behavior of the principal.* Unpublished doctoral dissertation, University of San Francisco.

Buetow, H. A. (1970). *Of singular benefit: The story of U.S. Catholic education.* New York: The Macmillan Co.

Buetow, H. A. (1988). *The Catholic school: Its roots, identity, and future.* New York: Crossroad Publishing.

Burns, J. A. (1912). *The growth and development of the Catholic school system in the United States.* New York: Benziger Brothers.

Byrd, P. (1997). *Job satisfaction of Catholic school and public school principals in Arkansas, 1997.* Unpublished doctoral dissertation, University of Arkansas.

Cababe, L. (1997). *A qualitative study of power and empowerment as perceived by women Catholic school superintendents.* Unpublished doctoral dissertation, Fordham University.

Camarena, M. (1987). *A comparison of the organizational structures of public and Catholic high schools.* Unpublished doctoral dissertation, Stanford University.

Carey, M. (1987). *Lay administrators in Jesuit secondary schools: Sharing both vision and responsibility in genuine collaboration.* Unpublished doctoral dissertation, Gonzaga University.

Carr, K. (1995). *Catholic elementary school leadership: A study of principals' motivation, efficacy and satisfaction.* Unpublished doctoral dissertation, The Catholic University of America.

Carroll, H. F. (1984). *Parish school board involvement in policy-making.* Unpublished doctoral dissertation, Fordham University.

Cibulka, J., O'Brien, T. J., & Zewe, D. (1982). *Inner-city private elementary schools.* Milwaukee, WI: Marquette University Press.

Cody, F. J. (1980). *Policy boards in Jesuit secondary schools, 1976.* Unpublished doctoral dissertation, The Ohio State University.

Coleman, J., & Hoffer, T. (1987). *Public and private high schools: The impact of communities.* New York: Basic Books.

Coleman, J. S., Hoffer, T., & Kilgore, S. (1982). *High school achievement: Public, Catholic, and private schools compared.* New York: Basic Books.

Coley, K. (1993). *Transformational and transactional leadership and the school principal: An analysis of selected private secondary school principals in Maryland.* Unpublished doctoral dissertation, University of Maryland.

Convey, J. J. (1992). *Catholic schools make a difference: Twenty-five years of research.* Washington, DC: National Catholic Educational Association.

Convey, K. (1987). *A comparison of attitudes of avowed religious and lay teachers and parents toward avowed religious and lay principals in the Christian brothers high schools of the St. Louis district.* Unpublished doctoral dissertation, University of San Francisco.

Costello, C. (1981). *Differences in burnout between Roman Catholic religious administrators and teachers in California.* Unpublished doctoral dissertation, University of San Francisco.

Cusack, S. (1983). *Lay administration of Catholic schools in the New York City area.* Unpublished doctoral dissertation, Teachers' College, Columbia University.

DeWalt, H. (1965). *An analysis of the status and the functions of the diocesan school superintendency in the United States.* Unpublished doctoral dissertation, University of Minnesota.

Diamond, D. (1997). *An analysis of leadership behavior and self-efficacy of principals of Catholic secondary schools.* Unpublished doctoral dissertation, The Catholic University of America.

Dias, O. J. (1994). *Principals' and teachers' perceptions of the extent of shared decision-making in urban and suburban Catholic elementary schools.* Unpublished doctoral dissertation, St. John's University.

Dixon, J. (1987). *The Catholic school superintendent: A national profile.* Unpublished doctoral dissertation, Gonzaga University.

Donovan, B. (1980). *A study and comparison of the expectations for the decision-making role of the Catholic secondary school principal in New York State on the part of teachers, students, parents, and the incumbent principals.* Unpublished doctoral dissertation, St. John's University.

Dygert, W. (1998). *A study of the president/principal administrative model in Catholic secondary schools in the United States.* Unpublished doctoral dissertation, University of Dayton.

Fichter, J. H. (1958). *Parochial school: A sociological study.* Notre Dame, IN: University of Notre Dame Press.

Ford, J. (1989). *A qualitative study of Catholic school superintendent evaluation procedures.* Unpublished doctoral dissertation, University of Wisconsin.

Gardner, H. (1999). *Intelligence reframed: Multiple intelligence for the 21st century.* New York: Basic Books.

Greeley, A. (1982). *Catholic high schools and minority students.* New Brunswick, NJ: Transaction Books.

Greeley, A., & Rossi, P. (1966). *The education of American Catholics.* Chicago: Aldine Publishing Co.

Guerra, M. (2000). *CHS 2000: A first look.* Washington, DC: National Catholic Educational Association.

Harkins, W. (1993). *Introducing the Catholic elementary school principal: What principals say about themselves, their values, their schools.* Washington, DC: National Catholic Educational Association.

Haymon, D. (1990). *Relationships among elementary school principals' leadership style, school climate, and student achievement in differing racial-ethnic and socioeconomic status contexts.* Unpublished doctoral dissertation, University of Southern California, Los Angeles.

Helm, C. (1989). *Cultural and symbolic leadership in Catholic elementary schools: An ethnographic study.* Unpublished doctoral dissertation, The Catholic University of America.

Hersey, P., & Blanchard, K. H. (1988). *Management of organizational behavior: Utilizing human resources.* Englewood Cliffs, NJ: Prentice-Hall.

Higgins, D. (1993). *The relation of participative leadership style to two measures of school effectiveness in the Catholic high schools of the archdiocese of San Antonio.* Unpublished doctoral dissertation, Texas A & M University.

Hines, E. (1999). *The perceptions of lay Catholic elementary school principals and superintendents of the faith leadership formation of principals.* Unpublished doctoral dissertation, University of San Francisco.

Hocevar, R. (1989). *An investigation of the internal governance structures of selected exemplary Catholic high schools.* Unpublished doctoral dissertation, Kent State University.

Holland, P. B. (1985). *The Catholic high school principalship: A qualitative study.* Unpublished doctoral dissertation, Harvard University.

Hood, R. (1991). *The leadership in Rockford, Illinois diocesan elementary schools.* Unpublished doctoral dissertation, Northern Illinois University.

Howe, W. S. (1995). *Instructional leadership in Catholic elementary schools: An analysis of personal, organizational, and environmental correlates.* Unpublished doctoral dissertation, Stanford University.

Hunt, T. C. (1998). *Doctoral dissertations on Catholic schools in the United States, 1988–1997.* Washington, DC: National Catholic Educational Association.

Iaffaldano, L. (1985). *Existing and preferred practices of evaluation of principals in the archdiocese of Omaha.* Unpublished doctoral dissertation, University of Nebraska.

John, R. (1984). *Attitudes of priests, elementary school principals, and school parents toward lay administrators and lay teachers in Catholic elementary schools.* Unpublished doctoral dissertation, University of San Francisco.

Johnson, A. (1995). *Frames and effective leadership: A study of the use of organizational frames by elementary principals.* Unpublished doctoral dissertation, University of La Verne, California.

Jones-Stewart, P. (1986). *Stress factors as perceived by principals in Chicago's Catholic elementary schools.* Unpublished doctoral dissertation, Southern Illinois University.

Kealey, R. (1999). *Balance sheet for Catholic elementary schools: 1999 income and expenses.* Washington, DC: National Catholic Educational Association.

Keane, D. (1983). *Typologies and leadership systems in Roman Catholic parishes.* Unpublished doctoral dissertation, Fordham University.

Kettenbach, G. (1994). *The implementation of collegial governance in archdiocesan high schools following the Second Vatican Council.* Unpublished doctoral dissertation, Saint Louis University.

Kobasa, S. C. (1979). Stressful life events, personality, and health: An inquiry into hardiness. *Journal of Personality and Social Psychology, 37,* 1–11.

Kobasa, S. C., & Maddi, S. R. (1976). Existential personality theory. In R. Corsini (Ed.), *Current personality theories* (pp. 243–276). Itasca, IL: Peacock.

Kushner, R. (1982). *Action theory congruence and the exercise of transformational leadership in Catholic elementary schools.* Unpublished doctoral dissertation, Fordham University.

Lamb, M. (1997). *A study of excellence: Principals in urban Catholic elementary schools.* Unpublished doctoral dissertation, Fordham University.

Leithwood, K. A., & Jantzi, D. (1992, January). *Tranformational leadership and school restructuring.* Paper presented at the International Effectiveness and Improvement conference, Victoria, British Columbia.

Lipsitz, J. (1984). *Successful schools for young adolescents.* New Brunswick, NJ: Transaction Books.

Maddi, S. R. (1997). Personal views survey II: A measure of dispositional hardiness. In C. P. Zallaquett & R. J. Wood (Eds.), *Evaluating stress: A book of resources* (pp. 293–309). Lanham, MD: The Scarecrow Press.

Maddi, S. R. (1998). Hardiness in health and effectiveness. In H. S. Friedman (Ed.), *Encyclopedia of mental health* (Vol. 2, pp. 323–335). San Diego: Academic Press.

Maddi, S. R., & Kobasa, S. C. (1984). *The hardy executive: Health under stress.* Chicago: Dorsey Professional Books.

Manno, B. (1985). *Those who would be Catholic school principals: Their recruitment, preparation, and evaluation.* Washington, DC: National Catholic Educational Association.

Mastalerz, L. (2000). *The dynamics of burnout in Catholic school principals.* Unpublished doctoral dissertation, Roosevelt University, Chicago.

Matan, L. (1999). *A profile of the effective Catholic high school administrator.* Unpublished doctoral dissertation, University of San Francisco.

McCluskey, N. G. (1964). *Catholic education in America: A documentary history.* Unpublished doctoral dissertation, Columbia University.

McCormick, P. (1985). *A comparison of the school's Catholic identity, the principal's instructional leadership, and the overall school effectiveness in Catholic elementary schools administered by members of religious institutes with those schools administered by lay principals.* Unpublished doctoral dissertation, University of Cincinnati.

McDonald, D. (1999). *U.S. Catholic elementary and secondary schools 1999–2000: The annual report on schools, enrollment, and staffing.* Washington, DC: National Catholic Educational Association.

McGraw, B. (1981). *A comparison of inservice interest between Catholic and public school principals in central Illinois, 1981.* Unpublished doctoral dissertation, Saint Louis University.

McIlmurray, D. B. (1980). *A determination and comparison of the ideal role expectations for principals of Roman Catholic secondary schools in the New York archdiocese on the part of the lay teachers, the religious teachers and the principals themselves.* Unpublished doctoral dissertation, St. John's University.

McLaughlin, T., O'Keefe, J., & O'Keeffe, B. (1996). *The contemporary Catholic school: Context, identity and diversity.* Washington, DC: Falmer Press.

Melton, M. (1981). *Role expectations for the board of trustees and school principals in the incorporated secondary schools in the diocese of Brooklyn, New York.* Unpublished doctoral dissertation, St. John's University.

Mignacca, E. (1988). *A comparison of leadership styles of Catholic and public elementary school principals, and organizational effectiveness, teacher loyalty, and job satisfaction, 1988.* Unpublished doctoral dissertation, Wayne State University.

Moriarty, J. K. (1989). *Leadership, structure, and effectiveness of parochial secondary schools.* Unpublished doctoral dissertation, Rutgers University.

Muccigrosso, R. (1983). *Catholic elementary school decisional discrepancy, parent-teacher satisfaction, and student academic achievement.* Unpublished doctoral dissertation, Fordham University.

Muccigrosso, R. (1996). Nurturing faith: The principal's trust. In M. J. Ciriello (Ed.), *Formation and development for Catholic school leaders* (Vol. II, pp. 3–7). Washington, DC: United States Catholic Conference.

Mullen, R. J. (1998). *The president-principal model in United States Catholic high schools: A profile of schools, roles and responsibilities.* Unpublished doctoral dissertation, Spaulding University.

Neuwien, R. (Ed.). (1966). *Catholic schools in action: A report.* Notre Dame, IN: University of Notre Dame Press.

O'Brien, J. S. (1987). *Mixed messages: What bishops and priests say about Catholic schools.* Washington, DC: National Catholic Educational Association.

O'Donnell, D. (1983). *Insightful evaluation: The development of a theory for the evaluation of educational administrators.* Unpublished doctoral dissertation, Fordham University.

O'Donnell, M. (1982). *An analysis of the leader behavior dimensions of women Catholic elementary school principals.* Unpublished doctoral dissertation, St. John's University.

Olsen, J. D. (1975). *Doctoral dissertations on Catholic education, 1968–1975.* Washington, DC: National Catholic Educational Association.

Ouellette, F. M. (1989). *Interdependent administrative linkages between the diocesan education office and diocesan schools.* Unpublished doctoral dissertation, Boston College.

Peshkin, A. (1978). *Growing Up American.* Chicago: University of Chicago Press.

Peters, L. (1984). *Perceptions of the principalship in Catholic elementary schools.* Unpublished doctoral dissertation, Saint Louis University.

Petersen, W. (1991). *Making sense of purpose: The principal's role.* Unpublished doctoral dissertation, University of California, Los Angeles.

Petro, J. (1982). *The effects of Catholic education on attitudes toward selected issues, with implications for the lay leader in the Catholic schools.* Unpublished doctoral dissertation, Florida Atlantic University, Boca Raton.

Petty, G. (1992). *Administrative decision-making in public, independent, and parochial elementary schools.* Unpublished doctoral dissertation, Columbia University.

Politz, A. (1991). *Leadership styles of principals and student achievement in selected Catholic schools of Indiana.* Unpublished doctoral dissertation, Ball State University.

Poupard, D. (1982). *Job-related stress and coping strategies as perceived by twelve principals of center city Catholic schools.* Unpublished doctoral dissertation, University of Michigan.

Puglisi, G. (1983). *The impact of administrative training on the leadership of Catholic elementary schools.* Unpublished doctoral dissertation, Fordham University.

Puma, M. (1994). *A study of the boards of trustees of nine religiously affiliated elementary and secondary schools.* Unpublished doctoral dissertation, Columbia University.

Quinn, R. (1985). *The relationship of commitment on the part of lay Catholic elementary school principals in the United States to selected personal variables.* Unpublished doctoral dissertation, The Catholic University of America.

Rocchio, D. (1993). *The mentoring and socialization of selected Catholic high school principals.* Unpublished doctoral dissertation, Fordham University.

Sergiovanni, T. J. (1987). *The principalship: A reflective practice perspective.* Boston: Allyn & Bacon.

Seymour, D. (1990). *Perceptions of leadership styles of principals in the archdiocese of Detroit.* Unpublished doctoral dissertation, Western Michigan University.

Sheehan, M. L. (1981). *A study of the functions of school boards in the educational system of the Roman Catholic Church in the United States.* Unpublished doctoral dissertation, Virginia Polytechnic Institute and State University.

Traviss, M. P. (1989). *Doctoral dissertations on Catholic schools, K–12, 1976–1987.* Washington, DC: National Catholic Educational Association.

Ubokudom, S. (1981). *A comparative study of the self-perceived leadership behavior of public and Catholic high school administrators.* Unpublished doctoral dissertation, The Catholic University of America.

Vanders, N. (2000). *Catholic school superintendents: An investigation of motivation and job satisfaction.* Unpublished doctoral dissertation, University of San Francisco.

Vitullo-Martin. T. (1977). *Catholic inner-city schools: The future.* Washington, DC: United States Catholic Conference.

Voelker, J. M. (1935). *The diocesan superintendent of schools: A study of the historical development and functional status of his office.* Unpublished doctoral dissertation, The Catholic University of America.

Walch, T. (1996). *Parish school: American colonial parochial education from colonial times to the present.* New York: Crossroad Publishing.

Wallace, T. (1995). *Assessment of the preparedness of lay Catholic high school principals to be faith leaders.* Unpublished doctoral dissertation, University of Dayton.

Weaver, E. (1997). *The self-managing school: A case study of school-based decision-making with regard to curriculum, power, and human resources.* Unpublished doctoral dissertation, Immaculate College, Pennsylvania.

Yeager, R., Benson, P., Guerra, M., & Manno, B. (1985). *The Catholic high school: A national portrait.* Washington DC: National Catholic Educational Association.

Yeager, R., Benson, P., Guerra, M., & Manno, B. (1986). *Catholic schools: Their impact on low-income students.* Washington DC: National Catholic Educational Association.

Chapter 6

A Role Analysis Based on Church Documents, Dissertations, and Recent Research

Gini Shimabukuro

INTRODUCTION

Catholic school leaders are focusing on identity crises. In a society that is driven by unprecedented scientific and technological innovation, in tandem with "a crisis of values" (Congregation for Catholic Education [CCE], 1997, #1), an understanding of the role of the Catholic school teacher is pivotal to the future of Catholic education. The dramatic shift from a teaching corps of religious to an overwhelming majority of lay teachers (Convey, 1992; Guerra, 1998; Kushner & Helbling, 1995), has heightened the need for role definition. In earlier days, the majority of Sister-teachers naturally instilled their spiritual formation in their students (Jacobs, 1998; Keating & Traviss, in press; Meyers, 1941; Traviss, 2000; Walch, 1996). Today, many lay teachers are in the process of discerning their contemporary roles in Catholic schools. This chapter will review the literature and scant empirical research that can provide insight into this foundational area, and conclude with a discussion of applications and implications pertinent to future research.

Catholic Literature on Education

Although secular and Catholic educational communities converge at many common points of interest in teacher and student development, the Catholic school's approach to the education of the child, with its strong emphasis on teacher formation (which includes the religious and the spiritual dimensions), is distinctive.

Pre–Vatican II: Christian Education of Youth

Pius XI issued the first encyclical on education in 1929, in reaction to fascism and national socialism abroad, which subjugated the lives of children to the state. Accentuating the moral and religious education of the child, roles that the state ignored, this encyclical established the primacy of a Christian education.

Since education consists essentially in preparing man for what he must be and for what he must do here below, in order to attain the sublime end for which he was created, it is clear that there can be no true education which is not wholly directed to man's last end, and that in the present order of Providence, since God has revealed Himself to us in the Person of His Only Begotten Son, who alone is "the way, the truth and the life," there can be no ideally perfect education which is not Christian education. (p. 5)

The thinking of the times posited universal truth as independent of the human mind, existing beyond in an objective realm. Thus, the imagery of humanity walking the earth below, reaching outside of itself for truth, was reflected in this encyclical. Although self-centeredness, the antithesis to God-centeredness and the supernatural, was scorned during this time, this document laid the groundwork for the Second Vatican Council's celebration and formation of the personhood of the student and teacher, as evident in the following excerpt: "Christian education takes in the whole aggregate of human life, physical and spiritual, intellectual and moral, individual, domestic and social, not with a view of reducing it in any way, but in order to elevate, regulate and perfect it, in accordance with the example and teaching of Christ" (Pius XI, 1929, p. 36).

After the release of this encyclical, the Catholic school began to focus on its aims and objectives, thereby formulating beginning typologies descriptive of the role of the Catholic school teacher. For example, the Secondary School Department of the Catholic Educational Association (Policies Committee, 1940) advanced seven broad aims of Catholic secondary education: the development of intelligence, spiritual vigor, culture, personal health, vocational readiness, social-mindedness, and adherence to American principles. Although translation of these goals into objectives that could be implemented in the classroom was left to the individual educator, the formulation and release of *The Christian Education of Youth* (Pius XI, 1929) signified the birth of a shift in emphasis in Catholic education from depersonalized acquisition of truth to person-centered Christian formation. This shift developed into a full-grown movement of institutional transformation with the convocation of the Second Vatican Council (Vatican II), which occurred from 1962 to 1965.

Paradigm Shift in the Church

Vatican II brought in a new paradigm of thinking. Hastings (1991) recalled that once Pope John XXIII called the Council "the consequences were inevitable: the foundations of many hundred years were going to be rocked upon every side" (p. 4). Hastings related that "the world of the twentieth century again necessitated a quite extraordinarily different Church and theology from that appropriate in the past" (p. 7). Twenty years following the commencement of the Second Vatican Council, Naisbitt (1982) wrote the celebrated *Megatrends,* in which he declared that change was becoming a constant in a world that required its members to function in new and often disorienting ways. He characterized the new paradigm as a basic transition from dualistic, vertical, hierarchical models to those that were participative, horizontal, and multifaceted. This extraordinary shift greatly impacted the role of the Catholic school teacher. Table 6.1 displays a summarized version of the paradigm shift of the role of the Catholic school teacher as reflected in the literature of this period.

Vatican II to the Present

Vatican II marked the beginning of a series of contemporary statements, both Roman and American, on Catholic education. Of special interest was the U.S. bishops' interpretations of Roman statements on the role of the Catholic school teacher, as translated for the American Catholic population within the context of post-conciliar documents. This section will examine the Roman and American documents between the years of 1965 and 1997 (see Table 6.2).

The *Declaration on Christian Education* (Flannery, 1988), with related Vatican II documentation, and *To Teach as Jesus Did* (National Conference of Catholic Bishops [NCCB], 1972) communicated radical messages for implementation in the Catholic educational world. These two documents on education, one Roman and the other American, were among the first written results of Vatican II, and symbolized the major shift occurring in Catholic education. Consequently, these two documents received a plethora of scholarly commentary and are utilized, to the present day, as seminal pieces of Church literature on education. Surprisingly, there exists a scarcity of erudite review of Church documentation published after 1972. In light of this deficiency of scholarly comment, a review of remaining documents from the perspective of the role of the Catholic school teacher seems appropriate.

Declaration on Christian Education (1965)

The *Declaration on Christian Education* (Flannery, 1988) was but one Vatican II document within a culture of documentation that addressed the issue of Catholic education. Petty (1967) expressed his conception of Vatican II as "The Council on Education," claiming that the *Pastoral Constitution of the Church in the Modern World* was one such conciliar document that was "more powerful and deep sighted" than many of its counterparts (p. 89). For example, Walters (1966) chronicled 24 references to the importance of the person in one chapter of this document.

Table 6.1
Paradigm Shift in the Role of the Catholic School Teacher (Pre-Vatican to Post-Vatican)

From:	To:
Traditional pedagogy	Progressive pedagogy
Teacher-centered	Learner-centered, with focus on personalization of learning
Objectified role of teacher and student	"Personhood" of the teacher and student
Authoritarian	Participative, encouraging personal responsibility
School as institutional	School as experience of community, concerned with building a Christian atmosphere
Academic achievement of students	Integral Christian formation of students *and* teachers; lifelong learning; personal wholeness
Depersonalized view of students	Strong emphasis on dignity of students, based upon teacher-student relationships
Rote teaching and learning	Teaching for understanding; meaningful learning that includes thinking, creativity, moral decision making
Uniformity of curriculum and its delivery	Teaching methodologies that address the individual needs of students
Silence in schools	Communication, dialogue, cooperative learning, collaboration among teachers
Religious instruction relegated to religion class; dogmatic; indoctrinating	Permeation of Christian atmosphere throughout the school; religious instruction that is relevant to the spiritual lives of learners
Parochialism	Global awareness; promotion of social justice; teaching peacemaking skills

Conciliar literature, particularly in regard to Catholic education, carried two major thrusts that characterized the paradigm shift in Catholic pedagogical thinking, one that was inner-directed emphasizing personal wholeness, and the other that was outer-directed accentuating ecumenism, the development of global consciousness, and relationships with others. Bradley (1966), referring to the *Declaration on Christian Education*, stated that teachers must be able to change

Table 6.2
Contemporary Conciliar and Post-Conciliar Documentation on Catholic Education

Date of Publication	Document
1965	*Declaration on Christian Education*
1972	*To Teach as Jesus Did*
1976	*Teach Them*
1977	*The Catholic School*
1979	*Sharing the Light of Faith*
1982	*Lay Catholics in Schools: Witnesses to Faith*
1988	*The Religious Dimension of Education in a Catholic School*
1997	*The Catholic School on the Threshold of the Third Millennium*

themselves, "rather than shaping the students and the surroundings into a pattern that has been cut out in advance" (p. 439); they must represent the human community for the learner; and, they must keep the school aware of the contemporary world.

Walters (1966) identified the importance and dignity of the person as a central concern of the Council. She advocated that "The teacher is called upon at every level of the educational ladder to help children achieve a sense of being persons" (p. 367). Cultivation of the dignity of students, moreover, was contingent upon the personhood of the teacher. "If she sees herself only as a functionary serving an institution . . . her sense of being a person will have undergone disintegration. This is so because an individual who is defined by a role rather than as a person will be seen as an object, a thing. When the role displaces the personhood of the sister, she is seen as just a thing in a category" (pp. 369–370). Walters noted that over the several decades prior to Vatican II, increasing depersonalization occurred in Catholic schools. Teachers tended to view students from the perspective of the bureaucrat, "not so much as persons but as objects to be handled and taken care of in one way or another" (p. 372). When this attitude invaded classrooms, it sometimes caused animosity among children toward teachers, schools, and, ultimately, the Church.

According to Joseph (1966), the documents of Vatican II displayed "the overwhelming concern of our times for the human person" (p. 330). An outgrowth of this concern was the science of human relations, an interdisciplinary study whose objective was the development of awareness of the feelings of others, along with a concomitant flexibility of behavior. Joseph claimed that awareness and flexibility of behavior depended upon communication, necessary for both teachers and students, potential communicators of the Gospel message in a world in dire need of dialogue. Thus, the refinement of communication skills, both for sending and receiving, was vital to teacher attentiveness to the feelings of students, and constituted living out Christ's command to love one another.

Moreau (1966) expanded teacher concern for students to include consideration of the environmental, psychological, social, and spiritual needs of each individual in the classroom.

As classroom teachers, supervisors, and administrators, we must not say, or think, that we fully understand these young people if we simply instruct them in class in the areas of what the syllabus demands. We should reflect on their lives in the home before and after school, on the way to and from school, and their mode and style of living while in the association of their peer groups and away from parental and authoritative influences. (p. 377)

Personalization also included curriculum development. McGreal (1966) described the curriculum as an "instrument of renewal" (p. 346), in light of Vatican II's call for renewal, and described it as "not a mass of facts and skills tossed together but an orderly relationship of learning experiences selected and organized for definite purposes" (p. 347). The teacher held the key to this through day-to-day instruction. McGreal claimed that individualization or personalization of curriculum involved two factors: first, establishment of good relationships with students so that learning would be received; and second, that teachers adapt curriculum to the capacities of different learners. She cited a recurring theme in conciliar documents, that of "human freedom, matched by responsibility" (p. 347), and applied this theme to the teacher's ability to experiment with curriculum in an effort to create meaningful learning for the student, as well as the development of student freedom in the classroom toward the goals of thinking, creativity, and moral decision making.

Closely linked to human relations was the fostering of a spirit of community within the Catholic school. Thaddeus (1966) stated that the *Declaration on Christian Education*, as well as the *Dogmatic Constitution on the Church*, gave Catholic educators guidelines for creating an atmosphere in the school that would "concretize the unity of persons in the formation of a better world" (p. 331). He asserted that students were intimately a part of the school community, "not outside or below it" (p. 332), and that community was not taught and imposed from outside the school, but rather experienced.

To Teach as Jesus Did (1972)

In November of 1972, the Catholic bishops of the United States issued their collective pastoral statement on Catholic education, *To Teach as Jesus Did* (NCCB, 1972). Bishop William McManus, then an auxiliary bishop in the Archdiocese of Chicago and reputed to be a primary drafter of this document, alluded to the wide range of consultation within the Church that went into its preparation. *"To Teach as Jesus Did* represents not only the bishops speaking to the Church but the Church speaking through the bishops" (D'Alessio & Shaw, 1973, p. 11). Heath (1973) predicted that implementation of *To Teach as Jesus Did* in the Catholic school would "turn out to be an historic turning point in American Catholic life" (p. 284). Attempting to capsulize the purposes of Catholic education, the bishops put forth three powerful words: message, community, and service, a threefold formula that Heath defined as a "priceless and flexible instrument for summarizing the activities and objectives of Christian education" (p. 288).

In this pastoral message, Catholic education was viewed as a most significant way for the Church to fulfill its dedication to the dignity of the individual and the building of community. Educational leaders were called to form "persons-in-community" (NCCB, 1972, #13) in an environment in which "one person's problem is everyone's problem and one person's victory is everyone's victory" (#22). This focus on community, which formed the heart of Christian education, was a reality to be lived, in addition to a concept to be taught. Integral personal growth was only possible through integral social life. This concept represented a high form of learning, the crucial task of Catholic education. As stated in *To Teach as Jesus Did*, "Building and living community must be prime, explicit goals of the contemporary Catholic school" (#108). However, community included, but was not limited to, the environment within the school or immediately surrounding the school. It embraced "the larger community of people on this planet" (#26), advising teachers to educate students in the skills of peacemaking in order to develop globally conscious and active witnesses of Gospel values.

Teach Them (1976)

Aligned with the educational guideposts from *To Teach as Jesus Did*, of message, community, and service, *Teach Them* (NCCB, 1976) continued with the theme of integral personal growth. "Appreciation has increased for the fact that the Catholic school is not simply an institution, which offers academic instruction of high quality, but, even more important, is an effective vehicle of total Christian formation. The tendency to emphasize one aspect at the expense of the other has given way to recognition that both are necessary and possible, and indeed are being accomplished in Catholic schools" (p. 5). In this document, teachers were urged to implement instructional methodologies that responded to the individual needs of students. The movement toward personalized learning, emphasizing the total educational environment, "makes clear that the atmosphere and relationships in the school are as much the focus of the Catholic school as is the formal religious education class" (p. 7).

The educational changes introduced by Vatican II were of a philosophical and psychological nature, offering the opportunity for substantive growth in awareness to those in Catholic education. Duplass (1975) commented, "One of the most important results of Vatican II was the growth in awareness of the church with regard to the psychological needs of man and in particular youth, and its reaffirmation of man as a cognitive-affective person capable of reflection and the making of deliberate choices based on a set of values" (p. 281). In contrast to the pre–Vatican II classroom, teacher-directed and indoctrinating, the post–Vatican II classroom was child-centered, concerned with building an atmosphere of community and characterized by the living-out of the Gospel message.

The Catholic School (1977)

Linked to its Vatican II predecessor, the *Declaration on Christian Education, The Catholic School* (CCE, 1977) stated its purpose in its first paragraph, to develop further the ideas put forth in the 1965 document. "In the Council's Declaration *Gravissimum Educationis* it [the Catholic school] is discussed in the wider sphere of Christian education. The present document develops the idea of this Declaration, limiting itself to a deeper reflection on the Catholic school" (#1). Donohue (1977) found this document particularly relevant in two ways: as an anthology of the central themes pertaining to Catholic schools from Vatican II; and, as a measure for appreciating the advancement of Catholic educational theory during the past half century.

Elaborating what the development of the whole person meant in practice, this document advocated the simultaneous development of the student's psychological growth and moral consciousness. "The school must begin from the principle that its educational program is intentionally directed to the growth of the whole person" (CCE, 1977, #29). This mission called for the development of persons who were responsible and inner-directed within the context of a school community, with emphasis placed on the interpersonal and sincere relationships of its members. In this environment, the student "experiences his dignity as a person before he knows its definition" (#55). Teachers were called to "form the mind[s] and heart[s] of . . . pupils and guide them to develop a total commitment to Christ" (#40) and, in imitation of the greatest teacher, Christ, to "reveal the Christian message not only by word but also by every gesture of their behaviour" (#43). Furthermore, teachers were urged to constantly update themselves in developments in the fields of child psychology and pedagogy, and to foster an authentic, child-centered atmosphere in the Catholic school. Teachers were charged with the important role of safeguarding the Christian atmosphere of the school, which was the foundation of academic education.

Sharing the Light of Faith (1979)

Adding to the threefold purposes of Catholic education as stated in *To Teach as Jesus Did, Sharing the Light of Faith* (NCCB, 1979), the national catechetical directory for Catholics of the United States, encouraged ongoing catechesis for faculty members in order to accomplish the fourfold dimensions of Catholic education: message, community, worship, and service. The bishops added the dimension of "worship" to the threefold purposes stated in *To Teach as Jesus Did*. This document continued to refine the concept of the dignity of the human person, the fundamental concept in Catholic social teaching. "In Catholic teaching the concept of human dignity implies not only that the person is the steward of creation and cooperates with the creator to perfect it, but that the rest of creation, in its material, social, technological, and economic aspects, should be at the service of the person. Human dignity is secure only when the spiritual, psychological, emotional, and bodily integrity of the person is respected as a fundamental value" (#156).

Having a dignity of their own, students were regarded with importance not only for their future accomplishments, but "for what they are here and now— for their intrinsic value and their value in relation to the common good" (NCCB, 1979, #181). To adequately acknowledge their dignity in the here and now, teachers were encouraged to understand their students; to communicate with them by listening to them with respect and sensitivity; and to empower them to live as fully as possible, while facilitating their acceptance of individual strengths and weaknesses. In this way, the teacher was called upon to build the integrity of his or her students and to create community in the classroom, teacher and students together, learning "the meaning of community by experiencing it" (#209).

Lay Catholics in Schools: Witnesses to Faith (1982)

The 1982 document, *Lay Catholics in Schools: Witnesses to Faith* (CCE), raised the issue of the lay teacher, initially put forth in Vatican II's *Declaration on Christian Education*, with the intent to "expand on its contents and deepen them" (#1).

This document delivered a challenge to the soul of the Catholic school lay teacher. It called for a deep-felt recognition of continuous self-development, with a firm commitment to personal action, acknowledging the causal relationship between the development of the teacher and the contingent effectiveness in the area of student formation.

The teacher under discussion here is not simply a professional person who systematically transmits a body of knowledge in the context of a school; "teacher" is to be understood as "educator"—one who helps to form human persons. The task of a teacher goes well beyond transmission of knowledge, although that is not excluded. Therefore, if adequate professional preparation is required in order to transmit knowledge, then adequate professional preparation is even more necessary in order to fulfill the role of a genuine teacher. It is an indispensable human formation, and without it, it would be foolish to undertake any educational work. (CCE, 1982, #16)

The use of the phrase "genuine teacher" in this document is noteworthy. Educator is derived from the Latin root *educere*, which means "to draw out."

The genuine teacher, the true educator, successfully draws out the person in the learner in a loving and respectful context. This is only possible after the teacher internally experiences his or her own personhood as a learner, with love and respect for self. By so doing, the teacher is able to recognize what it is he or she is attempting to draw out of his or her students. The "genuine teacher" typified one who was dedicated to the task of forming students who would make the "civilization of love" (CCE, 1982, #19) a reality. The more a teacher gave concrete witness to modeling the ideal person to students, the more students would believe and imitate it. Again, the dignity of the individual person was paramount to the Christian vision. It must never be forgotten that, in the crises "which have their greatest effect on the younger generations," the most important element in the educational endeavor was "always the individual person: the person, and the moral dignity of that person which is the result of his or her principles, and the conformity of actions with those principles" (#32). Direct and personal contact between teachers and students was crucial, identified by the Church as a privileged opportunity for giving witness. True education stepped beyond the imparting of knowledge, as it promoted human dignity and fostered genuine human relationships. The atmosphere of a Catholic school should be marked by sincere respect and cordiality, a place where authentic human relationships flourished.

The Religious Dimension of Education in a Catholic School (1988)

The Religious Dimension of Education in a Catholic School (CCE, 1988) expanded the concept of the Catholic school teacher to one of climate-setter. The distinctive characteristic of a Catholic school was "its attempt to generate a community climate . . . permeated by the gospel spirit of freedom and love" (#1). In this document, the Church emphasized that teachers were primarily responsible for creating a unique Christian school climate, to be accomplished through a variety of vehicles, such as individual behavior, friendly and harmonious relationships, and ready availability to students. In fact, students should come to regard the school "as an extension of their own homes, and therefore a 'school-home' ought to have some of the amenities which can create a pleasant and happy family atmosphere. When this is missing from the home, the school can often do a great deal to make up for it" (#27). This statement affirmed the power of the individual teacher to affect the lives of students. The teacher not only possessed the power to make a difference in the lives of students, but also, to make the decisive difference in a student's life. This potential rested upon the developing personhood of the teacher.

In addition, this document restated an important theme found in previous documents, that of basing a genuine educational philosophy on the nature of the human person. A philosophy of this genre takes into account all of the physical and spiritual powers of each student, inviting each one to be an active and creative agent in service to society. Moreover, "teachers should help students begin to discover the mystery within the human person" (CCE, 1988, #76). "The educational value of Christian anthropology is obvious. Here is where students discover the true value of the human person: loved by God, with a mission on earth and a destiny that is immortal. As a result, they learn the virtues of self-respect and self-love, and of love for others—a love that is universal" (CCE, 1988, #76).

Teachers were asked to teach students what it means to be human, including the display of affection, understanding and compassion, tactfulness, serenity of spirit, patience in listening to others, and the use of balanced judgment in one's response. This document urged the teacher's availability for personal meetings and conversations with students (CCE, 1998).

The Catholic School on the Threshold of the Third Millennium (1997)

The most recent Roman document to speak to the Catholic educational community was *The Catholic School on the Threshold of the Third Millennium* (CCE, 1997). Roman authors acknowledged that the role of the teacher in the Catholic school on the threshold of the third millennium has become more complex and specialized. "The sciences of education, which concentrated in the past on the study of the child and teacher training, have been widened to include the various stages of life and the different spheres and situations beyond the school. New requirements have given force to the demand for new contents, new capabilities and new educational models besides those followed traditionally. Thus education and schooling become particularly difficult today" (#2). Supportive of previous documents on education, this document emphasized that the contemporary Catholic educator is called to "prudent innovation" in a social context that is characterized by a "crisis of values" that in our highly technological society "assumes the form, often exalted by the media, of subjectivism, moral relativism, and nihilism" (#1). Thus, today's Catholic school teacher, more than ever before, is called to a "missionary thrust, the fundamental duty to evangelize, to go towards men and women wherever they are" (#3) to impart a solid, integral Christian formation, and to integrate teaching and learning with the faith dimension. The document reiterated the need for teachers to create unique Christian climates in their schools: "Teaching has an extraordinary moral depth and is one of man's most excellent and creative activities, for the teacher does not write on inanimate material, but on the very spirits of human beings" (#19).

Empirical Literature on the Role of the Catholic School Teacher

Empirical research on the role of the Catholic school teacher is minimal. Presse and Bills (1981) surveyed 185 Catholic school teachers to determine their ideal teacher role concepts, as compared with their public school counterparts. Five bipolar factors became the basis of this study: I. "Opening" (teacher behavior that opened the student to the world of learning) or "Focusing" (directed the student's attention toward specific educational goals); II. "Planning" (teacher engaged in decision making for and with students); III. "Monitoring Learning" (teacher established classroom management, as well as facilitated an atmosphere that motivated students toward self-learning); IV. "Responsibility for Learning" (teacher assumed responsibility for teaching and encouraged students to be responsible for their own learning); and V. "Guided Learning" (teacher expectations were clearly defined; teacher had rapport with students, and was open to their suggestions). The data indicated a high degree of alignment between Catholic and public school teachers in factors I, II, III, and V and a lesser degree of alignment between factor IV, thus supporting the conclusion that "although much agreement is present in the ideal teaching role of the two groups, significant differences are present" (p. 110). According to the researchers, this had particular importance in consideration of the trend toward uniformity in teacher preparation programs, since the diversity in factor descriptions suggested that "professional education is not close to agreement on what constitutes an ideal teacher" (p. 110). The findings indicated that Catholic school teachers idealized a more facilitative role in their relationships with students, dictated less in the classroom than public school teachers, and tended to encourage an atmosphere of openness, cooperation, and student self-monitoring with more frequency than their public school counterparts.

Bryk and Holland (1984), researchers associated with the Harvard Graduate School of Education, sought to discover the distinctive features of good Catholic schools. Criteria in defining "good schools" consisted of academic achievement, affective and social development, and personal values orientation. Findings revealed: (1) that Catholic schools tended to emphasize a core academic curriculum with a modest range of electives; (2) that teacher expectations for student mastery of core academic curriculum were strongly supported by both parents and students; (3) that students were held accountable for academic performance; (4) that the social environment was supportive, that is, teachers were available to assist students before and after school (data indicated that Catholic school students rated their teachers high in terms of their interest in students inside and outside of class); and (5) that teachers were dedicated, "concerned with the kind of persons their students become as well as what they know. Many described their work as a kind of ministry and their role as one of shaping young adults" (p. 16).

In their 1993 study of the Catholic high school, Bryk, Lee, and Holland noted the distinctive "sense of community" (p. 275) displayed in these schools, which attributed to the high levels of teacher commitment, as well as student engagement in learning. The researchers characterized Catholic schools as "communally organized" (p. 278), with social relations typifying Noddings' (1984) "ethic of caring." They documented that faculty tended to describe their work from a moral perspective, noting "a diffuse teacher role" in which faculty accepted a host of responsibilities that extended beyond their normal classroom duties. Bryk, Lee, and Holland interpreted the effects of a diffuse role for teachers: "Schools in which the adults are expected to take on diffuse roles recognize that the explicit and implicit objectives of schooling extend beyond the intellectual to include students' social and personal development. Adults see students as 'whole persons' to be educated rather than as distinct intellectual capacities to be advanced or particular problems to be solved" (p. 278). These studies (Bryk & Holland, 1984; Bryk, Lee, & Holland, 1993; Presse & Bills, 1981) supported the distinctive role of the Catholic school teacher.

A small number of dissertations have expounded upon the role of the post–Vatican II Catholic school teacher. Mayock (1979) extracted nine themes from Vatican II literature that she believed to be new emphases in the philosophy of Catholic education with direct application for the teacher: (1) Modern methods of research; (2) Religious existence in a secular world; (3) Involvement in the secular world; (4) Dignity of the person; (5) Religious liberty; (6) People of God; (7) Lay persons in the Church; (8) Church, the sacrament of the world's salvation; and (9) Unity of Christians and all people. She later restated: "Five of these themes came into prominence in the early post-conciliar period and, in our view, retain to this day an importance for the post-conciliar school. These five key motifs are: service, unity of Christians and of all persons, dignity of the person, responsible freedom and community" (Mayock & Glatthorn, 1980, p. 7).

Luebking (1981) analyzed conciliar and post-conciliar documents in order to establish authenticated standards for Catholic schools. He extracted six teacher standards, two of which pertained to teacher-parent relationships. The remaining four stated that:

35. Catholic school teachers must bear testimony to Christ by their lives as all the teachers share in the religious educational ministry.

36. Catholic school teachers must be current in educational practices.

37. Catholic school teachers form the minds and hearts of students and guide them to total commitment to Christ.

38. Catholic school teachers safeguard and develop the Christian atmosphere of the school. (p. 93)

Mayock's and Luebking's findings mutually relied on Church documents in extracting distinguishing characteristics of the Catholic school teacher.

Daues (1983) sought to define the role of the contemporary Catholic teacher through role theory and conciliar and post-conciliar documents. She developed three teacher roles: traditional, emergent, and enduring, which were utilized in her study. The traditional teacher role was characterized by behaviors typical of pre–Vatican II, while the emergent teacher role was descriptive of post–Vatican

II. The enduring teacher role complemented the traditional role and the emergent role, by incorporating behaviors that were not bound by time. Although perception of the role of the teacher varied according to specific groups (such as laity, clergy, parents, board members), Daues' major conclusion was that Catholic school educators assimilated conciliar and post-conciliar educational directives into their perceptions of the role of the Catholic teacher.

Ciriello (1987) examined the motivation for teaching of Catholic elementary school teachers. Three facets of commitment were identified: (1) organizational (commitment to Catholic education; teaching as ministry; opportunity to witness to faith; personal educational background in Catholic schools); (2) teaching (desire to work with young people; love of teaching; personal growth and development; personal experience in and with schools); and (3) job (desire to work in home parish; salary and benefits offered by the school; school requested assistance; opportunity to work in a school close to home). Findings demonstrated that most teachers in the study had high organizational commitment, as well as high commitment to teaching. This study revealed the self-awareness of the typical Catholic school teacher whose organizational commitment distinguished him or her from that of a professional to that of a minister.

Also studying commitment of Catholic elementary and secondary teachers, Tarr (1992) distinguished three dimensions of commitment: commitment to the organizational mission of Catholic schools; commitment to teaching; and commitment to job-specific characteristics. She found that both length of tenure in a Catholic school and the importance of religion were hallmarks of organizationally committed Catholic lay teachers. Organizationally committed teachers perceived relationships with colleagues more positively, displayed higher levels of mission-related efficacy, and derived more satisfaction from their work than either teaching- or job-committed teachers.

The author (Shimabukuro, 1993) discovered five major themes that emerged from a textual analysis of a corpus of Roman and American Vatican II and post-Vatican II documents on education (1965–1990) that characterized the role of the Catholic school teacher. Emergent themes consisted of the following: (1) The teacher forms the Christian spirituality of students; (2) The teacher is vocationally prepared; (3) The teacher is a builder of community; (4) The teacher forms the humanity of students; and (5) The teacher is professionally prepared. It was noted that themes representative of teacher characteristics and expectations, although displayed hierarchically and quantitatively, represented parts of a holistic, organic approach to education that is distinctively Catholic. A typology of the ideal Catholic school teacher was formulated, including 31 sub-themes, that addressed Catholic teacher expectations in the following contexts: religious, spiritual, moral, intellectual, psychological, developmental, interpersonal, social, environmental, global, and technological.

Gross (1994) sought to determine the extent to which the attributes that distinguish Catholic elementary school teachers—namely, proclaiming the gospel message, building a faith community, and leading others to service—were present in teachers working in elementary Catholic schools of the Archdiocese of Omaha. Findings indicated a significant presence of all three of the attributes among religious, lay Catholic, and lay non-Catholic teachers.

Recognizing the radical shift from religious to lay teachers during the past 50 years, Galetto (1996) studied the religious knowledge, beliefs, and practices of a sample of Catholic elementary lay teachers. He investigated their knowledge in four areas: general Christian dogma; Catholic Church discipline (juridical and canonical issues); Catholic positions on morality; and Catholic dogma. Results indicated that generally lay teachers were well-informed in some areas of religious knowledge but not in others, and that, although they generally believed certain tenets of the Catholic Church, there were areas of belief that they did not accept. Galetto recommended that if religious knowledge and belief are important factors in lay teachers, that background in religious education be considered in their hiring.

Related Literature

The identity of the Catholic school, as reflected in popular literature, is currently under examination in Catholic education with the realization that clarifying, strengthening, and communicating a shared vision of the Catholic school will ensure its survival. This has direct implications for the role of the teacher. Barrett (1979), asserting that the survival of Catholic schools is intimately linked to the Catholicity of the school, defined this Catholicity as "the ability to instill a loving faith in all aspects of a child's education; to fire the children with the Gospel message of faith, love and brotherhood" (p. 7). He stated that the teacher was the transmitter of Catholicity through every aspect of behavior and was judged accordingly by the child.

Bell (1984), former U.S. Secretary of Education, recognized Catholic schools as child-centered "communities of faith" (p. 10). He credited Catholic educators as "supporters of an ethic that rewards diligence, achievement and high personal standards, and discourages satisfaction with mediocrity" (p. 11). He applauded Catholic schools and Catholic educators as an "indispensable national resource."

The ideal Catholic school teacher was further conceptualized by McBride (1984) who challenged Catholic school teachers to find ways "to kindle within our schools the flame of the love of learning with the love of God," and attributed the success of the Catholic school to hinge on maintaining the "spark of loving commitment" (p. 4). Raftery (1985), identifying the distinctive characteristic of the Catholic school teacher as one of commitment, contended, "Teaching in a Catholic school is not a job, but a way of life—a commitment" (p. 5). At its most fundamental level, Catholic school teaching consists of sharing one's faith with students, while concurrently deepening one's own faith.

McDermott (1985) attributed the uniqueness of the Catholic school to its inherent configuration, that of "a religious community within an academic community" (p. 11) whose twofold purpose existed in learning and believing. He related Erickson's (1981) *Gemeinschaft* Model, "an association of people who have special commitment, a sense of unity, a consensus on goals and an awareness of their specialness" (p. 16), as characteristic of the superior social climate identified in Catholic schools. This superior social climate was restated in Coleman and Hoffer's (1987) research as the "functional community" (p. 214), which distinguished the Catholic school from its public counterparts.

Buetow (1988), in his comprehensive work *The Catholic School*, provided extensive philosophical background to the role of the Catholic school teacher, particularly in his chapter entitled "Who Gets Catholic Schools There: Teachers." He defined "teacher" in a Catholic sense as "one who has authority over others for the purpose of improving them in knowledge, skills, habits, attitudes, or ideals consonant with their true nature, ultimate end, and highest good" (p. 245). However, the authority of the teacher is not authoritarian, which Buetow characterizes as tyrannical, domineering control. It is, rather, "the dynamic influence and wholesome guidance of the mature person over the less mature" (p. 245), which necessitates a "personal presence" (p. 245) of the teacher characterized by awareness, trust, and willingness to serve others. He quoted a profound statement directed to teachers by John Paul II: "Through you, as through a clear window on a sunny day, students must come to see and know the richness and the joy of a life lived in accordance with his [Jesus'] teaching. . . . To teach means not only to impart what we know, but also to reveal who we are by living what we believe. It is this latter lesson which tends to last the longest" (p. 245).

The Catholic Education Futures Project (O'Gorman, 1988), as well as the National Congress on Catholic Schools for the 21st Century (Keating, 1991), represented contemporary attempts to explore Catholic school identity. O'Gorman created a portrait of the present-day Catholic, reiterative of the paradigm shift brought about by Vatican II and pertinent to the role of the Catholic school teacher.

Catholics' faith relationships are horizontal (not just the vertical "me and God"); Catholicism is identified as public (not just a private, parochial matter). In addition, 1988 Catholics are intentional about being Catholic (not just cultural Catholics); the mission of their church belongs to them (not just the priest); their religion is experiential and critical (not rote and simply deductive). Contemporary Catholicism is an adult life style (not completed at eighth grade). It is symbolic, imaginative, rational. Catholics now respond to the authority of the church based upon its competence (not its power); their religion is centered, in touch with the transcendent. It has a preferential option for the poor and it is ethnically diverse. (1988, p. 20)

Literature emanating from the National Congress explicated Catholic school identity. Reck (1991) claimed that before Vatican II the Catholic school was viewed as an institution. Since then, it has been regarded as a community. She elaborated seven elements of Catholic school identity, which categorically suggested areas of role definition for the Catholic school teacher: mission of Church, religious formation, gospel values, community, climate, service, and global concern. Exemplifying reflection on teacher identity that has ensued of late, Keating (1991) pondered, "I wonder if to awaken the transcendent or contemplative dimension of the young is not, in fact, the principal challenge and contribution of a Catholic school?" (p. 10). Link (1991) further elaborated, "As Catholic educators, we should be tremendously concerned about the self-image [of the student]. It is one of the marks that should distinguish our approach to education" (p. 30).

More recently, Catholic school researchers McLaughlin, O'Keefe, and O'Keeffe (1996) published a volume entitled *The Contemporary Catholic School, Context, Identity and Diversity*, consisting of a rich variety of authors who contributed to the research on the role of the Catholic school teacher. As a case in point, Groome (1996), succinctly and profoundly, explored "What Makes a School Catholic?", noting that the primary function of the Catholic school, with direct application to the teacher, is "to educate the very 'being' of . . . students, to inform, form, and transform their identity and agency—who they are and how they live—with the meaning and ethic of Christian faith" (p. 188). In his well-received book *Educating for Life* (1998), Groome further provided teachers with extensive background material in the Catholic, Christian tradition, with applications for personal and professional growth of the teacher, strategies for use in the classroom and school, and suggestions for implementation with parents. Additionally, Jacobs (1996) wrote a monograph to explore the vocational aspects of the Catholic educator, inquiring into the essence of the Catholic educational ministry.

The current literature on the Catholic teacher abounds, establishing that papal and episcopal concerns are shared in the local incarnations of Catholic education.

Future Research

Based on this review of the literature, descriptive of the distinctive role of the Catholic school teacher, two major concerns immediately surface, which suggest further research in this area. First, empirical studies are warranted which would determine the extent to which Catholic school teachers are actualizing their distinctive roles in classrooms. The future of Catholic education hinges on this distinctive reality. Such data, uncovering areas of needed teacher formation, could intelligently drive faculty development efforts and serve to preserve the Catholic identity of schools.

Second, research is needed to determine the nature and design of teacher preparation that would best serve the Catholic sector. State teacher certification standards, designed to promote the distinctive role of the public school teacher, have been sought after by the Catholic educational community since the Third Plenary Council in Baltimore in 1884, in an effort to raise the quality of Catholic education at that time (Dolan, 1985; Kraushaar, 1972; Walch, 1996). Walch quoted the Catholic educator Ralph Hayes, who wrote for the *CEA Bulletin* of 1922, confirming the widespread endorsement for state certification of Catholic school teachers: "It will serve to maintain and elevate the standard of our schools by providing additional incentive for higher teacher preparation . . . and will protect our prestige and reputation against the insinuations of those who through ignorance or malice regard our Catholic schools with unfavorable eyes" (pp. 147–148). Since that time, the value placed upon state certification has increased, with few voices in the Catholic educational community expressing concern regarding issues of pedagogical incompleteness, inconsistencies, and even areas of inappropriateness in state-determined preparation for Catholic educators.

One voice was Kraushaar (1972) whose subtitled section "The Defects of the Teacher Certification Process" introduced a litany of questions pertinent to this discussion, such as: "Should teachers of private schools be required to undergo the same training and acquire the same knowledge and skills as teachers in public schools?" (p. 321).

Another voice was Buetow, who, in 1988, articulated the need for a special Catholic teacher preparation. He wrote, "Catholic teacher-training should be especially exacting" (p. 251), asserting that the requirements of the Catholic school teacher surpass their public school counterparts: "the Catholic-school teacher trainee should be substantially exposed to, in addition to the liberal arts, programs in religious studies. These religious programs should encourage formational activities like discussion groups, retreats, prayer groups, and communal liturgy celebrations" (p. 251).

Traviss (1999) is embarking upon a study with colleagues from Boston College and Creighton University to determine the extent of teacher preparation specifically aimed at the Catholic educator by Catholic colleges and university teacher education programs. A preliminary demographic survey of Catholic colleges and universities in the United States revealed a 76% return from a universal population of 160 institutions. In response to the item, "Does your program have a Catholic school component/track, that is, does it prepare teachers for the Catholic schools?" 26 institutions (11%) replied in the affirmative. To the dismay of the researchers, accompanying written comments to these affirmative responses indicated that Catholic teacher preparation was perceived in a myriad of ways, such as: the offering of an elective on the teaching of religion; an allusive curricular emphasis of the Catholic tradition; and, a preparation that embraced both Catholic and public pre-service teachers. Traviss (1999) concluded, "There is a great deal of additional research to be done in this area if it is to be useful to the leadership of the Catholic schools, but even this [*sic*] scant data suggests that, if the Catholic schools are to continue to be staffed by prepared personnel, the bishops, superintendents, Catholic colleges and universities will have to cooperate in working on this apostolic challenge. It is a need that will not resolve itself" (p. 15). In answer to the challenge of determining the best means of guaranteeing the preparation of Catholic school teachers, Traviss (2000) convincingly wrote that "The answer is not the teaching credential as determined by the state" (p. 153). She recommended that Catholic teacher preparation involve religious learning experiences that have been analyzed and updated and subsequently linked to academic curricula. These would involve "immersion in the culture of the Catholic schools which places value on common prayer and faith sharing, cooperative learning integrating Christian belief and secular knowledge, a life of ministry in the service of others, the practice of virtue, and activities which emanate from the truth that all peoples are sisters and brothers and that God is their father" (p. 153).

In light of the extensive documentation that has been published to define Catholic pedagogy, forming the heart of this chapter, the area of Catholic teacher preparation clearly demands immediate attention.

REFERENCES

Barrett, F. (1979). Spiritual preparation of teachers. *Momentum, X (3)*, 7–8.

Bell, T. (1984). Catholic schools are an important national resource. *Momentum, XV (3)*, 10–11.

Bradley, R. (1966). The council: Renewal of education. *National Catholic Educational Association Bulletin, 63*, 439–446.

Bryk, A., & Holland, P. (1984). Research provides perspectives on effective Catholic schools. *Momentum, XV (3)*, 12–16.

Bryk, A., Lee, V., & Holland, P. (1993). *Catholic schools and the common good.* Cambridge, MA: Harvard University Press.

Buetow, H. (1988). *The Catholic school, its roots, identity and future.* New York: Crossroad Publishing.

Ciriello, M. (1987). *Teachers in Catholic schools: A study of commitment.* Unpublished doctoral dissertation, The Catholic University of America.

Coleman, J., & Hoffer, T. (1987). *Public and private high schools: The impact of communities.* New York: Basic Books.

Congregation for Catholic Education (CCE). (1977). *The Catholic school.* Washington, DC: United States Catholic Conference.

Congregation for Catholic Education (CCE). (1982). *Lay Catholics in schools: Witnesses to faith.* Boston: Daughters of St. Paul.

Congregation for Catholic Education (CCE). (1988). *The religious dimension of education in a Catholic school.* Boston: Daughters of St. Paul.

Congregation for Catholic Education (CCE). (1997). *The Catholic school on the threshold of the third millennium.* Boston: Daughters of St. Paul.

Convey, J. (1992). *Catholic schools make a difference: Twenty-five years of research.* Washington, DC: National Catholic Educational Association.

D'Alessio, E., & Shaw, R. (1973). The pastoral and the school. *Homiletic & Pastoral Review, LXXIII (11–12)*, 10–15.

Daues, M. (1983). *The modern Catholic teacher: A role analysis in the post–Vatican II schools.* Unpublished doctoral dissertation, Fordham University.

Dolan, J. (1985). *The American Catholic experience.* New York: Doubleday.

Donohue, J. (1977). A Vatican statement on education. *America, 137 (4)*, 67–70.

Duplass, J. (1975). Marginal difference in Catholic education. *Religious Education, LXX (3)*, 278–288.

Erickson, D. (1981). The superior social climate of private schools. *Momentum, XII (3)*, 5–8.

Flannery, A. (Ed.). (1982). *Vatican Council II* (Vol. 2). Northport, NY: Costello Publishing.

Flannery, A. (Ed.). (1988). *Declaration on Christian education (Gravissimum educationis).* In *Vatican Council II: Vol. 1* (Rev. ed., pp. 725–737). Northport, NY: Costello Publishing.

Galetto, P. (1996). *Building the foundations of faith: The religious knowledge, beliefs, and practices of Catholic elementary school teachers of religion.* Washington, DC: National Catholic Educational Association.

Groome, T. (1996). What makes a school Catholic? In T. McLaughlin, J. O'Keefe, & B. O'Keeffe (Eds.), *The contemporary Catholic school: Context, identity and diversity* (pp. 107–125). London: The Falmer Press.

Groome, T. (1998). *Educating for life.* Allen, TX: Thomas More Publishing.

Gross, D. (1994). *Teachers in Catholic schools: A study of the attributes of teachers that foster the identity of the Catholic school in the elementary schools of the archdiocese of Omaha.* Unpublished doctoral dissertation, University of Nebraska.

Guerra, M. (1998). *CHS 2000: A first look.* Washington DC: National Catholic Educational Association.

Hastings, A. (Ed.). (1991). *Modern Catholicism, Vatican II and after.* New York: Oxford University Press.

Heath, M. (1973). To teach as Jesus did: A critique. *The Living Light, 10 (1)*, 284–295.

Jacobs, R. (1996). *The vocation of the Catholic educator.* Washington, DC: National Catholic Educational Association.

Jacobs, R. (1998). U.S. Catholic schools and the religious who served them: Contributions of the 18th and 19th century. *Catholic Education: A Journal of Inquiry and Practice, 1 (4)*, 364–383.

Joseph, G. (1966). Human relations in the dynamics of the group. *National Catholic Educational Association Bulletin, 63*, 330–331.

Keating, K., & Traviss, M. (in press). *Pioneer mentoring in teacher education: From the voice of women.* St. Cloud, MN: North Star Press.

Keating, T. (1991). Catholicity: A tradition of contemplation. In F. D. Kelly (Ed.), *What makes a school Catholic?* (pp. 10–13). Washington, DC: National Catholic Educational Association.

Kraushaar, O. (1972). *American nonpublic schools, patterns of diversity.* Baltimore, MD: Johns Hopkins University Press.

Kushner, R., & Helbling, M. (1995). *The people who work there: The report of the Catholic elementary school teacher survey.* Washington, DC: National Catholic Educational Association.

Link, M. (1991). Facilitating students' self-image. In F. D. Kelly (Ed.), *What makes a school Catholic?* (pp. 30–40). Washington, DC: National Catholic Educational Association.

Luebking, T. (1981). *An authenticated categorization of standards promulgated for United States Catholic schools since Vatican Council II.* Unpublished doctoral dissertation, The Catholic University of America.

Mayock, L. (1979). *The influence of the Second Vatican Council on the American Catholic school.* Unpublished doctoral dissertation, University of Pennsylvania.

Mayock, L., & Glatthorn, A. (1980). NCEA and the development of the post-conciliar Catholic school. *Momentum, XI (4),* 7.

McBride, A. (1984, August). Why go to a Catholic school? *Catholic Update.* Cincinnati: St. Anthony Messenger Press.

McDermott, E. (1985). *Distinctive qualities of the Catholic school.* Washington, DC: National Catholic Educational Association.

McGreal, N. (1966). Curriculum for renewal. *National Catholic Educational Association Bulletin, 63,* 346–352.

McLaughlin, T., O'Keefe, J., & O'Keeffe, B. (Eds.). (1996). *The contemporary Catholic school: Context, identity and diversity.* London: The Falmer Press.

Meyers, B. (1941). *The education of sisters.* New York: Sheed and Ward.

Moreau, G. (1966). Directions for the future. *National Catholic Educational Association Bulletin, 63,* 375–381.

Naisbitt, J. (1982). *Megatrends.* New York: Warner.

National Conference of Catholic Bishops (NCCB). (1972). *To teach as Jesus did.* Washington, DC: United States Catholic Conference.

National Conference of Catholic Bishops (NCCB). (1976). *Teach them.* Washington, DC: United States Catholic Conference.

National Conference of Catholic Bishops (NCCB). (1979). *Sharing the light of faith.* Washington, DC: United States Catholic Conference.

Noddings, N. (1984). *Caring: A feminine approach to ethics and moral education.* Berkeley: University of California Press.

O'Gorman, R. (1988). Catholic education and identity: The future in light of the past. *Momentum, XVIV (3),* 18–21.

Petty, M. (1967). The council on education. *The Catholic Educator, XXXVII (7),* 89–95.

Pius XI. (1929). *The Christian education of youth.* Washington, DC: National Catholic Welfare Conference.

Policies Committee, Secondary School Department, National Catholic Educational Association. (1940). Tentative statement of the objectives of Catholic secondary education in the United States. *Catholic School Journal, 40 (4),* 148–149.

Presse, N., & Bills, R. (1981). A comparison of role concepts between public and parochial school teachers. *Psychology in the Schools, 18,* 107–111.

Raftery, F. (1985). *The teacher in the Catholic school.* Washington, DC: National Catholic Educational Association.

Reck, C. (1991). *The Catholic identity of Catholic schools.* Washington, DC: National Catholic Educational Association.

Shimabukuro, V. (1993). *Profile of an ideal Catholic school teacher: Content analysis of Roman and American documents, 1965 to 1990.* Unpublished doctoral dissertation, University of San Francisco.

Tarr, H. (1992). *The commitment and satisfaction of Catholic school teachers.* Unpublished doctoral dissertation, The Catholic University of America.

Thaddeus, Br. (1966). Fostering the spirit of community within the Catholic secondary school. *National Catholic Educational Association Bulletin, 63,* 331–333.

Traviss, M. (1999, September). Where have all the teachers gone? *NCEA Notes, 31 (1),* 15.

Traviss, M. (2000). Preparation of teachers for the Catholic schools. In T. Hunt, T.

Oldenski, & T. Wallace (Eds.). *Catholic school leadership: An invitation to lead* (pp. 141–156). London: The Falmer Press.

Walch, T. (1996). *Parish school, American Catholic parochial education from colonial times to the present.* New York: Crossroad Publishing.

Walters, A. (1966). Importance of the person. *National Catholic Educational Association Bulletin, 63,* 367–375.

Chapter 7

Guidance and Counseling in Catholic Schools

Patricia J. Polanski and Thomas W. Rueth

INTRODUCTION

It appears that the development of guidance and counseling programs in Catholic schools has mirrored that of public schools. For instance, in both Catholic and public schools, during the first half of the twentieth century, there was a shift from a strict vocational focus in school guidance to a broader approach that included psychological and developmental aspects of students (Hosinski, 1963; Paisley & Borders, 1995). Additionally, similar to public schools, there has been some outcry for Catholic schools to develop comprehensive, developmental guidance programs, to staff such programs with appropriately trained counselors, and to provide adequate staff for meeting the needs of students (Borders & Drury, 1992; Doyle, 1965; Doyle & Duffy, 1967; Hosinski, 1963; Zaffrann, 1985).

With regard to counseling in schools, it can be said that it is the "best of times and the worst of times." While it has been asserted that the field of school counseling is enjoying program expansion and renewal, at the same time questions remain about the appropriate role of school counselors and guidelines for effective practice in both public and Catholic schools (Borders & Drury, 1992; Stancato & McCabe, 1971). The purpose of this review is to summarize the research literature on guidance and counseling in Catholic schools from the 1960s through 1998, to determine the current status of the roles and practice of Catholic school counselors and to examine directions for future research and development.

METHOD

Although research on Catholic schools reportedly blossomed between 1965 and 1990 (Convey, 1992), very little theoretically grounded, methodologically sophisticated research was generated pertaining specifically to guidance and counseling in Catholic schools. In compiling this review, the authors conducted computerized and manual searches of indexes to Catholic educational journals and books, counseling and educational research journals, dissertations from Catholic colleges and universities, and ERIC documents from the 1960s through 1998. Predominantly conceptual articles and a few empirical studies were included in the review. Journals of particular interest were the *National Catholic Guidance Conference Journal*, and *Momentum*. While other counseling and educational research journals, such as *Counseling and Values*, the *Journal of Counseling and Development*, and school counseling journals, did not contain any articles specific to counseling in Catholic schools, some articles related to the field of school counseling were consulted to provide information about current standards of practice in guidance and counseling. The inclusion of these journals was deemed appropriate given the parallel between public and Catholic schools in the development of guidance and counseling programs.

BRIEF HISTORY

Vocational guidance began in 1908 and developed gradually but continually in the public high school system. Catholic schools also showed an early interest in this new field (Murray, 1938). Between 1918 and 1935, 16 studies focusing on Catholic guidance were conducted, and the interest of Catholic schools in vocational guidance was also evidenced by the fact that in 1932 and 1933, the proceedings of the National Catholic Educational Association (NCEA) devoted 20% and 15% of its focus on the area (Murray, 1938). Despite the early interest in the literature, it was found that that actual practice in schools lagged far behind. Murray (1938) felt this was due in part to the financial situation in Catholic schools, heavy teaching loads preventing teachers from giving time to guidance, and lack of persons with the necessary training. Much later Stack (1958), in a national study of Catholic high schools, found that Catholic schools had less complete and more poorly organized programs of guidance services then did public secondary schools. Effort in improving counseling programs was given a significant emphasis with the development of a national organization for guidance counselors.

The beginnings of a national Catholic guidance association took place in New York when the Catholic High School Guidance Council of the Archdiocese of New York was formed in 1951. By 1962, three groups, the National Conference of Catholic Guidance Councils, Catholic Counselors in the American Personnel and Guidance Association (APGA), and the editorial board of the national Catholic guidance journal the *Catholic Counselor*, were unified into a new national Catholic guidance organization, the National Catholic Guidance Conference (NCGC). The NCGC sponsored a national meeting every year, on the two days before and in the same city as the national APGA meeting. In 1964, the *National Catholic Guidance Conference Journal*, "a professional journal of theory, research, and opinion," replaced the *Catholic Counselor*, and was published quarterly (Lee & Pallone, 1966).

According to the meeting minutes published in the 1971 fall issue of the *National Catholic Guidance Conference Journal*, a discussion took place regarding the future direction of the NCGC. It appeared that a decision was made to align with the National Catholic Education Association (NCGC, 1971). However, contact with the NCEA via its web site and by phone elicited no specific information about the fate of NCGC beyond 1971. Given its alignment with the APGA, known as the American Counseling Association (ACA), it may be that NCGC was subsumed by the Association for Spiritual, Ethical, and Religious Values in Counseling (ASERVIC). Such speculation is based on the fact that the ASERVIC journal, *Counseling and Values*, has been listed as subsuming the *National Catholic Guidance Conference Journal* following 1971.

PRINCIPLES OF GUIDANCE AND COUNSELING PROGRAMS IN CATHOLIC SCHOOLS

The available research and commentary on counseling and guidance in Catholic education includes a primary focus on the need for establishing comprehensive guidance programs from kindergarten through high school (Doyle & Duffy, 1967; Inglese, 1971; Lee & Pallone, 1966; Zaffrann, 1984, 1985). In the general literature on school counseling, there is widespread agreement concerning the desired structure and function of school counseling programs (Borders & Drury, 1992). The results of this review reveal that a number of authors have suggested similar ideas regarding guidance programs in Catholic schools (Inglese, 1971; Lee & Pallone, 1966; Zaffrann, 1984, 1985). Indeed, it has been recommended that Catholic schools emulate the efforts of public schools when seeking to establish comprehensive guidance programs (Zaffrann, 1984). Essentially, four core principles have been identified as characterizing effective programs (Borders & Drury, 1992).

The first principle relates to the notion that counseling and guidance is a distinct, organized, and systematic program. Guidance is a learning process and, like other educational programs, its curriculum needs to be grounded in the philosophy or mission of the school (Lee & Pallone, 1966). Developmental guidance is not exclusively remedial; it's a planned intervention in the lives of students, arranged as a curriculum, and counselors reach out to students according to a planned schedule (Zaffrann, 1984). Effective programs are comprehensive, purposeful, sequential, and outcome-oriented (Borders & Drury, 1992). The developmental counselor is curriculum and program-oriented, available to all students, and is competent to teach important life skills (Sink & MacDonald, 1998).

Written guides for creating a comprehensive curriculum have become increasingly available at system and state levels. A review of written documentation from 41 states revealed that 24 states had produced, by March 1, 1997, some type of comprehensive guidance and counseling model (Sink & MacDonald, 1998). In general terms, these program models or frameworks are characterized by an overarching organizational structure with distinct elements, including student competencies, structural components, program components, and resources (ASCA, 1997; Gysbers & Henderson 1994).

An integral aspect to counseling and guidance constitutes the second core principle of effective guidance programs. While the program has its own distinct curriculum, guidance is infused in the school's total curricular program (Lee & Pallone, 1966). For example, communication skills aptly fit into the language arts curriculum, and problem solving into science and math (Gysbers & Henderson, 1994). This principle also implies that every school person participates in the counseling and guidance program and, as a member of that team, the counselor acts as the guidance specialist (Inglese, 1971; Lee & Pallone, 1966). An integrative approach helps teachers and other school staff to better understand and support the program and ensures that all students participate and benefit from counseling and guidance (Borders & Drury, 1992).

A solid grounding in theories of human development makes up the third core principle of effective counseling and guidance. These theories, including those of Piaget (1954) (cognitive), Erikson (1968) (psychosocial), Kohlberg (1981) and Gilligan (1982) (moral), outline sequential stages of functioning in various domains and provide a foundation upon which to construct age-appropriate, proactive programs geared to facilitate specific competencies and outcomes for students. A developmental program is designed to assist students with difficulties arising from their developmental needs before these "difficulties" erupt into problems (Lee & Pallone, 1966).

The final core principle asserts that successful school counseling and guidance serves all students in an unbiased way. All students includes those who are average; gifted and talented; low achieving, and those with handicaps and disabilities; those in all ethnic, cultural, and sexual orientation groups; boys and girls; athletes and non-athletes; and any other "special students" in the school (Borders & Drury, 1992). Each student has equal access to counselors, guidance curriculum, counseling resources, and all other direct and indirect services. While equity seems an obvious principle, there is evidence that school counseling services are not equally accessible to all students. In Catholic high schools, the number of qualified guidance counselors and amount of counseling services available in schools has been found to vary across regions of the country, size and type (diocesan, interparish, religious community) of school, and student population (Doyle & Duffy, 1967; Noyes, 1993).

PROGRAM RESOURCES

Guidance and counseling resources are often described in terms of the composition of the staff and their qualifications. A wide range of counselor-student ratios has been suggested in relation to the school level, student population, and content and goals of the counseling program (Borders & Drury, 1992). The ASCA (1997) has adopted a position statement asserting a realistic counselor-student ratio to be 1:250. A survey of a selected number of Catholic high schools in the metropolitan New York area revealed an estimated full- and part-time counselor-student ratio range of 1:1,000 to 1:680 (Doyle, 1965). These figures indicate a smaller number of school counselors in comparison to those found in various public schools across New York state with ratios ranging from 1:229 to 1:488. The counselors in this study also indicated that the higher the counselor-student ratio, the less adequate were the services provided (Duffy, 1965). Zaffrann (1984) surveyed 473 Catholic primary and secondary schools in Wisconsin to formulate a picture of attitudes, practices, and plans regarding guidance and counseling. Over 55% of the responding schools in this study had no one performing guidance functions and some had counselors who also taught part-time. Only two elementary counselors were listed (Zaffrann, 1984).

Doyle and Duffy (1966, 1967) sought to obtain a more complete picture of guidance in Catholic secondary schools by moving beyond quantitative measures such as counselor-student ratios and number of persons employed as guidance workers. The purpose of this study was to investigate the professional development of the personnel who perform guidance services. From the total number (N = 1767) of secondary schools nationwide responding to this study, 536 or 31% indicated that they either had no organized guidance program or no qualified personnel on their staffs. Of the remaining schools with programs (1,231) 2,589 faculty members responded that they were involved full- or part-time in their guidance programs. Among these, 45% were sisters, 26% were priests, 16% were lay persons, and 11% were brothers. Approximately 69% of the personnel in school counselor positions held a master's degree or higher, but 810 or 31% of these individuals had no graduate courses in guidance (Doyle & Duffy, 1967).

PROGRAM INTERVENTION

Program interventions in Catholic schools are essentially those that exist in public schools. The program interventions contained in the "ideal" school counseling program, as defined by middle and junior high school principals and counselors, include individual and group counseling, classroom guidance, consultation with parents and teachers, and coordination functions (Bonebrake & Borgers, 1984). Of these, high school teachers ranked individual counseling as the most important function of school counseling (Gibson, 1990). O'Brien (1985) identifies guidance and counseling as the two main elements of guidance services as they relate to the Catholic school community. He defines guidance as providing the students with information that will enable them to make decisions about their future. Counseling is described as an interpersonal relationship between a counselor and a student, designed to help improve the student's adjustment with self and others. Each of these has a distinct character in a Catholic school.

Etheredge (1988) states that a career guidance program in Catholic high schools should have three main elements: infusion of career information by classroom teachers into the overall curriculum, counselor-led group guidance process geared to the developmental needs of each level of students, and involvement and presentation by community members describing their work settings. While these elements are not dissimilar from those seen in public schools, they are presented in the unique philosophy of the Catholic value of work as a Christian service, which is necessary to build a better world. In this context, religion classes are seen as good places to present group guidance sessions establishing the relationship between work and spiritual development of the student.

Counseling, distinct from guidance, deals more with student problems of living than career choice. O'Brien (1985) describes the unique feature of counseling in a Catholic school as facilitating personal adjustment in the light of revealed truth taught by the Roman Catholic Church. He states that counseling interventions in Catholic schools are similar to those in public high schools in the number of White and minority students served, as well as students in higher and lower socioeconomic categories and in the specific services provided. However, Catholic schools have the additional mission of fostering the faith development of students and shaping the school into a living faith community.

Marino (1996) suggests that the individual counseling relationship is essentially the same in both public and Catholic schools, but that in the group counseling experience the difference is evidenced. In a Catholic school, there is the assumption that all members of the group have a set of common values. This assumption cannot be made about the more heterogeneous groups within the public school system. He points out that as the number of non-Catholic students attending parochial schools increases, this assumption is changing and it may be necessary to better educate non-Catholic students and parents about the mission and values of the school.

Empirical results have indicated that students receiving counseling have demonstrated improvement in their academic performance (Gerler, Kinney, & Anderson, 1985), in behaviors (Cobb & Richards, 1983), and attitudes (Gerler et al., 1985). Zaffrann (1984) has argued that counseling in Catholic schools is needed for all students, not just those at risk. He proposed a developmental approach in which every student is provided help and assistance in meeting age-related challenges.

Individual counseling has been shown to be effective with elementary students at risk in Catholic schools. Using a pretest/posttest design in which 56 first and second grade students, identified as having academic or behavioral problems, were compared before and after an average of 15 individual counseling sessions, Lavoritano and Segal (1993) determined that the students made significant gains in their self-perceptions of cognitive and social competence. While the design prevented the definitive conclusion that counseling was solely responsible for the changes, it was clear that individual counseling is a viable intervention with children of a young age for improving self-perceptions in the area of school competence.

Group counseling is often considered to be the most desirable intervention for guidance services. It is cost- and time-efficient (Myrick, 1987) and it has a sound rationale for use in educational settings (Dinkmeyer, 1971). Since groups play an important part in many elementary school activities, they serve as a natural modality for addressing the goals of elementary guidance (Dinkmeyer, 1971), described by Pietrofesa (1971) as understanding self and others.

Group counseling, using an application of Adlerian psychology, was shown to be effective with socially maladjusted 8th graders. Although significance on pre-post measures of several achievement and adjustment tests was not achieved, definite trends of improvement were observed in the better acceptance of authority, lessening of the degree of disrespect shown to others, and a greater ability to adhere to school rules and regulations (Ferinden & Seaber, 1971).

Long (1971) described an empirical study in which 67 senior high school students qualified to receive a specific level of disciplinary action were given intensive counseling. At the end of the project, 62% of the participants felt that the special counseling helped them remain in school and continue to work for a diploma; 80% felt that counseling was more beneficial in helping them change their behavior than was the discipline administered by the school; and 82% felt that talking things out with the counselor helped them perceive school in a different light. Also useful were the application of games as a way of providing a safe and comfortable atmosphere (Messing & Elliott, 1971), and the use of peer counseling to provide group counseling services to the entire student body (Dyer, Vriend, & Murphy, 1975). Whether the focus is on individual or group-based counseling, interventions must be altered to meet new challenges and problems.

Wolf (1982) has pointed out that as traditional family and social values change, there is a greater need for parochial schools to teach socialization skills. He describes a counseling program in a Catholic elementary school designed to foster interpersonal relationships leading to a Christian community, to improve academic achievement, enforce the student's self-discipline, and provide guidance for social and emotional growth. The primary emphasis is focused on the use of individual counseling; yet the group process was found to often be the most beneficial approach for counseling older students. Secondary emphasis focused on preventative and educational efforts utilizing a diocese-approved Family Life program conducted in individual classrooms.

Robbins and Carter (1998) also acknowledge that current social conditions require innovative counseling programs. They describe a program used throughout the Archdiocese of Louisville, KY, based on collaboration between school counselors and the families of students. The program is designed to move from the transitional individual counseling model, focusing on the dysfunctional behavior of an individual student, to a family-centered approach focusing on the interactional patterns of a family system, and designed to improve interfamily interaction and communication.

Catholic schools have, in addition, focused attention on dealing with specific problems such as teenage pregnancy (Hardebeck, 1987), children of divorced families (Prokop, 1990), and adolescent suicide (McCarty, 1993). Catholic school program interventions utilize methods appropriate for public school systems, but modify and adapt them in ways that fit the unique mission of Catholic education.

PROGRAM CLIMATE

The climate of the school counseling program is particularly significant given the sensitive nature of many of the program functions. Policies and procedures need to be constructed to ensure confidentiality and interactions with counseling staff must be characterized by trust, respect, and genuine interest (Lee & Pallone, 1966). In addition, the pervasive aspect of the counseling program facilitates influence on the overall school climate.

Research has shown that some school-related factors contribute to observed differences in student and teacher outcomes, and Catholic schools are more likely to evidence these factors than are public schools (Convey, 1992). These factors include the school's academic and curricular policies and the school's characteristic culture, its sense of community, its standard of order and discipline, and the collegiality, commitment, efficacy, and satisfaction of its teachers and staff. By virtue of their specialized training, school counselors are sensitive to environmental factors that impact the full development of students; they also have the skills to intervene. As consultants to teachers and staff, counselors enhance the goal of serving students by fostering collaborative relationships characterized by mutual respect, cooperation, and effective communication (Myrick, 1971).

The success of the counseling program is dependent upon the support of school administrators. Historically, Catholic school administrators have frequently equated professional guidance and counseling with moral guidance, administrative chores, or teaching and instructional responsibilities (Doyle & Duffy, 1967). Other misconceptions about guidance and counseling have included the notion that guidance is remedial and only needed in problematic cases, and thus outside agencies can meet these needs. In addition, some administrators have held the belief that guidance in Catholic schools is automatic with dedicated, involved professionals (Zaffrann, 1984). Pertinent literature suggests that there are structural characteristics within the organization of the school which prevent counselors from putting their training into practice (Stancato & McCabe, 1969).

One survey yielded results indicating that school counselors experience role conflict given the inconsistencies among the role expectations of counselor educators, pupils, parents, and the demands of the school setting (Stancato & McCabe, 1971). This survey of 455 full-time counselors from Catholic high schools in the United States obtained the following results: (a) the most pressing conflict results from their perception that more attention should be given to directing research to identify common student problems; (b) the highest conflict regarding public relations results from perceptions that more attention should be given to communicating with parents, community groups, and organizations; (c) the highest conflict regarding staff consultation results from perceptions that more attention should be given to contributing to an in-service program of guidance and counseling; (d) the highest conflict in the area of planning and development results from the perception that more attention should be given to establishing coordinated and continued guidance planning with staff at elementary and secondary levels; and (e) the highest conflict in the area of student appraisal is the perception that more attention should be given to collecting data using sociometric techniques.

It is imperative that counselors begin to educate administrators about their professional training and qualifications, and to take the initiative in working with administration and faculty to demonstrate the need for adequate comprehensive developmental guidance programs (Doyle & Duffy, 1967; Zaffrann, 1985). Counselors should meet with administrators regularly to clarify program goals and the appropriate use of the specialized skills (Gysbers & Henderson, 1994). Counselor educators need to support these efforts by providing school counselors with appropriate training in research and program evaluation, program development and delivery, and consultation and community collaboration. Through administrator conferences, teacher convention workshops and in-service sessions, and parish council and parent meetings, administrators, teachers, priests, and parents can begin to better understand the purpose and utility of school guidance and counseling programs (Zaffrann, 1985).

COUNSELING IN CATHOLIC SCHOOLS

Catholic schools are set apart from public schools by their mission of not only providing a rigorous academic curriculum but also fostering a faith community that integrates religious instruction, value formation, and faith development into the academic education of the students (Convey, 1992). Educators and supporters of Catholic schools have long spoken of a responsibility for the education of the whole person (Duffy & Doyle, 1967). These basic tenets of Catholic education clearly fall within the realm of a comprehensive developmental guidance program, and school counselors are in an optimal position to significantly contribute to Catholic schools achieving these goals (Lee & Pallone, 1966).

It has been suggested that qualitative differences exist between counseling in Catholic schools and in public schools (Marino, 1996; O'Brien, 1985). For example, in group counseling situations an assumption of common values among members reportedly exists in Catholic schools but not in public schools (Marino, 1996). Another difference relates to the context of Christian values in which counseling in Catholic schools takes place. While some believe that counselors need not be Catholic, it can be helpful in some situations, particularly those involving specific Church teachings (Marino, 1996). O'Brien (1985) has asserted that the counselor in a Catholic high school must be able to address the spiritual dimensions and aspects of a student's life within the framework and teachings of the Catholic Church. Perhaps a difference in the structure and content of a comprehensive developmental guidance program in a Catholic school may be the specific attention to students' spiritual development, along with the other developmental domains noted earlier. One model of development upon which to base programming might be Fowler's (1981) stages of faith.

With the recent interest in the integration of spirituality and religion with counseling, counselor education programs, along with professional development seminars, are increasingly addressing new theory and practice in this area (Kelly, 1995). These course offerings will undoubtedly enable better training of all counselors and in particular those who seek to provide services in religious-oriented settings such as Catholic schools.

CONCLUSION

The results of this literature review indicate that research on guidance and counseling in Catholic schools has fallen behind since the work of Doyle and Duffy in 1967, and that of Zaffrann in the 1980s. A current picture of the roles and practices of Catholic school counselors and the status of comprehensive developmental guidance programs in Catholic schools remains unclear. A number of the articles examined during this literature search, but not included in the review, indicated that teachers were performing some guidance tasks. This practice is not unusual in Catholic schools, where school personnel have historically worked part-time in the guidance function in addition to fulfilling their other responsibilities, such as teaching and administration (Doyle & Duffy, 1966, 1967). Also, while teachers and staff need to be involved in guidance work, it is imperative that guidance and counseling programs be directed by full-time persons with specific training in counseling (Doyle & Duffy, 1967; Lee & Pallone, 1966; Zaffrann, 1985).

With regard to future research, more information is needed about program resources (qualifications and composition of staff, availability of counseling service, facilities and materials) and program development and outcomes. In addition, the research priorities for Catholic education outlined by Convey (1992) also provide useful direction for the future research of guidance and counseling in Catholic schools. For instance, studies concerning the school as community, student leadership, values, parental involvement, and single-sex and coed schools could certainly involve the investigation of counseling program development and outcomes.

This review also found evidence that in many ways counseling in Catholic schools has kept pace with addressing the contemporary problems of society and their inevitable effect on students. The Contemporary Youth Concerns (CYC) survey revealed that principals and students agreed on the problems facing students, but disagreed on what help the schools provided (Elford & Feistritzer, 1982). The principals thought their schools were providing much more guidance than students saw being offered. Since this survey a number of innovative programs, some of which have been recognized by the NCEA's Special Programs for Improving Catholic Education (SPICE), have been and are being implemented to address family issues, drug education, teen pregnancy, and adolescent suicide.

REFERENCES

American School Counseling Association (ASCA). (1997). *The professional school counselor and comprehensive school counseling programs.* Alexandria, VA: Author.

Bonebrake, C. R., & Borgers, S. G. (1984). Counselor role as perceived by counselors and principals. *Elementary School Guidance and Counseling, 18,* 194–199.

Borders, L. D., & Drury, S. M. (1992). Comprehensive school counseling programs: A review for policymakers and practitioners. *Journal of Counseling & Development, 70,* 489–498.

Cobb, H. C., & Richards, H. C. (1983). Efficacy of counseling services in decreasing behavior problems of elementary school children. *Elementary School Guidance and Counseling, 7,* 180–187.

Convey, J. J. (1992). *Catholic schools make a difference: Twenty-five years of research.* Washington, DC: National Catholic Educational Association.

Dinkmeyer, D. (1971). Group approaches to understanding and changing behavior. *National Catholic Guidance Conference Journal, 15,* 163–166.

Doyle, R. E. (1965). Guidance services in metropolitan Catholic schools: A status report. *National Catholic Guidance Conference Journal, 9,* 227–229.

Doyle, R. E., & Duffy, J. C. (1966). The status of counseling and guidance in Catholic secondary schools. *National Catholic Guidance Conference Journal, 10,* 211–220.

Doyle, R. E., & Duffy, J. C. (1967). The counselor in Catholic secondary education: A national survey. *National Catholic Guidance Conference Journal, 11,* 155–203.

Duffy, J. C. (1965). *Guidance forum II.* New York: Society of Mary.

Dyer, W. W., Vriend, J., & Murphy, P. A. (1975). Peer group counseling: A total school approach. *Momentum, VI (4),* 8–15.

Elford, G., & Feistritzer, P. (1982). Report on the CYC survey. *Momentum, XIII (2),* 4–7.

Erikson, E. H. (1968). *Identity: Youth and crisis.* New York: Norton.

Etheredge, J. (1988). Making a difference. *Momentum, XVIV (4),* 56–58.

Ferinden, W. E., & Seaber, J. A. (1971). Adlerian psychology as a basis for group counseling of socially maladjusted students. *National Catholic Guidance Conference Journal, 15,* 106–112.

Fowler, J. W. (1981). *Stages of faith: The psychology of human development and the quest for meaning.* San Francisco: Harper & Row.

Gerler, E. R., Jr., Kinney, J., & Anderson, R. F. (1985). The effects of counseling on classroom performance. *The Journal of Humanistic Education and Development, 23*, 155–165.

Gibson, R. L. (1990). Teachers' opinions of high school counseling and guidance programs: Then and now. *The School Counselor, 37*, 248–255.

Gilligan, C. (1982). *In a different voice: Psychological theory and women's development.* Cambridge, MA: Harvard University Press.

Gysbers, N. C., & Henderson, P. (1994). *Developing and managing your school guidance program.* Alexandria, VA: American Counseling Association.

Hardebeck, P. L. (1987). A response to teenage pregnancy: Caring and consistency. *Momentum, XVIII (3)*, 45–47.

Hosinski, M. (1963). *Fifty years of Catholic writing on guidance and personnel work, 1909–1958.* Unpublished paper.

Inglese, S. (1971). Principles of guidance for public and Catholic schools. *National Catholic Guidance Conference Journal, 15*, 90–94.

Kelly, E. W. (1995). *Spirituality and religion in counseling and psychotherapy: Diversity in theory and practice.* Alexandria, VA: American Counseling Association.

Kohlberg, L. (1981). *The philosophy of moral development.* San Francisco: Harper & Row.

Lavoritano, J., & Segal, P. B. (1993). *A program evaluation of short term counseling with primary grade children* (Evaluative/Feasibility No. 142). Philadelphia, PA: READS, Inc.

Lee, J. M., & Pallone, N. J. (1966). *Guidance and counseling in schools: Foundations and processes.* New York: McGraw-Hill.

Long, T. (1971). A challenge: Counseling high school disciplinary cases. *National Catholic Guidance Conference Journal, 15*, 100–105.

Marino, T. W. (1996, September). Being a parochial school counselor presents benefits and challenges. *Counseling Today,* 1–6.

McCarty, R. J. (1993). Adolescent suicide: A ministerial response. *Momentum, XXIV (2)*, 61–65.

Messing, J., & Elliott, J. J. (1971). Game playing techniques in secondary school counseling groups. *National Catholic Guidance Conference Journal, 15*, 176–179.

Murray, G. (1938). *Vocational guidance in Catholic secondary schools: A study of development and present status.* Unpublished doctoral dissertation, Teachers College, Columbia University.

Myrick, R. D. (1971). The challenge of communication for the elementary school counselor-consultant. *National Catholic Guidance Conference Journal, 15*, 114–119.

Myrick, R. D. (1987). *Developmental guidance and counseling: A practical approach.* Minneapolis, MN: Educational Media Corporation.

National Catholic Guidance Conference (NCGC). (1971, April). *Minutes of the executive committee.* Atlantic City, NJ.

Noyes, B. R. (1993). Counseling climate: Effects of school type, minority enrollment, and community economic base (Doctoral dissertation, The Catholic University of America, 1993). *Dissertation Abstracts International, 54/02.*

O'Brien, T. F. (1985). *Counseling and religion: How they mix in a parochial school setting.* Paper presented at the annual convention of the American Association for Counseling and Development, New York. (ERIC Document Reproduction Service No. ED 275983.)

Paisley, P. O., & Borders, L. D. (1995). School counseling: An evolving specialty. *Journal of Counseling & Development, 74*, 150–153.

Piaget, J. (1954). *The construction of reality in the child.* New York: Basic Books.

Pietrofesa, J. (1971). Group work in the elementary school guidance program. *National Catholic Guidance Conference Journal, 15*, 121–125.

Prokop, M. S. (1990). Children of divorce: Relearning happiness. *Momentum, XXI (2)*, 72–73.

Robbins, T., & Carter, M. (1998). Family builders: Counseling families in Catholic schools. *Momentum, XXIX (3)*, 31–33.

Sink, C. A., & MacDonald, G. (1998). The status of comprehensive guidance and counseling in the United States. *Professional School Counseling, 2*, 88–94.

Stack, P. L. (1958). *A national study of guidance services in Catholic secondary schools.* Washington, DC: The Catholic University of America Press.

Stancato, F. A., & McCabe, S. P. (1969). Perceived obstacles of counselors in Catholic high schools. *National Catholic Guidance Conference Journal, 14*, 44–48.

Stancato, F. A., & McCabe, S. P. (1971). Role incongruity of counselors in Catholic high schools. *National Catholic Guidance Conference Journal, 15*, 95–99.

Wolf, T. J. (1982). Counseling program meets changing needs. *Momentum, XIII (4)*, 20–22.

Zaffrann, R. T. (1984). Developmental guidance in Catholic elementary schools: A realistic promise for educational growth. *Humanistic Educator and Development, 22*, 171–177.

Zaffrann, R. T. (1985). Developmental guidance in Catholic secondary schools: A call for change. *Journal of Humanistic Education and Development, 23*, 134–144.

Chapter 8

Enrollment in Catholic Schools in the United States

Jessica A. Greene and Joseph M. O'Keefe

This chapter examines the issue of enrollment in U.S. Catholic schools since their foundation. Enrollment is a more complex topic than one might suspect at first glance; a comprehensive overview must take into account a range of issues. To that end, we chose the following 10 variables to frame our discussion of the current reality: aggregate number of children in Catholic schools; school size; capacity of schools; geographic distribution of schools; ethnicity of students; gender composition of enrolled students; socioeconomic status of enrolled students and their families; academic issues; religious affiliation; and retention. We believe that it is important to put the current reality in its proper historical context. So, we begin with a historical perspective on enrollment from the outset of Catholic schools in North America. Next, we present our picture of students enrolled in U.S. Catholic schools at the present time, using both current literature and unpublished data collected in the 1995–1996 academic year at Boston College. We conclude with an analysis of major enrollment issues, speculation about possible futures, and avenues for further research.

HISTORICAL PERSPECTIVE ON ENROLLMENT IN U.S. CATHOLIC SCHOOLS

Catholic schools in the United States find their roots in three places: New Spain, New France, and the English Catholic colonies in Maryland. The Franciscans had a classical school and preparatory seminary for the Spanish in Saint Augustine, Florida, as early as 1606. Missions in Texas, Arizona, New Mexico, and California all had small schools for European and native children. The French established schools to teach the unlettered throughout their far-flung colonies in North America. There were, however, no Catholics of any sizable

Table 8.1
Aggregate Catholic School Enrollment, 1880–1965

1880	1900	1920	1930	1940	1950	1965
405,234	854,523	1,862,213	2,469,032	2,581,596	3,080,166	5,582,354

Sources: Dolan, 1987; McCluskey, 1969.

number in the Dutch, Swedish, or English colonies (Buetow, 1970; Burns, 1912). Maryland was the sole exception; its original settlers under Lord Calvert were Catholic refugees from a hostile Protestant England. In time, however, the number of Catholics decreased and the pressure for assimilation to the larger Protestant environment mounted. The growing Protestant majority eventually curtailed most of their civil rights by the end of the seventeenth century, and by the beginning of the eighteenth, "Catholicism became a distrusted and persecuted religious sect" (Dolan, 1987, p. 84). The tiny number of Catholics fared better in the more tolerant religious atmosphere of the new American republic. In 1788, for example, John Carroll opened Georgetown Academy, the first Catholic school in the United States. However, the educational institutions of the tiny minority of Catholics—merely 1.1% of the total population of the colonies in 1790—seem to be of little import (O'Gorman, 1987).

It was only with waves of European immigration in the nineteenth and early twentieth centuries that enrollment began to increase in Catholic schools. The generational effect of the waves of immigration was felt until the mid-1960s, when nearly 5.6 million children were enrolled in Catholic schools. While there are some discrepancies in precise enrollment figures among historians (Dolan, 1987; Grant & Hunt, 1992; Hennessey, 1981; McCluskey, 1969; McDonald, 2000), the basic story is consistent: a trajectory of steady growth that peaked in 1965. The figures in Table 8.1, taken from Dolan and McCluskey, tell the basic story.

While the debates about the precise reasons for such rapid growth are beyond the scope of this chapter, the mandate of the Third Council of Baltimore in 1884 no doubt played a central role.

After 1965, a period of decline began with a total of 4,367,000 students enrolled in Catholic schools in 1970, 3,139,000 in 1980, and 2,589,000 in 1990. As discussed in detail in the next section, enrollment grew slightly during the 1990s, with enrollment reaching 2,653,038 in the 1999–2000 academic year (McDonald, 2000). The decline was felt not only in raw numbers, but in what is called "market share." Convey (1992) estimated that in 1962 approximately 52% of Catholic children were in Catholic schools. That percentage decreased to 27% in 1987. Convey posited this decline to migration from urban centers where European immigrants had established schools a generation or two earlier; migration from the more heavily Catholic regions of the East and Midwest to the South and West (Morris, 1997); lower birth rates; and a lessening of ideological commitment. From the fortress ideology of previous generations, which was fed by Protestant hostility toward Catholics and an ultramontane self-perception, there developed an embrace of public schools (Harris, 1989).

From very small beginnings in informal educational settings in New Spain, New France, and Maryland, school size escalated with an increased number of students. By the turn of the nineteenth to twentieth centuries, most Catholic schools were overcrowded (Dolan, 1987). In 1957, the average Catholic elementary school had 390 students and the average class size was 45.9 (Fichter, 1958); in the 1950s many classes had more than 50 students (Walch, 1996). The years from 1946 to 1965 marked a period of unprecedented growth; many schools were at full capacity (Grant & Hunt, 1992). However, throughout their history Catholic schools have on average remained smaller than their public school counterparts. This may account, in part, for the spirit of community that many experience as the strength of these institutions (Reck, 1987).

Community is a much-used term in educational circles. In fact, the most important studies of student achievement have found that social capital, a set of resources that exist in the relationships between persons that are marked by trust (Bryk, 1996; Coleman & Hoffer, 1987), is the primary component of the positive "Catholic-school effect." Ingredients of community are many, but certain demographic features are prominent: ethnicity or race, class, and religion. These become, therefore, key features in a discussion of enrollment in Catholic schools.

A historian of religion, describing American Catholicism generally, wrote recently that the "manyness" of the lived reality balances the "oneness" of the Catholic tradition (Massa, 1999, p. 230). The manyness can refer to spiritual charisms or theological differences, but it is seen most starkly in ethnic heterogeneity. It can be argued that in the history of educational institutions in the United States, for example, Catholic schools have provided the most widespread and sustained example of bilingualism and biculturalism. Because they enrolled children from cultures other than that of the mainstream, they shaped their curriculum, instruction, ethos, and community relations to meet the needs of minorities. Indeed, Catholic immigrants, for the most part, desired to "hand on the faith according to their own cultural traditions" (Dolan, 1987, p. 276). The author of an overview of the education of African Americans in Catholic schools described the reality: "Regardless of the financial, political or cultural benefits that might have accrued from a united American Catholic Church, parish schools were allowed to flourish and fade within dozens of small ethnic communities. Catholics feared not only the taint of public education, but the taint of Catholic education that did not bear the unique print of their cultural identity" (York, 1996, p. 20).

Germans and French Canadians had the highest level of commitment to bilingualism and biculturalism. German support for parish education was motivated primarily by the fear that the public schools would "Anglicize" their children and turn them away from "heim and kirche"—home and church

(Walch, 1996, p. 51). The French Canadians, located mainly in New England, shared a similar concern (Sanders, 1985). These groups were followed closely by the Polish and the Irish, then the Slovaks, Czechs, Lithuanians, and Ukranians. The Italians and Mexican Americans were the least supportive. One could speculate that memories of anticlerical Italy dampened enthusiasm for the endeavor. Anticlericalism and poverty may account for the low rate among Mexicans; in 1906, of the 541 parishes nationwide that were Spanish-speaking, only six had a school (Dolan, 1987).

Despite different levels of commitment among immigrant groups, the commitment to bilingual and bicultural education was a prominent feature in the history of enrollment in Catholic schools. It began to decline in German-speaking areas with post–World War I xenophobia that was, for obvious reasons, directed against Germans. Among other groups, like the Polish, the decline began in the 1950s (Sanders, 1977). By century's end, there was virtually no trace of distinctive cultural and linguistic education for people of European descent. Concurrent with the demise of cultural distinctiveness among Europeans, Catholic schools were affected by waves of immigration from other continents, most notably South America. Moreover, the internal migration of African Americans from the rural South to the industrial centers of the Northeast and Midwest posed new cultural challenges to Church institutions (McGreevy, 1996). The issue of race complicated the issue of ethnic diversity. While it is beyond the scope of this chapter to discuss the appropriateness of race as a descriptor of human beings—race being a late-nineteenth-century construct based on faulty physiology—it is nonetheless a salient factor in the way people understand themselves and others. In the late twentieth century, ethnic diversity in Catholic schools became racial diversity. African Americans, Latinos, Asians, and Native Americans, called "ethnic minorities" in midcentury and "people of color" by the century's end, were, according to official pronouncements, to be welcomed into Catholic schools. The commitment was focused especially on Spanish-speakers, who have a greater tendency to be Roman Catholic. The U.S. bishops wrote: "Historically, the Church in the United States has been an 'immigrant Church' whose outstanding record of care for countless European immigrants remains unmatched. Today that same tradition must inspire in the Church's approach to recent Hispanic immigrants a similar authority, compassion and decisiveness" (National Catholic Conference of Bishops, 1983, p. 4).

The rhetoric did not always match the reality. First, although the Catholic Church had sponsored schools for Native Americans, African Americans, and Latinos for more than two centuries—often by religious communities who had a special apostolate to such groups—the efforts were limited in scope (Buetow, 1970). Second, people of color at times felt unwelcomed by Catholic parishes. Vitullo-Martin (1979) explained, "Because parishes form themselves so closely to the ethnic, cultural, economic and other characteristics of their parishioners, it is particularly difficult to incorporate newcomers with substantially different backgrounds and characteristics into the life of established parishes" (p. 45).

Third, a significant number of schools closed in inner-city areas populated by large numbers of people of color (O'Keefe, 1996).

Despite obstacles, the enrollment of children of color rose dramatically, especially in the 1970s. In 1970, 10.8% of students enrolled in Catholic schools were of color; by 1980 the number had nearly doubled, totaling 19.4% (McDonald, 2000). Moreover, the percentage of Hispanics and Asians in total school enrollment was higher in Catholic schools than in public schools; in 1983 Hispanics constituted 8.9% of the Catholic school population and only 8% of the public school population; Asians constituted 2.4% of Catholic school students and 1.9% of those in public school. That year, however, Blacks constituted 16% of public school students and only 8.6% of those in Catholic schools. Large urban areas had a relatively high percentage of minority enrollment: Newark, 74.1%; Los Angeles, 65.6%; Detroit, 58%; New York (Manhattan, Bronx, Staten Island), 55.2%; Chicago, 43.9%; Brooklyn, 40.2%; Cleveland, 26.5%; St. Louis, 25.7%; Philadelphia, 22.2%; Boston 16.8% (Manno, 1985). The percentage of Latino and Asian students was highest in the southwest (Convey, 1992). By 1986, on the secondary level, 17.7% of those in Catholic schools were of color as opposed to 18.8% of all secondary students. Moreover, the schools were less segregated (National Catholic Educational Association, 1986).

In summary, Catholic schools have a long history of respect for cultural differences, first among Europeans and later among people from all parts of the world. Historian Buetow (1988) put it well: "Catholic schools, with a long tradition of welcoming newcomers, continue to provide multicultural education to the new arrivals: the Hispanics, Blacks, Vietnamese, Koreans, Haitians and others have replaced the Irish, Germans, Italians and Poles of yore. Catholic schools, wary of attempting a 'melting pot' that might rob minority students of their identity, try instead for a sensitive course between isolationism and assimilation" (p. 283).

We have seen that ethnicity and race are important variables in an examination of enrollment in Catholic schools. The importance of socioeconomic status cannot be overlooked, however. Those members of ethnic minorities who were served by Catholic schools from the mid-nineteenth through the mid-twentieth centuries tended to come from lower socioeconomic classes. Catholic schools in the United States have a proud legacy of providing educational opportunities to children from low-income, poorly educated families. Throughout most of their history, U.S. Catholic elementary schools were not primarily supported by the families of their students, but by the entire community (i.e., the parish). Writing in 1958, Fichter reported that 42% of all Catholic elementary schools charged no tuition at all, and when they did, they charged modest tuition rates "that were affordable for an immigrant population, the majority of whom earned blue-collar wages" (Gillis, 1999, p. 203). High schools have always tended to be less accessible, a problem voiced by Crowley in 1935: "American Catholics have made heroic sacrifices to erect, equip and maintain Catholic elementary schools. They have long held the aim of providing Catholic elementary schools for all Catholic children, and if they are to be consistent it must be their aim to provide the same opportunity on the secondary-school level" (p. 13).

Crowley proposed that the parochial system be extended upward to secondary schools: "The real advantage of the parish high school is that the students may receive an education free or at a nominal cost, for the school is built, equipped and financed by members of the parish" (1935, p. 13). While this happened in some places—or was superceded by diocesan central schools—the more elite private Catholic schools, almost all sponsored by religious communities, were the norm. Yet even the Catholic elite high schools were more accessible than their counterparts in the broader world of private education, due to the volunteer labor provided by members of religious communities. They were, in fact, often called the "poor man's private school" (Lee, 1997, p. 154).

One could say, in summary, that Catholic schools were accessible to low-income students because of fiscal resources, provided through the local parish structure; and human resources, provided by members of religious communities. From the mid-1960s on, this way of proceeding became untenable. First, parishes provided less support (Harris, 1996), especially in the inner cities. Second, by the end of the twentieth century, traditional forms of religious life were in a period of extreme diminishment. It is remarkable that in 1920, for example, 92% of the professional staff in Catholic schools were members of religious communities; that figure fell to 7% at the outset of the new century (McDonald, 2000). Third, schools became more complicated endeavors (e.g., technology, physical infrastructure requirements, smaller class size, benefits packages for employees) that raised operating expenditures. The accessibility problem has forced Catholic schools to examine anew their mission and to come to a better self-understanding. In some ways, an "eliting" of Catholic schools is inevitable because of the expenditure requirements mentioned. In addition, the schools came to reflect the broader Catholic population, which was "no longer a poor, insolvent, non-cash available population . . . the mean incomes of Catholics had risen dramatically since the time of an earlier immigration" (McCready, 1989, p. 221). During the twentieth century, the Catholic community had indeed undergone a stunning upward mobility: "By the mid 1980s, only Episcopalians and Presbyterians outranked Catholics in the percentage of members in the $40,000 per year plus income bracket. And, given the relative size of the populations—Catholics 28% and Episcopalians 2% of the total U.S. population—Catholic affluence had a greater impact" (Gallup & Castelli, 1987, p. 4).

By the 1980s, the income level of families that attended Catholic high schools exceeded that of their public school counterparts by about $6,000 and the average parent had one more year of education (National Catholic Educational Association, 1986). On average, 13% of the students received some form of financial aid (National Catholic Educational Association, 1986). Elementary schools, while feeling the inevitable consequences of increased expenditures and a more elite sponsoring community, remained more accessible to low-income families (Convey, 1992). In the 1980s, the income of parents who sent their children to inner-city Catholic elementary schools was among the lowest. This created non-elitist, egalitarian institutions (Cibulka, O'Brien, & Zewe, 1982). However, many of these schools closed in time, and many more were in precarious circumstances (Vitullo-Martin, 1979). By the end of the century, the Church still struggled to find long-term support for schools that serve the poor. Diocesan and national philanthropic efforts, made possible by the wealth of U.S. Catholics and the friendship of affluent non-Catholics, have undoubtedly made a significant contribution. These efforts, along with increased avenues of government funding, will determine future enrollment patterns: "Catholic schools will not be able to serve all families who would choose them unless schools establish development and endowment programs that either reduce the percentage of their operating budgets supported by tuition or increase their capacity to provide financial aid to middle—as well as low—income families" (Guerra, 2000, p. 86).

Along with ethnicity and class, religion is an important enrollment variable. In fact, it is in the domain of religious affiliation that one sees the most remarkable transformation of Catholic school enrollment at the end of the twentieth century. Until the 1970s, virtually all students in Catholic schools were Catholic. In the academic year 1969–1970, for example, only 2.7% of those enrolled in Catholic schools were non-Catholic. That number rose dramatically in the 1970s, to 10.6% in the 1982–1983 academic year. Although the rate decreased, the trend toward religious diversity continued in the 1980s and 1990s. At the outset of the new century, 13.4% of Catholic school students are non-Catholics (McDonald, 2000). During the time of growth in the 1970s and 1980s, there were some sectoral differences to be noted: by level—high schools were more religiously diverse than elementary schools; by geography—those in the South and West more than other parts of the country; by ethnicity—African Americans, Asians, and Native Americans more than Hispanics and Whites (Convey, 1992). For example, only 35% of the African-American students in Catholic high schools in the mid-1980s were Catholic (National Catholic Educational Association, 1986). Religious diversity is not merely an interfaith issue but increasingly an intrafaith issue: How many nominal Catholics are, in fact, practicing? How does one define "Catholic" in the midst of competing ecclesiologies? How many children come from homes where there is a sense of spirituality? How many parents are, in fact, theologically illiterate, even about the most basic elements of Christian faith? As religious character becomes further diluted among the nominally Catholic, how will catechesis and spiritual formation change? Abundant anecdotal evidence points to an increase of intrafaith religious diversity, along with interfaith religious diversity.

Finally, single-sex education emerged in the broader educational realm of the 1980s and 1990s as an issue worthy of serious inquiry; gender is another important variable in Catholic school enrollment. The overwhelming majority of Catholic schools are coeducational: virtually all elementary schools are coeducational (McDonald, 2000), as well as most diocesan and parochial high schools.

Even in 1935, only 46% of Catholic schools were single-sex: 28% of single-sex schools were for boys, 72% for girls. Among the 46%, the overwhelming majority were private, Catholic secondary schools, often called academies, run by religious orders (Crowley, 1935). The percentage remained stable, at 46% in the 1940s, and declined to 40% in the 1980s (Convey, 1992). At the beginning of the new century, 35.8% of Catholic secondary schools were single-gender, and almost all of the religious order schools that are coeducational began as single-sex schools and converted only recently (Bryk, Lee, & Holland, 1993).

CURRENT PERSPECTIVE ON ENROLLMENT IN U.S. CATHOLIC SCHOOLS

Cognizant of enrollment trends in the past, it is time for us to look at the current reality. While a variety of sources exist which discuss Catholic school enrollment, its treatment is often cursory or, conversely, too site-specific to permit generalizable commentary. Therefore, the use of federally sponsored or nationally recognized organizations' datasets is typically desirable in that these data are often broad enough in scope to offer wide application, yet offer adequate detail to meet individual needs. Thus, for the discussion which follows, the results from the U.S. Department of Education's 1997–1998 Private School Universe Study and the National Catholic Educational Association's 1998–1999 and 1999–2000 Annual Statistical Reports on Schools, Enrollment, and Staffing are primarily used, in addition to other, smaller-scale studies.

Aggregate Number of Children in Catholic Schools

Of those private school students enrolled in Catholic schools during the 1997–1998 academic year, close to 73% (1,833,053) of the students were enrolled at the elementary level with a little over 24% (606,447) enrolled at the secondary level (Broughman & Colaciello, 1999). Enrollments increased slightly during the 1998–1999 academic year with over 75% of all private school students enrolled in Catholic elementary schools (1,990,947); Catholic secondary school enrollment remained steady at about 24% (McDonald, 1999). This growth has continued into the 1999–2000 academic year with over two million children enrolled in Catholic elementary schools and 639,954 children enrolled in Catholic secondary schools (McDonald, 2000). In fact, Catholic school enrollment has, in general, increased by close to 100,000 pupils since 1990 (McDonald, 1999). This growth trend stems in part from increases in the population of school-aged children, the economic prosperity of the 1990s, promotion of a Christian values-based education, the introduction of school choice (i.e., voucher programs), and enhanced marketing efforts by Catholic schools (Augenstein & Meitler, 1999).

It should be noted that these aggregate numbers are comprised of all major Catholic school types (i.e., parochial, diocesan, and private). When looked at individually, however, it is interesting to note the shift in enrollment by school type as students progress from the elementary to secondary levels. At the elementary level, for example, the majority of the students, about 68%, are enrolled in parochial schools with only about 3% of students enrolled in private Catholic schools; in contrast, about four-fifths of secondary-level students seek out diocesan or private Catholic secondary schools versus their parochial counterparts (Broughman & Colaciello, 1999). While this can be explained, in part, by the fact that fewer parochial schools exist at the secondary level, it is an interesting trend to consider due to the often prohibitive costs of private Catholic schools versus the more reasonable costs of parish-based schools.

Although growth in raw enrollment numbers has increased, it is important to view this growth in terms of the *overall* growth of the student-aged population in the United States. That is, has Catholic school enrollment kept pace with overall student enrollment? "A market share analysis controls for fluctuations in the size of the pool of consumers. This type of analysis relates the enrollment and number of Catholic schools to the number of potential students, thus giving the position of Catholic schools relative to other educational alternatives" (McLellan, 2000, p. 20).

As presented by Augenstein and Meitler (1999), "A comparison of Catholic school enrollment in 1988 and 1998 indicates an overall increase from 2,551,119 to 2,648,844 students, or 3.8%. However, during this time total K–12 enrollment in the United States increased from approximately 40.5 million to 47.0 million [students]. When evaluating the Catholic schools' 'market share,' it declined from 6.3% in 1988 to 5.6% in 1998" (p. 7).

The notion of market share is an important component to consider when discussing enrollment trends in that it helps to reveal actual versus perceived growth and can therefore be an important decision-making tool. As highlighted by McLellan, however, attention must be directed toward the method of market share calculation. For example, one approach is to estimate the number of Catholic children of school age in a given year and then compare the results with the number of children enrolled in Catholic schools; this method, however, may contribute to inconsistent estimates since it is difficult to approximate the *total* number of Catholic school-aged children (McLellan, 2000). An alternative approach is to calculate the proportion of total enrollment of school-aged children accounted for by Catholic schools; this method is advantageous in that it maintains measurement consistency and treats non-Catholic children as potential consumers of a Catholic education, an important sector of students to include as non-Catholic student enrollment continues to rise (McLellan, 2000).

School Size

With regard to school size, about one-fifth (19.4%) of all Catholic schools service less than 150 students, with the majority of schools (43.3%) enrolling between 150 and 299 students (Broughman & Colaciello, 1999). The largest

Table 8.2
Schools with Waiting Lists

Region	# of Schools	% in Region
New England	383	64.0%
Mideast	1,080	48.9%
Great Lakes	598	29.4%
Plains	306	33.0%
Southeast	571	57.2%
West/Far West	765	53.3%

Source: McDonald, 2000, p. 15.

schools, those with a student body of 750 students or more, only comprise 4.5% of the total Catholic school distribution (Broughman & Colaciello, 1999). Due to the steady increase of enrollments during the last decade, in combination with school closures and consolidations, close to half (45.4%) of all Catholic schools have admissions waiting lists (see Table 8.2) (McDonald, 2000, p. 15).

Capacity of Schools

As highlighted in the earlier discussion regarding school size, about 45% of all Catholic schools have admissions waiting lists, suggesting that many schools are at capacity (McDonald, 2000). This is largely explained by two opposing forces at work during the last decade (i.e., a decrease in the number of Catholic schools and an increase in Catholic school enrollment). Due to the merging and closing of Catholic schools in some areas, the number of Catholic schools in existence has decreased by about 650 schools, from 8,867 in 1988–1989 to 8,217 in 1998–1999 (McDonald, 1999). Conversely, many Catholic schools are at capacity due to increases in enrollment during the last decade; during the 1988–1989 academic year, for example, 2,551,000 students were enrolled in Catholic schools. A decade later, enrollment had increased by almost 100,000 students to 2,648,855 (McDonald, 1999). In fact, as explained by Augenstein and Meitler (1999), "if new Catholic schools were constructed in all areas with waiting lists, total Catholic school enrollment would be considerably higher than it is today" (p. 5). It is likely that current waiting list data actually underestimate demand in that they are often rarely reported; that is, in many schools with capacity enrollment, families neglect to include themselves on the waiting lists since enrollment is unlikely, thereby understating the true need (Augenstein & Meitler, 1999).

Table 8.3
Schools by Location

Location	# of Total	% of Total
Inner city	1,050	12.9%
Urban	2,669	32.8%
Suburban	2,683	32.9%
Rural	1,742	21.4%
Total	8,144	100.0%

Source: McDonald, 2000, p. 8.

Geographic Distribution of Schools

Of those students enrolled in Catholic schools, regardless of type, about half (52.1%) attend school in a central city (i.e., urban) location, with approximately 40% attending school on the fringe of an urban area or within the confines of a large town (Broughman & Colaciello, 1999). Less than 8% of Catholic school students are enrolled in rural or small town areas (Broughman & Colaciello, 1999). Redistributing enrollments by region so that inner-city and suburban areas are more clearly delineated, Table 8.3 shows that suburban-area Catholic schools have secured a strong presence, while inner-city schools have maintained their representation.

Although in aggregate, urban and suburban schools represent the location of one-third of Catholic schools respectively, research conducted by O'Keefe (1997) shows that, of those secondary schools with a 50% or more minority student enrollment, an overwhelming 73.7% of these schools are located in urban areas; in contrast, only 39.9% of the schools with greater than 50% non-minority student enrollment are located in such areas. Interestingly, when the percentage of non-minority versus minority students is expanded to 90% of the total student body, both types of schools reside in urban areas.

Noteworthy is the distinction between the locales of existing schools and new schools. For example, for the 1999–2000 academic year, 31.4% of Catholic elementary schools were located in urban areas, 13.6% in the inner city, 32.5% in suburban areas, and 22.5% of Catholic elementary schools were located in rural areas (McDonald, 2000). This contrasts starkly with the establishment of new Catholic elementary schools where over half (55%) are being opened in the suburbs and only 7% are being founded in the inner city (Augenstein & Meitler, 1999). Similar trends exist for Catholic high schools: 35.4% currently exist in suburban areas, although 42% of new secondary schools are being established in the suburbs; conversely, 9% of Catholic secondary schools are located in the inner city; however, only 8% of new Catholic secondary schools

Table 8.4
Geographic Distribution by Region

Region	1994-1995	1999-2000
New England	6.2%	6.2%
Mideast	29.5%	29.0%
Great Lakes	24.9%	24.2%
Plains	9.4%	9.5%
Southeast	12.7%	13.6%
West/Far West	17.4%	17.5%

Source: McDonald, 2000, p. 12.

are being established there (Augenstein & Meitler, 1999; McDonald, 2000). In fact, when asked to assess trends in enrollment over the past five years, 30.2% of principals of secondary schools with a greater than 50% minority student body reported a decrease, 25% reported no change, while 44.8% of the principals reported an increase in enrollment (O'Keefe, 1997). Notable are the responses of the principals of schools with a greater than 50% non-minority student body; of this group, only 13.1% reported a decrease in enrollment and only 17.5% reported no change (O'Keefe, 1997). A compelling 69.4%, however, reported an increase in school enrollment over the last five years. These data reinforce the unsettling trend of Catholic schools' movement out of the inner city and into select suburban areas. This suburbanization of new school establishment may simply be a function of overall population migration from urban to sub- urban areas; however, regardless of the impetus, the needs of inner-city and urban Catholic families must not be overlooked. That is, the maintenance and growth of inner-city and urban schools (even if limited) must not be wholly sacrificed in order to meet the demands of suburban-area expansion.

The National Catholic Educational Association's (NCEA) annual statistical report on schools, enrollment, and staffing also states that, during the 1989– 1990 academic year, 6.2% of the nation's Catholic schools were located in New England, 29.4% in the Mideast, 24.6% in the Great Lakes region, 9.0% in the Plains region, 11.6% in the Southeast, and 19.2% in the West and Far West areas of the United States (McDonald, 2000). This geographic distribution has not changed appreciably during the last five years, as presented in Table 8.4's comparison of Catholic schools' geographic distribution from the 1994–1995 to 1999–2000 academic years.

Noteworthy are the regional differences in growth from 1985 through 1999, likely due to attitudinal and population growth differences between regions. That is, where enrollment markedly declined in the New England, Mideast, and Great Lakes regions during this 15-year period, enrollment increased in the Plains,

Table 8.5
Student Enrollment by Ethnicity

Ethnicity	1995-1996	1999-2000
Black	7.7%	7.8%
Hispanic	10.3%	10.7%
Asian/Pacific Islander	4.3%	4.3%
Alaskan/Native American	0.5%	0.3%
Other/Multiracial	1.2%	1.6%
White	76.1%	75.1%

Sources: McDonald, 2000, p. 17; Savage & Milks, 1996, p. 17.

Southeast, and West/Far West regions of the United States (Augenstein & Mei-tler, 1999).

Ethnicity of Students

Not surprisingly, the majority of Catholic school students (76.6%) are of White, non-Hispanic descent with a fairly even breakdown of Black students (8.1%) and Hispanic students (10.6%) (Broughman & Colaciello, 1999). Students described as Asian/Pacific Islander comprise only 4.3% of the current Catholic school student body; Alaskan/Native American students represent less than one percent of the enrolled students (Broughman & Colaciello, 1999). Interesting to note is the relative consistency with which minority populations have been represented within Catholic schools over the last five years. As presented in Table 8.5, only slight, non-statistically significant differences exist between the 1995–1996 academic year's minority enrollment and that of the 1999–2000 academic year.

While adequate research does exist with regard to the minority and non-minority composition of the student body (ethnicity), little research has been done which focuses on students and their families' nationality, such as immigrant status or first language. This is somewhat interesting when one considers that the bedrock of Catholic schooling (of which there is ample research) rests on immigrants of the late nineteenth and early twentieth centuries. As explained earlier, today's "new" immigrants, Mexicans, Cubans, Central Americans, Haitians, Vietnamese, Koreans, and Filipinos, typically arrive in the United States with the "same ethno-religious aspirations as their predecessors, but they encounter a Catholic Church that has already assimilated the previous generations and is loathe to acknowledge, let alone accommodate, the need for 'national' parishes and schools" (Lawrence, 2000, p. 178). As the demographic characteristics of U.S. Catholic schools continues to evolve, the nationality of students will likely demand more attention; research pertaining to these groups' participation rates in Catholic schools will be necessary in order to help shape Catholic school policy and chart Catholic school growth.

Socioeconomic Status of Enrolled Students and Their Families

Analysis of the socioeconomic status of Catholic school students (or perhaps more appropriately, their families) is an interesting facet of Catholic school enrollment to study since it incorporates many issues, such as school choice, parent involvement, and the tuition dependence of schools. Historically, Catholic schools have been thought of as being fully accessible to the poor and working class, since children from these sectors of society had been the original attendees of Catholic schools. However, the changing status of American Catholics from the inception of Catholic schools to the present reveals a Catholic school student body that is less diverse in terms of socioeconomic standing. As explained by Riordan (2000), 12.3% of Catholic school students in 1972 were from the lowest socioeconomic (SES) quartile; by 1992 only 5.5% of the students attending Catholic schools represented the lowest SES quartile. In contrast, while 29.7% of Catholic school students were from the highest SES quartile in 1972, close to 46% of Catholic school students were from this quartile by 1992 (Riordan, 2000). "Not surprisingly, this transformation in the SES of students attending Catholic schools has been accompanied by a persistent and substantial increase in the average tuition at Catholic schools during this same period" (Riordan, 2000, p. 40).

For example, the average annual secondary school tuition has jumped from $2,800 per pupil in 1992 to $4,100 per pupil in 1999 (McDonald, 2000; Riordan, 2000). While tuition increases can be explained, in part, by the influences of inflation to which no commodity is immune, other factors contributing to rising tuition costs include less fiscal support via parish subsidies, fewer fund-raising events, and cost increases due to the abundance of lay teachers and administrators (Harris, 2000).

Socioeconomic status of students and their families is also a pertinent topic due to the unfortunate link between urbanicity, ethnicity, and poverty. Of the secondary school principals researched by O'Keefe (1997) with a non-minority student body, an overwhelming 87.8% reported that less than 10% of their students lived at or below the poverty line; only 44.6% of minority school principals could report the same (see Table 8.6).

This study also asked principals to estimate the percentage of students who do not have health care coverage. Similarly, the responses reveal the much harsher conditions under which the minority school students live. Principals in the non-minority secondary school sample report that only 7.7% of their students are without health care coverage, while the minority secondary school principals reveal that 17.1% of their students are without health care coverage (O'Keefe, 1997). Results regarding residence in low-income, government-subsidized hous-

Table 8.6
Distribution of Secondary School Students Living below the Poverty Threshold

% of Students	> 50 % Minority Schools	> 50 % Non-minority Schools
Less than or equal to 10%	44.6%	87.8%
11% to 20%	28.3%	8.5%
21% to 30%	10.9%	2.6%
31% to 40%	8.7%	0.6%
41% to 50%	3.3%	—
51% to 60%	3.3%	0.3%
61% to 70%	—	0.3%
71% to 80%	—	—
81% to 90%	1.1%	—
91% to 100%	—	—

Source: O'Keefe, 1997.

ing reinforce the trend. While principals within the non-minority Catholic secondary school sample report that only 2.2% of their students have endured life in low-income housing projects, principals within the minority school sample report that 13.9% of their students have lived in this type of housing situation (O'Keefe, 1997).

To further understand the dynamics present in students' lives, principals were asked to report on the percentage of students who come from single-parent families, foster homes, and homes in which grandparents are the primary caregivers. In addition, principals were asked to respond to four questions specifically about parents: Do the parents or guardians hold foreign citizenship? Do they have limited English proficiency? Did they graduate only from high school or earn a GED? Are they college graduates? Table 8.7 provides a summary of these data.

Much attention needs to be directed toward the fiscal needs of today's Catholic schools. The lack of serious innovation in this area will be marked by the inaccessibility of a Catholic school education for the less fortunate sectors of society, a trend certainly antithetical to the social justice mission of the Church.

Religious Affiliation

As expected, the religious affiliation of most students enrolled in Catholic schools is Catholic. When non-Catholic enrollment is broken out by school level, a more pronounced jump is seen within secondary schools. As researched by

Table 8.7
Parental Characteristics of Secondary School Students

Characteristic	> 50 % Minority Schools	> 50% Non-minority Schools
Caregivers: Single parents	37.5%	20.4%
Caregivers: Guardians	7.2%	3.7%
Caregivers: Grandparents	7.5%	1.8%
Caregivers: Foreign-born	16.1%	2.4%
Caregivers: Limited English Proficiency	14.6%	1.9%
Caregivers: HS/ GED only	38.2%	24.8%
Caregivers: College graduate(s)	34.8%	56.5%

Source: O'Keefe, 1997.

Riordan (2000), in 1992, the percentage of non-Catholic school enrollment was slightly over 21%. Recent findings note a slight decrease in non-Catholic student enrollment at the secondary level (at about 17%) during the 1999–2000 academic year (McDonald, 2000).

As explained by O'Keefe and Murphy (2000), however, the study of the religious identity of non-Catholics has largely remained unexamined beyond Catholic versus non-Catholic tallies. Their research demonstrates that while the bulk of students and adults in Catholic schools are Christian, "a significant and increasing number belong to non-Catholic denominations, especially African-American Baptist churches" (O'Keefe & Murphy, 2000, p. 134). For example, 73.2% of the students enrolling in predominantly (greater than 50%) minority secondary schools are Catholic, as opposed to 83.9% of the students enrolling in predominantly non-minority Catholic secondary schools (O'Keefe, 1997). Noteworthy is that when the percentage of minority versus non-minority students is expanded to 90% of the total student body, the percentage of Catholic students attending predominantly minority secondary schools drops to 66.5%; conversely, the percentage of Catholic students attending predominantly non-minority schools rises to 89.1% (O'Keefe, 1997). These ethnically diverse schools are also more religiously diverse. This tendency toward religious diversity prompts many questions regarding the ecumenical nature of these schools. "Depending upon one's theological perspective, denominationally diverse Catholic schools may present a wonderful opportunity for Christian dialogue or be a serious dilution of religious character (O'Keefe & Murphy, 2000).

Gender Composition of Enrolled Students

Overall, the gender composition of the Catholic school student body is roughly the same for males and females, with 51.4% of the enrollment being comprised of males and consequently 48.6% of the student body being comprised of females (Broughman & Colaciello, 1999). This fairly even breakdown is largely due to the nature of the schools; almost all (94.1%) are coeducational (Broughman & Colaciello, 1999). In fact, of all Catholic schools, regardless of level, only 3.3% are all-girl schools; 2.6% represent all-boy schools (Broughman & Colaciello, 1999). It should be noted, however, that these figures absorb the distribution of single-sex Catholic schools at the secondary level, where currently about 15% are single-sex male schools and approximately 21% are single-sex female schools (McDonald, 2000). These figures are in stark contrast to previous decades' single-sex school distribution where, for example, 60% of single-sex schools were all female (Convey, 1992).

Academic Issues

Using data from *High School and Beyond*, Coleman, Hoffer, and Kilgore (1982) concluded that a private school education results in higher cognitive outcomes for students than does a public school education. In addition, "students of parents with different educational backgrounds achieve at more nearly comparable levels in the Catholic schools than in the public schools, while the achievement levels are even more divergent in other private schools than in the public schools. And comparison of blacks and Hispanics in Catholic and public schools reveals that as sophomores these minority students achieve at a level closer to that of non-Hispanic whites in Catholic schools than in public schools" (Coleman et al., 1982, p. 177).

This last point has been particularly antagonistic to critics; note Coleman et al.'s (1982) claim that "altogether, the evidence is strong that the Catholic schools function much closer to the American ideal of the 'common school,' educating children from different backgrounds alike, than do the public schools" (p. 177). Their response to these arguments was based on the stratification of the American public school system, largely a result of the growth of suburban areas since World War II. "This stratification has in effect produced a 'public' school system which not only no longer integrates the various segments of the population of students, but appears no more egalitarian than private education, and considerably less egalitarian in outcome than the major portion of the private sector in America—the Catholic schools" (Coleman et al., 1982, p. 196). Citing failures at public school integration, such as bussing, Coleman et al. (1982) advocate school choice for all, regardless of social or economic resources.

Contrasting this, many researchers argue that the higher academic outcomes earned by students enrolled in private schools (including Catholic schools) stem not from these schools' superior administrative and teaching staffs, but more from the fact that the students themselves enjoy more advantages than do their public school counterparts, thereby making comparisons between public and private schools tenuous at best. As Greeley (1981) explains:

Even if the impressions of black and Hispanic parents are correct, and the young people who attend Catholic secondary schools do better academically, it does not necessarily follow that the Catholic schools are responsible for the superior academic outcome. Educational research in recent years has demonstrated that to a considerable extent, outcome is a function of input. Schools which feature young people from well-educated, powerfully-motivated, and affluent families will produce graduates who are very different from schools whose enrollees come from different family backgrounds. (p. 6)

Also to be considered are the admissions policies of private schools. Whereas public schools are responsible for educating students of all abilities (excluding extreme cases), private schools can restrict enrollments and expel those students who are unable to meet their academic and behavior standards. The option held by private schools to enroll only the "cream of the crop" also puts into question comparisons between public and private institutions. Critics of private and Catholic school research have also noted other explanations for differential effectiveness. First, parental involvement is often thought of as a source for the Catholic school advantage in that parents who actively choose their children's school(s) are likely to engage themselves more in their children's education. That is, "the high expectations that Catholic school parents have for their children, the extent to which they monitor their children's work, and their level of involvement in the school, each of which studies have shown is higher than that of the average public school parent, are important contributors to students' success" (Convey, 1992, p. 179). These qualities are reflective of the notion of social capital to which Coleman and Hoffer attribute much of the Catholic school advantage (Coleman & Hoffer, 1987).

Retention

Retention among Catholic school students is particularly healthy, especially for minority students enrolled in Catholic schools. In fact, "minority students in Catholic schools are less likely to drop out of school than are minority students in public schools" (Convey, 1992, p. 159). In addition, those who do drop out of Catholic schools do so at a lower rate than those attending public schools, with social class serving as little influence to the decision to drop out (Bryk & Thum, 1989). These findings are reflective of those from *High School and Beyond* (Coleman & Hoffer, 1987), which showed that at-risk students, such as those coming from single-parent, minority, or low-income homes, were less likely to drop out of their Catholic school than were similarly at-risk students attending public schools. Estimates of Catholic secondary school dropouts demonstrate that less than one percent of students choose to leave school during the academic year (O'Keefe, 1997).

CONCLUSION

This chapter has explored the issue of enrollment in U.S. Catholic schools, first from a historical perspective and then by looking at the current reality, based on federal studies, NCEA data, and data collected at Boston College during the 1995–1996 academic year. We explored aggregate numbers of students, recounting a history of steep growth from tiny beginnings at the earliest days of the Republic, to a peak in 1965, to a sharp decline that leveled off in the mid-1990s, to a slow rate of growth in raw numbers. We shed light on the meaning of these aggregate numbers by an investigation of market share and distribution by sector, level, and geography. In short, we attempted to answer the enrollment question, "How many are in Catholic schools?" Next, we identified key variables that provide insight into the identity of students: ethnicity, socioeconomic status, gender, and religion. We told the story of a religiously homogeneous population that swelled during a century of immigration from Europe (the mid-nineteenth to the mid-twentieth), that assimilated to dominant cultural patterns and experienced stunning upward mobility. In the last decades of the twentieth century, this population became increasingly polarized by income distribution, more representative of the entire globe in its ethnicity, and marked by inter- and intrareligious diversity. And, in the midst of these changes, we described institutions that are remarkably resilient as they serve contemporary needs. It was our aim to shed light on the question, "Who is in Catholic schools?"

Entering into the twenty-first century, one clearly marked by rapid social change and cultural transformations, the future of Catholic school enrollment is hard to predict. Undoubtedly, however, the following questions will be salient: Will the Church be able to finance the Catholic school to the extent that its services are accessible to a wide range of social classes? Will the Catholic school recover in a new way its long-standing commitment to cultural and linguistic diversity, especially for a burgeoning Latino population and other new immigrants? In a milieu marked by benchmarks, competition, efficiency, and technological savvy, will the Catholic school continue to offer a communitarian ethos for students, staff, and families? Finally, will the Catholic school be able to provide spiritual formation and theological literacy for a religiously diverse population?

Research will provide some answers to these key enrollment questions. Technology offers new possibilities for data collection at the federal, national Catholic, and local Catholic levels (e.g., an annual web-based census). Advances in electronic text analysis, voice-activated software, videography, and telecommunications will create new opportunities for qualitative studies conducted jointly by researchers and practitioners. These studies can complement demographic data in an ongoing exploration of class, ethnicity, religion, and gender; variables that will frame inquiry about Catholic school enrollment in the future.

REFERENCES

Augenstein, J., & Meitler, N. (1999). *Catholic school growth, 1985–1999.* Hales Corner, WI: Meitler Consultants.

Broughman, S. P., & Colaciello, L. A. (1999). *Private school universe survey, 1997–98.* Washington, DC: U.S. Department of Education, National Center for Education Statistics.

Bryk, A. S. (1996). Lessons from Catholic high schools in renewing our educational institutions. In T. McLaughlin, J. O'Keefe, & B. O'Keeffe (Eds.), *The contemporary Catholic school: Context, identity and diversity* (pp. 25–41). Washington, DC: Falmer Press.

Bryk, A. S., Lee, V. E., & Holland, P. B. (1993). *Catholic schools and the common good.* Cambridge, MA: Harvard University Press.

Bryk, A. S., & Thum, Y. M. (1989). The effect of high school organization on dropping out: An exploratory investigation. *American Educational Research Journal, 26,* 353–383.

Buetow, H. A. (1970). *Of singular benefit: The story of U.S. Catholic education.* London: The Macmillan Co.

Buetow, H. A. (1988). *The Catholic school: Its roots, identity and future.* New York: Crossroad Publishing.

Burns, J. A. (1912). *The principles, origin and establishment of the Catholic school system in the United States.* New York: Arno Press.

Cibulka, J., O'Brien, T., & Zewe, D. (1982). *Inner city private elementary schools: A study.* Milwaukee, WI: Marquette University Press.

Coleman, J. S., & Hoffer, T. (1987). *Public and private high schools: The impact of communities.* New York: Basic Books.

Coleman, J. S., Hoffer, T., & Kilgore, S. (1982). *High school achievement: Public, Catholic, and private schools compared.* New York: Basic Books.

Convey, J. J. (1992). *Catholic schools make a difference: Twenty-five years of research.* Washington, DC: National Catholic Educational Association.

Crowley, F. (1935). *The Catholic high school principal.* New York: Bruce Publishing Co.

Dolan, J. P. (1987. *The American Catholic experience.* New York: Image.

Fitchter, J. H. (1958). *Parochial school: A sociological study.* Notre Dame, IN: University of Notre Dame Press.

Gallup, G., & Castelli, J. (1987). *The American Catholic people.* New York: Doubleday.

Gillis, C. (1999). *Roman Catholicism in America.* New York: Columbia University Press.

Grant, M. A., & Hunt, T. C. (1992). *Catholic school education in the United States.* New York: Garland Publishing.

Greeley, A. M. (1981). Catholic high schools and minority students. In E. Gaffney (Ed.), *Private schools and the public good* (pp. 6–16). Notre Dame, IN: University of Notre Dame Press.

Guerra, M. (2000). Key issues for the future of Catholic schools. In T. Hunt, T. Oldenski, & T. J. Wallace (Eds.), *Catholic school leadership: An invitation to lead* (pp. 79–90). Washington, DC: Falmer Press.

Harris, J. C. (1989). *Enrollment patterns in Catholic schools: The past and the future, 1979–1992*. Washington, DC: National Catholic Educational Association.

Harris, J. C. (1996). *The cost of Catholic schools and parishes*. Kansas City, MO: Sheed and Ward.

Harris, J. C. (2000). The funding dilemma facing Catholic elementary and secondary schools. In J. Youniss & J. J. Convey (Eds.), *Catholic schools at the crossroads: Survival and transformation* (pp. 55–71). New York: Teachers College Press.

Hennesey, J. (1981). *American Catholics: A history of the Roman Catholic community in the United States*. New York: Oxford University Press.

Lawrence, S. (2000). "New" immigrants in the Catholic schools: A preliminary assessment. In J. Youniss & J. J. Convey (Eds.), *Catholic schools at the crossroads: Survival and transformation* (pp. 178–200). New York: Teachers College Press.

Lee, V. (1997). Catholic lessons for public schools. In D. Ravitch & J. Viteritti (Eds.), *New schools for a new century*. New Haven, CT: Yale University Press.

Manno, B. (1985, November 13). Stereotypes, statistics and Catholic schools. *Education Week*, p. 11.

Massa, M. (1999). *Catholics and American culture*. New York: Crossroad Publishing.

McCluskey, N. G. (1969). *Catholic education faces its future*. Garden City, NY: Doubleday.

McCready, W. C. (1989). Catholic schools and Catholic identity: Stretching the vital connection. *Chicago Studies, 28 (3)*, 217–231.

McDonald, D. (1999). *United States Catholic elementary and secondary schools 1998–99*. Washington, DC: National Catholic Educational Association.

McDonald, D. (2000). *United States Catholic elementary and secondary schools 1999–2000: The annual statistical report on schools, enrollment and staffing*. Washington, DC: National Catholic Educational Association.

McGreevy, J. (1996). *Parish boundaries: The Catholic encounter with race in the twentieth-century urban north*. Chicago: University of Chicago Press.

McLellan, J. A. (2000). Rise, fall and reasons why: U.S. Catholic elementary education, 1940–1995. In J. Youniss & J. J. Convey (Eds.), *Catholic schools at the crossroads: Survival and transformation* (pp. 17–32). New York: Teachers College Press.

Morris, C. R. (1997). *American Catholic*. New York: Times Books.

National Catholic Conference of Bishops. (1983). *The Hispanic presence: Challenge and commitment*. Washington, DC: Author.

National Catholic Educational Association. (1986). *Catholic high schools: Their impact on low-income students*. Washington, DC: Author.

O'Gorman, R. T. (1987). *The church that was a school: Catholic identity and Catholic education in the Untied States since 1790*. Monograph on the history of Catholic education in the United States, Catholic Education Futures Project.

O'Keefe, J. M. (1996). No margin, no mission. In T. McLaughlin, J. O'Keefe, & B. O'Keeffe (Eds.), *The contemporary Catholic school: Context, identity and diversity* (pp. 177–197). Washington, DC: Falmer Press.

O'Keefe, J. M. (1997). *The Catholic secondary school survey*. Chestnut Hill, MA: Boston College. Unpublished survey.

O'Keefe, J. M., & Murphy, J. (2000). Ethnically diverse Catholic schools: School structure, students, staffing, and finance. In J. Youniss & J. J. Convey (Eds.), *Catholic schools at the crossroads: Survival and transformation* (pp. 33–54). New York: Teachers College Press.

Reck, C. (1987). *Small Catholic elementary schools: An endangered species?* (ERIC Digest ED 296 815.)

Riordan, C. (2000). Trends in student demography in Catholic secondary schools, 1972–1992. In J. Youniss & J. J. Convey (Eds.), *Catholic schools at the crossroads: Survival and transformation* (pp. 33–54). New York: Teachers College Press.

Sanders, J. (1977). *The education of an urban minority: Catholics in Chicago, 1833–1965.* New York: Oxford University Press.

Sanders, J. (1985). Catholics and the school question in Boston: The Cardinal O'Connell years. In R. Sullivan & J. O'Toole (Eds.), *Catholic Boston: Studies in religion and community, 1840–1970.* Boston: Archdiocese of Boston.

Savage, F. X., & Milks, M. J. (1996). *United States Catholic elementary and secondary schools 1995–96.* Washington, DC: National Catholic Educational Association.

Vitullo-Martin, T. (1979). *Catholic inner-city schools: The future.* Washington, DC: U.S. Catholic Conference Department of Education Publications Office, U.S. Catholic Conference.

Walch, T. (1996). *Parish school: American Catholic parochial education from colonial times to the present.* New York: Crossroad Publishing.

York, D. E. (1996). The academic achievement of African Americans in Catholic schools: A review of the literature. In J. J. Irvine & M. Foster (Eds.), *Growing up African American in Catholic schools* (pp. 11–46). New York: Teachers College Press.

Chapter 9

Parenting and Child Development: Exploring the Links with Children's Social, Moral, and Cognitive Competence

James M. Frabutt

INTRODUCTION

As Pope John Paul II has stated, "The future of humanity passes by way of the family" (John Paul II, 1981, #86). The family is both foundational and fundamental to our vitality as a society and as a Church. Furthermore, a family is "our first community and the most basic way in which the Lord gathers us, forms us, and acts in the world" (National Conference of Catholic Bishops, 1993, p. 8). Within this first community, parents are undoubtedly their children's first teachers. As models and guides, parents provide the first crucial underpinnings that will support children's development in the years ahead. However, families today, and parents in particular, are faced with challenge and complexity manifested through society's continual social, economic, moral, and political changes (National Conference, 1972). While some critics have gone so far as to question whether parents matter in the lives of children (Harris, 1998), the research reviewed throughout this chapter illustrates the myriad ways that parents are truly instrumental in fostering child and adolescent development.

THE PROCESS OF PARENTING

Psychologist David Guttman has written, "For most adult humans, parenthood is still the ultimate source of the sense of meaning. For most adults the question 'What does life mean?' is automatically answered once they have children; better yet, it is no longer asked" (1975, p. 170). This statement begins to capture the depth and importance of the multifaceted commitment that is parenthood. Despite recent mainstream media contentions that the influence of parents is negligible (Cohen, 1999), parents foster all aspects of children's growth through nourishing, protecting, and guiding new life through the course of human development (Hamner & Turner, 1996; Jaffe, 1997; Lamb, Ketterlinus, & Fracasso, 1992). Brooks (1991) has summarized the main tasks of parents as establishing warm, nurturant, emotional relationships with children and providing opportunities for the development of competence and individuality. Through these processes, the ways that parents may influence their children are many and varied.

Research on parenting and child socialization for decades has attempted to delineate and understand the myriad pathways through which parents influence their children. Today, it is almost taken for granted that an interactional model of growth, suggesting that both biology and rearing guide children's adjustment, best explains overall development (Brooks, 1991; Kagan, 1994). This review focuses on one environmental factor, the process of parenting, which influences child and adolescent development. Specifically, findings are presented on the associations between parental factors and three distinct domains: children's social, moral, and cognitive competence.

Parenting and Children's Social Development

The analysis of children's interpersonal relations and their capacity for social interaction and relationships are the foci of social development research (Damon, 1983). Viewed from a developmental perspective, it is evident how varied and diverse children's social relationships can be. An infant's early attachment to a caregiver, a preschooler's emerging relationships with peers, a middle schooler's close bond with a sibling, an adolescent's first intimate relationship—each of these social relationships is characterized by a distinct purpose, quality, intensity, and emotional tone. In short, there is an incredible breadth in the nature and quality of children's relationships. Therefore, for the purposes of this review, the domain of peer relationships, and parents' influence upon children's development in this area, will be the primary focus.

One of the most critical psychosocial tasks of childhood is the development and maintenance of successful peer relations (Cohn, Patterson, & Christopoulos, 1991) and friendships (Sullivan, 1953; Youniss & Haynie, 1992). Moreover, a great deal of research supports the notion that children who adjust poorly to their peer groups are at risk for later social and academic problems. In their review, Parker and Asher (1987) documented that children who are rejected by their peers are at greater risk for a variety of difficulties, including increased risk of school dropout, poorer academic performance, increased delinquency, and mental health problems.

Despite the intriguing question of how children develop the knowledge and skills necessary to manage relationships with others, research documenting the role of parenting in children's social development is a fairly recent phenomenon. As Hartup wrote, "Quite possibly the most serious oversight in the literature on social development is the absence of information concerning the interdependen-

Figure 9.1
A Tripartite Model of the Linkages between the Family and Peer Contexts

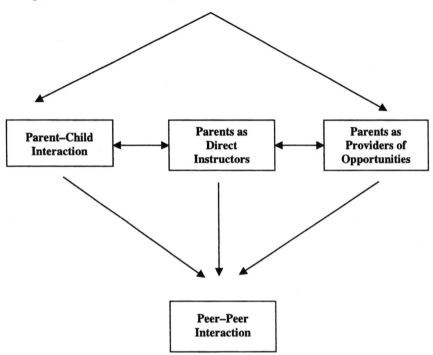

cies existing between experiences in one social world and experiences in others"
(1979, p. 944). However, two decades after that proclamation, the knowledge
base on the family–peer linkage has absolutely burgeoned. Scholars have begun
to describe and explain the interface of parenting and children's social development.

In a tripartite model of the connections across family and peer contexts (see
Figure 9.1), Parke and colleagues outlined three general categories that are inclusive of the multitude of research studies undertaken in the study of the linkages between family and peer contexts (Parke, Burks, Carson, Neville, &
Boyum, 1994; Parke, Cassidy, Burks, Carson, & Boyum, 1992). Direct effects
on children's peer–peer interaction are operationalized when parents serve as
direct instructors for their children's social behavior. Direct instruction can take
the form of advice, social coaching, or simply serving as a supervisor of peer
play. *Parents as providers of opportunities* is constituted by such factors as the
neighborhood context that parents provide for children and the arrangement of
social contacts with other play partners. Finally, parents are viewed as influencing their children's peer relationships indirectly through their *child-rearing
practices and interactive styles*. This pathway is generally described as

an indirect influence on peer behavior because parents are not explicitly guiding or instructing their children on appropriate peer social behavior. Research in accord with each of these components of the tripartite model is reviewed here.

Parents as Managers of Children's Peer Relationships

Parents can influence their children's relationships through their role as direct instructors who facilitate peer relations by means of monitoring, supervision, and advising (Hartup, 1979; Parke, 1978). Monitoring refers to parents' efforts to closely observe, regulate, and supervise children's choices of social settings, activities, and friends. Monitoring exerted by parents in the family context has long been studied and its impact is well documented (Loeber & Stouthamer-Loeber, 1986; Rollins & Thomas, 1979). Lack of child monitoring has clearly been linked to child conduct problems (Patterson, 1986; Patterson, Reid, & Dishion, 1992; Patterson & Stouthamer-Loeber, 1984; Rutter & Garmezy, 1983). Monitoring, as a form of parental management, is particularly evident as children move into preadolescence and adolescence, since this period marks a transition in the relative importance of family and peers as sources of influence on social relationships (Parke et al., 1998). Research has revealed that the more parents monitored their sons' behavior and whereabouts, the less likely it was that the adolescents engaged in court-reported delinquency, attacks against property, and rule breaking outside the home (Patterson & Stouthamer-Loeber, 1984). Finally, Patterson and colleagues (Dishion, Reid, & Patterson, 1988; Snyder, Dishion, & Patterson, 1986) argued that ineffective parenting, especially ineffective parental monitoring, leads children to acquire poor social skills, which in turn leads to association with deviant peers in childhood and adolescence.

Research has also been directed at a particular aspect of the role of parent as direct instructor, namely, as a supervisor of children's peer play. Based on observed sessions in a laboratory playroom, Bhavnagri and Parke (1985) found that 2-year-old children's social competence with an unfamiliar peer was rated higher during periods of parental (mother) supervision. When assisted by a parent, children exhibited more cooperation, turn taking, and longer play bouts than when playing without assistance. In a similar investigation, both mothers and fathers were effective facilitators of children's play with peers (Bhavnagri & Parke, 1991). Supervision had less impact on the quality of play for older (3½ to 6 years of age) than for younger (2 to 3½ years of age) children. This indicates that parental supervision and active facilitation may be most salient for younger children as they are beginning to acquire social skills. Among older children, "greater supervision and guidance on the part of parents of children's peer relationships may function more as a remediatory effort" (Parke et al., 1998, p. 93).

As children develop, the primary aspects of parental management shift from direct involvement or supervision of ongoing activities to a "less public form of management, involving advice or consultation concerning appropriate ways of handling peer problems" (Parke et al., 1994, p. 129). Ladd, LeSieur, and Profilet (1993) have termed this form of direct parental management *consultation*. In their role as consultants, parents may initiate conversations about many aspects of peer interactions and social relationships, including how to manage conflicts, start friendships, react to peer pressure, and deal with teasing. Parents may also react to a specific interpersonal problem that a child is experiencing with a friend or peer and offer assistance with problem solving (Kuczynski, 1984; Ladd, Profilet, & Hart, 1992). Cohen (1989) found that during middle childhood, some forms of mothers' consulting were associated with positive outcomes, whereas other forms were linked with poor social relationships. Specifically, when mothers were supportive and non-interfering, the outcomes were positive. In contrast, mothers who were too highly involved (interfering) had children who were socially withdrawn. It appears that high levels of control may inhibit children's efforts to develop their own strategies for dealing with peer relations (Cohen, 1989).

Parents as Providers of Opportunities for Peer Contacts

Parents are the undisputed architects of the social environment that their children occupy. Young children are especially dependent on their parents to provide opportunities for social contacts. Consequently, one pathway by which parents may exert an influence on children's social development is choice of neighborhood (Parke & Bhavnagri, 1989). For example, research on neighborhood ecology demonstrated that children's opportunities for peer–peer contact are greater in neighborhoods that have flat landscapes, amenities such as sidewalks and playgrounds, and a dense child population (Berg & Medrich, 1980; Medrich, Roizen, Rubin, & Buckley, 1982). Moreover, these investigations showed that children have larger friendship networks and more spontaneous play arrangements when houses are closely spaced and have few barriers between them.

Beyond selection of neighborhood, parents influence children's social development through the arrangement of informal peer contacts and regulation of peer play partners. Ladd and colleagues (Ladd, 1992; Ladd & Golter, 1988; Ladd & Hart, 1991) hypothesized that by initiating play opportunities with peers, parents may facilitate children's entrance into the peer culture. In research with preschool children, parents who initiated and arranged peer contacts, as compared to those who did not, had children with larger networks of playmates and more consistent partners (Ladd & Golter, 1988). Further, boys with more parent-initiated contacts were more likely to be accepted by their classmates following entrance into kindergarten.

Parent–Child Interaction

A third distinct line of research has documented that parents influence their children's social relationships indirectly through ongoing parent–child interaction patterns. This pathway is generally described as an indirect influence on peer behavior because parents are not explicitly guiding their children's social development. However, as articulated by Parke et al. (1994), "the foundation of this line of research has been the assumption that parent–child face-to-face interaction may provide opportunities to learn, rehearse, and refine social skills that in turn will be useful in children's interactions with peers" (p. 116).

The linkage of the affective quality, or emotional expressiveness, of the parent–child relationship with children's social outcomes has received much attention. Parke and colleagues (Burks, Carson, & Parke, 1987; MacDonald & Parke, 1984) found that among 3- to 5-year-olds, popular boys have parents who are engaging, verbally stimulating, and who elicit positive affect during play; popular girls also tend to have affect-eliciting fathers. Another investigation showed that greater self-reported parental expressiveness is associated with children's greater peer competence; the more expressive the parents, the more prosocial and less shy the child (Cassidy, Parke, Butkovsky, & Braungart, 1992). Carson and Parke (1996) examined the extent to which affect displayed during parents' physical play with their children was related to their concurrent peer competence. Findings suggested that parents who were more likely to engage in negative affect sequences had children who were also likely to do so. Fathers who were more likely to respond to their children's negative affect displays with reciprocal negative affect had children who avoided others more, were more physically and verbally aggressive, and shared less (Isley, O'Neil, & Parke, 1996).

Investigators have also proposed that parents' disciplinary styles may influence the nature of children's social relations (Cohn et al., 1991; Putallaz & Heflin, 1990). Early studies demonstrated that parents who employed power-assertive disciplinary techniques (e.g., commands, physical force) tended to have children who were more aggressive and domineering with peers. In contrast, parents who utilized more inductive methods of discipline had children that exhibited more prosocial orientations toward peers (Becker, 1964; Hoffman, 1960; Zahn-Waxler, Radke-Yarrow, & King, 1979). More recent investigations have supported these findings, such that "extreme levels of control (both high and low levels), as expressed through disciplinary strategies, may have a deleterious effect on children's social competence" (Campbell, 1999, p. 17). Specifically, Hart, Ladd, and Burleson (1990) found that children whose parents used power-assertive discipline strategies were more likely to believe that unfriendly strategies would lead to successful outcomes. These children were also more likely to be rejected by their peers. Finally, additional evidence of a connection between parents' disciplinary styles and children's social outcomes derives from a series of investigations by Dishion and colleagues (Dishion, 1990,

1994; Dishion, Patterson, Stoolmiller, & Skinner, 1991; Vuchinich, Bank, & Patterson, 1992). Taken together, these studies documented that coercive, inconsistent disciplinary styles would encourage children to develop antisocial behavior, which in turn would lead children to be rejected by peers.

PARENTING AND CHILDREN'S MORAL DEVELOPMENT

Empirical research has examined the association of parental characteristics and socialization practices with a variety of morally relevant behaviors in children. While not exhaustive, this review focuses on four critical aspects of parenting that have been linked with children's moral development: disciplinary practices, the affective quality of the parent–child relationship, parental modeling, and promotion of autonomous thinking.

Parents' Disciplinary Practices

Comprehensive reviews of modes of discipline and their relation to children's moral development have been published by Hoffman (1970) and Brody and Shaffer (1982). These reviews, as well as subsequent discussions of parental disciplinary practices, have made clear the differential effects of power-assertive versus inductive disciplinary techniques. Power-assertive disciplinary practices are those in which parents use threats, commands, or physical force to achieve compliance. In contrast, inductive discipline involves pointing out the effects of the child's misbehavior on others ("She feels so sad because you won't give her back her doll") (Hoffman, 1988). In general, Hoffman (1970, 1983) and Brody and Shaffer (1982) found that inductive reasoning practices are associated with higher levels of morality; power-assertive practices undermine children's moral reasoning.

More recent studies have upheld the positive association between inductive parental practices and moral reasoning in offspring (de Veer & Janssens, 1992; Janssen, Janssens, & Gerris, 1992; Janssens & Gerris, 1992). Further, parental inductions that underscore the consequences of the child's behavior for another (e.g., "Now you've made Matthew cry") have been associated with children's empathy and prosocial behavior (Karylowski, 1982; Moore & Eisenberg, 1984; Radke-Yarrow, Zahn-Waxler, & Chapman, 1983). One investigation found that for children as young as two years of age, mothers who reported using inductions had children who exhibited relatively high levels of prosocial behavior toward others (Zahn-Waxler et al., 1979). In sum, it appears that inductive techniques are related to higher levels of empathy in children, which in turn are related to children's prosocial behavior.

Power-assertive (physical punishment, deprivation of privileges) disciplinary practices, in contrast, exhibit negative associations with children's moral reasoning, prosocial orientation, and resistance to temptation (Brody & Shaffer, 1982; Hoffman, 1983; Moore & Eisenberg, 1984). Using both maternal reports and observations of mother-child interaction, Kochanska (1991) examined mothers' disciplinary practices in toddlerhood, then correlated these measures with children's reports of moral behaviors at ages 8 through 10. Results indicated that mothers who emphasized power assertion and coercive discipline, rather than democratic modes of discipline, had children who manifested lower levels of guilt and moral orientation. Despite the evident trend in these findings, researchers have noted that the occasional, measured, and rational use of power-assertive techniques within the context of a positive parent–child relationship is associated with children's socially responsible behavior (Baumrind, 1971; Hoffman, 1983).

The Affective Climate of the Parent–Child Relationship

Theorists have emphasized the salience of the affective context in which parental socialization efforts are embedded (Dix, 1991; Hoffman, 1970). Quite simply, Hoffman postulated that the optimal environment for socialization is one in which the parents exhibit high levels of warmth. Children would be more likely to attend to and care about pleasing their parents in socialization environments that are warm and supportive (Eisenberg & Murphy, 1995). These theoretical suppositions have received some support (Buck, Walsh, & Rothman, 1981; Speicher, 1992). In one investigation, children's moral growth was associated with a supportive and positive family environment during family discussions (Walker & Taylor, 1991).

Others studies have presented less definitive support for the role of parental warmth and nurturance upon children's moral reasoning and development. For example, Hoffman and Saltzstein (1967) found that paternal affection was unrelated to children's moral reasoning. Smart and Smart (1976), examining school-age children, uncovered differential effects of parental support on levels of children's moral reasoning, documented by a significant association for boys but not girls. A longitudinal investigation of males from 10 to 30 years of age found that paternal affective involvement correlated with males' moral reasoning until age 26, although significant relations were not found for mothers (Hart, 1988). Given the mixed support for the association between parental warmth and various moral outcomes, it has been suggested that warmth does not exert a direct effect on children's moral development. Instead, parental warmth may function as a moderator variable, influencing the overall effectiveness of other parental strategies that exert direct effects on children's moral development (Eisenberg & Murphy, 1995).

Parental Modeling

Modeling refers to providing examples of behaviors for others to imitate. Accordingly, a reasonable line of inquiry in this area of research would be whether the behavioral examples that parents provide for their children are related to aspects of children's moral development. Unfortunately, few studies involving children and parents have directly examined this linkage. Results from laboratory studies have shown, however, that children exposed to dishonest models were more likely to act dishonest themselves (Burton, 1976). Furthermore, parental honesty was associated with children's honesty across situations (Hartshorne & May, 1928), and mothers of liars were more likely to report lying themselves than mothers of non-liars (Lewis, 1931; Stouthamer-Loeber, 1986).

It is clear from laboratory work, however, that subjects (children and adults) who have viewed a prosocial model are more prosocial themselves than are those that have not viewed a prosocial model (Eisenberg & Mussen, 1989; Moore & Eisenberg, 1984; Radke-Yarrow et al., 1983). Particularly compelling evidence of the effects of parental modeling upon children's moral outcomes derives from two real-life situations. First, studies of Europeans who saved Jews from the Nazis during World War II found that rescuers reported coming from families in which helpfulness and generosity were routinely modeled (London, 1970; Oliner & Oliner, 1988). Second, a study of the "freedom riders" of the late 1950s and early 1960s reported similar findings. Freedom riders were young adults who became involved in civil rights activities to increase opportunities for African Americans in the southern United States. Often at much danger to themselves, these individuals routinely sacrificed jobs and homes to support the civil rights cause. Rosenhan (1970) reported that these highly committed individuals described their parents as models of prosocial behavior who were devoted to working for worthy causes and often discussed their activities with their children. In sum, there appears to be sufficient evidence to contend that parental modeling of prosocial behavior is associated with children's willingness to demonstrate concern for others, even at a cost to themselves.

Promotion of Autonomous Thinking

A final research area considered here has demonstrated an association between parenting practices that promote children's autonomy and autonomous thinking and higher levels of children's moral reasoning. For example, parents who encouraged children's decision making and participation in discussions were more likely to have children with relatively higher levels of moral reasoning (Holstein, 1972). For adolescent boys, the level of moral reasoning increased when maternal punitiveness and control was low and when mothers placed little emphasis on maintaining boundaries between the child and others (Leahy, 1981). Eisenberg (1977) found that high school girls' increased reasoning about moral dilemmas was associated with their reports of maternal emphasis on autonomy granting.

Studies of observed styles of parent–child interactions have also supported this general trend. For example, Buck et al. (1981) examined parenting practices during a discussion of how to handle sons' aggression and linked these observations to preadolescent boys' moral reasoning. Results indicated that higher-reasoning boys had parents who used reasoning themselves, took into consideration their son's view, and encouraged the son to express his view. Similarly, Walker and Taylor (1991) investigated parents' interaction style during a discussion of moral issues with their 1st, 4th, 7th, or 10th grade child and used this information to predict their moral reasoning two years later. A Socratic questioning style, supportive interactions, and the presentation of higher-level reasoning were the parenting behaviors that best predicted children's moral growth. Notably, parenting behaviors such as critiquing, directly challenging the child's reasoning, or simply providing information were not associated with children's moral growth. Thus, across several studies it appears that children's moral development is best facilitated when parents encourage the consideration of autonomous, higher-level moral thinking in a supportive, non-confrontational manner.

PARENTING AND CHILDREN'S COGNITIVE DEVELOPMENT

Studies reviewed by Plomin (1988) suggested that at least half the variance in general cognitive ability as measured by IQ is due to genetic factors. In contrast, Sternberg and Williams (1995) have made the contention that "the existence of a genetic contribution to intelligence does not prevent you [parents] from intervening in your child's cognitive growth" (p. 260). Regardless of the role of genetics, parents still exert an influence on the cognitive competence of children. This section presents two parenting research foci that have been associated with children's cognitive outcomes: child-rearing styles and parental involvement.

Child-Rearing Styles and Cognitive Development

In a series of landmark studies, Baumrind (1966, 1967, 1975, 1978) collected information on child-rearing styles through direct observations of parents and children in laboratory and natural settings, structured interviews, and standardized psychological tests. Cluster and factor analytic techniques applied to these observations yielded two broad dimensions of child rearing: demandingness (or control) and responsiveness (Baumrind, 1991). From these two dimensions, Baumrind created the widely known typology of parenting styles (see Table 9.1).

Authoritative parents are demanding and responsive, and they employ a rational, democratic approach in which parents' and children's rights are respected. Authoritarian parents are demanding but are low in responsiveness to children's rights and needs. Thus, conformity and obedience are valued over open communication with the child. Permissive parents are responsive but undemanding and they exhibit an overly tolerant approach to child rearing.

Table 9.1
A Two-Dimensional Typology of Parenting Styles

	Responsive	Unresponsive
Demanding	Authoritative Parent	Authoritarian Parent
Undemanding	Permissive Parent	Uninvolved Parent

Subsequently, an extensive line of research has linked authoritative, authoritarian, and permissive parenting to child and adolescent cognitive competence (Melby & Conger, 1996; Wentzel, 1994). Using large samples of adolescents who varied in ethnicity, family structure, socioeconomic status, and community type, research has demonstrated that adolescents whose parents are accepting, firm, and democratic (i.e., authoritative) score higher on measures of academic performance (Dornbusch, Ritter, Leiderman, Roberts, & Fraleigh, 1987; Lamborn, Mounts, Steinberg, & Dornbusch, 1991; Steinberg, Elmen, & Mounts, 1989; Steinberg, Mounts, Lamborn, & Dornbusch, 1991). The authoritative style predicted higher grades, whereas authoritarian and permissive styles were associated with lower grades. Of all child-rearing styles, an inconsistent approach (a mix of authoritarian and permissive techniques) predicted the poorest school performance (Dornbusch et al., 1987). Finally, Patterson and colleagues (Dishion, 1990; Patterson & Bank, 1990) also documented significant associations between parenting styles and early adolescent boys' school success. Their results indicated that inconsistent and harsh discipline is associated with the lowest levels of academic achievement.

What accounts for these associations between styles of parenting and child and adolescent cognitive competence? Authoritative parenting styles likely promote cognitive development by encouraging independent problem solving and critical thinking. In contrast, authoritarian styles are believed to detract from cognitive competence by discouraging active exploration and problem solving and encouraging dependence on adult control and guidance (Hess & McDevitt, 1984; Wentzel, 1994). Other explanations have been offered for the efficacy of authoritative parenting. Authoritative parents are most likely to adjust their expectations to match their children's capacity to take responsibility for their own behavior. For example, parents who engage in joint decision making with their adolescents and gradually permit more autonomy with age, have children who achieve especially well (Dornbusch, Ritter, Mont-Reynaud, & Chen, 1990). Parental warmth and firmness, when accompanied by open discussion, contributes to adolescents' constructive thinking and self-control and allows adolescents to feel competent and valued. Each of these factors is then related, in turn, to independent effort and achievement among high school students (Baumrind, 1991; Carlson, Hsu, & Cooper, 1990; Wentzel & Feldman, 1993).

Parental Involvement: Association of Specific Parenting Practices with Cognitive Development

Parental involvement in schooling is related to children's achievement (Dornbusch et al., 1987), and consequently has been a key concern in research (Eccles & Harold, 1996; Epstein, 1987b). A diversity of definitions of parental involvement has emerged within this line of research. As Keith (1991) noted, some investigators have used parental involvement to refer to parental participation in school activities (Cervone & O'Leary, 1982), whereas others use the term to refer to a more general interest in students' academic and social lives (Keith, Reimers, Fehrmann, Pottebaum, & Aubey, 1986). However, despite methodological and definitional contrasts, research is generally consistent in suggesting positive effects for parental involvement on student learning (Keith, 1991). For example, in research on early adolescents, researchers proposed that authoritative parenting has its effects on adolescent achievement primarily by way of its relation to parental involvement in school activities (Steinberg, Lamborn, Dornbusch, & Darling, 1992). Results from that investigation showed that parents who attended school programs and extracurricular activities and participated in course selection had children who earned high grades, spent a significant amount of time on homework, had high expectations for their own achievement, and had strong academic self-concepts.

The following paragraphs review three areas of parent involvement and parenting practices that exhibit documented effects on children's cognitive competence: literacy-related parenting practices, homework-related parenting practices, and parents' educational expectations and aspirations for their children. Literacy-related parenting practices are one of the critical means through which parents can influence their children's academic competence (Connors & Epstein, 1995; Scott-Jones, 1995). For example, professionals have urged parents to establish a rich oral language environment in the home from infancy in order to increase the chances of children's school success (Morisset, 1993; Young & Marx, 1992). Further, researchers found that children's reading ability was associated with the amount of reading material in the home (Hess, Holloway, Dickson, & Price, 1984). Overall, the number and types of educational resources provided to elementary-aged children in the home have been linked to various aspects of academic and intellectual success (Hess & Holloway, 1984; Stevenson & Lee, 1990). Parents can also create a stimulating and rich print or written language environment by serving as model readers for their children (Nickerson, 1992; Strickland & Cullinan, 1990). Topping (1985) identified concrete practices that parents may employ to facilitate children's reading success. The specific factors included (1) allowing more time for children to practice reading at home, (2) making reading more valued and enjoyable, (3) giving children feedback or praise, and (4) modeling reading and writing behaviors at home. Finally, parents may influence children's reading skills through listening to a child read and from exploring and sharing books (Evans, 1993; Wolfendale, 1985).

Another area in which parents exert an effect upon their children's learning is through homework-related parenting practices. Teachers often give homework to facilitate students' independence and responsibility in their academic endeavors and to share classroom activities with parents (Epstein, 1987a; Parsons, Adler, & Kaczala, 1982). Moreover, parents and teachers are in agreement that parents have a role to play in children's homework (Epstein & Dauber, 1991). Given these observations, findings on parents' involvement in and monitoring of homework activities are especially critical. Clark (1993) examined the parenting practices in predominantly African-American and Hispanic families with high- and low-achieving 3rd graders. The findings delineated the distinguishing qualities of the homes of high-achieving students, in that these parents: (1) checked homework for neatness and accuracy, (2) were knowledgeable about how to help with homework, and (3) demonstrated how to use the dictionary and reference materials. Generally, parents of elementary school children report spending more time helping their children and feel more capable of helping with homework than parents of students in the middle grades (Dauber & Epstein, 1993). For 8th graders in the National Education Longitudinal Survey of 1988, 45% reported that parents often checked their homework. Parental checking of homework was positively related to the amount of time students spent on homework, but was not related to students' grades (Muller & Kerbow, 1993). In sum, parental monitoring and involvement in homework-related activities contribute to children's achievement. Ideally, parental monitoring will eventually lead to self-monitoring and self-management strategies in the child (Scott-Jones, 1995).

A third research focus has examined the association of parents' beliefs about their children with their children's cognitive and academic accomplishments. Early work in this area documented significant relations between parents' educational expectations and aspirations and children's school performance (Crandall, 1963; Hess & Holloway, 1984; Miller, 1988; Seginer, 1983). Generally, high-achieving children tend to have families who hold high educational expectations (Seginer, 1983). For example, in an Australian sample, parents' expectations for post-secondary education were positively related to 9th graders' achievement, intentions to remain in school past 10th grade, and educational plans (Ainley, Foreman, & Sheret, 1991). Similarly, students' science achievement was correlated more highly with parental educational aspirations than SES (Reynolds & Walberg, 1992), and parental expectations were found to mediate the association between math and science achievement and prior achievement (Reynolds & Walberg, 1991). Parents' expectations for post-secondary education are also significant predictors of college attendance (Davies & Kandel, 1981; Hossler & Stage, 1992). Carpenter and Fleishman (1987) determined that students are more likely to attend college when their parents expect them to go to college, encourage them to explore options, and help them prepare for college. Lastly, one study demonstrated that a consistent "yes" response over three years to the question, "Is it taken for granted in your home that you will attend post-secondary education?" was positively associated with college attendance (Conklin & Dailey, 1981).

CONCLUSION

Underpinning all of this research, it is safe to say that we study parenting mainly because we are interested in, and concerned about, children's development. There are several beneficiaries of parenting research, perhaps most obviously, parents themselves (Jaffe, 1997; National Conference, 1972). Parents benefit from having good, sound information on topics such as effective discipline methods. Teachers, as interactors who work with both children and parents, benefit from parenting research through support they provide to parents and through knowledge of children's developmental capabilities. Knowledge that results from the study of parenting is of potential use to anyone who works with children and parents, including coaches, guidance counselors, psychologists, social workers, and pediatricians. Ultimately, however, the primary beneficiaries of parenting research are children themselves, especially when we utilize this knowledge base to create healthy, supportive, and nurturant family and community environments in which children are allowed to reach their full potential.

REFERENCES

Ainley, J., Foreman, J., & Sheret, M. (1991). High school factors that influence students to remain in school. *Journal of Educational Research, 85,* 69–80.

Baumrind, D. (1966). Effects of authoritative parental control on child behavior. *Child Development, 37,* 887–907.

Baumrind, D. (1967). Child care practices anteceding three patterns of preschool behavior. *Genetic Psychology Monographs, 75,* 43–88.

Baumrind, D. (1971). Current patterns of parental authority. *Developmental Psychology Monographs, 4,* 1–103.

Baumrind, D. (1975). Early socialization and adolescent competence. In S. E. Dragastin & G. H. Elder (Eds.), *Adolescence in the life cycle: Psychological change and social context* (pp. 117–143). Washington, DC: Hemisphere.

Baumrind, D. (1978). Parental disciplinary patterns and social competence in children. *Youth & Society, 9,* 239–276.

Baumrind, D. (1991). Effective parenting during the early adolescent tradition. In P. A. Cowan & M. Hetherington (Eds.), *Family transitions* (pp. 111–163). Hillsdale, NJ: Lawrence Erlbaum.

Becker, W. C. (1964). Consequences of different kinds of parental discipline. In M. L. Hoffman & L. W. Hoffman (Eds.), *Review of child development research* (Vol. 1, pp. 169–208). New York: Russell Sage Foundation.

Berg, M., & Medrich, E. A. (1980). Children in four neighborhoods: Physical environment and its effects on play and play patterns. *Environment and Behavior, 12,* 320–348.

Bhavnagri, N., & Parke, R. D. (1985, April). *Parents as facilitators of preschool peer-peer interaction.* Paper presented at the Biennial Meeting of the Society for Research in Child Development, Toronto.

Bhavnagri, N., & Parke, R. D. (1991). Parents as direct facilitators of children's peer relationships: Effects of age of child and sex of parent. *Journal of Personal and Social Relationships, 8*, 423–440.

Brody, G. H., & Shaffer, D. R. (1982). Contributions of parents and peers to children's moral socialization. *Developmental Review, 2*, 31–75.

Brooks, J. B. (1991). *The process of parenting* (3rd ed.). Mountain View, CA: Mayfield.

Buck, L. Z., Walsh, W. F., & Rothman, G. (1981). Relationship between parental moral judgement and socialization. *Youth and Society, 13*, 91–116.

Burks, V. M., Carson, J. L., & Parke, R. D. (1987). *Parent–child interactional styles of popular and rejected children.* Unpublished manuscript, University of Illinois, Urbana, IL.

Burton, R. V. (1976). Honesty and dishonesty. In T. Lickona (Ed.), *Moral development and behavior: Theory, research, and social issues* (pp. 173–197). New York: Holt, Rinehart and Winston.

Campbell, J. J. (1999). *Familial antecedents to children's overt and relational aggression.* Unpublished doctoral dissertation, University of North Carolina at Greensboro.

Carlson, C., Hsu, J., & Cooper, C. R. (1990, March). *Predicting school achievement in early adolescence: The role of family process.* Paper presented at the Conference on Human Development, Atlanta, GA.

Carpenter, P. G., & Fleishman, J. A. (1987). Linking intentions and behavior: Australian students' college plans and college attendance. *American Educational Research Journal, 24*, 79–105.

Carson, J. L., & Parke, R. D. (1996). Reciprocal negative affect in parent-child interactions and children's peer competency. *Child Development, 67*, 2217–2226.

Cassidy, J., Parke, R. D., Butkovsky, L., & Braungart, J. (1992). Family-peer connections: The roles of emotional expressiveness within the family and children's understanding of emotions. *Child Development, 63*, 603–618.

Cervone, B. T., & O'Leary, K. (1982). A conceptual framework for parent involvement. *Educational Leadership, 40 (2)*, 48–49.

Clark, R. M. (1993). Homework-focused parenting practices that positively affect student achievement. In N. F. Chavkin (Ed.), *Families and schools in a pluralistic society* (pp. 85–106). Albany: State University of New York Press.

Cohen, D. B. (1999). *Stranger in the nest: Do parents really shape their child's personality, intelligence, or character?* New York: Wiley.

Cohen, J. S. (1989). *Maternal involvement in children's peer relationships during middle childhood.* Unpublished doctoral dissertation, University of Waterloo, Waterloo, Canada.

Cohn, D. A., Patterson, C. J., & Christopoulos, C. (1991). The family and children's peer relations. *Journal of Social and Personal Relationships, 8*, 315–346.

Conklin, M. E., & Dailey, A. R. (1981). Does consistency of parental encouragement matter for secondary students? *Sociology of Education, 54*, 254–262.

Connors, L. J., & Epstein, J. L. (1995). Parent and school partnerships. In M. H. Bornstein (Ed.), *Handbook of parenting* (Vol. 4, pp. 437–458). Mahwah, NJ: Lawrence Erlbaum.

Crandall, V. J. (1963). Achievement. In H. W. Stevenson (Ed.), *Child psychology: The sixty-second yearbook of the National Society for the Study of Education* (pp. 416–459). Chicago: University of Chicago Press.

Damon, W. (1983). *Social and personality development: Infancy through adolescence.* New York: W. W. Norton.

Dauber, S. L., & Epstein, J. L. (1993). Parents' attitudes and practices of involvement in inner-city elementary and middle schools. In N. F. Chavkin (Ed.), *Families and schools in a pluralistic society* (pp. 53–72). Albany: State University of New York Press.

Davies, M., & Kandel, D. (1981). Parental and peer influences on adolescents' educational plans: Some further evidence. *American Journal of Sociology, 87*, 363–387.

de Veer, A.J.E., & Janssens, J.M.A. (1992). Victim-oriented discipline and the child's internalization of norms. In J. M. Janssens & J. R. Gerris (Eds.), *Child rearing: Influence on prosocial and moral development* (pp. 145–168). Amsterdam: Swets & Zeitlinger.

Dishion, T. J. (1990). The family ecology of boys' peer relations in middle childhood. *Child Development, 61*, 874–892.

Dishion, T. J. (1994). The world of parents and peers: Coercive exchanges and children's social adaptation. *Social Development, 3*, 255–268.

Dishion, T. J., Patterson, G. R., Stoolmiller, M., & Skinner, M. L. (1991). Family, school, and behavioral antecedents to early adolescent involvement with antisocial peers. *Developmental Psychology, 27*, 172–180.

Dishion, T. J., Reid, J. B., & Patterson, G. R. (1988). Empirical guidelines for a family intervention for adolescent drug use. *Journal of Chemical Dependency Treatment, 2*, 181–216.

Dix, T. (1991). The affective organization of parenting: Adaptive and maladaptive processes. *Psychological Bulletin, 100*, 3–25.

Dornbusch, S. M., Ritter, P. L., Leiderman, P. H., Roberts, D. F., & Fraleigh, M. J. (1987). The relation of parenting style to adolescent school performance. *Child Development, 58*, 1244–1257.

Dornbusch, S. M., Ritter, P. L., Mont-Reynaud, R., & Chen, Z. (1990). Family decision making and academic performance in a diverse high school population. *Journal of Adolescent Research, 5*, 143–160.

Eccles, J. S., & Harold, R. D. (1996). Family involvement in children's and adolescents' schooling. In A. Booth & J. F. Dunn (Eds.), *Family-school links: How do they affect educational outcomes?* (pp. 3–34). Mahwah, NJ: Lawrence Erlbaum.

Eisenberg, N. (1977). The development of prosocial moral judgment and its correlates. *Dissertation Abstracts International, 37*, 4753B (University Microfilms No. 77–444).

Eisenberg, N., & Murphy, B. (1995). Parenting and children's moral development. In M. H. Bornstein (Ed.), *Handbook of parenting* (Vol. 4, pp. 227–257). Mahwah, NJ: Lawrence Erlbaum.

Eisenberg, N., & Mussen, P. (1989). *The roots of prosocial behavior in children.* Cambridge, England: Cambridge University Press.

Epstein, J. L. (1987a). *Homework practices, achievements, and behaviors of elementary school students* (Report No. 26). Baltimore, MD: Johns Hopkins University, Center for Research on Elementary and Middle Schools.

Epstein, J. L. (1987b). Toward a theory of family-school connections: Teacher practices and parent involvement across the school years. In K. Hurrelmann, F. Kaufmann, & F. Losel (Eds.), *Social intervention: Potential and constraints* (pp. 121–136). New York: de Gruyter.

Epstein, J. L., & Dauber, S. L. (1991). School programs and teacher practices of parent involvement in inner-city elementary and middle schools. *Elementary School Journal, 91,* 289–303.

Evans, C. A. (1993, April). *Who's teaching what to whom? Parents and young fluent readers.* Paper presented at the annual meeting of the American Educational Research Association, Atlanta, GA.

Guttman, D. (1975). Parenthood: A key to the comparative study of the life cycle. In N. Daton & L. H. Ginsberg (Eds.), *Life-span developmental psychology: Normative life crises* (pp. 167–184). New York: Academic Press.

Hamner, T. J., & Turner, P. H. (1996). *Parenting in contemporary society* (3rd ed.). Boston: Allyn & Bacon.

Harris, J. R. (1998). *The nurture assumption: Why children turn out the way they do.* New York: The Free Press.

Hart, C. H., Ladd, G. W., & Burleson, B. R. (1990). Children's expectations of the outcomes of social strategies: Relations with sociometric status and maternal disciplinary styles. *Child Development, 61,* 127–137.

Hart, D. (1988). A longitudinal study of adolescents' socialization and identification as predictors of adult moral judgment development. *Merrill-Palmer Quarterly, 34,* 245–260.

Hartshorne, H., & May, M. (1928). *Studies in the nature of character: Vol. 1. Studies in deceit.* New York: The Macmillan Co.

Hartup, W. W. (1979). The two social worlds of childhood. *American Psychologist, 34,* 944–950.

Hess, R. D., & Holloway, S. D. (1984). Family and school as educational institutions. In R. D. Parke (Ed.), *Review of child development research* (pp. 179–222). Chicago: University of Chicago Press.

Hess, R. D., Holloway, S. D., Dickson, W. P., & Price, G. G. (1984). Maternal variables as predictors of children's school readiness and later achievement in vocabulary and mathematics in sixth grade. *Child Development, 55,* 1902–1912.

Hess, R. D., & McDevitt, T. M. (1984). Some cognitive consequences of maternal intervention techniques: A longitudinal study. *Child Development, 55,* 2017–2030.

Hoffman, M. L. (1960). Power assertion by the parent and its impact on the child. *Child Development, 31,* 129–143.

Hoffman, M. L. (1970). Moral development. In P. H. Mussen (Ed.), *Carmichael's manual of child development* (Vol. 2, pp. 261–359). New York: Wiley.

Hoffman, M. L. (1983). Affective and cognitive processes in moral internalization. In E. T. Higgins, D. N. Ruble, & W. W. Hartup (Eds.), *Social cognition and social development* (pp. 236–274). Cambridge, England: Cambridge University Press.

Hoffman, M. L. (1988). Moral development. In M. H. Bornstein & M. E. Lamb (Eds.), *Developmental psychology: An advanced textbook* (2nd ed., pp. 497–548). Hillsdale, NJ: Lawrence Erlbaum.

Hoffman, M. L., & Saltzstein, H. D. (1967). Parent discipline and the child's moral development. *Journal of Personality and Social Psychology, 5,* 45–57.

Holstein, C. (1972). The relation of children's moral judgment level to that of their parents and to communication patterns in the family. In R. C. Smart & M. S. Smart (Eds.), *Readings in child development and relationships* (pp. 484–494). New York: Macmillan.

Hossler, D., & Stage, F. K. (1992). Family and high school experience influences on the postsecondary educational plans of ninth grade students. *American Educational Research Journal, 29*, 425–451.

Isley, S., O'Neil, R., & Parke, R. D. (1996). The relation of parental affect and control behaviors to children's classroom acceptance: A concurrent and predictive analysis. *Early Education and Development, 7*, 7–23.

Jaffe, M. L. (1997). *Understanding parenting* (2nd ed.). Needham Heights, MA: Allyn & Bacon.

Janssen, A. W., Janssens, J. M., & Gerris, J. R. (Eds.). (1992). Parents' and children's levels of moral reasoning: Antecedents and consequences of parental discipline strategies. In J. M. Janssens & J. R. Gerris (Eds.), *Child rearing: Influence on prosocial and moral development* (pp. 169–196). Amsterdam: Swets & Zeitlinger.

Janssens, J. M., & Gerris, J. R. (1992). Child rearing, empathy, and prosocial development. In J. M. Janssens & J. R. Gerris (Eds.), *Child rearing: Influence on prosocial and moral development* (pp. 57–75). Amsterdam: Swets & Zeitlinger.

John Paul II. (1981). *Familiaris consortio*. [On the family]. Washington, DC: Office of Publishing Services, United States Catholic Conference.

Kagan, J. (1994). *The nature of the child*. New York: Basic Books.

Karylowski, J. (1982). Doing good to feel good v. doing good to make others feel good: Some child-rearing antecedents. *School Psychology International, 3*, 149–156.

Keith, T. A., Reimers, T. M., Fehrmann, P. G., Pottebaum, S. M., & Aubey, L. W. (1986). Parental involvement, homework, and TV time: Direct and indirect effects on high school achievement. *Journal of Educational Psychology, 78*, 373–380.

Keith, T. Z. (1991). Parent involvement and achievement in high school. In B. A. Hutson (Series Ed.) & S. B. Silvern (Vol. Ed.), *Advances in reading/language research. Vol. 5: Literacy through family, community, and school interaction* (pp. 125–141). Greenwich, CT: JAI Press.

Kochanska, G. (1991). Socialization and temperament in the development of guilt and conscience. *Child Development, 62*, 1379–1392.

Kuczynski, L. (1984). Socialization goals and mother-child interaction: Strategies for long-term and short-term compliance. *Developmental Psychology, 20*, 1061–1073.

Ladd, G. W. (1992). Themes and theories: Perspectives on process in family-peer relationships. In R. D. Parke & G. W. Ladd (Eds.), *Family-peer relationships: Modes of linkage* (pp. 3–34). Hillsdale, NJ: Lawrence Erlbaum.

Ladd, G. W., & Golter, B. S. (1988). Parents' management of preschoolers' peer relations: Is it related to children's social competence? *Developmental Psychology, 24*, 109–117.

Ladd, G. W., & Hart, C. H. (1991). *Parents' management of children's peer relations: Patterns associated with social competence*. Paper presented at the 11th Meeting of the International Society for Behavioral Development, Minneapolis, MN.

Ladd, G. W., LeSieur, K., & Profilet, S. M. (1993). Direct parental influences on young children's peer relations. In S. Duck (Ed.), *Learning about relationships* (Vol. 2, pp. 152–183). London: Sage.

Ladd, G. W., Profilet, S. M., & Hart, C. H. (1992). Parents' management of children's peer relations: Facilitating and supervising children's activities in the peer culture.

In R. Parke & G. Ladd (Eds.), *Family-peer relationships: Modes of linkage* (pp. 215–253). Hillsdale, NJ: Lawrence Erlbaum.

Lamb, M. E., Ketterlinus, R. D., & Fracasso, M. P. (1992). Parent-child relationships. In M. H. Bornstein & M. E. Lamb (Eds.), *Developmental psychology: An advanced textbook* (3rd ed., pp. 465–518). Hillsdale, NJ: Lawrence Erlbaum.

Lamborn, S. D., Mounts, N. S., Steinberg, L., & Dornbusch, S. M. (1991). Patterns of performance and adjustment among adolescents from authoritative, authoritarian, indulgent, and neglectful families. *Child Development, 62,* 1049–1065.

Leahy, R. L. (1981). Parental practices and the development of moral judgment and self-image disparity during adolescence. *Developmental Psychology, 17,* 580–594.

Lewis, M. (1931). How parental attitudes affect the problem of lying in children. *Smith College Studies in Social Work, 1,* 403–404.

Loeber, R., & Stouthamer-Loeber, M. (1986). Family factors as correlates and predictors of juvenile conduct problems and delinquency. In M. Tonry & N. Morris (Eds.), *Crime and justice: An annual review of research* (Vol. 7, pp. 29–149). Chicago: University of Chicago Press.

London, P. (1970). The rescuers: Motivational hypotheses about Christians who saved Jews from the Nazis. In J. Macaulay & L. Berkowitz (Eds.), *Altruism and helping behavior* (pp. 241–250). New York: Academic Press.

MacDonald, K., & Parke, R. D. (1984). Bridging the gap: Parent-child play interaction and peer interactive competence. *Child Development, 55,* 1265–1277.

Medrich, E. A., Roizen, J. A., Rubin, V., & Buckley, S. (1982). *The serious business of growing up: A study of children's lives outside school.* Berkeley: University of California Press.

Melby, J. N., & Conger, R. D. (1996). Parental behaviors and adolescent academic performance: A longitudinal analysis. *Journal of Research on Adolescence, 6,* 113–137.

Miller, S. (1988). Parents' beliefs about children's cognitive development. *Child Development, 59,* 259–285.

Moore, B., & Eisenberg, N. (1984). The development of altruism. In G. Whitehurst (Ed.), *Annuals in child development* (Vol. 1, pp. 107–174). New York: JSI Press.

Morisset, C. E. (1993). *Language and emotional milestones on the road to readiness* (Report No. 18). Baltimore, MD: Johns Hopkins University, Center on Families, Communities, Schools and Children's Learning.

Muller, C., & Kerbow, D. (1993). Parent involvement in the home, school, and community. In B. Schneider & J. S. Coleman (Eds.), *Parents, their children, and schools* (pp. 13–39). Boulder, CO: Westview.

National Conference of Catholic Bishops. (1972). *To teach as Jesus did: A pastoral message on Catholic education.* Washington, DC: United States Catholic Conference.

National Conference of Catholic Bishops. (1993). *Follow the way of love: A pastoral message of the U.S. Catholic bishops to families.* Washington, DC: United States Catholic Conference.

Nickerson, R. S. (1992). On the intergenerational transfer of high-order skills. In T. G. Sticht, B. A. McDonald, & M. J. Beeler (Eds.), *The intergenerational transfer of cognitive skills* (Vol. 2, pp. 159–171). Norwood, NJ: Ablex.

Oliner, S. P., & Oliner, P. M. (1988). *The altruistic personality: Rescuers of Jews in Nazi Europe.* New York: The Free Press.

Parke, R. D. (1978). Children's home environments: Social and cognitive effects. In I. Altman & J. F. Wohlhill (Eds.), *Children and the environment* (pp. 33–81). New York: Plenum.

Parke, R. D., & Bhavnagri, N. P. (1989). Parents as managers of children's peer relationships. In D. Belle (Ed.), *Children's social networks and social supports* (pp. 241–259). New York: Wiley.

Parke, R. D., Burks, V. M., Carson, J. L., Neville, B., & Boyum, L. A. (1994). Family-peer relationships: A tripartite model. In R. D. Parke & S. G. Kellam (Eds.), *Exploring family relationships within other social contexts* (pp. 115–145). Hillsdale, NJ: Lawrence Erlbaum.

Parke, R. D., Cassidy, J., Burks, V. M., Carson, J. L., & Boyum, L. (1992). Familial contribution to peer competence among young children: The role of interactive and affective processes. In R. D. Parke & G. W. Ladd (Eds.), *Family-peer relationships: Modes of linkage* (pp. 107–134). Hillsdale, NJ: Lawrence Erlbaum.

Parke, R. D., O'Neil, R., Isley, S., Spitzer, S., Welsh, M., Wang, S., Flyr, M., Simpkins, S., Strand, C., & Morales, M. (1998). Family-peer relationships: Cognitive, emotional, and ecological determinants. In M. Lewis & C. Feiring (Eds.), *Families, risk, and competence* (pp. 89–112). Mahwah, NJ: Lawrence Erlbaum.

Parker, J. G., & Asher, S. R. (1987). Peer relations and later personal adjustment: Are low accepted children at risk? *Psychological Bulletin, 102*, 357–389.

Parsons, J. E., Adler, T. F., & Kaczala, C. M. (1982). Socialization of achievement attitudes and beliefs: Parental influences. *Child Development, 53*, 310–321.

Patterson, G. R., & Bank, L. (1990). Some amplifying mechanisms for pathologic processes in families. In M. R. Gunnar & E. Thalen (Eds.), *The Minnesota symposia on child psychology* (Vol. 22, pp. 167–209). Hillsdale, NJ: Lawrence Erlbaum.

Patterson, G. R., Reid, J. B., & Dishion, T. J. (1992). *Antisocial boys*. Eugene, OR: Castalia.

Patterson, G. S. (1986). Maternal rejection: Determinant or product for deviant child behavior? In W. W. Hartup & Z. Rubin (Eds.), *Relationships and development* (pp. 73–94). Hillsdale, NJ: Lawrence Erlbaum.

Patterson, G. S., & Stouthamer-Loeber, M. (1984). The correlation of family management practices and delinquency. *Child Development, 55*, 1299–1307.

Plomin, R. (1988). The nature and nurture of cognitive abilities. In R. J. Sternberg (Ed.), *Advances in the psychology of human intelligence* (Vol. 4, pp. 1–33). Hillsdale, NJ: Lawrence Erlbaum.

Putallaz, M., & Heflin, A. H. (1990). Parent-child relations and peer rejection. In S. R. Asher & J. D. Coie (Eds.), *Peer rejection in childhood*. New York: Cambridge University Press.

Radke-Yarrow, M., Zahn-Waxler, C., & Chapman, M. (1983). Prosocial dispositions and behavior. In P. Mussen (Series Ed.) & E. M. Hetherington (Vol. Ed.), *Manual of child psychology: Vol. 4: Socialization, personality, and social development* (pp. 469–545). New York: Wiley.

Reynolds, A. J., & Walberg, H. J. (1991). A structural model of science achievement. *Journal of Educational Psychology, 83*, 97–107.

Reynolds, A. J., & Walberg, H. J. (1992). A structural model of science achievement and attitude: An extension to high school. *Journal of Educational Psychology, 84*, 371–382.

Rollins, B., & Thomas, D. (1979). Parental support, power, and control techniques in the socialization of children. In R.H.W. Burr, F. I. Nye, & I. Reiss (Eds.), *Contemporary theories about the family* (pp. 317–364). New York: The Free Press.

Rosenhan, D. L. (1970). The natural socialization of altruistic autonomy. In J. Macaulay & L. Berkowitz (Eds.), *Altruism and helping behavior* (pp. 251–268). New York: Academic Press.

Rutter, M., & Garmezy, N. (1983). Developmental psychopathology. In E. M. Hetherington (Ed.), *Handbook of child psychology* (Vol. 4, pp. 775–912). New York: Wiley.

Scott-Jones, D. (1995). Parent-child interactions and school achievement. In T. P. Gullotta (Series Ed.) & B. A. Ryan, G. R. Adams, T. P. Gullotta, R. P. Weissberg, & R. L. Hampton (Vol. Eds.), *Issues in children's and families' lives: The family-school connection: Theory, research, and practice* (Vol. 2, pp. 75–107). Thousand Oaks, CA: Sage.

Seginer, R. (1983). Parents' educational expectations and children's academic achievements: A literature review. *Merrill-Palmer Quarterly, 29,* 1–23.

Smart, R. C., & Smart, M. S. (1976). Preadolescents' perceptions of parents and their relations to a test of responses to moral dilemmas. *Social Behavior and Personality, 4,* 297–308.

Snyder, J., Dishion, T. J., & Patterson, G. R. (1986). Determinants and consequences of associating with deviant peers during preadolescence and adolescence. *Journal of Early Adolescence, 6,* 29–43.

Speicher, B. (1992). Adolescent moral judgment and patterns of family interaction. *Journal of Family Psychology, 6,* 128–138.

Steinberg, L., Elmen, J. D., & Mounts, N. S. (1989). Authoritative parenting, psychosocial maturity, and academic success among adolescents. *Child Development, 60,* 1424–1436.

Steinberg, L., Lamborn, S. D., Dornbusch, S. M., & Darling, N. (1992). Impact of parenting practices on adolescent achievement: Authoritative parenting, school involvement, and encouragement to succeed. *Child Development, 63,* 1266–1281.

Steinberg, L., Mounts, N. S., Lamborn, S. D., & Dornbusch, S. M. (1991). Authoritative parenting and adolescent adjustment across varied ecological niches. *Journal of Research on Adolescence, 1,* 19–36.

Sternberg, R. J., & Williams, W. M. (1995). Parenting toward cognitive competence. In M. H. Bornstein (Ed.), *Handbook of parenting* (Vol. 4, pp. 259–275). Mahwah, NJ: Lawrence Erlbaum.

Stevenson, H. W., & Lee, S. (1990). Contexts of achievement. *Monographs of the Society for Research in Child Development, 55* (1–2, Serial No. 221).

Stouthamer-Loeber, M. (1986). Lying as a problem behavior in children: A review. *Clinical Psychology Review, 6,* 267–289.

Strickland, D., & Cullinan, B. (1990). Afterword. In M. J. Adams (Ed.), *Beginning to read: Thinking and learning about print* (pp. 426–434). Cambridge, MA: MIT Press.

Sullivan, H. S. (1953). *The interpersonal theory of psychiatry.* New York: W. W. Norton.

Topping, K. (1985). Parental involvement in reading: Theoretical and empirical background. In K. Topping & S. Wolfendale (Eds.), *Parental involvement in reading* (pp. 17–31). London: Croom Helm.

Vuchinich, S., Bank, L., & Patterson, G. R. (1992). Parenting, peers, and the stability of antisocial behavior in preadolescent boys. *Developmental Psychology, 28,* 510–521.

Walker, L. J., & Taylor, J. H. (1991). Family interactions and the development of moral reasoning. *Child Development, 62,* 264–283.

Wentzel, K. R. (1994). Family functioning and academic achievement in middle school: A social-emotional perspective. *Journal of Early Adolescence, 14,* 268–291.

Wentzel, K. R., & Feldman, S. S. (1993). Parental predictors of boys' self-restraint and motivation to achieve at school: A longitudinal study. *Journal of Early Adolescence, 13,* 183–203.

Wolfendale, S. (1985). An introduction to parent listening. In K. Topping & S. Wolfendale (Eds.), *Parental involvement in reading* (pp. 35–41). London: Croom Helm.

Young, K., & Marx, E. (1992). *What does learning mean for infants and toddlers? The contributions of the child, the family, and the community* (Report No. 3). Baltimore, MD: Johns Hopkins University, Center on Families, Communities, Schools, and Children's Learning.

Youniss, J., & Haynie, D. L. (1992). Friendship in adolescence. *Journal of Developmental and Behavioral Pediatrics, 13,* 59–66.

Zahn-Waxler, C., Radke-Yarrow, M., & King, R. (1979). Childrearing and children's prosocial initiations toward victims of distress. *Child Development, 50,* 319–330.

Chapter 10

Pluralism and Public Policy: Catholic Schools in the United States

Dale McDonald

We are a religious people whose institutions presuppose a Supreme Being. When the state encourages religious instruction or cooperates with religious authorities by adjusting the schedule of public events to sectarian needs, it follows the best of our traditions. For then it respects the religious nature of our people and accommodates the public service to their spiritual needs. To hold that it may not would be to find in the Constitution a requirement that the government show a callous indifference to religious groups.
—*Zorach v. Clauson*, 343 U.S. 306, 313, 1952

In framing the U.S. Constitution, the Founders faced a dilemma: how to create a secular federal government in the milieu of a society of essentially religious people. Within the specific historical circumstances of the period, the Founders attempted to solve the problem by devising a concept of disestablishment that institutionalized a form of governance that would not prefer, discriminate against, or oppress any particular religion. This concept was incorporated into the First Amendment to the Constitution, creating a legal framework for protecting religious freedom while distancing the federal government from religious institutions (Mooney, 1990). Significantly, the cultural context in which this occurred was dominated by a Protestant ethos, a de facto establishment of Protestant hegemony, creating, in effect, a Christian nation in which religious and political values became interrelated in the public mind. "Protestants generally accepted the separation of church and state, but stoutly resisted any sense of separation of moral from public well-being" (Handy, 1984, p. 334). This had enormous consequences for American society, among which was "the creation of patriotic and civil institutions through which Protestantism could inject the teachings and practices of the mainline churches" (Mooney, 1990, p. 52).

THE ROLE OF RELIGION IN AMERICAN PUBLIC LIFE

An examination of the role of religion in American public life entails an exploration of the impact, influence, and interplay of the sectarian on the secular in a pluralistic society and its consequences for shaping the public agenda, particularly as it affects religious schools.

Murray (1960) produced the seminal work in this area with a creative study of American and Catholic traditions and their independence and interdependence. His philosophical exploration of the coexistence within one political community of disparate religious groups led to the exposition of principles needed to facilitate the participation of all religious groups as a single community in which individual groups retain their own identities. He expounded a public philosophy rooted in the sacredness of the human person and situated law as the driving force of justice that ultimately serves to educate the public conscience to greater public morality.

This was further developed by Reichley (1985) who provides insight into the interplay between religious groups and American society, demonstrating the historic connections between religion and the practice of democracy and concluding that the most important service organized religion has played in the society was to nurture moral values that help humanize capitalism and give direction to democracy. Dunn (1989), however, takes a different viewpoint in his examination of the contributions of religious participation in society. He notes that the advent of pluralism as Catholics, Jews, other immigrant groups, and liberal Protestantism, challenged traditional conservative Protestantism and ascertains that the secularization of society and politics has generally reduced religion to another competing force within America's pluralistic democracy.

Determination of what role, if any, religious discourse should play in public life has taken the form of a debate in the popular culture as well as among contemporary political philosophers. On one side, Rawls (1993) premises a liberal understanding of acceptable religious discourse as one in which individuals "bracket" their religious conviction in secular, impartial, or neutral terms in order to engage individuals outside the sectarian community. Perry (1991), Carter (1993), and Neuhaus (1984) counter by addressing the problem of the proper relation of religious belief to political life. They expound on the ideal of "ecumenical politics" in which an accommodationist view of the First Amendment will allow religious morality to be introduced in productive ways into political discourse. Contemporary sociological surveys, such as that of Wolfe (1998), indicate that while 84% of the people interviewed expressed belief in God, they felt religion should be removed from politics. This he calls a "quiet faith" that remains private.

Today we see evidence of the subtle conflict that strikes at the heart of the democratic enterprise: the personal and public nature of religion's place in American life. Legal interpretations of the intent of disestablishment have fostered within the nation a pluralism of religious commitments, creating a privatization of religion and an ambiguity concerning the role of religious institutions and their interaction with the government in forming culture (Bellah, Madsen, Sullivan, Swidler, & Tipton, 1985; Carter, 1993). As a result, the entry of religious groups into the civic arena has usually been interpreted as an effort to impose religious policy, and thus inhibits church and state from discussing values and commitments that could be shared in the public sector. Rosen (2000) argued that the 2000 presidential election campaign would change that by fostering a greater erosion of the wall of separation as candidates vie for the votes of a populace that vocalizes support for cooperation between church and state, particularly in the provision of welfare and education services. Glenn (2000) forcibly advances this issue, building a case for faith-based organizations to play a more active role in delivery of social services for the mutual benefit of both church and society.

LEGAL BATTLES OVER SEPARATION OF CHURCH AND STATE ISSUES

The Jeffersonian metaphor of "a wall of separation between church and state" forms the central concept in the dialogue on church–state relations. Curry (1986) argues that the wall metaphor, which historically serves as the basis for constitutional interpretations of church–state relations, bifurcates the religion clauses by implying that cases pursuant to establishment should not include arguments with regard to free exercise. Exploring the ramifications of applying the wall metaphor to the issue of governmental aid to private, particularly parochial, schools, Oaks (1963) makes a useful distinction between two aspects: the desirability and the constitutionality of the question. The former is a matter of legislative public policy, the latter a subject for judicial opinion. This constitutional dichotomy is explored from a public policy perspective by Drinan (1963), who articulates intertwined theories of the legal aspects of church–state relations by defining the issue as: "absolute separation, state neutrality between religion and irreligion, cooperation between church and state, and state refusal to employ religion or irreligion as a basis for classification" (p. 220).

Several authors have explored different aspects of these themes on the constitutional issues. Bennett (1986) argues the cooperation aspect, connecting religious liberty and political liberty as the indispensable consensus in the minds of the Founders. Mooney (1990) examines the intersection of law, religion, and education and provides a historical understanding of the enigmatic nature of the establishment clause. His analysis describes the legacy of the Founders from what they said about the separation of religion and government, the revisionist interpretation provided in the wake of the Fourteenth Amendment, and subsequent Supreme Court decisions, and concludes with an appeal for a dialogue that avoids categorical imperative and absolutist approaches at either end of the spectrum. Russo and Orsi (1992) argue that in the current educational reform movement, the state should not use religion as a basis for classification, but this has been strenuously countered by anti-parochaid voices expounding rationale for a more absolute separation (Anthony, 1990; Bryson & Houston, 1990; Doerr & Mendez, 1991; James & Levin, 1983).

The Supreme Court's religion-clause case law has reached the stage where it is confused, inconsistent, and incoherent when attempting to analyze the application of the First Amendment to various types of religious institutions. Unraveling the confusion has captured the attention of legal scholars on several fronts. Anthony (1990), McConnell (1990), Veverka (1985), and Wilson (1989) examined the ambiguity in the interpretation of intentionality in the minds of the Founders, in their formulation of the concept of disestablishment and the consequent determination of the relationship of private schools to the state. The legality of using public monies for religious-sponsored education was examined extensively by Weber and Gilbert (1981), who studied the issue from the perspective of policy implications of fiscal neutrality as it related to the limitations and control of financial aid to religious schools. Bryson and Houston (1990) have focused on the same issue, analyzing how the Supreme Court decided the vast number of cases litigated before it during the past two decades. This aspect has been further explored in a multidisciplinary analysis of the question of state aid and the religion clause conducted by Stravinskas (1982). He has added theological, sociological, and philosophical insights to the legal and historical research regarding an understanding of the composite picture of Catholic schools that is in the mind of the Court, the sources from which such a profile is derived, and how it affects the Court's decisions. Stronks (1995) pursued this further, analyzing the perceptions justices make about the definition of religion and the inconsistencies of their assumption. For some justices, religion means belief in an extratemporal reality; others assume it to be evidenced in religious activity; and still others argue that religious belief can be legally separated from public expression.

McGrath (1962) points to the constitutional distinctions made by the Court when the law is applied unevenly to religious charities and to schools. The former case law, applicable to health and child-care institutions, determines the differences according to organizational constructs: religious-affiliated institutions are in conformity with the separation clause if they have an independent corporate existence apart from the church or religious order which conducts them. Generally speaking, religious schools have a closer identification with and hierarchy of control within the official church than do health and child care institutions (McGrath, 1962). The distinctions become ever more blurred when applied to the various levels of educational institutions. In *Edwards v. Aguillard* (1987) the Court applied a higher standard when interpreting the establishment clause in K–12 settings because of the impressionability of young children and the presumption of susceptibility to indoctrination (Underwood, 1989).

For the first century and a half of the nation's history, there was a general acceptance of a pattern of church–state relations which constituted this informally established Protestantism, attested to by the fact that the U.S. Supreme

Court did not rule in any substantial way on the meaning of the establishment clause until the *Everson v. Board of Education* decision in 1947 (Drinan, 1963). In *Everson*, the Court ruled favorably on the constitutionality of providing public transportation for non-public school students and attempted to strike a balance between the two clauses of the First Amendment: prohibition of the establishment of religion (separation) and prohibition of limitations of religious freedom (accommodation). While the theory of strict separation holds that the government may do nothing by program, policies, or laws to aid or support religion or religious activities, the accommodationist view allows for a zone of indirect aid through "permissible" public welfare benefits. In American jurisprudence today, disestablishment prohibits sponsorship and interference; it sanctions permissible promotion of religious freedom while outlawing impermissible promotion of religious belief (Mooney, 1990). In reality, there has developed a judicial tendency to create a dichotomy between the two clauses and rule, at times, in favor of one over the other, creating tension and an inability to predict the constitutionality of public policy directions in church and government relations.

THE CATHOLIC CHURCH'S RELIGIOUS AND SOCIAL MISSION IN A PLURALISTIC SOCIETY

Paramount in developing an appreciation of the social activist role of the Catholic Church is an understanding of the mission of the Church as it was defined by the Second Vatican Council (Vatican II) in two key documents, *Dignitatis Humanae* and *Gaudium et Spes* (Abbott, 1989). The former accepted religious pluralism as integral to human freedom and the condition under which the Church would structure church–state relationships; the latter articulated a theological conception of the promotion and protection of human dignity which situated social ministry at the center of the Church's life (Hehir, 1986).

While *Gaudium et Spes* describes a "public church" as one entering into dialogue with the human family about all of its different problems (Abbott, 1989, #3), the manner in which it exercises that role is debated. An exploration of the political activity of the bishops and the premises on which they have intensified participation in the public debates has been the subject of several works, with conflicting conclusions about how to mediate Christian vision to a pluralistic world.

The focus on Vatican II ideology as rationale for insertion of the American bishops into the life of society is given concrete expression through the institutional framework of the National Conference of Catholic Bishops and the United States Catholic Conference. (NCCB/USCC). These organizations have been the subject of several studies.

The early history of the development of the National Catholic Welfare Conference was portrayed by Keeler (1991) and McKeown (1980). Sunshine (1988), also, traced the NCCB/USCC origins as an outgrowth of the National Catholic

War Council, formed during World War I to coordinate Catholic groups in cooperation with the war effort. In 1923, the National Catholic Welfare Conference was formed as a legal body to handle pastoral, educational, and social programs, and to unify the bishops in the coordination of Catholic charity and give Catholics a united voice in the public forum. In the wake of Vatican II, two new organizations were created: the National Conference of Catholic Bishops, which deals primarily with the internal life of the Church, and the United States Catholic Conference, which directs the civil and public policy activities. When they wish to speak or act on national policy issues, they do so as USCC. In the latter mode, they influence public policy through public statements, through their lobbyists on Capitol Hill, and through litigation in the courts (Reese, 1992).

The bishops have repeatedly attempted to avoid appearances of choosing sides in campaigns while asserting the right to be visible in the debate about the broad range of policy choices. Because the moral content of public choice is so central today, the religious communities are inevitably drawn more deeply into the public life of the nation.

As president of the National Conference of Catholic Bishops, James Malone, then bishop of Youngstown, Ohio, addressed the 1984 NCCB assembly regarding the Church's call to work at the intersection of public opinion and public policy. He discussed how the Church's moral vision should be used to address the key issues of life in American society, reminding the bishops that "we should demonstrate that one can combine profound conviction of moral principles and abiding civil courtesy toward allies and adversaries in the public debate" (Malone, 1984, p. 39). Every four years, USCC issues a statement on political responsibilities of Catholics to society, urging the faithful to bring their commitment to human life, dignity, and care for the poor and vulnerable to debates in the electoral process in public life. (USCC, 1999).

HISTORICAL ORIGIN AND DEVELOPMENT OF THE AMERICAN CATHOLIC SCHOOL SYSTEM

In early nineteenth-century America, the common school movement was begun to ensure the continuance of the fragile democracy through a process of educating citizens in civic responsibility, useful knowledge, and a common Christianity. The growth of the common school movement was first chronicled by Cubberley (1919), who portrayed the triumphs of public education in transmitting the dominant culture of the new democracy. In the common school movement, the social ideals embodied in Protestantism and the Social Gospel converged to shape a common moral and religious ideal that would produce a political consensus and homogenize the newly arriving immigrant masses (Spring, 1990, 1991).

By the middle of the nineteenth century, Catholics were experiencing the system of public schools as non-denominational Protestant and increasingly anti-

Catholic and discriminatory in nature (O'Keefe, 1991). The Church began to oppose an education that attempted to teach "common Christianity"; it did not want children exposed to other religions, "for with a Catholic, religion forms a vital part of education" (Ravitch, 1988, p. 44). Consequently, it dissented from the common school consensus as the "one best system" and sought to create an alternative form of schooling which gave the Church control over its own educational destiny.

The Catholic dissent from the common school movement and the accompanying struggles between interest groups to control the schools have been chronicled by Tyack (1974) and Ravitch (1983, 1988), both of whom studied the religious, cultural, and class animosities present in the debates surrounding the contest for control of the schools in New York City in the 1830s and 1840s. The "Great School Wars," as Ravitch dubbed them, were focused in the major urban areas: New York, Chicago, and Boston. Ravitch's (1988) research has focused extensively on New York City, which serves as an archetype of the patterns of hostility met by Catholic schools elsewhere when need forced them to petition for public subsidy for their schools. Clear and strong evidence of religious prejudice in the acrimonious debates surrounding the hearings before the Board of Aldermen and in city-wide elections in 1841–1842, coupled with a blatant unwillingness to compromise, forced Archbishop Hughes to abandon efforts to secure public support and to pursue Catholic education independent of state support (Burns, 1969).

The historiography of the Catholic school system portrays its origins in the story of the patterns of immigration history (Buetow, 1970, 1985, 1988; Burns, 1969; Walch, 1996). By the 1840s, the growing American resistance to increased immigration, expressed as anti-Catholicism, was organized into the Nativist movement, which eventually culminated in the formation of the Know-Nothing political party (Higham, 1968). Amid this increasing hostility of the Protestant majority, and under threats of loss of ability to hand on the faith in the traditions of the European cultural heritage, the Catholic bishops formalized, in 1884 at the Third Plenary Council of Baltimore, their commitment to the establishment of a separate school system, and required parents to send their children to these schools. The growth and development of American Catholic schools in the nineteenth and first half of the twentieth centuries was rooted in a clear sense of purpose and identity. Defense of the faith, enculturation, and escape from religious and ethnic prejudice were significant factors in the creation of these schools (Buetow, 1985, 1988).

While the goal of erecting a school within every parish was never realized, the growth of the system was steady and extraordinary. By 1965, the peak year, there existed almost 11,000 elementary schools (4.5 million students) and 2,500 secondary schools (1.1 million students). The year 2000 figures, however, document that a significant diminishment has occurred within those three decades. The data show a present system of 6,923 elementary schools and 1,221 secondary schools, with a combined student population of 2.5 million students (McDonald, 2000).

The growth and diminishment of the Catholic schools, accompanied by the rise in non-Catholic student population (currently 24.7%) illustrate a fundamental ambiguity in understanding the nature of Catholic education in the second half of the twentieth century: the necessity of preserving Catholic schools as a means for communicating a distinctly Catholic worldview, while at the same time being perceived as genuinely American institutions serving the public good. The United States Bishops' Pastoral, *To Teach as Jesus Did* (USCC, 1972), reiterated the importance of Catholic education in service to the nation, indicating that the bishops considered the schools as part of the American system: "partners in the total American educational enterprise" (USCC, 1972, #111). Banks (1999) underscores this theme, emphasizing the relevance of offering a Catholic education to non-Catholics as inherent in the theological vision that focuses on the promotion of the dignity of all persons.

Catholic Schools and the Common Good

The creation of a system of education in both the public and private sectors, legitimized by the *Pierce v. Society of Sisters* decision, has resulted in a diversity of educational opportunities and a variety of ideologies concerning the role of education in a democratic pluralistic society.

Several authors have examined the nature of and purpose of schooling and conclude that all schools, regardless of how they are financed or administered, are institutions that serve public purposes. Buetow (1985) suggests that the term "private" connotes separation from public purposes and participation in the common weal. He argues that there is no such thing as a private school: "every school takes students from the public and returns them to the public; uses texts and materials from publishers who are public; forms curricula in accordance with a vision of public needs; abides by at least minimum public standards set by the state; accepts teachers from institutions publicly approved" (p. 5). He contends that it is more accurate to call such schools denominational rather than private.

The public function argument was also advanced by Herberg (1957), in his assertion that parochial schools are, in fact, public institutions that perform a public function and are seen as the equivalent of the education given in the public schools.

Today, the national agenda on school reform and restructuring is focusing public attention and academic scholarship on the question of school choice, with heated debates about the inclusion of private and religious school students and schools in such initiatives. The contribution of American Catholic schools to the common good through the education of almost three million children each year should be a significant part of the national dialogue.

Statistical data regarding Catholic school enrollments document major demographic changes in the Catholic schools over the past quarter century. Non-Catholic population in Catholic schools increased dramatically in the years between 1965 and 2000. The substantial and growing numbers of non-Catholic (14%) and minority students (24%) primarily served by inner-city parochial schools (McDonald, 2000), and their demonstrably higher levels of academic achievement, indicate that this issue is one which cannot be readily dismissed nor superficially investigated.

The research has demonstrated that Catholic schools provide an invaluable service to the public sector in the education of students. "The very existence of private schools prevents education from becoming a government monopoly . . . they provide educational alternatives and successful models in such academic areas as reading, math and science; in values education; in drop-out prevention; and in serving the needs of minority students" (McNamee, 1989, p. 2). In addition, significant financial contributions are made in savings to the government on educational expenses. The estimated operating expenses for all Catholic schools in 1999–2000 indicate that Catholic school parents save the nation more than $17.2 billion while, at the same time, contributing their share of taxes for public school education (McDonald, 2000).

Catholic Schools in the Public Policy Arena

From the outset of the common school movement, some Church leaders have been involved in public debates about the nature of the schools, public and private, and their funding sources. At first, some state funding was provided for religious schools, but over time, changing political and social circumstances led to re-interpretations of the establishment clause that effectively eliminated direct support for all non-public schools (Ravitch, 1988; Sanders, 1977).

In the last century, constitutional battles were fought over compulsory public education and the liberty to choose alternatives, culminating in the legitimization of a dual system of education (*Pierce v. Society of Sisters*, 1925; *Yoder v. Wisconsin*, 1972). As these alternative systems began to reflect upon their service to the common good and examined the fiscal costs in providing such public service, they began to challenge the inequities inherent in denial of funding because of educational choices exercised by parents. Ultimately, some benefits in the form of the National School Lunch Act, provisions for public transportation (*Everson v. Board of Education*, 1974), and student textbook loans (*Board of Education v. Allen*, 1968; *Cochran v. Louisiana*, 1930) were upheld by the Supreme Court if the state constitution permitted. Other attempts to secure direct public assistance for non-public schools resulted in a series of Supreme Court decisions which became increasingly unfavorable in the 1970s. Argued together, *Lemon v. Kurtzman* and *Earley v. DiCenso* (1971) resulted in a Court decision that denied reimbursement for secular educational services and payment of teacher salaries and, in *Meek v. Pittenger* (1975) prohibited the loan of instructional materials other than textbooks.

Ultimately, the leadership of the Catholic educational community, represented by the USCC and the NCEA, shifted its strategy away from aid to institutions to one of assistance to individual students and parents, primarily in the form of greater participation in federal programs and tax credits or vouchers for school tuition payments.

Participation in Federal Education Programs

As early as the 1940s, attempts were made to enact federal legislation to provide assistance to elementary and secondary schools. These attempts failed because of lack of agreement on several ideological grounds that related to state and local autonomy, civil rights, and inclusion of private and religious schools in proposed legislation. While general aid was being debated, limited programs of assistance, the National School Lunch (1946) and National Defense Education Act (1958) were enacted (Davis, 1998). The Elementary and Secondary Education Act (ESEA) of 1965 was the first step in the passage of federal legislation to aid elementary and secondary school education. In 1964, however, President Johnson requested legislation for federal aid to education and, in an attempt at compromise to secure passage, Congress and the president agreed to two very important principles for providing services to students in public, private, and religious schools. These principles were: (1) "child benefit" that provides "special types" of assistance or services primarily for needy students and only incidentally for the school they attended; and (2) the aid would be channeled through "public trustees," (i.e., public authorities who would receive the ESEA funds and, in turn, would act as accountable trustees on behalf of the eligible children in their community, regardless of the type of school they attended) (Davis, 1998).

McAndrews (1991) intensively analyzed the process of the passage of the Act. His study focuses on the attempt of the bishops to exert political influence in public policy affecting education. This study analyzed the activities of the National Catholic Welfare Council (NCWC) related to the Elementary and Secondary Education Act of 1965. The struggle to resolve the "religious issue" and include non-public school children in the federal aid bill resulted in a series of compromises by NCWC that "acquiesced in a program which omitted the provision for private administration which NCWC had demanded, included the poverty approach which NCWC had abandoned, and amounted to little more than the shared time to which NCWC had refused to resign itself" (p. 55). McAndrews asserts that this failure was attributable to both legislative realism and inherent problems with the NCWC lobbying effort. He asserts that NCWC's lack of political muscle was the product of four factors: (1) no unanimity of voice on the part of the bishops, (2) lack of clearly defined objectives and frequently changing positions, (3) inability to master the machinations of Congress and the White House, and (4) poor timing given the religious and political climate of the country.

In the five subsequent reauthorizations of ESEA, and other federal assistance legislation, the USCC has been in the forefront, testifying before several congressional committees to secure the delivery of more equitable services to private school students, particularly those burdened by educational, economic, and social disadvantage. Its basic premise is expressed in the document *Principles for Educational Reform in the United States* (USCC, 1995). The bishops argue that when services are available to students and teachers in public schools, equitable services should be made available to their counterparts in religious schools, since these schools also serve the common good.

The current reauthorization of ESEA in the 106th Congress represents the first time that a Republican majority in both houses controlled the process. While radical changes, such as block granting of funding have been proposed, the opposition of a Democratic president and active public school lobby in an election year casts doubt on the ability of either party to enact major changes (Davis, 1999).

In addition to congressional tampering with aspects of the overall constructs of ESEA, two legal challenges to parts of the program have reached the U.S. Supreme Court, and USCC has been active in opposing litigation that challenged the participation of private school students in federal programs (USCC, 1995). An attempt to exclude students in religious schools from participation in Title I services was partially remedied in *Aguilar v. Felton* (1985), when the Court ruled that services were permissible as long as they were delivered at a neutral site so as not to give the impression that religion was being endorsed by the presence of public school teachers on religious property. This was overturned in *Agostini v. Felton* (1997), when the Court changed its views on the establishment clause and allowed services to be delivered back in the religious schools because the program was viewed as aid to children, not direct aid to institutions.

In June 2000, the U.S. Supreme Court decided *Mitchell v. Helms*, a case concerning the use of Title VI funds that supply instructional materials, including computers and software, to both public and private schools. Private schools received about 25–30% of the $375 million spent in the last fiscal year on this program. Opponents argue that computers may be diverted for religious purposes and used to further the religious mission of the school; supporters argue that computers are the modern equivalent of textbooks, which have been provided by the government for more than 30 years (Stream, 2000). The Court's favorable decision indicated some optimism about achieving success on a variety of taxpayer issues for religious schools, including vouchers.

Tax Policies and Catholic Schools

During the 1972 presidential campaign, the role of the federal government in education and the option for inclusion of private schools in funding proposals began to surface as a viable issue. The release of the final report of President

Nixon's *Panel on Non-Public Education* urged tuition tax credits for parents along with a future share of federal tax subsidies to be given to the states (House Committee Report, 1972). Nixon had appeared at the annual convention of the Knights of Columbus in August 1971 and that of the NCEA in 1972, and at both pledged his support of constitutional ways of obtaining assistance for non-public schools. The Republican Party platform for the 1972 presidential election campaign included similar references. While the Democratic platform avoided the issue, George McGovern, the presidential nominee, did release a statement pledging his support for constitutional measures to aid non-public schools (McGovern-Shriver Campaign press release, September 15, 1972). In the 20 years following the 1972 presidential election campaign, several pieces of federal legislation were introduced into Congress, each of which appeared to have significant congressional and presidential support, but ultimately failed to be enacted into law: (1) Mills-Byrnes Act of 1973; (2) Tuition Tax Credits Act of 1978; and (3) Educational Opportunity and Equity Act in 1983.

According to an analysis (McDonald, 1995) of the lobbying efforts of the Catholic school community's pursuit of tax credits at the federal level, several factors contributed to lack of success. The results of the analysis revealed that despite strong presidential support for some measures and congressional support for others, bipartisan support could not be maintained and tax credits became identified solely with the Republican Party, which did not deliver on its promises. When examined as an interest group lobbying to impact public policy formation regarding tuition tax credits, the data show that the Catholic school community was not a monolithic organization, was reactive rather than proactive, was conflicted in its leadership, and engaged in short-lived and episodic activities.

While the ultimate objective was the same for all of the constituent private and religious school groups, attainment of tuition tax credits or voucher assistance, the constructs of the individual groups resulted in differences of opinion about: (1) strategies to be used to influence policymakers, (2) with whom to form alliances, (3) how much individual effort and membership support each organization was willing to contribute, and (4) perceptions about the need for consensus and uniformity of action.

Politicians developed the tax credit agenda and appealed to the religious interests for support. When success seemed possible, the Catholic school community mobilized in support of specific legislation, but there has been no long-term commitment to work actively to formulate an agenda and aggressively pursue it.

No consensus has been sought from the Catholic school community regarding what the pursuit of federal (or state) tax-assisted support for non-public schools should entail. The ramifications of accepting public funding on the independence of the schools surfaced frequently in the tax credit debates but were not explored fully. Untested assumptions about the type of government regulations that might ensue and how they would impact separation of church and state were introduced into House and Senate floor debates. Ambiguity and fear about the impact of regulations on the independence of the non-public schools were used by opponents as indicative of a lack of support, by the non-public school community, for assistance. At the other end of the spectrum, fear of regulation was countered with naive assertions about the government's legal inability to impose any regulations or measures of public accountability (McDonald, 1995).

State Educational Tax Credit Legislation. Greater success in securing tax relief for parents who educate children in private and religious schools has been achieved at the state levels. Minnesota (1955), Iowa (1987), and Illinois (1999) state legislatures have approved legislation that allows taxpayers deductions or credits against state income tax liability for expenses incurred in educating their children. These laws are written to allow parents of children educated in public as well as non-public schools the same opportunities for tax relief. Inclusion of benefits to public school parents is essential if a law is to avoid the legal problems that invalidated a New York State credit law that benefited only private school parents (*Committee for Public Education*, 1973). The 1978 challenge to the Minnesota law, *Mueller v. Allen*, reached the U.S. Supreme Court where it was validated and serves as the precedent for other tax credit legislation (Chopko, 1999).

In 1997, Arizona policymakers established two non-refundable individual income tax credits. Taxpayers may claim a tax credit of up to $500 for contributions to a non-profit organization that distributes scholarships or tuition grants to private and parochial schools. In addition, taxpayers may claim a tax credit of up to $200 as reimbursement for fees paid to a public school for extracurricular activities (i.e., school-sponsored activities that require enrolled students to pay a fee to participate, including fees for band uniforms or equipment, uniforms for varsity athletic activities, and scientific laboratory materials) (Shokraii-Rees, 2000).

Arizona's tax credit law was challenged in court. In January 1999, the Arizona Supreme Court ruled that the law does not violate state and federal constitutional prohibitions against government aid to religion. This decision was appealed to the U.S. Supreme Court. In October 1999, the U.S. Supreme Court declined to review the case, thus allowing the Arizona Supreme Court's ruling that the program is constitutional.

School Choice in the Educational Reform Debates

Parental choice in the selection of schools for their children has become an intensely debated issue in the literature of school reform. The term "choice" refers to a variety of options among different kinds of constructs: public school choice which permits intra- as well as cross-district selections; public funds for private institutions and public funding for religiously affiliated schools. The *Carnegie Report* (Carnegie Foundation, 1992), while highly critical of some school choice programs, raised public consciousness of the significance of choice in its multifaceted forms.

For the most part, the literature on school choice makes very little distinction among the options as such and focuses, instead, on consideration of the impact of choice through such concepts as marketplace competition to improve accountability and effectiveness; parental rights and distributive justice; equity, elitism, racism, and the social and democratic perspectives of a common school education; organization and administration of the control of choice initiatives, and scarce resources and issues of civil liberties and separation of church and state.

In the Catholic school community, a long-standing commitment to working for full and fair educational choice for all parents is rooted in the conviction that it is a justice issue, and, therefore, good public policy for the United States. Catholic school leaders believe that all parents should have the right to select the best educational environment for their children and that fundamental right should not be conditional upon parents' ability to pay tuition or to afford to live in neighborhoods where the public school system meets the needs of their children.

In America, the financially disadvantaged cannot exercise their right to select alternative schooling for their children, since public policy today is formulated to offer parents choices that are restricted to public school options only. Parents who wish to send their children to parochial or private schools are financially penalized for exercising their right. While the United States is the only Western democracy that does not provide parents with a fair share of their education tax dollars so they may choose a non-public school education, the tide of public opinion is beginning to turn in support of publicly funded school choice initiatives.

The present momentum is building around the school choice movement, but the leadership is in the hands of politicians and philanthropists who are not part of the Catholic school community. Numerous private scholarship programs, under the leadership of corporate America, are providing millions of dollars for tuition grants to disadvantaged children, and Catholic schools are the primary constituents and beneficiaries of the parents' choices. Theoretically, this may be a good thing, as it will help to focus the choice debates on the justice and educational merits, and not make it simply a "Catholic issue" (McDonald, 1999).

Market Metaphors

Chubb and Moe (1990) advance the use of the marketplace economy metaphor to create a climate responsive to accountability and reform. They make a sophisticated political case for the failure of any education reforms, based on restructuring, within the present bureaucratic monopoly of the public school system. Key to their findings about effective and ineffective schools is the degree of autonomy and freedom from bureaucratic restraints. These authors report that effective schools are those most similar to private schools in organizational autonomy. Utilizing the latest data from government, business, education, and the work of Chubb and Moe, Reinhart and Lee (1991) analyze the legacy of public education and the government's inability to produce quality education for all students. They advocate a move to privatization of public schools. The business community, reflecting on the goals of the National Education Summit, also advanced a move to a market economy model as the means to effect systemic change in a government monopoly impervious to change (Ball & Hume, 1990). Lieberman (1989, 1991, 1993), an outspoken critic of the public school system, has been a consistent supporter of school choice as a market mechanism for effecting improved service and lower costs in the reform of schools.

Ideological opposition to the concept of schools as market-driven enterprises has been advanced by Bryk, Lee, and Holland (1993). They view the market metaphor as defeating the concept of school as community, which their work demonstrates is paramount to school effectiveness. Likewise, O'Keefe (1995a, 1995b) repudiates a market philosophy approach, arguing that the market philosophy is antithetical to a Jesuit religious identification of solidarity with the poor, which values community and cooperation over competition and individualism.

Cookson (1991, 1994) attempts to bring balance to the debate through an examination of choice in its historical and contemporary contexts. He analyzes the major choice plans in effect in the United States and examines the major assumptions of the market model of educational reform in each of these initiatives. A detailed historical evaluation is presented by Coulson (1999), whose premise is that the common schools have failed students, in many instances segregating them into haves and have-nots, creating a learning chasm that cannot be bridged in an educational monopoly. While the demand side of school choice is demonstrably high by every measure in public opinion polls and applications for vouchers and scholarships, the actual experience with choice has been based on a constrained supply and demand situation. In a universal choice program, the supply side will emerge as a serious concern. Hill (1999) examines the assumptions about availability of schools and what kinds of schools might become available, and urges the creation of opportunities for developing new schools through political, legal, and financial challenges that must be addressed if more than the already advantaged are to experience choice.

PARENTAL RIGHTS

Coons and Sugarman (1978) produced the seminal work in the field of parental rights, as the basis of choice in education, and argue the ethical as well as practical ends of school choice. Their emphasis on family values and the primacy of the parent in the choice of schooling is claimed to be an individual, democratic freedom rooted in the civil libertarian ideals of Locke. They advocate the social wisdom of providing all families, especially those of lower incomes, with the opportunity and means to choose among a wide range of government and private schools through vouchers. The use of education vouchers to promote exercise of parental rights and advance distributive justice has been further expanded in Coons' analyses of government polices, particularly in the inner cities, which de facto isolate children by class and race with destructive consequences for families (Coons & Monahan, 1991; Coons & Sugarman, 1991, 1999).

Leonard DeFiore, former president of the NCEA, views parental rights to direct the education of their children as the arbiter of justice and hope. He reasons that when parents are empowered to choose the schools their children attend, they can demand and will get better schools, and the act of choosing strengthens families in an educational partnership in which they determine their own futures. His contention is that while the *Pierce* decision promoted liberty in education, taxpayer-supported school choice will effect justice (DeFiore, 1999).

Equity and Equality

The most volatile aspect of the choice debate centers around notions of civil rights, racism, elitism, and the common school as the safeguard against such injustices. The sanctity of public schools as the arbiter of social equality has been challenged by several authors. Kozol (1991) examined the "savage inequalities" of educational opportunity provided for poor children confined in urban public schools, and the apparent acceptability of ineffective schools as a permanent reality in the social policies of the public school system. Kozol concluded, however, that conditions would further deteriorate if choice initiatives siphoned off monies from these institutions. While Glenn (1991) discovered some expanded options for the poor and some pressure on poorer schools to improve through controlled choice initiatives, he notes that both opponents and proponents of school choice do not agree on the ability of choice to safeguard and promote equity. He raises an interesting question, not often addressed, regarding whether or not sanctions would ever be imposed on schools and staff that fail to attract students in a market-controlled option. Despite such indictments of inadequate school systems, especially for the poor, critics of school choice plans, particularly those which included private school options, continue to stress their perceived notions of the elitist nature of such schools and continue to argue for the social values of the common school movement (Boyd & Walberg, 1990; Levy, 1986; Lynch, 1990; Puckett, 1983).

Proponents of funded choice initiatives, particularly those which include private school options, advocate them as a means of attaining equity for disadvantaged students through expanding their educational opportunities. Schneider (1989) examines the schooling of poor and minority children from an equity perspective, and finds that private schools offer greater socially equalizing opportunities for youth than do comparable inner-city public schools. Bauch (1989) addresses a critical issue in the public policy debate over choice: the question as to whether or not parents, especially the poor, can make wise educational decisions. Based on a study of inner-city Catholic schools, she concludes that there is strong evidence to support parental ability to choose the best schools for their children. Howell and Peterson (2000), who have done extensive studies on school choice, have found that alarm about the equity issue, particularly the skimming of the best and the brightest, is not founded. They have discovered that voucher families in their studies were the more disadvantaged than non-voucher families in terms of initial test scores of students and family income.

Viteritti (1999) reviews a variety of policy initiatives enacted in the name of school reform and finds that they do not provide an adequate education for most disadvantaged children. Acknowledging that there are legal and civic challenges inherent in public support to the poor to attend private schools, he argues that successfully meeting them would foster the redistributive and social agenda present in American social and public policy goals.

The 1992 *People's Poll on Schools and School Choice*, commissioned by the NCEA (1992), provides valuable information regarding public opinion on school choice. The Gallup Organization polled over 1,200 Americans regarding their perceptions of the quality of education offered in public, private, and parochial schools and their attitudes toward parental choice in education. Seventy percent of the respondents in the sample indicated that they favored the government allotting a certain amount of money to parents to send their children to the public, private, or parochial school of their choice; 54% stated that they had sufficient information about the schools in their community to make the best choice for their children. The 30th annual Phi Delta Kappan poll (Rose & Gallup, 1999) demonstrated rising support for publicly supported choice. Support among the general public rose from 35% in 1995 to 51% in 1999; support among minorities is at 68%.

The most comprehensive presentation of the political and policy objectives of choice and their impact on organizational changes in American schools is contained in the two-volume publication of the symposium on *Choice and Control in American Education* (Clune & Witte, 1990). This work provides insight into the many nuances within the debate over quality and equality in education and how choice may affect both goals.

CHURCH AND STATE

Finally, much of the debate centers about "parochaid," the inclusion of religiously affiliated schools in public choice initiatives. Doerr and Mendez (1991) offer vituperative attacks, based on old stereotypes of Catholic schools, as rationale for denying inclusion of private or religious schools in the interest of retaining the "wall of separation" between church and state. Curley (1988) and Devins (1989) explored the constitutional issues in historical context and support the retention of the *Lemon* test (*Lemon v. Kurtzman*, 1971) for prevention of excessive entanglement of church and state. Wilson (1989) examined the Supreme Court's interpretations of cases involving education and religion in light of the First Amendment and the Founders' intentions. Attention is paid to the manner in which the Court's decisions created conflict and inconsistency, and he offers a framework for "intentional theory" review rather than the *Lemon* test currently used. McConnell's (1990) analysis of constitutional grounds for challenging vouchers for private or religious schools also deals with ambiguity of interpretation and argues for a more permissive attitude toward religious, pre-collegiate schools. Bolick and Bullock (1999) and Chopko (1999) have written and litigated on the constitutionality of carefully constructed voucher programs. In their analyses of cases that have been argued in federal courts, they note that when benefits under a voucher program are determined by neutral criteria that neither advance nor impede religion and are made equally available to religious and secular beneficiaries, they do not violate the establishment clause. This theory was confirmed in *Jackson v. Benson* (1998) when the U.S. Supreme Court declined an appeal of the Milwaukee voucher program and allowed it to stand as constitutional.

Glenn (1989) argues that the de facto removal of the issue of public funding for private schools from the political arena and relegating it to the constitutional lacks foundation in the Constitution and discriminates against religious believers. Glenn surveyed the provisions for diversity, including religious diversity, of publicly funded education in six nations, and concludes that in "most Western democracies the right of parents to choose a school based on their religious convictions and to have that schooling supported with public funds is legally protected" (p. 214).

Publicly Funded Vouchers. Currently, three states have established limited voucher programs for students to attend other public schools outside their home district, or private and religious schools. These programs exist statewide in Florida and in Milwaukee, Wisconsin, and Cleveland, Ohio. These programs have started with targeted populations, based on financial need or consideration of the failing nature of the assigned public school. All have been under legal challenge since their inception, with the Milwaukee program making it to final validation in the U.S. Supreme Court in *Jackson v. Benson* (1998). Litigation is pending in federal courts regarding the Ohio and Florida programs (Shokraii-Rees, 2000).

In Maine and Vermont, a long-standing program of tuitioning has been in effect whereby small towns that do not maintain a secondary school pay for students to be educated in other districts. Originally, private and religious schools were included in such programs but were eventually declared unconstitutional in state courts and those decisions upheld by the U.S. Supreme Court. The history and specifics of these variations of publicly funded vouchers will be presented elsewhere (Milton and Rose Friedman Foundation, 2000).

Suffice it to say that at present, voucher programs are experimental, in their early stages, and subject to the biases of the researchers who criticize the scholarship of other scholars who reach differing conclusions. One of the more thorough early analyses of the Milwaukee program has been conducted by Witte

(2000). His work provides a detailed framework for understanding the broader implications of a market approach to American education. He asserts that while the voucher program seems to be working in Milwaukee, there is no evidence that success, in terms of achievement and equal education, would necessarily translate to a universal voucher approach to education.

CONCLUSION

Catholic educational leaders must be a more articulate and assertive force in shaping both the direction and content of public policy debates that impact Catholic schools. Unfortunately, there is a great deal of apathy and ignorance about the conceptual and practical aspects of parental rights in education as a public policy issue among Catholic school leaders and consumers. Consequently, the debate is largely defined and shaped by those who do not have the interests of private and religious schools as a significant concern: the Clinton administration and U.S. Department of Education, as well as the various education associations and agencies representing public schools' interests in Washington, DC.

The misperceptions about Catholic schools as elitist, as divisive and segregationist, as successful with minorities due to the selectivity of the recruitment and retention policies, and as generally harmful to public schools need to be aggressively countered. Too frequently, the language of the congressional floor debates and Supreme Court rulings have reflected these stereotypes. Often overlooked is the research of Greene (1998b), who analyzed data from the U.S. Department of Education's National Education Longitudinal Study (NELS) of 12th graders and their parents, school administrators and teachers, and found that, on average, private schools are not only better integrated but also display greater racial tolerance, and generally convey stronger democratic values than do public schools (Greene, 1998a).

Unfortunately, public schools have assumed a status synonymous with democratic civic culture and any questioning of the role of public education evokes highly charged emotional response. What is needed is an effective public relations campaign to provide accurate information about Catholic schools to policymakers, as well as the general public, that will focus the debate on the issue of the value and the need for a pluralistic system of education in a pluralistic society.

REFERENCES

Abbott, W. M. (Ed.). (1989). *The documents of Vatican II*. New York: Crossroad Publishing.

Agostini v. Felton, 117 U.S. 2016 (1997).

Aguilar v. Felton, 483 U.S. 105 (1985).

Anthony, P. G. (1990, January 18). Conservative judicial activism and parochaid: An open-door policy towards funding religious schools? *Education Law Reporter, 57*, 13–27.

Ball, C., & Hume, J. (1990, Fall). In search of excellence: Business leaders discuss school choice and accountability. *Policy Review, 54*, 54–59.

Banks, R. J. (1999). The Catholic Church's involvement in the educational choice movement. In D. McDonald (Ed.), *Partners for justice: Catholic schools and school choice* (pp. 8–25).Washington, DC: National Catholic Educational Association.

Bauch, P. (1989). Can poor parents make wise educational choices? In E. Boyd & J. Cibulka (Eds.), *Private schools and public policy: International perspectives* (pp. 285–314). London: The Falmer Press.

Bellah, R., Madsen, R., Sullivan, W., Swidler, A., & Tipton, S. (1985). *Habits of the heart: Individualism and commitment in American life*. Berkeley: University of California.

Bennett, W. J. (1986). *Religious belief and the constitutional order*. Paper presented at the Paine Lectures in Religion, University of Missouri.

Board of Education v. Allen, 393 U.S. 236 (1968).

Bolick, C., & Bullock, S. G. (2000). *State of the Supreme Court: The justices' record on civil and economic liberties*. Washington, DC: Institute for Justice. [On-line]. Retrieved from the World Wide Web: http://www.ij.org/publications/other/SupCt.shtml.

Boyd, W. L., & Walberg, H. (1990). *Choice in education: Potential and problems*. Berkeley: McCutchan Publishing.

Bryk, A. S., Lee, V., & Holland, P. (1993). *Catholic schools and the common good*. Cambridge, MA: Harvard University Press.

Bryson, J. E., & Houston, S. H. (1990). *The Supreme Court and public funds for religious schools*. Jefferson, NC: McFarland & Company.

Buetow, H. (1985). *A history of United States Catholic schooling*. Washington, DC: National Catholic Educational Association.

Buetow, H. A. (1970). *Of singular benefit: The story of Catholic education in the United States*. New York: Macmillan.

Buetow, H. A. (1988). *The Catholic school: Its roots, identity and future*. New York: Crossroad Publishing.

Burns, J. A. (1969). *The principles, origin and establishment of the Catholic school system in the United States* (Vol. 1). New York: Arno Press.

Carnegie Foundation. (1992). *School choice: A special report*. New York: Carnegie Foundation for the Advancment of Teaching.

Carter, S. L. (1993). *The culture of disbelief: How American law and politics trivialize religious devotion*. New York: Basic Books.

Chopko, M. (1999). A favorable environment for voucher programs. *Catholic Education: A Journal of Inquiry and Practice, 3 (1)*, 87–96.

Chubb, J. E., & Moe, T. M. (1990). *Politics, markets & America's schools*. Washington, DC: The Brookings Institution.

Clune, W., & Witte, J. (Eds.). (1990). *Choice and control in American education* (Vol. 1). London, New York: The Falmer Press.

Cochran v. Louisiana State Board of Education, 330 U.S. 1 (1947).

Committee for Public Education and Religious Liberty v. Nyquist, 413 U.S. 756 (1973).

Cookson, P. W. (1991, February). Private schooling and equity: Dilemmas of choice. *Education and Urban Society, 23 (2)*, 185–199.

Cookson, P. W., Jr. (1994). *School choice: The struggle for the soul of American education*. New Haven, CT: Yale University Press.

Coons, J., & Monahan, F. J. (1991). *Political action, public policy and Catholic schools*. Washington, DC: National Catholic Educational Association.

Coons, J. E., & Sugarman, S. D. (1991). *Education by choice: The case for family control*. Berkeley: University of California Press.

Coons, J. E., & Sugarman, S. D. (1999). *Making school choice work for all families*. San Francisco: Pacific Research Institute for Public Policy.

Coulson, A. (1999). *Market education: The unknown history*. Washington, DC: The Brookings Institution.

Cubberley, E. P. (1919). *Public education in the United States: A study and interpretation of American educational history*. New York: Houghton Mifflin Co.

Curley, J. R. (1988, July). Education interest groups and the lobbying function in the political process. *Urban Education, 23 (2)*, 162–172.

Curry, T. (1986). *First freedoms: Church and state in America to the passage of the First Amendment*. New York: Oxford University Press.

Davis, W. F. (1998). *Making federal dollars work for Catholic school students and staff*. Washington, DC: United States Catholic Conference

Davis, W. F. (1999). The reauthorization of the Elementary and Secondary Education Act in a Republican-controlled Congress: A view from the bishops' conference. *Catholic Education: A Journal of Inquiry and Practice, 3 (1)*, 97–106.

DeFiore, L. (1999). Choice and justice. *Momentum, XXXI (1)*, 5–8.

Devins, N. E. (Ed.). (1989). *Public values, private schools*. Bristol, PA: The Falmer Press.

Doerr, E., & Mendez, A. (1991). *Church schools and public money*. Buffalo: Prometheus Books.

Drinan, R. F. (1963). *Religion, the courts and public policy*. New York: McGraw-Hill.

Dunn, C. W. (Ed.). (1989). *Religion in American politics*. Washington, DC: CQ Press.

Edwards v. Aguillard, 482 U.S. 575 (1987).

Everson v. Board of Education, 330 U.S. (1947).

Glenn, C. (1991). Controlled choice in Massachusetts public schools. *The Public Interest, 103*, 88–105.

Glenn, C. (2000). *The ambiguous embrace: Government and faith-based schools and social agencies*. Princeton, NJ: Princeton University Press.

Greene, J. P. (1998a). *Civic values in public and private schools*. Paper presented at the meeting of the American Political Science Association, Boston, MA.

Greene, J. P. (1998b). *Integration where it counts: A study of racial integration in public and private school lunchrooms*. Paper presented at the meeting of the American Political Science Association, Boston, MA.

Handy, R. T. (1984). *A Christian America: Protestant hopes and historical realities* (2nd ed.). New York: Oxford University Press.

Hehir, J. B. (1986). *Church-state and church-world: The ecclesiological implications*. Paper presented at the Catholic Theological Society of America: Proceedings of the Forty-First Annual Convention, Chicago.

Herberg, W. (1957, November 16). Justice for religious schools. *America, XCVIII (7)*, 190–193.

Higham, J. (1968). *Strangers in the land: Patterns of American nativism 1860–1925*. New York: Atheneum.

Hill, P. (1999). The supply-side of school choice. In S. Sugarman & F. Kemerer (Eds.), *School choice and social controversy: Politics, policy and the law* (pp. 140–174). Washington, DC: The Brookings Institution.

House Committee Report. (1972). *Tax credits for nonpublic education, Part 1, 2* (Y4.W36:T19/57/pt. 1; pt. 2) Publication 72–603097. Washington, DC: U.S. Government Printing Office.

Howell, W. G., & Peterson, P. E. (2000, March). *School choice in Dayton, Ohio: An evaluation after one year*. Paper prepared for the Conference on Vouchers, Charters and Public Education, sponsored by the Program on Education Policy and Governance, Harvard University.

Jackson v. Benson, 119 S. Ct. 466 (1998)

James, T., & Levin, H. M. (Eds.). (1983). *Public dollars for private schools*. Philadelphia: Temple University Press.

Keeler, W. (1991, July 18). Tracing the development of a bishops' conference. *Origins 21 (9)*, 149–152.

Kozol, J. (1991). *Savage inequalities*. New York: Crown Publishers.

Lemon v. Kurtzman, Early v. DiCenso, 403 U.S. 602 (1971).

Levy, D. C. (Ed.). (1986). *Private education: Studies in choice and public policy*. New York: Oxford University Press.

Lieberman, M. (1989). *Privatization and educational choice*. New York: St. Martin's Press.

Lieberman, M. (1991). *Public school choice: Current issues, future prospects*. Lancaster, PA: Technomic.

Lieberman, M. (1993). *Public education: An autopsy*. Cambridge, MA: Harvard University Press.

Lynch, R. (1990, November 15). The climate of choice in American education. *Origins, 21 (23)*, 373–377.

Malone, J. (1984, November 29). The intersection of public opinion and public policy. *Origins, 14 (24)*, 384–390.

McAndrews, L. (1991, Spring). A closer look: The NCWC and the elementary and secondary education act. *Records 102*, 45–65.

McConnell, C. C. (1990). *A legal analysis of issues related to educational vouchers and public funds for private elementary and secondary schools*. Unpublished doctoral dissertation, University of North Carolina at Greensboro.

McDonald, D. (1995). *Towards full and fair choice: An historical analysis of the lobbying efforts of the Catholic school community in support of federal tax-supported choice in education 1972–1992*. Unpublished doctoral dissertation, Boston College.

McDonald, D. (Ed.). (1999). *Partners for justice: Catholic schools and school choice*. Washington, DC: National Catholic Educational Association.

McDonald, D. (2000). *United States Catholic elementary and secondary schools 1999–2000: Annual statistical report on schools, enrollment and staffing*. Washington, DC: National Catholic Educational Association.

McGrath, J. (Ed.). (1962). *Church and state in American law*. Milwaukee: Bruce Publishing Co.

McKeown, J. (1980, October). The national bishops' conference: An analysis of its origins. *Catholic Historical Review, 66*, 565–583.

McNamee, C. T. (1989, September). A matter of choice. *Momentum, XX (3)*, 2.

Meek v. Pittenger, 421 U.S. 348 (1975).

Milton and Rose Friedman Foundation. (2000). *The ABC's of school choice*. Indianapolis, IN: Friedman Foundation.

Mitchell v. Helms, 120 S. Ct. 2530 (2000).

Mooney, C. (1990). *Boundaries dimly perceived: Law, religion, education and the common good*. Notre Dame, IN: University of Notre Dame Press.

Murray, J. C. (1960). *We hold these truths*. New York: Sheed and Ward.

National Catholic Educational Association (NCEA). (1992). *People's poll on school and school choice*. Washington, DC: Author.

Neuhaus, R. (1984). *The naked public square: Religion and democracy in America*. New York: Eerdmans Books.

Oaks, D. (Ed.). (1963). *The wall between church and state*. Chicago: University of Chicago Press.

O'Keefe, J. M. (1991). *Higher achievement scholars: A study of the experience of minority and low-income students*. Unpublished doctoral dissertation, Harvard University.

O'Keefe, J. M. (1995a). *A Jesuit perspective on school choice*. Unpublished manuscript, American Association of Colleges of Teacher Education.

O'Keefe, J. M. (1995b). No margin, no mission. In T. McLaughlin, J. O'Keefe, & B. O'Keeffe (Eds.), *The contemporary Catholic school: Context, identity and diversity* (pp. 177–197). London: The Falmer Press.

Perry, M. (1991). *Love and power: The role of religion and morality in American politics*. New York: Oxford University Press.

Pierce v. Society of Sisters, 268 U.S. 510 (1925).

Puckett, J. L. (1983, Fall). Educational vouchers: Rhetoric and reality. *Educational Forum, 48*, 7–26.

Ravitch, D. (1983). *The troubled crusade: American education 1945–1980*. New York: Basic Books.

Ravitch, D. (1988). *The great school wars* (2nd ed.). New York: Basic Books.

Rawls, J., (1993). *Political liberalism*. New York: Columbia University Press.

Reese, T. J. (1992). *A flock of shepherds: The National Conference of Catholic Bishops*. New York: Sheed and Ward.

Reichley, A. J. (1985). *Religion in American public life*. Washington, DC: The Brookings Institution.

Reinhart, J. R., & Lee, J. F. (1991). *American education and the dynamics of change*. New York: Praeger.

Rose, L. C., & Gallup, A. M. (1999). Phi Delta Kappa/Gallup 31st annual poll of the public's attitudes toward the public school. *Phi Delta Kappan, 81 (1)*, 41–56.

Rosen, J. (2000, January 30). Is nothing secular? *New York Times Magazine*, Sec. 6-40.

Russo, C. J., & Orsi, M. P. (1992, September). The Supreme Court and the breachable wall. *Momentum, XXIII (2)*, 42–45.

Sanders, J. W. (1977). *The education of an urban minority*. New York: Oxford University Press.

Schneider, B. (1989). Schooling for poor and minority children: An equity perspective. In W. L. Boyd & J. G. Cibulka (Eds.), *Private schools and public policy: An international perspective* (pp. 73–90). London: The Falmer Press.

Shokraii-Rees, N. (2000). *School choice 2000: What's happening in the states.* Washington, DC: The Heritage Foundation.

Spring, J. (1990). *The American school: 1642–1990.* New York: Longmans.

Spring, J. (1991). *American education: An introduction to social and political aspects.* New York: Longmans.

Stravinskas, P. M. (1982). *The constitutional possibilities for governmental financial assistance to nonpublic school parents.* Unpublished doctoral dissertation, Fordham University.

Stream, C. (2000). Do computers cross the church-state divide? *Christianity Today, 4 (2),* 44–46.

Stronks, J. (1995). *The legal definition of religion: Judges, statutory interpretation and neutrality.* Unpublished doctoral dissertation, University of Maryland, College Park.

Sunshine, E. R. (1988). *Moral argument and American consensus: An examination of statements by U.S. Catholic bishops on three public policy issues, 1973–1986.* Unpublished doctoral dissertation, Graduate Theological Union.

Tyack, D. B. (1974). *The one best system.* Cambridge, MA: Harvard University Press.

Underwood, J. K. (1989, November 9). Establishment of religion in primary and secondary schools. *Education Law Reporter, 807,* 195–226.

United States Catholic Conference (USCC). (1972). *To teach as Jesus did.* Washington, DC: National Conference of Catholic Bishops.

United States Catholic Conference (USCC). (1995). *Principles for educational reform in the United States.* Washington, DC: Author.

United States Catholic Conference (USCC). (1999). *Faithful citizenship: Civic responsibility for a new millennium.* Washington, DC: Author.

Veverka, F. (1985, Winter). The ambiguity of Catholic educational separatism. *Religious Education, 80 (1),* 65–100.

Viteritti, J. P. (1999). *Choosing equality: School choice, the constitution, and civil society.* Washington, DC: The Brookings Institution.

Walch, T. (1996). *Parish school: American Catholic parochial education from colonial times to the present.* New York: Crossroad Publishing.

Weber, J., & Gilbert, D. (1981). *Private churches and public money: Church-government fiscal relations.* Westport, CT: Greenwood Press.

Wilson, R. (1989). *The Supreme Court, religion and education: An investigation of intention.* Unpublished doctoral dissertation, University of Washington.

Witte, J. F. (2000). *The market approach to education: An analysis of America's first voucher program.* Princeton, NJ: Princeton University Press.

Wolfe, A. (1998). *One nation after all.* New York: Viking Press.

Yoder v. Wisconsin, 406 U.S. 205 (1972).

Zorach v. Clauson, 343 U.S. 306, 313 (1952).

Chapter 11

Catholic School Finance:
A Review of Research

Barbara M. De Luca

INTRODUCTION

While there is a plethora of public school finance research available, there is a dearth of research which addresses Catholic school finance. This chapter includes reviews of some of the available studies completed by individual researchers, the National Catholic Educational Association (NCEA), as well as the National Center for Educational Statistics (NCES).

The study of school finance generally includes three major areas: revenue sources, allocation strategies, and expenditure patterns. The study of revenue sources includes the origins of the incoming dollars and addresses such questions as: From where does the money come? What proportion of the money comes from each source? How stable is each source? What impact does the source have on dioceses, communities, parishes, schools, and families?

Research studies on revenue sources for Catholic schools are legion. This review includes not only the sources of revenue, but also, in some cases, the proportion of support from each source. Also included in this chapter are studies which investigated the effects of inadequate revenue.

Allocation strategies, the second major area of study in school finance, refers to how the money which is centrally collected is distributed to individual districts and from the district to the individual schools. In the public sector, tax money is collected both locally and at the state level. In most states the local money stays in the local district and the state money is distributed by using some type of formula. Studies exploring allocation strategies in public education often involve examining the formula used and analyzing its component parts with respect to equity and adequacy of distribution. Only recently has noteworthy research been done in the public school arena on allocation strategies from district levels to individual schools within the district. One of the reasons for the paucity of work in this area is the lack of available data. In the case of Catholic schools, studying allocation strategies would involve analyzing the various approaches for apportioning revenue from the diocesan level, religious community level (for schools operated by religious communities), or the parish level (in cases of one parish supporting more than one school) to the individual schools. It would seek answers to questions such as: What is the formula for distributing money? If there is no formula, how are specific allotments determined? Who makes the decisions? Are there winners and losers as a result of the distribution strategies used? Is there a relationship between allocation strategies and student achievement?

Finally, little investigation involving expenditure patterns has been undertaken by researchers in school finance. Expenditure patterns refers to the building-level methods used to allocate funds. Such studies could address the following questions: How are dollars spent once they reach the individual schools? Is there a pattern? Is there a relationship between expenditure patterns and achievement? Very little work has been undertaken in this area, primarily because of the tremendous lack of school-level data. Some states are trying to collect such data to fill this void. When they are available, studying expenditure patterns from school to school and comparing public and private schools, in particular Catholic schools, will likely prove very informative. Funding decisions in many private schools are site-based, while much decision making in public schools is done centrally.

Ideally, the remainder of this chapter would be divided into five sections: revenue sources, allocation strategies, expenditure patterns, and a section identified as "other," which will look at studies which either combine revenues and expenditures or cannot be put into one category or another. However, most of the research in Catholic school finance is descriptive in nature and much of it is all-inclusive; that is, it addresses more than one of the relevant finance topics, and often, all are included. As much as possible, the following reviews are separated into the topics identified earlier.

REVENUE

In a report entitled *Public and Private Schools: How Do They Differ?*, NCES (1997) data were used to look at differences in revenue sources, students, teachers, organization, management, school climate, academic programs, and support services between public and private schools. This review will only address the finance components of the report. One way the two types of schools differ is in their sources of revenue. Revenue sources identified were tuition, endowments, grants, charitable donations, and public funds for certain services in some states.

Average non-sectarian private school tuition in 1993–1994 was slightly more than 67% higher than average Catholic school tuition, and 56% higher than average tuition of other religious schools. The average tuition for Catholic schools was $1,628 for elementary schools and $3,643 for secondary. At the same time, tuition for other religious schools averaged $2,606 for elementary and $5,261 for high school students. Private non-sectarian average annual tuition was the highest of all three private groups: $4,693 for elementary students and $9,525 for secondary students (NCES, 1997).

In a qualitative study designed to examine issues associated with changes undertaken in Catholic, inner-city Black elementary schools in Chicago in 1997, Nelson (1994) used interviews and case studies to investigate the "relationship between resource dependency, autonomy, and institutional legitimacy" (p. 209). The changes that had occurred were an effort to avoid closure, a fate that affected 117 schools in the area beetween 1965 and 1985. Of the 62 schools available, interviews were conducted at 33. Each school in the sample experienced a severe decrease in revenue and substantial reorganization, resulting from changes in local socioeconomic conditions. The schools were divided into four categories based on the adjustments made to address the changing environment: parish-centered (13), isolated (8), cooperatively linked (7), and externally linked (6). A case study was developed for one school in each category.

Parish-centered schools received 86% of their budget from tuition and fees even as enrollment dropped 50%. They were able to maintain this level of support through very active parish, community, and teacher involvement. Isolated schools essentially had been abandoned by their parishes. Because of declining enrollment, they could no longer support themselves, and any significant parish support would arguably have required a major commitment of parish resources. Many of the survival tactics undertaken by the isolated schools were a result of fiscal deficiencies (Nelson, 1994). For example, in order to attract a sufficient number of students to generate enough revenue to keep the school open, a more generalist curriculum was devised, compared to the expected Catholic school program containing many religious concepts.

Cooperatively linked schools consisted of schools in the same area which chose to work together. Each retained a weak connection to its local parish. In the restructuring process, the archdiocese rather than the parish was responsible for the fiscal needs of the schools. Financial responsibilities were centralized so they were no longer the focus of the individual school principals. Externally linked schools, despite keeping very weak links to local parishes, generated revenue from sources external to the local parish or archdiocese. Most of the students in externally linked schools were from areas outside the immediate neighborhood. More than 55% of the schools' budgets was met by outside supporters (Nelson, 1994). This, along with externally provided scholarship money, allowed for lower tuition rates which, in turn, prevented the schools from closing.

Following her description of each category of schools, Nelson (1994) discussed the implications of the four different revenue sources she identified. Although being assured of supplemental revenue from the parish or archdiocese, parish schools could still face financial problems if the parish or diocese faced decline. Because of the ties to the larger Church, such schools would not be free to make adjustments in mission or focus to attract a wider population. The threat of closure still existed.

Although the isolated schools enjoyed more local decision-making power, they faced the greatest threat of closure in cases of serious finance deficits (Nelson, 1994). These schools were completely dependent on the environment—a poor, inner-city environment.

Externally linked schools had the greatest potential for maintaining and even increasing revenue. However, the broader the revenue sources, the more generic in nature the curriculum became in each school (Nelson, 1994). Furthermore, because of the compulsion to please funders so as not to lose the revenue source, principals were torn between designing programs to please funders and meeting student needs. Also, generating revenue became a major component of the principal's job.

Cooperatively linked schools remained under the authority of the archdiocese. As a result, not only did they have little autonomy, but because the newly formed linkages were not yet strong, there was little resistance when the archdiocese decided to close some schools and reorganize others (Nelson, 1994).

Nelson (1994) concluded that each model has advantages and disadvantages with respect to its ability to generate revenue and secure its own future. More study is required to see if, in fact, one model does fit the "Chicago-type" situation better than another, or if decisions are best made on an ad hoc basis.

Although tuition and fees are the primary revenue source for Catholic schools, some revenue comes from the federal government. McDonald (1995) investigated the efforts made by the Catholic school community to encourage public funding for Catholic schools during the early 1970s, when political campaigns were addressing aid to non-public schools. McDonald summarizes the evolution of Catholic schools and public funding for them, including the school lunch program, public transportation, and student textbook programs. Also included is mention of proposed assistance which did not pass the constitutional test: monies for non-religious educational services, teacher salaries, and non-text instructional materials.

Given the public agenda to advocate school choice during the early 1970s, Republicans began promoting tuition tax credits. Also at this time, McDonald (1995) explains, the United States Catholic Conference (USCC) and the NCEA shifted efforts from trying to secure funding for schools and particular activities to securing funds for individuals. McDonald's research is an investigation of the efforts of Catholic leaders (USCC and NCEA) and several non-Catholic private organizations to lobby for choice in education (tuition tax credits being one way of providing choice) from 1972 through 1992. Questions addressed by the research included: Did the Catholic school community engage in lobbying efforts to promote the school choice movement? Did the community take advantage of the political climate at the time? If yes, why were school choice legislation efforts ineffective?

McDonald (1995) used a historical methodology and a modified case study approach. Primary data sources included archival materials, public records, and interviews. Some secondary data sources were also used. By tracing activities undertaken by legislators, Catholic leaders, and other relevant parties with respect to the 1973 Mills-Byrnes Bill, the Moynihan-Packwood Bill of 1978, the Educational Opportunity and Equity Act of 1983, and America 2000 Excellence in Education Act/Neighborhood Schools Improvement Act (1991), McDonald was able to identify patterns of behavior by Catholic community leaders which resulted in the failure of lobbying efforts. Her research resulted in the identification of 14 reasons for the lack of success of the school choice proposals promulgated from the early 1970s through the early 1990s. The reasons ranged from existing legal restrictions to the principles of group dynamics; available level of resources; skill level, experience, and traditional roles of the Catholic community with respect to lobbying, communicating, and so forth; and attitudes of participants with respect to tuition tax credits or vouchers.

Six conclusions based on the findings are identified (McDonald, 1995). In general, the conclusions suggest that there is much work needed if the Catholic community anticipates playing a major role in affecting future legislation. Effective lobbying is an art as well as a science, and leaders in the Catholic community must realize this to be effective in the political arena.

Carlson (1970) investigated public aid as a possible revenue source to help solve the financial woes of Catholic schools in the 1960s. His thesis begins with an explanation of why Catholic school enrollment declined in the 1960s. Because there were fewer religious, schools were forced to hire lay teachers at salaries substantially higher than those paid to religious. This drove costs up, which, in turn, forced student tuition and fees up, which led to decreases in enrollment. Furthermore, because the Second Vatican Council put less emphasis on parochial education, families began to question the worth of the extra expenditure. While these two phenomena were occurring, there was a decline in the Catholic birth rates and families were moving to places where fewer Catholic schools existed, generally the suburbs.

Lower enrollments led to major financial crises. Fewer children in each classroom meant the cost increased. At the same time, church operating expenses were increasing as a result of inflation, and revenue was not keeping up with increased expenses, so churches were less able to subsidize schools. Finally, as enrollments decreased, schools and churches were not able to maintain payments on capital debt incurred when enrollments were up. Specifically, expenditures for Great Falls Central High for 669 students in 1968–1969 totaled $195,750; income for that same year was $175,006, creating a $20,744 deficit. Budget figures for 1969–1970 (643 students) identified expenditures of $245,008 and income of $156,717, a deficit of $88,291 (Carlson, 1970).

Through a series of simple calculations, Carlson (1970) showed that costs to the public increase as children leave Catholic schools and go to public institutions, resulting in a need for increased millage to support the public schools.

Cost increases were caused by the need for more staff and expanded facility needs to accommodate the additional children. Such cost increases without comparable revenue increases cannot exist long term in any system. Revenues must increase or costs decrease; with an influx of children from Catholic schools, costs cannot decrease.

Proposed solutions to the problem at Great Falls High School included reducing operating expenses, increasing revenue, requesting greater support from the Catholic community, looking for federal assistance, and investigating local city and public school district assistance. Carlson (1970) administered a survey to a random sample of voters in Great Falls, Montana to solicit opinions and attitudes regarding the proposed solutions. Catholics and non-Catholics favored assistance in the form of aid for transportation and textbooks in order to save the local Catholic high school. Rather than increase millage by four points to support all children going to public schools, the survey indicated that the people would be willing to support the Catholic school at a district and county level of 1.16 mills. A cost-benefit analysis indicated that public support was feasible. If public aid were provided, there would be no need to increase tuition, which would reduce or eliminate enrollment declines (and, in fact, might even increase enrollment) and eliminate increased enrollment in public schools. Because it is less expensive to operate a Catholic school than a public school (lower salaries), it would cost less for the people to subsidize the Catholic school than pay increased taxes to expand public schools. Carlson determined that a level of public support that would allow tuition to be cut in half would induce this reaction.

Survey results also showed that Catholics were willing to provide greater financial support to the school than was being provided currently. Furthermore, Carlson (1970) concluded that the solution of public aid had merit and suggested several methods of providing public aid: tax credits, tuition grants, and shared time plans.

A small proportion of school revenue comes from the federal government. Chapter 1 (of Title I of the Elementary and Secondary Education Act in 1965) monies come from the federal government to both public and private schools to assist in educating disadvantaged children. Haslam and Humphrey (1993) completed a study for the U.S. Department of Education investigating the services provided to students in religious schools using Chapter 1 money. They gathered data from several sources. The Sectarian School Survey garnered information from a nationally representative sample of religious schools with students participating in Chapter 1. The School District Survey provided information from public schools providing Chapter 1 services. Finally, the School Services Survey collected data from a non-representative sample of religious schools not participating in Chapter 1, although they had eligible students. Other data sources, including case studies, were also used.

A historical and legal review of various issues surrounding the use of Chapter 1 monies in religious schools is provided. Of all students served through Chapter 1, only 3% were from religious schools in 1990–1991 (Haslam & Humphrey, 1993). Religious school student participation in Chapter 1 fluctuated over time and from district to district. Participation rates were greatest for schools located in large, urban districts. Private school participation rates peaked in 1980–1981 and hit a low in 1985–1986. This was one year after the *Aguilar v. Felton* (1985) legal case in which Title I programs on religious schools' premises were declared unconstitutional. Participation rates increased slowly through the late 1980s and early 1990s. About 20% of the districts providing Chapter 1 services to students in religious schools experienced an increase in the number of students served as a result of the *Felton* decision. Conversely, about 33% realized a decline. The study recognized that factors beyond the *Felton* decision also affected Chapter 1 participation rates: changes in total school enrollment, the number of Chapter 1 students enrolled, and parent willingness to allow children to participate.

Increased participation after *Felton* was attributed to several factors: clarification of permissible method of delivery and instruction, the willingness to use computer-aided instruction, and district efforts to encourage student participation (Haslam & Humphrey, 1993). More recent increases in participation were found to be the result of a strong commitment by public and religious schools to work together to provide services, more secure and convenient service delivery systems, use of third-party contractors, and the availability of capital funds. However, service is still refused by many, and some school districts choose not to service religious schools for one of a variety of reasons, many of which are either financial or practical in nature.

Chapter 1 services were and continue to be provided through the public school district in which the religious school is located. The funds are not provided to the religious school itself. Therefore, to fully understand the financial value of the in-kind services provided, the researchers would have had to assign a dollar value to each service. No attempt was made to do this in the study. In reality, however, the services provided to religious schools via Chapter 1 grants secured by the public school district constitute revenue. Thus, the inclusion of this study is appropriate in this chapter. The study (Haslam & Humphrey, 1993) includes an in-depth look at the nature of the Chapter 1 services provided to religious school students. Districts serving a larger number of religious-school students (31–1000+) were more likely to use computer-aided instruction as one component of their delivery system than were districts serving small numbers of religious-school students (1–30). The latter districts were much more likely to service the religious-school students in a public school facility. Vans or portable classrooms were used extensively by districts serving large numbers of religious-school students, and nearly half of the districts serving 1,000 or more students used facilities at a neutral site.

Most Chapter 1 instruction to religious-school students was in reading and mathematics and 90% of the student participants were in grades K–6. About 60% of the students received Chapter 1 instruction at least three days per week; 9% reported receiving instruction only one day per week. The study report included the length of instructional sessions and the time of day instruction was provided. It also included a comparison of both schools and students from public and private settings participating in the study in the 1987–1988 school year (Haslam & Humphrey, 1993).

The participant selection process for each school and the level and nature of coordination between the Chapter 1 services and the regular instruction program were also investigated in this study (Haslam & Humphrey, 1993).

The Hawkins-Stafford Amendments authorized funds for capital expenses incurred as a result of service adaptations for religious-school students necessitated by the *Felton* decision. Federal funds are initially distributed to the state and made available to districts via a grant process. Funds are available to cover costs of transporting students, purchasing equipment, leasing property, payment of costs incurred to increase participation rates, and payment of other, eligible current expenses. The money may not be used for instruction purposes, only for administrative expenses (Haslam & Humphrey, 1993).

Haslam and Humphrey (1993) discovered that appropriations for capital expenses routinely fell short of actual expenses incurred. For example, the late 1989 appropriation covered only 31% of the eligible expenditures. Of the money appropriated for 1988, nearly 50% was spent on mobile vans, about 27% was spent on securing other appropriate neutral sites, 19% on portable classrooms, and almost 5% on public school sites.

From 1988 through 1992, between 80% and 90% of districts serving 1,000+ religious-school students received capital expense funds. Furthermore, districts serving 1,000 or more students spent large portions of their money on purchase and lease of real and personal property, as did higher-poverty districts (Haslam & Humphrey, 1993). Districts serving a smaller number of students and poor districts spent much of their money on transportation. Funds were also used for upgrading existing facilities, particularly for computer-assisted instructional needs.

Unfortunately, the researchers (Haslam & Humphrey, 1993) did not report district cost per pupil for providing Chapter 1 services. However, in situations where the funding bypasses the state (for one reason or another) and flows directly from the federal level to local districts, the expenditure per pupil was higher than in non-bypass states, due to additional administrative expenses. In the bypass states as well as in a variety of other circumstances, third-party contractors were hired to deliver the Chapter 1 program. The school district, however, retains fiscal responsibility.

The costs of delivering Chapter 1 services by third-party contractors in non-bypass states were generally less than the cost to school districts for providing the same service. Third-party contractors paid lower wages and often were able to use part-time staff. Lower per-pupil cost allows more pupils to be served. The privatizing of Chapter 1 services provided religious schools with a more responsible partner than some school districts proved to be (Haslam & Humphrey, 1993). Third-party contractors recognized that their lack of cooperation could result in a loss of revenue.

Equity has been and continues to be a major issue in matters of school finance. Equity refers to both equal amounts of money spent and equal services provided per pupil across a program. Both types of equity were difficult to assess. In one case study, more money was being spent on public- than religious-school participants, but this was because more computer-assisted instruction was employed for religious-school children. Haslam and Humphrey (1993) recommended that these and other equity issues be given more attention in future research.

The final section in the research report discussed options for improving Chapter 1 programs for students in religious schools. Several recommendations were mentioned with respect to the capital grant procedure, including simplifying the state grant programs, providing assistance in the grant application process to smaller schools with small administrative staffs, and eliminating funds for past expenditure and focus on the future (Haslam & Humphrey, 1993).

The purpose of a 1997 study conducted by the NCEA was to investigate the growth of Catholic schools from 1985 to 1995 and to provide data regarding facilities, finances, and sponsorship. In an effort to develop a comprehensive database about Catholic schools opened since 1985, the researchers collected data on a variety of topics including some finance matters, specifically sources of funding for buildings, cost of facilities, and sources of funding for the 1994–1995 operating budgets of schools. Data were collected through surveys sent to principals of the 138 schools newly opened between 1985 and 1995. (Schools reopened and consolidated schools were eliminated from the study.) Diocesan superintendents were asked to verify information provided by principals. The sample of 138 schools consisted of 120 elementary schools, 14 middle schools, and four pre-K–12 facilities.

Survey respondents reported that matters related to finances presented the greatest obstacles to opening new schools. Of the 58 respondents identifying "securing capital" as an obstacle, 21 identified it as one of the greatest obstacles. Nearly 27% (21 of 79 respondents) reported "obtaining support for annual operating budgets" as one of the greatest obstacles. All other challenges were nonfinancial in nature and were considered to be only "minor obstacles" by a majority of respondents (NCEA, 1997).

Several different sources were identified for securing the facility. About 30% of the new elementary schools were started in parish buildings with no additions while 29% were new buildings. The remaining 41% of the new elementary schools fell between these two extremes: 18% used existing parish buildings with additions, 8% leased a building, 8% erected a modular building, and 7% purchased an existing structure (NCEA, 1997).

Twenty-three respondents reported the cost of building a new elementary school. One school cost over $6 million and three cost under $1 million. However, caution must be taken when comparing these dollar values; the study covered a 10-year period of time and the costs were not adjusted for inflation (NCEA, 1997).

Funding sources for the new buildings included "cash from diocese," "cash from parish," "fund drive," "borrowed," and "other." In all geographic districts except the Plains, the single greatest source of funding for a new elementary school facility was a "fund drive." The second most frequently cited funding source was borrowing. Only new schools in the Mideast, West/Far West, and South received "cash from diocese" for the facility. New schools in the Plains, Southeast, West/Far West received some cash directly from a parish. In the New England region, 100% of the money for new facilities came from a "fund drive." Additionally, it was the only region in which no borrowing was done. Excluding the New England region, the average percentage of funding generated through borrowing was slightly over 37% (NCEA, 1997).

When asked about future building additions, 23 respondents anticipated a future addition at less than $1 million. Seven expected a needed addition between $1 and $2 million. Six respondents were planning additions exceeding $2 million (NCEA, 1997).

Average 1995–1996 tuition for the first child was highest in the West/Far West ($1,966) and lowest in the Mideast ($1,135). Average tuition for all six regions was about $1,529 (NCEA, 1997).

About 29% (26 of 91) reported no parish subsidy for the school budget. Ten of those schools were in the West/Far West where tuition was highest. About one-fourth of the schools received 1% to 20% of their budgets from the parish. About 26.4% of the new elementary schools reported 21% to 40% of their budgets being subsidized by parishes (NCEA, 1997). The Plains had the greatest number of schools (10) receiving over 40% of their budgets from parishes.

Fourteen new secondary schools were opened between 1985 and 1996. None was located in New England or the Mideast. One was in the Great Lakes region, four in both the Plains and West/Far West, and five in the Southeast (NCEA, 1997).

The major difficulties encountered when opening the new secondary schools were financial. Eight respondents cited "securing capital" as the major obstacle; none reported it as a minor hurdle. Three reported "obtaining support for annual operating budget" as a major obstacle; six reported it as a concern and none considered it a minor problem (NCEA, 1997). Sixty-two percent of the secondary facilities were built new, 23% were leased, and 15% were renovated existing buildings.

Of the eight new facilities built (for which data were reported), four cost between $2.5 million and $4.5 million; four were over $10 million, including the costliest at $26 million. The diocese paid 100% of the cost of the one new facility in the Great Lakes region. As with the new elementary schools, fund drives played an important role in financing new secondary facilities. Half of the money needed in the West/Far West was borrowed. The majority of the schools planning additions anticipated costs under $1 million (NCEA, 1997). A second addition was planned by seven schools.

The average 1995–1996 tuition for the first child was highest in the West/Far West at $3,990 and the lowest was in the Great Lakes at $2,200 (NCEA, 1997).

A 1963 (Greeley & Rossi, 1966) and a replicate 1974 (Greeley, McCready, & McCourt, 1976) study were conducted through the National Opinion Research Center (NORC) to investigate the role of a Catholic school education in students' adult lives. While the early study contained very little about finances, the 1976 "replication" directly addressed financial support for schools. An initial sample of 1,128 American adult Catholics was surveyed through interviews by trained staff from NORC; 927 surveys were usable, a completion rate of 81% (Greeley et al., 1976).

When asked if they would be willing to give additional money to prevent a Catholic school from closing, 80% of the respondents said they would give more. Of those with more than 10 years of Catholic education, 86% would give more. But, interestingly enough, 79% of the respondents with no Catholic education would give more. When asked how much more they would be willing to give, responses ranged from under $5 to over $500. Projecting the response rates onto the entire 1975 population, the researchers determined that only 2% would be willing to give over $500 and only 3% under $5. About 28% would be willing to contribute between $51 and $100 to keep the school open (Greeley et al., 1976).

Correlation coefficients between willingness to give and various religious beliefs and practices were low. The correlation coefficients between willingness to give and age as well as between willingness to give and education were .00. "Anticlericalism" ($-.18$) and "rigid sexual morality" ($-.16$) had a negative relationship with willingness to give, although neither was strong (Greeley et al., 1976).

When asked why they did not send their children to Catholic schools, 24% of the respondents claimed that they were too expensive. The cost was the "most compelling deterrent for urban dwellers" (Greeley et al., 1976, p. 230). Cost was also mentioned by parents with less education and lower income. Only 8% of the parents with 1974 incomes over $20,000 and sending their children to non-Catholic schools identified cost of Catholic schools as the reason for sending children elsewhere. About 45% of the Spanish-speaking parents identified cost as the reason.

Of the total sample, 76% believed schools should get federal aid. About 62% thought parents with children in Catholic schools should get a tax refund while only 30% believed the government should provide vouchers for children to attend any school. Using correlation analysis, Greeley et al. (1976) concluded that "an individual's current involvement in the activities of the Catholic Church, combined with acceptance of the teachings of the church, is more likely to influence his or her support for Catholic schools" (pp. 241–242) than either number of years of Catholic education or highest education level of respondent.

Average tuition in 1974 was $343. Respondents reported spending an average of 3.32% of their income on Catholic schools. Other financial data are included in both the 1963 and 1974 reports, but the focus of these findings is on the Church rather than the schools (Greeley et al., 1976).

The next two research studies (Hensley, 1995; Plante, 1991) were undertaken for Ph.D. dissertations. Unfortunately, because no institution would lend the original works, the reviews included in this chapter are based on abstracts.

To investigate knowledge of and attitude toward funding revenues for parish Catholic elementary schools, Plante (1991) surveyed pastors, principals, and laity of parish schools with Sisters of Mercy as principals. Survey questions asked about tuition, fund-raising, development, and government sources of revenue. Plante found that principals had the most knowledge about the revenue sources. Overall, the least amount of knowledge was held regarding development revenue activities. She concluded that if development programs are going to become an important source of revenue for Catholic elementary schools, principals, pastors, and laity must gain knowledge about development.

Hensley (1995) undertook a study to analyze equity in Catholic elementary schools in the St. Louis Archdiocese. She used both the McLoone Index and the Gini Index to test equity of educational opportunity in 67 schools. County schools were the most equitable while the greatest inequities existed at a regional level. Hensley also found that dependence on local wealth decreased during the study period of the 1993 to the 1995 fiscal years. In yet another part of her analysis, a correlation analysis showed no significant relationship between per-pupil expenditures and achievement outcomes.

EXPENDITURES

Larson (1995) looked at religious elementary schools in the Phoenix area and compared the nature of the students, mission or goals, programs offered, and expenditures to those of public elementary schools in the same area. Of the 50 religious elementary schools in the Phoenix area, 12 were willing to participate in her study. Data consisted of information collected through interviews with administrators and from secondary sources available to the researcher such as mission or goal statements and curricular and program offerings. The specific goal of the research was to "provide data on the actual costs of religious elementary education" (p. 5).

Descriptive data collected included student ethnicity, class size, teacher salaries, principal salaries, and expenditure per pupil. Teacher and principal salaries were substantially higher in public than in private schools. Principal salaries were generally higher in non-Catholic private schools, but this was not necessarily the case with teacher salaries. Expenditure per pupil in non-Catholic private schools ranged from $1,714 to $4,600 (Larson, 1995). Eliminating the extreme of $4,600, the range would be $1,714 to $2,464. Expenditure per pupil in Catholic schools ranged from $1,612 to $2,545.

Using data collected from all sources, Larson (1995) created three typical classrooms, one to represent the Catholic elementary schools, another to represent the non-Catholic religious schools, and the third to typify the public schools in her sample. All costs (except capital costs) for operating and maintaining the three classrooms were prorated for a class of 25 students. Total expenditures for the typical Catholic school classroom were $41,196 ($1,647.84 per pupil). For non-Catholic religious schools, total costs for the typical classroom came to $40,299.09 ($1,611.96 per pupil). Expenditures for a typical public school classroom totaled $64,021.46 ($2,560.86 per pupil).

In comparing the "ingredient" costs (Larson, 1995) for public and private religious schools, all teacher costs were lower in the private sector, as were utilities and communications, supplies and materials, and benefits (private less than 9% of public); but administrative (principal) and student services personnel (secretary, custodian) costs were higher in the private religious schools.

To adjust for the scale differences in the typical public school size (630 pupils) and private religious school size (195.38 pupils), Larson (1995) developed a second public school expenditure model using the private school size. Total expenditures for this typical classroom equaled $74,199.53 ($2,967.98 per pupil). After the scale adjustment was made, all expenditures for the ingredients in a typical private religious classroom were less than the public school counterpart. A marginal analysis was also done for each classroom model to compare costs of additional services such as librarians, day care, and computers.

With respect to finance, Larson (1995) concluded that expenditure differences did indeed exist between Catholic and non-Catholic private schools as well as between private and public schools included in the study. When scale of the institution was considered and program offerings were held constant in the calculations, "projected public school costs were over 50% greater than in nonpublic schools" (p. 98), primarily due to teacher salaries and benefits.

ALLOCATION PATTERNS

A study by David (1972) was designed to examine the management procedures of Catholic schools. David was interested in investigating the Planning-Programming-Budgeting (PPBS) method of management and superintendents' level of familiarity with it. PPBS is a process of management that includes attention to objectives, goals, inputs, outputs, and alternatives, rather than just focusing on the level of financial revenue available. Using a seven-point, Likert-type scale, David interviewed superintendents of 10 dioceses in Louisiana, Alabama, Mississippi, and Florida to garner information regarding personal characteristics of parish leaders, factual data regarding dioceses and schools, structures of authority, budgeting procedures, and superintendents' opinions about past and future events.

With respect to degree of familiarity with PPBS, three superintendents claimed to have studied and implemented the technique while another had never heard of it. Three were familiar with the name only and three had little familiarity (David, 1972).

All respondents reported financial problems. Some reported that poorer parishes were having to close schools. The need to pay competitive salaries to lay teachers because of the availability of fewer religious led to an increase in tuition. The tuition increases caused children to leave Catholic schools. Through his interviews, David (1972) discovered that 30 elementary schools had been closed within the previous three years and no new schools were planned.

When questioned about the future, all superintendents agreed that change was necessary and would be coming. However, there was little consensus on the nature of the change. When asked how they viewed the financial crises facing diocesan systems, three superintendents felt resources were being used efficiently; the remaining seven did not agree (David, 1972).

When asked about a uniform accounting system for all schools in the diocese, eight superintendents said they had one, one had none, and one said a "partial" system was in place. With respect to the school budgets, some superintendents reported being completely removed from the process while others were deeply involved. In some cases, the school principal prepared the budget and sent it to the diocese for approval while in others, the school boards prepared the budget, and in still others, the pastor developed the budget. One superintendent reported that the high school budgets were done at the diocesan (bishop) level. In some cases, the pastor, principal, and lay board prepare the budget together. Although all superintendents reported that tuition was the main source of revenue for the schools, they also reported that parishes supplemented revenue for elementary schools. Annual deficits were not uncommon. They were often due to revenue levels (from tuition) that did not cover expenditures or parent inability to pay the full tuition. Deficits were covered by either general funds of the parish or diocese (David, 1972).

The PPBS model requires the identification of objectives prior to budget development. Seven superintendents reported that school faculty worked on objectives. Self-assessment is also critical to the PPBS model. Five superintendents reported no form of self-evaluation was in place, four reported some form existed, and one superintendent said the district was working on it (David, 1972).

Respondents were also given the opportunity to address other management issues. The interviewing process included considerable opportunity for respondents to provide a variety of unstructured information.

David (1972) drew 10 conclusions from his study. Those related to finance included: "management (leadership style) is authoritarian" (p. 98); "accountability for decisions on the use of resources will increase in number and accuracy" (p. 98); "state aid to Catholic education will begin or increase in every state in the foreseeable future" (pp. 98–99); "innovation is expensive, and so, funds will be made available only when there is a high expectation of success" (p. 100); "systems analysis emphasizes approaches to decision-making which allow better choices to be made" (p. 100); "systems analysis in the form of PPBS will be necessary to Catholic schools in the pursuit of better organizational and financial management" (p. 100); and "cost/effectiveness (benefits) studies in the decision-making of the allocation of scarce resources to the best choice among alternatives will increase in volume and importance" (pp. 100–101).

The final study reviewed in this section addressed both expenditures and allocation patterns in an effort to compare efficiency in private and public schools. Meier's study (1994) utilized the Micro-Financial Cascade Model to compare one Catholic and two other non-sectarian private schools to 422 diverse public schools. After tracking the expenditures to the classroom level, Meier sorted allocations and expenditures for all 425 schools into 10 functions. His analysis showed that the private schools allocated between 41% and 60% of their funds to the classroom. Public schools allocated between 54% and 63% to the classroom. Private schools spent an average of 18.57% of their funds on administration while public schools spent only 11.55% on administration. Meier concluded that private schools were not necessarily more efficient than public schools.

A COMBINED VIEW

Lundy (1999) began his research with a rather lengthy history of Catholic school enrollments and the factors affecting enrollments, not the least of which was financial. Although many urban Catholic elementary schools were forced, by a lack of revenue, to close their doors, some Catholic elementary schools in low-income urban areas have thrived over time. The purpose of Lundy's study was to attempt to identify differences between the schools forced to close or consolidate (non-survivor schools) and those able to remain open (survivor schools). Schools studied were in the Chicago Archdiocese, and the study ran from 1991 to 1994.

The study consisted of three components. First, a comparison of finances was done between the survivor and non-survivor schools. A discriminant analysis was then done to determine if survival rates could have been predicted. Finally, strong predictor variables from the discriminant analysis were correlated with responses to a survey completed by school principals (Lundy, 1999).

Several financial features were identical for both types of schools. There was no difference in the amount of tuition collected per student between the survivor and non-survivor schools. Both types of schools received 84% of their revenue from tuition and fees and 9% from fund-raising. Compensation constituted 82% of the expenditures for both survivors and non-survivors (Lundy, 1999).

Parish subsidies for non-survivor schools averaged $138,000 compared to $160,000 for survivor schools. Other differences between the two types of schools included average enrollment, 345 for the survivors and 175 for the non-survivors (Lundy, 1999). Regular annual collection of the sponsoring church was $480,000 for the survivors and $313,000 for the non-survivors. While the percentage of expenditures committed to compensation was identical for the two types of schools, the percent of income was quite different. About 53% of income of survivor schools went to compensation, but slightly more than 77% of non-survivor school income went to compensation. The churches of the non-survivors had an average of 7.5% of their revenue available for the schools, while the churches of the survivors contributed an average of 26.2% of their revenue as subsidy to schools.

Other financial comparisons were made. Non-survivors spent an average of 22.68% more per pupil than survivors. Non-survivors' average parish deficit was $104,099; survivors' average parish surplus was $4,312 (Lundy, 1999).

After discussing the details of an archdiocesan grant program targeted at needy parishes and schools, Lundy (1999) concluded that the factor that most effectively distinguished survivors from non-survivors was the relationship between revenues and expenditures for both the parish and school, rather than the sociodemographic characteristics of parishioners and students.

The discriminant analysis included 22 independent variables, two of which were demographic and 20 of which were financial. The dependent variable was school status, either survivor or non-survivor. Eight variables were eliminated by the analysis because of high intercorrelation. The remaining 14 variables correctly predicted survivor status 93% of the time. Lundy's (1999) statistical analysis predicted survivor rates considerably better than non-survivors, which suggested that other elements were involved in closure and consolidation decisions that the 14 variables used in the analysis encompassed. Lundy speculated on the "other elements."

Further analysis suggested that variables related to staff compensation (either parish or school) were the most important individual predictors of survival status. Size was important, but not as important as the compensation component. Results indicated that the wealth of the parish was not an important determinant in closure decisions (Lundy, 1999).

Finally, six themes identified from the survey phase of the research were correlated with the 14 variables used in the discriminant analysis. Findings from this phase of the research suggested that verbal support from the pastor, "clear articulation of the role of the school in the parish mission" (Lundy, 1999, p. 104), and implementation of good financial management practices contributed to the survival of schools.

Kealey (1990, 1994, 1996, 1998) undertook four NCEA-sponsored studies of the financial status of Catholic elementary schools. In order to make comparisons more easily through the years, all four studies will be examined together in this chapter. A 100-item survey was used for data collection in each of the four study years. The original instrument was designed for the 1988–1989 school year and was adjusted as needed for each subsequent study. Information gathered included details on school demographics, finances, compensation, and other special issues. Surveys were sent to a random sample of elementary schools for each study year. A selected review of Kealey's work has been compiled and presented in tables developed by the author of this chapter. Table 11.1 summarizes the revenues from each year. Table 11.2 shows the expenditures. Using

Table 11.1
Revenue Sources from Kealey (1990, 1994, 1996, 1998) NCEA Surveys

Item of Information	1989	1993	1995	1997
Number of surveys distributed	1,200	1,021	1,018	1,012
Percent of surveys returned usable	75.58%	60%	60%	68.1%
Percent of all Catholic elementary schools	12.09%	9%	8%	9.8%
Percent with students eligible for Chapter 1	72.91%	80.2%	73.2%	75.6%
Income of school families $15,001–$25,000 $25,001–$35,000 $35,001–$50,000	Not included	21.5% 21.1% 23.4%	21.0% 33.6% 22.2%	30.4%* 32.3%** 22.3%***
Percent of schools charging no tuition	About 2.5%	Less than 3%	About 1%	Not given
Average tuition Lowest	$762 (Great Lakes)	$809 (Great Plains)	$1,244 (Mideast)	$977 (Plains)
Highest	$1,177 (Far West/West)	$1,456 (Far West/West)	$1,657 (Far West/West)	$1,894 (Far West/West)
National average tuition Lowest	$658 (rural)	$851 (rural)	$907 (rural)	$970 (rural)
Highest	$1,096 (urban)	$1,334 (suburban)	$1,394 (suburban)	$1,702 (suburban)
Average tuition by school size Lowest	$833 (1–199)	$915 (1–199)	Size not included	$835 (1–99)
Highest	$1,031 (200–299)	$1,330 (200–299)	Size not included	$1,655 (200–349) $1,653 (500+)
Average tuition by sponsorship Lowest	Not included	$1,071 (diocesan)	$1,249 (diocesan)	$1,456 (parish)
Highest	Not included	$2,389 (private)	$2,542 (private)	$2,760 (private)

*Income bracket from $0 to $25,000 for 1997 data; **income bracket from $25,001 to $40,000 for 1997 data; ***income bracket from $40,001 to $60,000 for 1997 data.

Table 11.1 (continued)

Item of Information	1989	1993	1995	1997
Tuition for Catholic non-parish students By region: Lowest	75% of schools 1–40% higher (Northeast)	$1,355 (Great Plains)	$2,053 (Far West/West)	$1,541 (Plains)
Highest	20% of schools 100%+ higher (Great Lakes, Plains)	$1,748 (Southeast) $1,752 (Far West/West)	$2,109 (Southeast)	$2,313 (Far West/West)
By local area: Lowest	Not included	$1,073 (rural)	$1,231 (rural)	$1,401 (rural)
Highest		$1,702 (suburban)	$1,998 (suburban)	$2,255 (suburban)
By school size: Lowest	Not included	$1,264 (1–199)	Not included	$1,221 (1–99)
Highest		$1,773 (300–499)		$2,170 (200–349)
National average	59.09% had special rates	$1,504	$1,766	$2.005
Tuition for non-Catholics By region: Lowest	30.98% (1–24 percentage pts. higher)	$1,353 (Plains)	$1,499 (Plains)	$1,558 (Plains)
Highest	13.58% (100%+ higher)	$1,929 (Southeast)	$2,468 (Far West/West)	$2,565 (Southeast)
By local area: Lowest	Not included	$1,193 (rural)	$1,343 (rural)	$1,560 (rural)
Highest		$1,860 (suburban)	$2,088 (suburban)	$2,430 (suburban)

Table 11.1 (continued)

Item of Information	1989	1993	1995	1997
By school size: Lowest	Not included	$1,355 (1–199)	Not included	$1,312 (1–99)
Highest		$1,920 (300–499)		$2,298 (200–349) $2,275 (500+)
National average	63.11% had special rates	$1,631	$1,884	$2,112
Percent of schools with tuition assistance By region: Lowest	59.09% overall	65.81% (Mideast)	70.0% (Mideast)	70.6% (Mideast)
Highest		90.11% (Far West/ West)	94.2% (Far West/West)	83.3% (Great Lakes)
By local area: Lowest		69.44% (inner city)	73.3% (urban)	76% (suburban)
Highest		75–76% (each: urban, suburban, rural)	86% (suburban)	83.1% (rural)
By school size: Lowest	55.28% (1–199)	67.18% (1–199)	Not included	74.4% (1–99)
Highest	63.54% (200–299)	81.45% (300–499)		82.1% (100–199)
Fund-raising Percent of schools with Fund-raisers	84.5%	96%	Not included	97%+
Most common fund-raisers	candy sales (54.7%)	candy sales (65.1%)	candy sales (57%)	candy sales (59.6%)
Party responsible for fund-raising	parent group (74.52% of schools)	parent group (73% of schools)	Not included	parent group (52% of schools)
Percent of schools with endowments	Not included	37%	40%	44%

Table 11.1 (continued)

Item of Information	1989	1993	1995	1997
By region: Lowest	9.85% (Mideast) (37.93% of revenue)	Not included	Not included	24.5% (Mideast) (0.59% of revenue)
Highest	33.33% (Southeast) 37.93% of revenue)	Not included	Not included	62.85 (Plains) (2.29% of revenue)
By local area: Lowest	19.97% (suburban) (45.17% of revenue) 20% (inner city) (46.43% of revenue)	28.8% (inner city) (4.4% of revenue)	33.3% (suburban) (0.84% of revenue)	Not included
Highest	31.01% (rural) (61.07% of revenue)	54.9% (rural) (6.6% of revenue)	44.9% rural (2.95% of revenue)	Not included
By sponsor: Lowest	Not included	35.6% (parish)	37.3% (parish)	33.3% (diocesan) (0.74% of revenue)
Highest		50.1% (private)	60.0% (private)	46.2% (private) (1.61% of revenue)
By school size: Lowest	18.18% (500+) (42.86% of revenue)	31.8% (300–499)	Not included	24.4% (1–99) (1.97% of revenue)
Highest	26.47% (200–299) (50% of revenue)	44.4% (1– 199 & 500+)		37.5% (200– 349) (0.98% of revenue) 37.6% (350– 499) (1.23% of revenue)
National average	22.74% of schools	37.1% of schools (4.9% of revenue)	39.8% of schools (1.34% of revenue)	43.6% of schools (1.26% of revenue)

Table 11.2
Expenditure Patterns from Kealey (1990, 1994, 1996, 1998) NCEA Surveys

Item of Information	1989	1993	1995	1997
Expenditure per pupil By region: Lowest	$1,614 (Far West/West) (72.92%)*	$1,857 (Northeast) (60.47%)*	$1,886 (Northeast) (63.7%)*	$2,162 (Northeast) (79.2%)*
Highest		$2,192 (Great Lakes) (37%)*	$2,286 (Southeast) (69%)* $2,276 (Far West/West) (81.6%)	$2,589 (FarWest/ West) (80.5%)*
By local area: Lowest	Not included	$1,906 (rural) (38.82%)*	$2,018 (rural) (45.6%)*	$2,331 (rural) (42.6%)*
Highest		$2,141 (inner city) (54.69%)*	$2,221 (urban) (61%)*	$2,455 (urban) (69.6%)* $2,466 (suburban) (70.1%)*
By sponsor: Lowest	Not included	$1,992 (interparoch) (84.63%)*	$1,192 (interparoch) (57.9%)*	$2,288 (interparoch) (68.2%)*
Highest		$2,711 (private) (105.94%)*	$3,144 (private) (94.7%)*	$3,861 (private) (74.5%)*
By school size: Lowest	Not included	$1,889 (500+) (64.32%)*	Not included	$2,219 (500+) (75.2%)*
Highest		$2,147 (1–199) (34.56%)*	Not included	$2,639 (1–99) (35.1%)*
National Average	$1,476	$2,044 (54.11%)*	$2,145 (59.7%)*	$2,414 (64.8)*

Table 11.2 (continued)

Item of Information	1989	1993	1995	1997
Average Principal's salary: Rel. Nun	Not included	$16,206	$20,274	$22,768
Lay	Not included	$32,160	$34,520	$37,403
Average Assistant Principal's salary: Rel. Nun	Not included	$14,618	$18,068	$21,588
Lay	Not included	$28,033	$30,762	$31,395
Average starting teacher salaries, bachelor's degree By area: Lowest	Not included	$14,337 (New England)	$15,448 (New England)	$16,414 (Plains)
Highest		$17,122 (Far West/West)	$18,303 (Far West/West)	$19,533 (Far West/West)
By sponsor: Lowest	Not included	$14,763 (diocesan)	$16,214 (diocesan)	$16,830 (interparoch)
Highest		$16,940 (private)	$16,795 (interparoch)	$19,048 (private)
By size of school: Lowest	Not included	$14,358 (1–199)	Not included	$14,708 (1–99)
Highest		$16,799 (200–299)		$18,753 (500+)
National average	Not included	$15,676	$16,602	$17,683

Table 11.2 (continued)

Item of Information	1989	1993	1995	1997
Average salary of highest-paid teachers	Not included	$24,114 ($10,000)**	$25,706 ($11,000)**	$27,646 ($11,000)**
Percent of schools with benefits Health care	Not included	92%	92%	94%
Retirement plan	Not included	84%	89%	90%
Life insurance	Not included	58%	64%	63%
Unemployment Compensation	Not included	57%	64%	66%
Dental Plan	Not included	44%	49%	55%

*Percent of expenditures covered by tuition and fees; **Amount higher of highest public school teacher salary.
Interparoch = interparochial.

a table format allows the reader to compare findings from one study year to the next.

The 1995 and 1997 surveys (Kealey, 1996, 1998) asked for comments by the respondent. The most common comment provided in 1995 was the need for financial assistance. Respondents were also interested in the distinction between fund-raising and development activities. In 1997, the most common remark was that fund-raisers keep schools going financially. Respondents recognized the need for greater effort in the area of development. Finally, comments reflected a concern on the part of principals regarding the financial status of the school.

Using a variety of data sources, Harris (1996) developed a financial profile of Catholic parishes and schools in an effort to study the decline in the number of Catholic schools and in Catholic school enrollment. He examined revenues, expenditures, and the relationship between them with respect to the continued viability of Catholic schools and parishes. Harris contended that suburbanization led to the decline of Catholic school enrollments in urban areas. Decreased enrollments required tuition increases to cover costs, increases which led to greater enrollment declines. He also studied Catholic schools in rural settings. The inability of small rural parishes to meet the subsidizing needs of their schools because of escalating costs caused small rural schools to close.

From a random sample of 712 parishes, Harris (1996) collected data from the 142 parishes which contributed information in 1991 and 1993. He also used data from parish records, diocesan offices, private studies at Catholic universities, ETS, and the NCEA. Harris' work includes descriptive and forecasted findings, as well as possible solutions to potential problems faced by Catholic institutions. Although much information is included in this volume, it is sometimes difficult to determine what is primary versus secondary research, what numbers are the result of Harris' analyses versus analyses of others which he is reporting, and what methods were used for the primary analyses undertaken.

Using estimation techniques, Harris (1996) determined that while elementary school expenses increased an average of 8.7% annually from 1980 to 1993, parish revenue increased an average of only 3.1% annually. Further, he estimated that parishes subsidized an average of 63% of elementary school budgets in 1969, but only 33% in 1996. From these data, Harris concluded that parish subsidies decreased as a percentage of school expenditures because school expenses rose more rapidly than parish revenues. The cost increases resulted from a variety of phenomena, including implementation of smaller class sizes, provision of special services, and decreased numbers of religious on faculties in elementary schools.

Harris (1996) discovered, however, that not only have parish subsidies to elementary schools decreased in relative terms, but in absolute ones, also. Between 1986 and 1988, parish subsidies increased an average of $17,003 in current dollars; the increase between 1988 and 1990 averaged only $7,308.

Harris (1996) also looked at school-sponsored fund-raising and tuition as sources of revenue. Fund-raising supported an average of 11% of elementary school expenditures in 1980 and 15% of expenditures in 1996. In 1980, an average of 40% of total elementary program expenditures was covered by tuition, while in 1993, 67% was covered by tuition. Average tuition generated per school in 1980 was $125,000. In 1993, the average per-school revenue from tuition was $275,000. (Both numbers are after inflation.) Another way to study the economic impact of tuition is to evaluate the effect on households. Harris calculated that tuition payments consumed 2.3% of gross household income in 1980 and 3.6% in 1993.

Average secondary school expenditures increased by $578,372 per school from 1987 to 1993. This represented an 81% increase. Between these same years, tuition increased an average of $181,225 beyond inflation. Generally, tuition increases covered increases in expenditures during this time period. Harris estimated that the average tuition per secondary school pupil in 1993 was $3,226, about "7.8% of an estimated Catholic household income" (Harris, 1996, p. 119). In 1987, the household burden per pupil in Catholic high schools was about 7% of income.

Like tuition, secondary school fund-raising dollars also increased beyond inflation from 1987 to 1993. Further analyses showed that 8.5% of secondary school revenue came from fund-raising money in 1987 and 9.5% in 1993. Increases in subsidy and other income did not keep up with inflationary increases between the two years studied (Harris, 1996).

Concerned that his analysis was not useful to practitioners, Harris (1996) used NCEA data in a separate chapter to provide a disaggregated picture of Catholic school finances. His review is similar to that previously included in this chapter (Guerra, 1993; Guerra & Donahue, 1990, 1995; Kealey, 1990, 1994, 1996, 1998).

Harris (1996) identified and discussed two ways to address the need for more money for Catholic schools. He proposed increasing parish collections and promoting a publicly funded voucher system. Although he found little evidence that Catholic giving had decreased through the years, he found substantial documentation that Catholics gave less than most members of other religious denominations. Harris included case studies to describe successful funding models for both Catholic schools and parishes.

OTHER

Cibulka (1988) was interested in the Catholic Church's response to the problem of closing inner-city Catholic schools considering the inordinate impact on African Americans. Besides using data from the NCES, the NCEA, and the U.S. Bureau of the Census, he interviewed administrators at 32 dioceses, including the 25 largest. The dioceses targeted had a large minority enrollment in the Catholic schools.

There were three primary reasons for the school closures: poor conditions of the facilities, urban blight, and poor financial positions. Cibulka (1988) found that initial school closings were both revenue and expenditures driven. That is, revenues decreased because of decreasing enrollments and expenditures increased because of the increasing need to hire lay staff members as the number of religious dwindled. He concluded that the closures were an economically efficient response to the immediately existing conditions.

Cibulka (1988) found, however, that over the long run, the closure response was not as efficient as initially thought. He determined that the Catholic Church felt an obligation to a particular population, that is, the minority population, which generally resides in inner-city neighborhoods. He also found that careful planning for the future could have a major impact on closure decisions. Finally, Cibulka found that the Catholic Church was very interested in avoiding negative publicity in the local communities.

After a discussion on the authoritative hierarchy of the Catholic Church with respect to the status of individual schools, Cibulka (1988) identified six patterns of authority which surfaced in his data analysis. In the first type, "centralized initiative," the superintendent of the diocesan schools made the decisions regarding closings. Under the style entitled "central initiative, local participation," schools earmarked for possible closure were identified by the central authority. However, in planning for a school's closure or continuance, local input was not only solicited but mandated. The response pattern labeled "local initiative, mutual decision making" was characterized by less involvement (than the previous pattern) on the part of the diocese in making closure decisions. Some closure decisions were dubbed "collaborative," describing a decision effort involving both local and diocesan officials.

Cibulka (1988) found that some closure decisions were initiated by the pastor, and the bishop either ratified or reversed the local decision. This was referred to as the "local initiative, central ratification" pattern. The final decision-making pattern identified was simply called "local initiative." Closure decisions were initiated locally by a parish or a religious community with no external input.

Cibulka (1988) concluded that the more decentralized decision-making patterns resulted in greater responsiveness to local interests and desires. Thus, the last pattern discussed above would be the most responsive. However, according to Cibulka, because of a responsiveness-efficiency trade-off, in such extremely responsive systems, efficiency is sacrificed. Also, in such systems, equity is often sacrificed. That is, when diocesan involvement occurs, schools serving diverse populations are less likely to be closed.

Cibulka (1988) suggested alternatives to closing schools: targeting new populations, searching for different sources of revenue, searching for ways to reduce costs, and consolidation. He concluded that future challenges exist for Catholic school officials when making decisions regarding school closures, particularly in predominantly African-American, non-Catholic urban centers. These challenges focus on whether responsiveness, efficiency, or equity should dominate the decision process.

McLaughlin and Broughman (1997) used data from the NCES School and Staffing survey to examine private schools in the United States. Although nine different categories of private schools are described in the report, this review includes only information for three types of Catholic schools: parochial (affiliated with a parish), diocesan (affiliated with the larger diocese), and private order (affiliated with a specific Catholic group). Furthermore, although a wide range of data are included in this NCES volume, this review will look only at financial data. About 8,351 Catholic schools were included in this study, 61% of which were parochial, 29% diocesan, and 10% conducted by a private order.

Slightly over 63% of Catholic school teachers have a bachelor's degree, while nearly 30% have a master's. One percent have a doctorate, and about 84% are state certified. Average base salary for Catholic school teachers was $21,652; the highest average was for private order schools ($26,950), and the lowest average ($19,695) was for parochial schools. Of all teachers surveyed in Catholic schools, 68% had medical insurance. About 54% had retirement plans, about 40% had dental insurance, and 40% had life insurance. Tuition benefits were available to 20% of the teachers. The average number of years of principal experience was just over nine years, but the average number of years of teaching experience for principals was slightly over 17. Although the average Catholic school principal salary was $28,058, over 73% had a master's degree.

McLaughlin and Broughman (1997) reported that only 13% of the principals in Catholic parochial schools earned $40,000 or more per year, while 24% in all private schools earned at least $40,000. Thirty-five percent of the Catholic parochial school principals earned less than $20,000. Of teachers, 46% of those in Catholic schools earned less than $20,000.

Nearly 99% of the Catholic schools charged tuition. About 95% allowed for tuition reductions. Average Catholic elementary school tuition in 1993–1994 was $1,572. Average tuition at private order schools was substantially higher than at parochial or diocesan schools. Revenue in the form of tuition ranged from $3,500 or more (2% of the Catholic elementary schools) to less than $1,500 (47% of Catholic elementary schools). About 51% charged tuition between $1,500 and $3,500. Average secondary tuition was $3,699. About 45% of the Catholic non-elementary schools charged less than $3,000 for tuition (McLaughlin & Broughman, 1997).

The average student–teacher ratio in Catholic schools was 19:1, the highest being in parochial (20.4:1) and the lowest in private order (14.7:1) schools. McLaughlin and Broughman (1997) included a more detailed breakdown of these numbers as well as a comparison to other types of private schools.

Reports in earlier editions of this same NCES document suggested that tuition is generally lower in Catholic schools because class size is larger than in other private schools. Thus, there was an inverse relationship between class size and tuition rates.

Guerra (1993) and Guerra and Donahue (1990, 1995) investigated Catholic school finances for the NCEA. Six studies have been completed, one for each of the following school years: 1984–1985, 1985–1986, 1987–1988, 1989–1990, 1991–1992, and 1993–1994. For the sake of space and to avoid redundancy, only the last three will be discussed in this chapter. Although some earlier trends will be masked by the decision to exclude the first three studies, others will surface by comparing the latest three years.

Each year a survey was sent to a stratified random sample (based on region and enrollment size) of Catholic high schools in the United States. Each study more or less followed the same format, although survey and data adjustments were made each year to reflect more accurately the changes and current conditions in Catholic high schools. The review discussed in this chapter addresses only descriptive information. However, using the descriptive information collected, the researchers developed several "typical school designs" to give the reader a better picture of what the whole school might look like from the pieces of data available. A selected review of their work has been compiled and presented in tables developed by the author of this chapter (see Tables 11.3 and 11.4). The reader is reminded that although this review includes a great deal of data, it is only a summary. Much more information than that reported herein is included in the original volumes previously cited.

In an effort to look at long-term financial effects of children attending Catholic schools, Greeley (1977) attempted to answer the question: "Is the expenditure

Table 11.3

Revenue Data for Catholic High Schools in the United States, 1990, 1992, 1994

Item of Information	1990	1992	1994
Sample—Useable return rate	222/500 = 44.4%	278/500 = 55.6%	293/500 = 58.6%
Revenue Sources—Dollar amount (percent of total revenues)			
Tuition and fees	$1,240,000 (72%)	$1,489,200 (73%)	$1,859,800 (75%)
Contributed services	$65,500 (4%)	$68,700 (3%)	$65,200 (3%)
Subsidies	$125,400 (7%)	$150,300 (7%)	$158,700 (6%)
Fund-raising	$145,700 (8%)	$174,400 (9%)	$226,600 (9%)
All other income	$148,800 (9%)	$162,500 (8%)	$161,000 (7%)
Total	$1,725,400	$2,045,100	$2,471,300
Percent of schools participating in federal programs			
Chapter 1	15%	21%	21%
Chapter 2	80%	78%	77%
Upward Bound	8%	5%	7%
Vocational Programs	6–8%	4–6%	5019%
Percent of schools participating in state programs			
Bus transportation	41%	40%	39%
Drug education	42%	54%	50%
Education of the handicapped	11%	13%	13%

Table 11.3 (continued)

Item of Information	1990	1992	1994
Education of low income	4%	3%	4%
Guidance and counseling	16%	20%	24%
Health services	28%	37%	36%
Media resources	57%	55%	54%
Textbooks	48%	50%	54%
Development			
Percent of schools with development office	84%	84%	89%
Average revenue from: Alumni	$34,500	$38,500	$51,300
Parents	$26,000	$24,600	$26,900
Other contributions to annual fund	$34,400	$41,300	$57,100
Special events	$51,200	$73,000	$91,400
Annual fund-raising revenue			
Principal-led schools: Alumni		$24,700	$42,200
Parents		$16,800	$20,500
Total revenue	Not included	$149,500	$201,300
President-led schools: Alumni		$95,600	$78,900
Parents		$58,00	$46,600
Total revenue		$292,800	$303,800

Table 11.4

Expenditure Data for Catholic High Schools in the United States, 1990, 1992, 1994

Item of Information	1990	1992	1994
Averaging operating expenses (percentage of total operating expenses)			
Salaries—lay	$746,600 (44%)	$934,200 (46%)	$1,135,200 (47%)
Salaries—religious	$118,600 (7%)	$111,500 (5%)	$130,900 (5%)
Contributed services	$45,300 (3%)	$49,900 (2%)	$46,000 (2%)
Other salaries	$151,300 (9%)	$158,300 (8%)	$184,200 (8%)
All benefits	$199,300 (12%)	$242,900 (12%)	$300,700 (12%)
Other operating expenses	$455,000 (26%)	$552,900 (27%)	$634,800 (26%)
Total	$1,716,100	$2,048,800	$2,431,800
Median tuition as percent of total expenditures			
By region: Lowest	53% (Plains)	49% (Plains)	54% (Plains)
Highest	79% (West/ Far West)	81% (New England)	81% (West /Far West)
By sponsor: Lowest	62% (par/interpar)	57% (par/interpar)	72% (par/interpar)
Highest	74% (private)	73% (private)	79% (private)
By enrollment: Lowest	59% (under 300)	53% (under 300)	60% (under 300)
Highest	80% (over 750)	85% (751+)	81% (501+)
By gender: Boys' school	79%	73%	81%

Table 11.4 (continued)

Item of Information	1990	1992	1994
Girls' school	71%	74%	75%
Coed school	66%	68%	72%
All Catholic high schools	65%	73%	75%
Average principal salary			
Lay principal	$41,300	$45,800	$51,000
Religious principal	$21,200	$25,600	$27,300
Public high school	$55,700	$61,800	$65,000
Average lay starting teacher salary—BS or BA			
All Catholic high schools	$16,200	$17,700	$19,000
With bargaining representation	$16,900	$18,800	$20,100
Without bargaining representation	$15,900	$17,300	$18,500
All public high schools	$20,500	$22,200	$24,000
Highest lay salary—MA or MS			
All Catholic high schools	$29,000	$32,000	$34,400
All public high schools (not including years of experience)	$34,300	$39,800	$43,800
Financial aid			

Table 11.4 (continued)

Item of Information	1990	1992	1994
Number of schools with none	13 (7%)	1	8 (3%)
Average percentage of students receiving aid in schools where offered	17%	19%	24%
Value of grants by enrollment: Lowest	$799 (over 750)	$851 (under 300)	$977 (301–500)
Highest	$995 (under 300)	$1,061 (over 750)	$1,192 (501–750)
Average salaries in principal- vs. president-led high schools			
Lay teachers	Not included	$26,400 (president) $24,200 (principal)	$28,700 (president) $26,200 (principal)
Development Director		$34,900 (president) $30,000 (principal)	$38,900 (president) $31,600 (principal)

of Catholic schools less a drain on the resources of the Church than it might seem precisely because those who have gone to Catholic schools are likely to be more generous in their contributions?" (pp. 43–44).

Using data from two earlier studies, one a national study done by the NORC and the other a local one done in the Chicago Archdiocese, Greeley (1977) employed multiple regression analysis to predict future contributions to Catholic schools. The dependent variable was dollars of annual contribution; independent variables included number of years of Catholic schooling, children in Catholic schools, and income.

Greeley (1977) found that on a national level the subsidies churches contributed to their associated Catholic schools were greater than the contributions made to the Church by families with children in Catholic schools and Catholic school children as adults. In fact, the loss was about 4%. However, using the data collected in the Chicago Archdiocese, his analysis showed a profit of 51%.

That is, the revenue as a result of Catholic school attendance was 51% greater than the subsidy to Catholic schools.

Greeley (1977) further found that using only years of attendance in Catholic schools as the independent variable, each additional year yielded $8.31 in contributions in the NORC sample and $14.23 in the Chicago sample. Each year after eight yielded a contribution of $27.60 for the national sample and $23.78 for Chicago. He also looked at the impact of attendance at Mass, parish loyalty, level of participation, and obligation to contribute.

Findings suggested that generalized decisions not to build Catholic schools might be unwise from a profitability standpoint for Catholic churches. Rather, each diocese should assess its own situation in terms of profitability of new schools to accommodate a growing demand.

The research studies included in this chapter do not constitute an exhaustive review of Catholic school finance research. It is selective rather than exhaustive. Other studies exist which analyze parish rather than school finances. Other studies look at the socioeconomic status of families who send their children to Catholic schools. There is much Catholic school literature available which discusses finance but is not based on research. The exclusion of these works is not to suggest that they are not valuable, but simply that they did not fit the purpose of this chapter. Clearly, the area of financial administration will remain a pressing concern for the Catholic community in relation to its operation of schools.

REFERENCES

Aguilar v. Felton, 105 S. Ct. 3232 (1985).

Carlson, P. R. (1970). *Is public aid the answer to parochial education's finance woes? A study of Great Falls Central Catholic High School.* Unpublished master's thesis, University of Montana.

Cibulka, J. G. (1988). Catholic school closings: Efficiency, responsiveness, and equality of access for Blacks. In D. T. Slaughter & D. J. Johnson (Eds.) *Visible now: Blacks in private schools* (pp. 143–156). Westport, CT: Greenwood Press.

David, R. (1972). *A study of the perceptions of selected diocesan superintendents of education relative to school management in the planning-programming-budgeting (PPBS) method of system analysis.* Unpublished doctoral dissertation, University of Miami.

Greeley, A. M. (1977). A preliminary investigation: The "profitability" of Catholic schools. *Momentum, 8 (4)*, 43–49.

Greeley, A. M., McCready, W. C., & McCourt, K. (1976). *Catholic schools in a declining church.* Kansas City, MO: Sheed and Ward.

Greeley, A. M., & Rossi, P. H. (1966). *The education of Catholic Americans.* Chicago: Aldine Publishing Co.

Guerra, M. J. (1993). *Dollars and sense: Catholic high schools and their finances 1992.* Washington, DC: National Catholic Educational Association.

Guerra, M. J., & Donahue, M. J. (1990). *Dollars and sense: Catholic high schools and their finances 1990.* Washington, DC: National Catholic Educational Association.

Guerra, M. J., & Donahue, M. J. (1995). *Dollars and sense: Catholic high schools and their finances 1994.* Washington, DC: National Catholic Educational Association.

Harris, J. C. (1996). *The cost of Catholic schools.* Kansas City, MO: Sheed and Ward.

Haslam, M. B, & Humphrey, D. C. (1993). *Chapter 1 services to religious-school students.* Washington, DC: U.S. Department of Education.

Hensley, P. D. (1995). The archdiocesan elementary school system of St. Louis: An equity analysis of financing with a correlational study of achievement outcomes versus fiscal spending (Missouri). *Dissertation Abstracts International, 56* (09), 3392. Retrieved August 23, 2000 from the World Wide Web: http://wwwlib.umi.com/dissertations/.

Kealey, R. J. (1990). *United States Catholic elementary schools & their finances: 1989.* Washington, DC: National Catholic Educational Association.

Kealey, R. J. (1994). *Balance sheet for Catholic elementary schools: 1993 income and expenses.* Washington, DC: National Catholic Educational Association.

Kealey, R. J. (1996). *Balance sheet for Catholic elementary schools: 1995 income and expenses.* Washington, DC: National Catholic Educational Association.

Kealey, R. J. (1998). *Balance sheet for Catholic elementary schools: 1997 income and expenses.* Washington, DC: National Catholic Educational Association.

Larson, M. (1995). *Public and religious elementary school costs and programs.* Unpublished doctoral dissertation, Arizona State University.

Lundy, G. F. (1999). School-parish financial linkages and the viability of urban Catholic elementary schools. *Journal of Research on Christian Education, 8 (1),* 85–106.

McDonald, D. (1995). *Toward full and fair choice: An historical analysis of the lobbying efforts of the Catholic school community in pursuing federal tax-supported choice in education, 1972–1992.* Unpublished doctoral dissertation, Boston College.

McLaughlin, D. H., & Broughman, S. (1997). *Private schools in the United States: A statistical profile, 1993–94.* Washington, DC: National Center for Educational Statistics, NCES 97-459.

Meier, E. C. (1994). Efficiency and cost effectiveness in private and public schools: Micro-financial expenditure analysis (private schools). *Dissertation Abstracts International, 55* (11), 3370. Retrieved August 23, 2000 from the World Wide Web: http://wwwlib.umi.com/dissertations/.

NCEA. (1997). *New Catholic school: 1985–1995.* Washington, DC: Author.

NCES. (1997). *Public and private schools: How do they differ?* Washington, DC: U.S. Department of Education, Office of Educational Research and Improvement, NCES 97-983.

Nelson, S. (1994). Catholic elementary schools in Chicago's Black inner city: Four models of adaptation to environmental change. *Nonprofit and Voluntary Sector Quarterly, 23 (3),* 209–225.

Plante, M. M. (1991). A study of pastor, principal, and laity's knowledge of and attitude toward financial sources for parish Catholic elementary schools. *Dissertation Abstracts International, 52* (12), 4221. Retrieved August 23, 2000 from the World Wide Web: http://wwwlib.umi.com/dissertations/.

Chapter 12

Catholic Schools and the Law

Charles J. Russo

INTRODUCTION

The U.S. Supreme Court's 1925 decision in *Pierce v. Society of Sisters* is arguably the most important ruling in the history of Catholic and other non-public schools in America. *Pierce* involved a successful challenge to Oregon's compulsory attendance law, which required parents or guardians of "normal" children to send them "to a public school for the period of time a public school shall be held during the current year" (*Pierce*, 1925, p. 530). In the suit, filed by the Society of Sisters and the Hill Military Academy, the Court unanimously affirmed that Oregon's compulsory attendance law was unconstitutional because it "unreasonably interfere[d] with the liberty of parents and guardians to direct the upbringing and education of children under their control" (*Pierce*, pp. 534–535).

In addition to upholding the right of Catholic schools to operate, *Pierce* established a key principle in the relationship between non-public schools and the state. In *Pierce*, the Court acknowledged the power of the state "reasonably to regulate all schools, to inspect, supervise, and examine them, their teachers and pupils" (1925, p. 534). A myriad of subsequent opinions by federal and state courts have interpreted *Pierce* to mean that while individual states, and the federal government, may regulate non-public schools, they may not do so to any extent greater than they impose on public institutions. In fact, Catholic and other non-public schools have come to have significant freedom from most forms of governmental oversight.

Pierce is also interesting from a legal perspective because while the case, in part, involved state regulation over a Catholic school, the Court sidestepped the difficult First Amendment issues, reaching its judgment on the basis of the Fourteenth Amendment. More specifically, the Court ruled that since the religious community that operated the Catholic school had a property interest in its continuing existence, the state law that would have forced the school to close violated the Fourteenth Amendment because it violated their right to due process.

The freedom that Catholic schools have from most forms of governmental regulation notwithstanding, administrators need to be mindful of the parameters of the legal system, as it should help them to maintain effective, efficient, and safe learning environments. Accordingly, this chapter is divided into four sections. The first part reviews the nature and structure of the American legal system. The next section examines legal issues surrounding state aid to Catholic schools. The third section examines the rights and duties of teachers and other personnel in Catholic schools. The fourth part looks at the rights of students and, by extension, their parents. The author hopes that this review of relevant case law will provide researchers with a review of the current legal status of Catholic schools at the dawn of the new millennium.

SOURCES OF LAW

In reviewing the sources of law that affect Catholic schools, it is important to recognize that understanding the legal system is not an end in itself. Rather, knowledge of the law comes into play as the most important factor in developing sound policies that contribute to the smooth, efficient, and safe operations of the schools.

Simply stated, the U.S. Constitution is the law of the land. As the primary source of American law, the Constitution provides the basic framework within which our entire legal system operates. To this end, all actions taken by the federal and state governments, including state constitutions (which are supreme within their jurisdictions as long as they do not contradict or limit rights protected under their federal counterpart), statutes, regulations, and common law are subject to the Constitution as interpreted by the Supreme Court.

As important as education is, it is not mentioned in the Constitution. Consequently, under the Tenth Amendment, according to which "the powers not delegated to the United States by the Constitution, nor prohibited by it to the States, are reserved to the States respectively, or to the people," education is primarily the concern of individual states. It is important to note that the federal government can intervene in disputes, such as *Brown v. Board of Education* (1954), when the government deprives individuals of rights protected under the Constitution. In *Brown*, the Supreme Court struck down state-sanctioned racial segregation on the ground that it violated the students' rights to equal protection under the Fourteenth Amendment to the U.S. Constitution.

The Constitution also protects Americans from arbitrary and capricious acts of the government. This is essential in the public schools since, as extensions of the government, the full weight of the Constitution protects their students and teachers. However, since Catholic and other non-public schools are private entities, students and teachers are generally not afforded constitutional protections. The major exception is that the federal government can become involved when protected constitutional rights, such as the right of parents to direct the upbringing of their children (as in *Pierce*), are involved, or when rights are explicitly extended by statute such as Title I, which offers educational services for specifically identified children based on socioeconomic need.

Along with delineating the rights and responsibilities of all Americans, the Constitution establishes the three co-equal branches of government that exist on both the federal and state levels. The legislative, executive, and judicial branches of government, in turn, give rise to the other three sources of law.

The legislative branch makes the law. In other words, once a bill completes the legislative process, it is signed into law by a Chief Executive who has the authority to enforce the new statute. Keeping in mind that a statute is not unlike the frame of a house, the executive branch fleshes out a law by providing details in the form of regulations. For example, a typical compulsory attendance law requires that "except as provided in this section, the parent of a child of compulsory school age shall cause such child to attend a school in the school district in which the child is entitled to attend school" (Ohio Revised Code, 3321.03, 1999). Even in recognizing exceptions for parents who wish to send their children to Catholic schools, statutes are typically silent on such important matters as the content of the curriculum and the length of the school day. Consequently, these essential elements are addressed by regulations which are developed by personnel at administrative agencies who are well versed in their areas of expertise. Given their extensiveness, it is safe to say that the professional lives of educators, at least in public schools, are more directly influenced by regulations than by statutes.

The fourth and final source of law, judge-made or common law, is perhaps the most important for Catholic schools. Common law refers to judicial interpretations of the law that have evolved over time when dealing with issues that may have been overlooked in the legislative or regulatory process, or that may not have been anticipated when the statute was enacted. In *Marbury v. Madison* (1803), the Supreme Court asserted the authority to review the constitutional validity of actions taken by the other branches and in so doing has the ability to establish precedent. Although there is an occasional tension between the three branches of government, the legislative and executive branches generally defer to judicial interpretations of their actions.

Precedent stands for the proposition that a majority ruling of the highest court in a given jurisdiction is binding on lower courts within its jurisdiction. In other words, a ruling of the U.S. Supreme Court is binding throughout the nation while a decision of the Supreme Court of Ohio is binding only in Ohio. Persuasive precedent, a majority ruling from another jurisdiction, is actually not precedent at all. For example, a ruling of the Supreme Court of Ohio is only persuasive precedent in New York. In other words, as judges in New York seek to resolve a novel legal issue, they typically review precedent from other jurisdictions to determine whether it has been addressed elsewhere. However, a court is not bound to follow precedent from another jurisdiction.

Two forms of common law are especially important for Catholic schools: contracts and torts. Contracts are significant because unlike the public schools, where education, as a matter of right, is controlled by the state, most of the rights of teachers, students, and parents are created by entering into contracts. In order to be binding, a contract must consist of an offer and acceptance on mutually agreed terms, the parties must offer consideration (such as tuition in return for an education or salary in return for teaching), the parties must have the authority to enter into the agreement, the subject matter must be legal, and, depending upon its length and what it addresses, a contract may have to be in writing. Oral contracts are valid but, in the absence of a written agreement, the burden of proving its existence falls upon the party seeking its enforcement.

Torts are civil, as opposed to criminal, wrongs other than breaches of contracts. Intentional torts and negligence are the two most important types of torts that occur in the schools. Intentional torts include assault (fear of unwanted physical contact), battery (the actual contact), false imprisonment, and concerns over defamation (which may overlap with free speech). In order for a school (or its employees or volunteers) to be liable for negligence, or inadequate supervision, which is, by definition, not intentional, the party bringing suit must prove four related items. First, the party must show that a school had a duty which required it to take reasonable steps to foresee and prevent an injury from taking place. Second, the school must have breached, or failed to meet its duty. Third, there must be an injury for which compensation can be awarded. Finally, the school must be the proximate, or actual, cause of the injury. However, even if a school appears to be at fault, it may escape liability if it applies a defense such as assumption of risk, contributory negligence, or charitable immunity.

In sum, other than applicable federal and state anti-discrimination laws that may have limited applicability, Catholic schools operate largely free of governmental regulation. Even so, authors of personnel manuals and student policies for Catholic schools would be wise to be knowledgeable about developments in the wider spectrum of education law and to adopt practices similar to those followed in the public schools, as they typically have been developed over time and are sensitive to safeguarding the rights of both the schools and their personnel. In light of the heavy influence of litigation on Catholic schools, the remainder of this chapter primarily examines key Supreme Court cases that impact directly on Catholic schools.

LEGAL ISSUES AFFECTING CATHOLIC SCHOOLS

State Aid to Religious Schools

Of the legal issues affecting Catholic schools, none is even close to matching the impact of disputes under the Establishment Clause of the First Amendment and the extent to which public funds can be used to aid Catholic schools and their students. According to the relevant language in the Establishment Clause, "Congress shall make no law respecting an establishment of religion, or prohibiting the free exercise thereof." As simple as these words sound, they have led to a plethora of litigation in federal and state courts over the "original intent" of its authors. Put another way, there are two distinct schools of thought, with varying ranges of attitudes in between for those who, on the one hand (such as this author), believe that the government can make reasonable accommodations to religious institutions consistent with the First Amendment, and those, on the other hand, who follow Thomas Jefferson's letter of January 1, 1802 to A Committee of the Danbury Baptist Association (as cited in Russo, 1999), wherein he called for a wall of separation between church and state. Moreover, the development of the Supreme Court's Establishment Clause jurisprudence, reflecting the attitudes of its members at different times in its history, does not follow anything resembling a straight line of judicial reasoning.

The first case directly involving state aid to Catholic school was *Cochran v. Louisiana State Board of Education* (1930), and did not involve the Establishment Clause. In *Cochran*, the Supreme Court unanimously upheld a state law from Louisiana which required the expenditure of public funds to provide free textbooks for all children regardless of where they attended school. In a prelude (of sorts) of what developed into the Child Benefit Test, the Court rejected a challenge to the law which claimed that the textbook loan program violated the Fourteenth Amendment because it was a taxation for the purchase of school books that constituted a taking of private property for private purposes. The Court affirmed lower court rulings which refused to issue an injunction to prevent the program from going into effect on the ground that children, rather than their schools, were the beneficiaries of the statute.

The Supreme Court first addressed a case on the merits of the Establishment Clause in *Everson v. Board of Education* (1947), wherein it upheld a state statute from New Jersey that permitted parents to be reimbursed for the cost of transporting their children to religiously affiliated non-public schools. In *Everson*, the Court enunciated the so-called Child Benefit Test, which is based on the premise that under certain circumstances, aid is constitutional when it is provided primarily to students and not the religiously affiliated schools that they attend. The Court reasoned that since transportation was paid for by the tax dollars of all parents, regardless of where their children attended school, and the aid primarily benefitted the students, albeit through their parents, rather than the schools, it was constitutionally permissible. In the only other case involving a challenge to transportation, *Wolman v. Walter* (1977), the Court ruled that while school buses could be used to transport children to and from religiously affiliated non-public schools in Ohio, they could not be used to take them on field trips. The Court struck down the use of buses for field trips on the basis that this could have created excessive entanglement between religious schools and the state.

After *Everson*, the next Supreme Court case involving aid to non-public schools did not occur until 21 years later, in *Board of Education v. Allen* (1968). Prior to *Mitchell v. Helms* (1999), *Allen* was generally considered the outer limit of state aid to religious schools. In *Allen* the Court upheld a law from New York State that required school boards to loan textbooks for secular subjects to all students on the ground that it applied to all children, regardless of whether they attended public or non-public schools. The Court relied heavily on the fact that regulations overseeing the programs specified which books on officially approved lists could be used.

Three years later, the Court's ruling in *Lemon v. Kurtzman* (1971) ushered in an almost 20-year period during which its interpretations of both federal and state actions have generally maintained that the Establishment Clause prohibits governmental sponsorship of or aid to any religion. In *Lemon* the Court considered the constitutionality of programs from Rhode Island and Pennsylvania. The case from Rhode Island centered on a state statute that paid salary supplements to certified teachers in non-public schools who taught only subjects that were offered in the public schools. Similarly, the dispute from Pennsylvania involved a state law that provided reimbursements for teachers' salaries, textbooks, and instructional materials for courses as long as they did not contain "any subject matter expressing religious teaching, or the morals or forms of worship of any sect" (*Lemon*, 1971, p. 610). In invalidating both programs, the Court added a third element, from *Walz v. Tax Commission of New York City* (1970), wherein the Court upheld New York State's practice of providing state property tax exemptions for church property that is used in worship services, to create the tripartite test that it has since relied upon in virtually all cases involving the Establishment Clause, to the two-part purpose and effect test that it enunciated in *Abington v. Schempp* and *Murray v. Curlett* (*School District*, 1963), cases involving the constitutionality of prayer and Bible reading in public schools. Chief Justice Burger's majority opinion in *Lemon* (1971) stated that "Every analysis in this area must begin with consideration of the cumulative criteria developed by the Court over many years. Three such tests may be gleaned from our cases. First, the statute must have a secular legislative purpose; second, its principal or primary effect must be one that neither advances nor inhibits religion; finally, the statute must not foster 'an excessive government entanglement with religion' " (pp. 612–613, internal citations omitted). Even though the first two parts of the increasingly unworkable *Lemon* test were developed in the context of prayer cases, it continued to be applied just as widely in disputes involving aid to non-public schools over the next 15 years. For example, in *PEARL v. Nyquist* (1973), the Court struck down a state program from New York that would have not only provided direct payments to religious schools for the repair and maintenance of equipment, but also would have permitted tuition reimbursements and income-tax credits for low-income parents whose children attended these schools. The Court feared that these programs violated the effects and entanglement prongs of *Lemon*. In addition, in *Sloan v. Lemon*

(1973), the Court struck down another statute from Pennsylvania that would have reimbursed religious schools for the cost of teaching secular classes, based on its concern that the law had the impermissible effect of advancing religion.

Levitt v. PEARL (1973) and *PEARL v. Reagan* (1980) provide an interesting example of the interaction between the judiciary and legislature. In *Levitt v. PEARL*, the Court invalidated a statute from New York that would have provided reimbursement to non-public schools for state-mandated student testing on the ground that there were insufficient safeguards in place to ensure that public funds were not used for impermissible religious purposes, including teacher-made tests dealing with religion. Subsequently, the Court upheld that revised statute in *PEARL v. Reagan*, since it was satisfied that appropriate safeguards were set in place to ensure that religious institutions did not receive impermissible assistance.

In *Meek v. Pittenger* (1975), a case from Pennsylvania, the Court upheld textbook loans while striking down the loan of instructional equipment such as laboratory materials and maps and the on-site delivery of auxiliary services for students in religiously affiliated non-public schools. The Court struck down the on-site programs because it feared that such arrangements might have created excessive entanglements between religious schools and the state. Similarly, in *Wolman v. Walter* (1977), the Court upheld an Ohio statute that permitted textbook loans, reimbursement for standardized testing, the on-site delivery of diagnostic testing, and off-site delivery of therapeutic services. However, the Court vitiated provisions that would have permitted the disbursement of instructional materials and the use of public school buses to take children from religiously affiliated non-public schools on field trips, in light of its ongoing fears of excessive entanglement.

In 1983, the Court addressed the constitutionality of a state law from Minnesota that granted state income tax deductions to parents for the costs of tuition, textbooks, and transportation regardless of whether their children attended religiously affiliated non-public schools or public schools. The Court, in *Mueller v. Allen* (1983), upheld the statute even though the vast majority of parents who benefitted from the deductions had children in religious schools. The Court reasoned that the law was constitutional because it managed to pass all three prongs of the *Lemon* test.

Two years later, the Court reached major decisions in the companion cases of *Grand Rapids v. Ball* (1985) and *Aguilar v. Felton* (1985). In *Ball* the Court struck down a program from Michigan that was designed to provide supplementary classes in non-public schools that were taught by full-time public school employees, and educators from the non-public schools who were hired on a part-time basis. Further, the classes were offered in predominantly religiously affiliated non-public schools in classrooms leased from public schools. The Court argued that while the program had a secular legislative purpose, it was unconstitutional because it had the impermissible effect of advancing religion.

In *Aguilar* the Court banned the on-site delivery of remedial educational serv-

ices under Title I of the Elementary and Secondary Education Act for economically disadvantaged students in religiously affiliated non-public schools in New
York City. The Court concluded that this program was constitutional based on
the unproven fear that it risked violating the excessive entanglement clause of
the *Lemon* test. In a strident dissent, Justice O'Connor argued (correctly in
hindsight, from this author's perspective) that the Court was "throwing the baby
out with the bath water" since so many children would have been deprived of
greatly needed educational services.

Witters v. Washington Services for the Blind (1986) was a harbinger of developments to come. Although set in the context of higher education, *Witters* is
significant for religious schools because in it the Court ruled that a vocational
rehabilitation program that provided financial assistance to a blind student as he
studied for the ministry at a Bible college did not violate the Establishment
Clause. In essentially expanding the Child Benefit Test to higher education, the
Court was convinced that since the student could have relied on the program to
fund his education in a variety of different institutions, it was constitutional
since he, not his college, was the primary beneficiary of the state aid.

The Court's 1993 ruling in *Zobrest v. Catalina Foothills School District*
(1993) provided an unexpected boon for supporters of Catholic schools. In *Zobrest*, the Court reversed lower court rulings and relied on the Child Benefit
Test to permit a sign language interpreter to provide services on-site in a Roman
Catholic high school in Arizona, under the auspices of the Individuals with
Disabilities Education Act (1990), which opened the door for millions of children with disabilities. Along with ensuring that all students with disabilities are
entitled to free appropriate public education in the least restrictive environments,
the Act includes substantive and procedural safeguards to assist children and
their parents in safeguarding their rights. In any event, in *Zobrest*, the Court
decided that since the interpreter was a mere conduit of information, the student
was entitled to receive the services on-site because he, not the school, was the
primary beneficiary of the aid.

Most recently, in *Agostini v. Felton* (1997), the most important case on state
aid to Catholic schools since *Lemon*, the Supreme Court took the unusual step
of striking down an injunction that had been entered pursuant to its own earlier
decision in *Aguilar v. Felton*. Writing for a closely divided Court in a five-to-
four decision, Justice O'Connor, author of a stinging dissent in the original
Aguilar, joined by Chief Justice Rehnquist and Justices Scalia, Kennedy, and
Thomas, reasoned that the New York City Board of Education's Title I program
did not violate the Establishment Clause since there was no governmental indoctrination, there were no distinctions between recipients based on religion,
and there was no excessive entanglement. Thus, the Court was of the opinion
that as a federally funded program that offers supplemental, remedial instruction
to disadvantaged children on a neutral basis, the program's delivery of services
in religiously affiliated non-public schools did not run afoul of the Establishment
Clause, because it had appropriate safeguards in place. Dissenting opinions by

Justices Souter and Ginsburg, joined in parts by Justices Stevens and Breyer, voiced fears that the Court further blurred the line separating aid to religiously affiliated non-public schools by permitting aid that was direct and substantial.

In *Mitchell v. Helms* (2000), the Supreme Court, in a case from Louisiana, held that a federal statute that permits states to loan educational materials and equipment (including film strip and overhead projectors, television sets, motion picture projectors, videocassette recorders, video camcorders, computers, printers, library books, and periodicals) to students in religiously affiliated non-public schools did not run afoul of the Establishment Clause. Further, subject to the discussion below about the fact that *Helms* is a plurality opinion, Justice Thomas' opinion also reversed those parts of *Meek v. Pittenger* (1975) and *Wolman v. Walter* (1977) that struck down programs providing many of the same types of materials as Chapter 2 of the Elementary and Secondary Education Act. *Meek* and *Wolman* were resolved during the high–water mark of the Court's limiting state aid to religious schools.

One of two cases involving religion that the Court resolved in June 2000, *Helms* appears to be more far-reaching than *Sante Fe Independent School District v. Doe* (2000), wherein the Court struck down student-led prayer prior to the start of high school football games, for two reasons. First, *Helms* is likely to have a greater impact than *Sante Fe*, not only because estimates are that more than one million children in the United States benefit from Chapter 2, but also because it may open the door to other forms of governmental aid, such as vouchers. Although such a result is certainly speculative at this time, Justice Thomas' opinion added fuel to the fire because he relied on the principles of neutrality and the private choices of parents in deciding where to send their children to school, buzzwords that are often used by supporters of vouchers.

The second reason why *Helms* appears to be of greater significance is that *Helms* continues to expand the boundaries of permissible state aid to religious schools in striking down cases to the contrary. At the same time, as important as *Helms* appears to be, it is worth noting that as a plurality, with less than the requisite majority of five justices joining the opinion of the Court, questions can be raised about its applicability as binding precedent in similar situations.

Evolving case law over the questions of vouchers and tax credits may present Catholic schools with interesting alternatives. In *Jackson v. Benson* (1998), the Supreme Court of Wisconsin reversed an appellate tribunal and upheld the constitutionality of the Milwaukee Parental Choice Program (MPCP). The court reasoned that the MPCP, which was designed to provide publicly funded vouchers that enable low-income parents to send their children to private schools, including those that are religiously affiliated, did not violate the Establishment Clause of the First Amendment to the U.S. Constitution or the establishment provisions of the Wisconsin Constitution. As to tax credits, in *Kotterman v. Killan* (1999) the Supreme Court of Arizona recently upheld a statute that permitted state tax credits to be used to support attendance at private schools, relying on both *Lemon v. Kurtzman* (1971) and *Mueller v. Allen* (1983) in finding that the law was constitutional. Although the Supreme Court's refusal to hear appeals in *Jackson* (1998) and *Kotterman* (1999) are of no precedential value outside of Wisconsin and Arizona respectively, it is likely that similar programs may well pass constitutional muster. While many Catholic school leaders are reluctant to accept public funds for fear of subjecting themselves to increased levels of state oversight, the status of vouchers and tax credits is an issue that certainly bears watching.

EMPLOYEE RIGHTS

Insofar as the rights of Catholic school personnel are largely grounded in contract, rather than statutory law, it is important to maintain sound employment policies that provide a detailed review of the rights of all parties. With that in mind, this section reviews the salient features of key federal statutes dealing with employment-related matters that can help to provide workable guidelines for leaders in Catholic schools.

Perhaps the most important federal law dealing with hiring is Title VII (Mawdsley, 2000). This far-reaching statute, which applies regardless of whether an employer receives federal financial assistance, prohibits practices that discriminate in hiring, firing, or classifying workers based on race, color, religion, sex, or national origin (Title VII, 1999). At the same time, Title VII does permit religious employers to set bona fide occupational qualifications that include religion, and also allows them to limit hiring in key areas to members of their faith.

Other important federal statutes that apply, regardless of whether a school receives financial aid, include the Equal Pay Act of 1964 (EPA) (1999), Age Discrimination in Employment Act (ADEA) (1999), and the Family and Medical Leave Act (FMLA) (1999). Subject to a number of exemptions including seniority and merit, the EPA requires employers to pay women and men at the same rate for the same job. The ADEA, which applies to workers who are 40 or older, prohibits employers from using age as the determining factor in hiring, firing, classifying, or paying employees. The FMLA, which is designed to protect workers who may be forced to choose between caring for their families or themselves and job security, requires employers to establish leave policies to cover such circumstances.

A second category of federal laws applies, based on whether a school receives federal financial assistance. Perhaps the most important of these laws, and one which also applies to students, is Section 504 of the Rehabilitation Act of 1973 (1999). Section 504 declares that "no otherwise qualified individual with a disability . . . shall, solely by reason of her or his disability, be excluded from participation in, be denied the benefits of, or be subjected to discrimination under any program or activity receiving Federal financial assistance." Section 504 requires schools to provide reasonable accommodations to individuals with disabilities. Under Section 504, accommodations may involve modest adjustments such as permitting an employee to sit rather than stand while teaching or allowing a student with a visual impairment to occupy a seat in the front, rather than the back, of a classroom. However, schools are not required to make accommodations that are unduly costly, create an excessive monitoring burden, expose others to excessive risk, or fundamentally alter the nature of a program. Similarly, Title I of the Americans with Disabilities Act (1999), which deals with employment, and Title III, which deals with public accommodations (including education), may also impact upon the operation of Catholic schools.

Other statutes that may cover Catholic schools that receive federal financial assistance include Titles VI (1999) and IX (1999). Title VI, which does not contain an exemption for religious practices, prohibits discrimination based on race, creed, or national origin. Title IX outlaws discrimination based on gender. As case law emerges in coming years, the extent to which these statutes apply to Catholic schools will become clearer.

Unfortunately, the other end of the hiring spectrum involves discipline or dismissal of employees. The most common grounds for adverse employment actions in public schools are incompetence, neglect of duty, and conduct unbecoming an educator. While state laws do not apply to Catholic schools, administrators would be wise to borrow from the procedures they outline and thoroughly document their acts, as this will make them more legally defensible. Further, to the extent that many Catholic schools do not confer tenure, the rights of teachers are governed by their contracts and policy manuals. Even where tenure is not available, the evolving common law doctrine of the expectation of continuing employment may apply. Under this legal construct, the longer that an employee has provided satisfactory service, the greater the evidence that a school will have to produce in dismissing an individual.

Tenure is arguably granted more frequently in Catholic high schools that are represented by some form of teachers' union or association. Yet, the Church's stance with regard to unions is curious. Beginning with Pope Leo XIII's *Rerum Novarum* in 1891, the Church has consistently affirmed the right of all workers to organize and bargain collectively. Even so, the Church has consistently relied on the Supreme Court's ruling in *National Labor Relations Board v. Catholic Bishop of Chicago* (1979), which held that since Church-related institutions are outside of the scope of the National Labor Relations Act, they are not required to bargain with their employees.

In 1985, the American Catholic bishops, in their pastoral letter, *Economic Justice for All*, explicitly extended this right when they proclaimed that "all Church institutions must also fully recognize the rights of employees to organize and bargain collectively with the institution through whatever association or organization they freely choose (U.S. National Conference of Catholic Bishops, 1986, p. 176)." The eloquent language of *Economic Justice for All* notwithstanding, leaders in Catholic schools have continued to oppose teachers who sought to assert their right to organize and bargain collectively. However, relying on state rather than federal law, the High Courts of New York and New Jersey, in

New York State Labor Relations Board v. Christ the King Regional High School (1997) and *South Jersey Catholic School Teachers Organization v. St. Theresa of the Infant Jesus Church Elementary School* (1997), respectively, rejected arguments advanced by Catholic school officials that permitting teachers to organize and bargain collectively would have impacted negatively on their managerial authority and missions. While neither supporting nor opposing the right of teachers to organize, one can only wonder why Church leadership has been so reluctant to put its espoused teachings into practice (Gregory & Russo, 1999).

STUDENT RIGHTS

Just as educators in Catholic schools are not protected by the full array of federal laws, the same is true of students. Even so, just as awareness of federal law applicable to employees is useful, the same applies to students. In light of trends at the Supreme Court, perhaps the most significant issues affecting students is how administrators in Catholic schools apply discipline, search students and their property for drugs and other contraband, and deal with free speech and expression. Briefly stated, the heart of any discipline policy should focus on procedural due process and fairness. In other words, consistent with a wide variety of Supreme Court cases applicable to public schools, most notably *Goss v. Lopez* (1975), administrators should not only outline the range of unacceptable behaviors, but must also detail with specificity any penalties that might attach for violations. Moreover, to the extent that administrators can identify a range of penalties wherein the "punishment fits the crime," the more likely they are to prevail in the face of a challenge.

Search and Seizure

In light of growing problems with substance abuse, violence, and weapons, administrators in Catholic schools would be wise to familiarize themselves with the two Supreme Court cases involving searches and seizures of students.

New Jersey v. TLO (1985) examined the parameters of acceptable searches of students in public schools. In *TLO*, the Court held that the Fourth Amendment's prohibition against unreasonable searches and seizures applies to officials in public schools. The Court devised a two-part test to evaluate the legality of a search. According to the Court, "first, one must consider 'whether the . . . action was justified at its inception'; second, one must determine whether the search as actually conducted 'was reasonably related in scope to the circumstances which justified the interference in the first place' " (p. 341).

The Court added that a search is ordinarily justified at its inception when school officials have reasonable grounds for suspecting that a search will uncover evidence that the student has violated or is violating either school rules or the law. A subjective measure that must be based on specific facts, reasonable suspicion is a significantly lower standard than the probable cause standard that is applied to the police. Insofar as school, also known as administrative, searches are designed to ensure safety where there are generally large numbers of young people and reasonably few adults present, educators need only articulable justification before searching.

In considering the totality of circumstances, school officials may have to depend on the reliability of witnesses in determining whether to search. Keeping in mind that there is a wide spectrum of possibilities, it is more likely that a principal would proceed in searching a student or his locker based on a tip from a teacher who is well regarded than from a student who is frequently in trouble.

Turning to the scope of a search, the Court ruled that a search is permissible if its goals are reasonably related to its objectives, and if it is not excessively intrusive in light of the age and sex of a student and the nature of an infraction. For example, school officials will have to adopt less intrusive methods when searching younger students and may act in a more invasive manner if they are looking for a gun rather than a child's missing lunch.

Ten years after *TLO*, the Supreme Court revisited the Fourth Amendment rights of students in examining the implications of large-scale and suspicionless searches. In *Vernonia School District 47J v. Acton* (1995), the Court addressed the question of individualized suspicion that it left unanswered in *TLO*. *Acton* involved a seventh grade student in Oregon who was suspended from interscholastic athletics because he and his parents refused to comply with a district policy requiring them to sign a consent form allowing him to be tested for drug use. The family challenged his suspension, claiming that the district violated his Fourth Amendment rights and the state constitution since there was no reason to believe that he used drugs.

Responding to the perception of increased drug use on campus, the board created a policy which required all students trying out for interscholastic athletic teams to submit to a urinalysis drug test. As part of the policy, student athletes were tested individually at the beginning of each season and randomly throughout the year. The district also adopted elaborate procedures to safeguard the privacy rights of students. Students who tested positive were required to undergo a second examination. Those who tested positive on a second test were suspended from the team and sent for counseling. Subsequent violations led to mandatory suspensions from athletics.

The Supreme Court applied a three-part balancing test in affirming the constitutionality of the policy. First, it found that students have a lesser expectation of privacy than ordinary citizens. In fact, the Court reasoned that student athletes in particular have diminished privacy expectations because they are subject to physical examinations before becoming eligible to play, and dress in open areas of locker rooms. Second, the Court indicated the urinalysis was minimally intrusive since it was coupled with safeguards that allowed little encroachment on students' privacy. Finally, given the perception of increased drug use, the Court maintained that there was a significant need for the policy. However, a caution is in order, since *Acton* applies only to drug testing of student athletes. Consequently, it is unclear whether drug testing of any other groups would pass constitutional muster.

Even though these cases do not apply in Catholic schools, administrators would be wise to implement policies that are consistent with their rationales. Moreover, any policy dealing with searches of students, their lockers, and possessions should be clearly stated in the school's handbook as a means of avoiding problems when or if a search becomes necessary.

Student Free Speech

Tinker v. Des Moines Independent Community School District (1969), decided in the middle of the civil rights era that was ushered in by *Brown* and the social unrest of the 1960s, did much more than uphold the rights of students to wear arm bands as a protest against American involvement in Vietnam. The Court's often quoted words that "it can hardly be argued that students or teachers shed their constitutional rights to freedom of speech or expression at the schoolhouse gate" (p. 506), signaled the dawn of a new day in student rights.

The Court further defined the rights of students in *Goss v. Lopez* (1975). In *Goss*, the Court ruled in favor of students who did not receive procedural due process prior to their being suspended from school for 10 days. The Court found that since a suspension of 10 days (or longer) is more than a minimal deprivation of the rights of students to education, they "must be given some kind of notice and some kind of hearing" (p. 738). Although stopping short of mandating hearings for all disciplinary infractions, the Court suggested that longer suspensions or expulsions may require more formal procedures.

The Court cut back on the free speech rights of students in *Bethel School District v. Fraser* (1986). In *Fraser*, the Court ruled that educators could discipline a high school student who delivered a nominating speech at an assembly since it contained sexual innuendoes. The Court distinguished *Fraser* from *Tinker* on the basis that the non-disruptive, passive expression of a political viewpoint in the latter case intruded upon neither the work of the school nor the rights of other students.

The Court went full circle in a 1988 decision involving a dispute over a student newspaper. In *Hazelwood School District v. Kuhlmeier*, the Court concluded that educators could exercise "reasonable editorial control over the style and content of student speech in school sponsored expressive activities so long as their actions are reasonably related to legitimate pedagogical concerns" (p. 273). As such, the Court permitted educators to exclude an article on pregnancy from the newspaper at the high school, along with one about the divorce of a student's parents, because they believed that these topics were inappropriate.

CONCLUSION

Twenty-two years after the Supreme Court issued its monumental ruling in *Pierce v. Society of Sisters* (1925) acknowledging that Catholic and other non-public schools are generally free from state regulation, it directly addressed aid under the Establishment Clause in *Everson*, wherein it upheld a state law from New Jersey that permitted parents to be reimbursed for the cost of transporting their children to religiously affiliated non-public schools. Yet, since 1947 the Court has gone through periods during which it was more, or less, willing to extend aid to students in religious schools.

From *Everson* through *Allen*, wherein the Court, in 1968, upheld a state law from New York that provided textbooks for all students regardless of where they attended classes, it cautiously extended the boundaries of the Child Benefit Test. However, with the appearance of the tripartite *Lemon* test in 1971, the Child Benefit Test fell into an almost 20-year period of disuse. In fact, during this time, the Court perhaps reached its nadir in *Aguilar v. Felton* (1985), wherein it struck down the on-site delivery of Title I aid to students in religious schools based on the unproven fear that the program might have fostered excessive entanglement between the government and religious schools. It was not until *Zobrest v. Catalina Foothills School District* (1993) that the Court reinvigorated the Child Benefit Test in a K–12 setting. The Court further breathed life into the Child Benefit Test in 1997 when, in *Agostini v. Felton*, it dissolved an injunction from *Aguilar* and permitted the on-site delivery of Title I services for children in religious schools. As this chapter goes to press, supporters of Catholic and other religious schools are eagerly watching lower federal and state courts to see how they implement aid subsequent to *Helms* and whether they will follow its lead in continuing to expand the acceptable parameters of state aid under the Child Benefit Test.

Beyond cases involving state aid to religious schools and the Court's 1979 ruling in *National Labor Relations Board v. Catholic Bishop of Chicago*, which held that since Catholic institutions are outside of the scope of the National Labor Relations Act, they are not required to bargain with their employees, Catholic schools have had very little direct contact with the legal system. Even so, the more closely that Catholic schools comply with the dictates of civil law that protect the rights of students and employees, then the more closely they will bear witness to the Christian values that they represent.

REFERENCES

Age Discrimination in Employment Act, 29 U.S.C. § 623 (1999).
Agostini v. Felton, 521 U.S. 203 (1997).
Aguilar v. Felton, 473 U.S. 402 (1985).
Americans with Disabilities Act, 42 U.S.C. § §§ 12101 *et seq.* (1999).
Board of Education v. Allen, 392 U.S. 236 (1968).
Bethel School District No. 403 v. Fraser, 478 U.S. 675 (1986).
Brown v. Board of Education, 347 U.S. 483 (1954).
Cochran v. Louisiana State Board of Education, 281 U.S. 370 (1930).
Elementary and Secondary Education Act, 20 U.S.C. §§ 2701 *et seq.* (1999).

Equal Pay Act of 1964, 29 U.S.C. § 206 (d) (1999).

Everson v. Board of Education, 330 U.S. 1 (1947).

Family and Medical Leave Act, 29 U.S.C. §§ 2601 *et seq.* (1999).

Goss v. Lopez, 419 U.S. 565 (1975).

Grand Rapids v. Ball, 473 U.S. 373 (1985).

Gregory, D. L., & Russo, C. J. (1999). The first amendment and labor relations of religiously-affiliated employers. *Boston University Public Interest Law Journal, 8 (3)*, 449–467.

Hazelwood School District v. Kuhlmeier, 484 U.S. 260 (1988).

Helms v. Cody, 856 F. Supp. 1102 (E.D. La. 1994), aff'd in part and rev'd in part sub nom. *Helms v. Picard*, 151 F.3d 347 (5th Cir. 1998), opinion amended and re-hearing denied by *Helms v. Picard*, 165 F.3d 311 (5th Cir. 1999), cert. granted sub nom. *Mitchell v. Helms*, 119 S. Ct. 2336 (1999).

Individuals with Disabilities Education Act, 20 U.S.C.A. §§ 1400 *et seq.* (1990).

Jackson v. Benson, 578 N.W.2d 602 (Wis. 1998), *cert. denied*, 525 U.S. 997 (1998).

Jefferson, T. *Writings of Thomas Jefferson Vol. 16* (Andrew, ed. 1903).

Kotterman v. Killan, 972 P.2d 606 (1999), *cert. denied*, 120 S. Ct. 283 (1999).

Lemon v. Kurtzman, 403 U.S. 602 (1971).

Leo XIII. (1891/1987). *Rerum novarum: On the condition of the working class.* Boston: Daughters of St. Paul.

Levitt v. PEARL, 413 U.S. 472 (1973).

Marbury v. Madison, 5 U.S. 137 (1803).

Mawdsley, D. D. (2000). *Legal problems of religious and private schools* (4th ed.). Dayton, OH: Education Law Association.

Meek v. Pittenger, 421 U.S. 349 (1975).

Mitchell v. Helms, 120 S. Ct. 2530 (2000).

Mueller v. Allen, 463 U.S. 388 (1983).

Murray v. Curlett, 374 U.S. 203 (1963).

National Labor Relations Board v. Catholic Bishop of Chicago, 440 U.S. 490 (1979).

New Jersey v. TLO, 469 U.S. 325 (1985).

New York State Labor Relations Board v. Christ the King Regional High School, 660 N.Y.S.2d 359 (N.Y. 1997).

Ohio Revised Code, § 3321.03 (1999).

PEARL v. Nyquist, 413 U.S. 756 (1973).

PEARL v. Reagan, 444 U.S. 646 (1980).

Pierce v. Society of Sisters, 268 U.S. 510 (1925).

Russo, C. J. (1999, Winter). Prayer at public school graduation ceremonies: Exercise in futility or a teachable moment? *Brigham Young University Education and Law Journal*, 1–23.

Russo, C. J., & Mawdsley, R. D. (2000). Giving with one hand, taking with the other: State-aid to religiously affiliated nonpublic schools. *Education Law Reporter, 140 (3)*, 807–822.

Santa Fe Independent School District v. Doe, 120 S. Ct. 2266 (2000).

School District Of Abington Township v. Schempp, 374 U.S. 203 (1963).

Section 504 of the Rehabilitation Act of 1973, 29 U.S.C. § 794 (1999).

Sloan v. Lemon, 413 U.S. 825 (1973).

South Jersey Catholic School Teachers Organization v. St. Theresa of the Infant Jesus Church Elementary School, 696 A.2d 709 (1997).

Tinker v. Des Moines Independent Community School District, 393 U.S. 503 (1969).

Title VI, 42 U.S.C. § 2000d (1999).

Title VII, 42 U.S.C. § 2000e-2(a) (1999).

Title IX of the Educational Amendments of 1972, 20 U.S.C*.A. § 1681 (1999).

U.S. Constitution, Amendment X.

U.S. National Conference of Catholic Bishops. (1986). *Economic justice for all: Pastoral letter on Catholic social teaching and the United States economy.* Washington, DC: Author.

Vernonia School District 47 J v. Acton, 515 U.S. 646 (1995).

Walz v. Tax Commission of New York City, 397 U.S. 664 (1970).

Witters v. Washington Services for the Blind, 474 U.S. 481 (1986).

Wolman v. Walter 433 U.S. 229 (1977).

Zobrest v. Catalina Foothills School District, 509 U.S. 312 (1993).

Chapter 13

Research on Catholic School Effectiveness

Bruno V. Manno and Heather Graham

Beginning with the work of Rossi and Greeley in the early 1960s, rigorous empirical research has documented the effectiveness of Catholic schools on a variety of fronts, particularly in the academic and religious domains. Prior to 1980, however, most of these findings were of little interest to secular educators and policymakers. The mounting evidence of the efficacy of Catholic schools, particularly for disadvantaged students, has led to a growing interest in the organization and practices of Catholic schools and has inspired questions about what public education can learn from Catholic schools.

Unfortunately, much more research has been conducted on the effectiveness of Catholic high schools than their elementary counterparts. For that reason, this chapter devotes disproportionate attention to Catholic high school outcomes. The academic success of the Catholic high school is apparent particularly when one views its effectiveness for certain disadvantaged and minority children, whose persistently low achievement levels—especially in urban America—present perhaps the most pressing problem confronting American public education today. For example, the average mathematics test scores for Black and Hispanic public school students in the 12th grade are about the same as for White and Asian public school students in the 8th grade. Consider also that children from single-parent families in public schools are twice as likely to drop out as students from two-parent families; but in Catholic schools, dropout rates for both types of families are about the same, and that rate is nearly non-existent (Manno, 1999).

Why do Catholic high schools succeed so well in these different ways? How do they create advantaged educational opportunities for the most disadvantaged of our society? Much of the research demonstrates that the answer to these questions is both sound curriculum and sound communities. This chapter will review in a general way the research since the mid-1960s on the efficacy of

Catholic schools and conclude by offering a brief agenda for future research on Catholic schools.

EARLY RESEARCH ON CATHOLIC SCHOOLS

In 1966, two influential studies were released: *Catholic Schools in Action* (Neuwien) and *The Education of Catholic Americans* (Greeley & Rossi, 1966). Initiated in 1962, *Catholic Schools in Action* (also known as the Notre Dame Study of Catholic Education) was the first comprehensive study of Catholic schools in the United States, gathering data on 92% of Catholic elementary and 84% of Catholic secondary schools. The Carnegie Corporation funded the study, with data collected by the National Catholic Educational Association (NCEA) and the Education Department of the National Catholic Welfare Conference. Teachers and principals responded to a questionnaire that covered a variety of topics, including enrollment, tuition, organization, the further education of graduates, admission policies, and ownership patterns.

One of the most notable features of *Catholic Schools in Action* (Neuwien, 1966) was its Inventory of Catholic School Outcomes (ICSO), which measured students' knowledge of Catholicism and their religious values and attitudes. It tested how well students understood church law, doctrine, and liturgy; measured their religious values, civic attitudes, family values, and educational goals; and collected their opinions of Catholic school goals, the level of parental involvement in their religious schooling, and other factors affecting their religious development. Significantly, a high percentage of students reported at least average parental interest in their education (91%) with over one-third reporting very strong parental interest.

In addition, the study reported that girls were more likely than boys to espouse values similar to those of the Catholic Church and that individual and school differences influenced attitudes and aspirations. Weaknesses of the study include its descriptive, rather than evaluative, nature and the absence of supporting statistics. In addition, it was criticized because it lacked a random sample and did not fully utilize the ethnographic data collected. Nonetheless, as the first comprehensive work of its kind and scope, Neuwien's study offered a rich and descriptive portrait of students' religious knowledge and views (Convey, 1992).

The Education of Catholic Americans (Greeley & Rossi, 1966) was a more ambitious analytic study. It launched the effort to rigorously analyze the effects of Catholic schools on their graduates, using then "state-of-the-art" statistical methods. In this work, Greeley and Rossi used the 1963 National Opinion Research Center (NORC) study of the effectiveness of the value-based education of Catholic schools to evaluate whether Catholics who attended Catholic schools were better educated than those who attended public schools. They found greater levels of success among Catholics who had attended Catholic schools. The study's findings also challenged the widely held belief that Catholic school attendance had the effect of promoting intolerance of non-Catholics. It presented evidence that Catholic school graduates were as likely to associate with non-Catholics as their Catholic counterparts who attended public schools. To explain why Catholic schools were more effective for many students, Greeley and Rossi cited the schools' ability to integrate students into the Catholic community, which then provided them with the emotional well-being needed to excel. In addition, the authors found no particularly favorable effects associated with any one type of Catholic institution (elementary, secondary, or post-secondary).

The Greeley and Rossi study was criticized for various forms of sample bias (Hassenger, 1967; McCluskey, 1968). Given the authors' scrutiny and meticulous methodology, however, it is unlikely that any sample bias significantly affected their results (Convey, 1992). Another criticism was that the authors' conclusions rely on the association of variables to actually explain important relationships. In the words of John Convey (1992), "Because this study preceded the widespread use of regression analysis and path models, Greeley and Rossi were unable to estimate the cumulative effects of their predictors of adult religious behavior" (p. 15).

In 1976, *Catholic Schools in a Declining Church* (Greeley, McCready, & McCourt) confirmed the positive findings of the earlier study on the effectiveness of Catholic schools, *The Education of Catholic Americans*. This evaluation employed a more advanced statistical methodology, and relied on a nationally representative sample of 1,128 Catholic adults and data gathered from interviews with 927 Catholic adults. The researchers found that the importance and influence of Catholic schools to their graduates was growing, and that graduates of Catholic schools were more religious and more actively involved with the Church than they had been a decade earlier.

The authors also found that in spite of the growing evidence of the efficacy of parochial schools, declining enrollments and increasing costs were endangering the future of these schools. They attributed these challenges to the social unrest of the late 1960s and early 1970s, and the instability in the Church immediately following Vatican Council II. Nonetheless, the authors concluded that Catholic schools retained strong support among the American Catholic population, benefitted from increasing effectiveness, and were more important to the church during periods of traumatic transition (like Vatican Council II) than during times of peaceful stability (Greeley, McCready, & McCourt, 1976).

DESCRIPTIVE INFORMATION ON CATHOLIC SCHOOLS

The NCEA created another early source of data on Catholic schools in 1970 when it began collecting and publishing extensive statistical profiles of Catholic elementary and secondary schools. These annual reports use data collected from diocesan school offices to provide public and private school comparisons, as well as demographic data describing elementary and secondary Catholic school enrollment, staffing trends, and finances. A recent statistical report (McDonald, 1999) offers the following information:

- Total Catholic school enrollment nationwide during 1998–1999 was 2,648,844 with 1,990,947 students (75%) enrolled in elementary schools; 22,155 (1%) enrolled in middle schools; and 635,742 (24%) enrolled in secondary schools. Over 13% (355,832) of all students enrolled in Catholic schools were not Catholic.

- Nationally there were 8,217 Catholic schools during the 1998–1999 school year: 6,863 elementary schools; 127 middle schools; and 1,227 secondary schools. More than 41% of those schools had waiting lists and 33% were located in urban areas, 13% in inner-city neighborhoods, 33% in the suburbs, and 21% in rural areas.

- Student ethnicity is becoming increasingly diverse in Catholic schools, particularly in urban areas. In 1970–1971, minority enrollment was 11% of total enrollment; in 1980–1981, 19%; and it increased to 24.7% in 1997–1998 (see Table 13.1).

- There were 153,081 full-time professional staff at Catholic schools during the 1998–1999 school year with a student-teacher ratio of 17:1. Over 92% of professional staff were laity and 7.8% were religious or members of the clergy.

In addition to its annual statistical profile, the NCEA is supporting a multiyear project to survey Catholic high schools, *Catholic High Schools 2000 (CHS 2000)* that will provide "an informative benchmark picture of Catholic secondary schools at the end of what for all practical purposes is their first century" (Guerra, 1998, p. viii). This project follows up and attempts to update some parts of the NCEA's 1985 publication *The Catholic High School: A National Portrait*, which provided a detailed look at Catholic high schools in the early 1980s, collecting data from more than 900 schools in 1983–1984. *CHS 2000* surveys all 1,215 Catholic high schools in the United States. (Questionnaires were also sent to 38 schools in the Virgin Islands, Puerto Rico, the Caroline and Marshall Islands, and a few schools abroad.) By comparing the *CHS 2000* data with longitudinal data collected between 1983 and 1997, the NCEA will produce descriptive reports on school finances; governance and development; academic and co-curricular programs; religious education and formation; and the school community.

The first report in the series, *CHS 2000, A First Look* (Guerra, 1998), provides detailed information on institutional, student, staff, governance, academic, and religious characteristics of Catholic high schools. Here is a sampling of some of the information found in that report:

- Only 7% of the high schools are highly selective (accept 50% or less of those who apply); 32% are moderately selective (accept between 51% and 80% of those who apply); 47% are generally open (accept 81% to 98% of those who apply); and 14% accept nearly anyone who applies.

- Student religious affiliation is 81% Catholic, with the balance (19%) being non-Catholic. Race and ethnic enrollment includes 76% Caucasian; 8% African American; 10% Hispanic/Latino; 4% Asian/Pacific Islander; and 2% Other, with 230 schools serving student populations that are at least ⅓ minority.

Table 13.1
Catholic School Enrollment by Ethnic Background, 1997–1998

National	Elementary	%	Middle	%	Secondary	%	All Schools	%
Black	160,428	8.1	1,975	8.9	46,858	7.4	209,261	7.9
Hispanic	212,046	10.7	1,545	7.0	64,217	10.1	277,808	10.5
Asian/Pacific Islander	89,823	4.5	555	2.5	29,467	4.6	119,845	4.5
Native American	6,648	0.3	184	0.8	2,514	0.4	9,346	0.4
Multiracial	30,414	1.5	164	0.7	9,169	1.4	39,747	1.5
White	1,492,396	75.0	17,682	79.8	482,825	75.9	1,992,903	75.2
Total	1,983,534	100.0	22,191	100.0	635,742	100.0	2,641,467[1]	100.0

Percentages do not total 100 due to rounding.
[1]Ethnicity unreported: 7,377.

Source: McDonald, 1999.

- The income distribution of families is: 11% of families under $20,000; 32% between $21,000 and $40,000; 39% between $41,000 and $80,000; 13% between $81,000 and $120,000; and 5% over $121,000. Twenty-three percent of the students receive financial aid.

- Ninety-seven percent of the graduates attend college: 25% attend highly selective colleges; 55% attend moderately selective colleges; 17% attend community colleges. The remaining 3% immediately enter the workforce.

Additional analyses of enrollment, finance, staffing, and other operational trends appear in Youniss and Convey (2000). These evaluations include a study of enrollment trends in the 20 largest diocesan school systems as well as the use of three federal data sets to examine trends at the secondary school level over the last 25 years. The secondary school analysis by Riordan (2000) argues that over this time period, "these secondary schools have enrolled more economically elite, more non-Catholic, . . . more minority students . . . [and] more female students than . . . 25 years ago" (p. 13). The "eliting" charge has been disputed by other investigations (Greeley, 1998, 1999; Guerra, 1998; Youniss, Convey, & McLellan, 1999).

RESEARCH SPONSORED BY THE FEDERAL
GOVERNMENT

Perhaps the most controversial study of U.S public education ever commissioned by the federal government was James Coleman's *Equality of Educational Opportunity* (1966). It fueled public criticism of the nation's school systems, and compelled educators and policymakers to focus on what made some schools more effective than others. This interest in school efficacy led, in turn, to a heightened public scrutiny of the practices and outcomes of Catholic schools. While the earlier studies of Neuwien, Greeley, and Rossi were important to Catholics and Catholic schools, they did not have a significant impact on U.S. public policy.

In contrast, the research agenda of the U.S. Department of Education focused national attention on Catholic schools at a time when public dissatisfaction with U.S. public schools was high. As a result, Catholic schools were increasingly looked to for answers to the challenges facing secular educators. Of particular interest were their successes in educating disadvantaged youth and creating an environment conducive to learning.

The U.S. Department of Education's National Center for Education Statistics has been instrumental in facilitating the development of two important longitudinal data sources that provide information on Catholic schools: *High School and Beyond* (HS&B) and the *National Education Longitudinal Study of 1988* (NELS:88) (National Center for Education Statistics, 1996). Another important data set that offers rich historical trend information on student achievement at three age (ages 9, 13, and 17) and grade (4, 8, and 12) levels is the National

Assessment of Educational Progress (NAEP). The existence of these data sources has fostered more statistically rigorous and objective analyses of the effectiveness of Catholic schools.

HS&B collected longitudinal data from 1980 forward to document students' experiences and transitions during 10th and 12th grades and their subsequent post-secondary education. It collected base-year data from a nationally representative sample of 30,000 sophomores and 28,000 seniors and included data gathered from parents, teachers, and administrators. The HS&B survey included two cohorts: the 1980 senior class, and the 1980 sophomore class. Both cohorts were surveyed every two years through 1986, and the 1980 sophomore class was also surveyed again in 1992. The study's major objectives were to track changes in student achievement, attitudes, behaviors, and values over time; determine the variables that affected student outcomes; understand how these variables and their interactions affected education quality; and to inform the thinking of education policymakers.

Although Coleman's 1966 report did not look specifically at Catholic schools, the federal government asked Coleman to conduct a comparative evaluation of the outcomes of public and private schools using the HS&B base-year data. Coleman, along with his colleagues Hoffer and Kilgore, analyzed the HS&B 1980 data and concluded that students from Catholic schools consistently demonstrated higher cognitive achievement than their counterparts in public schools, regardless of parental backgrounds (Coleman, Hoffer, & Kilgore, 1982). The researchers considered both inputs (school, family, and student characteristics) and outputs (academic achievement), and found that the educational expectations, attendance, and participation of students in Catholic schools exceeded those of students in public schools. The authors suggested that Catholic school students' greater achievement levels, attendance, and study of more rigorous subjects was due to the discipline, structure, high faculty expectations, and quality instruction found in parochial schools. They concluded that public schools had much to learn from private schools.

The study was controversial due to both its methodology and the implications of the authors' findings (Goldhaber, 1999). Critics objected to the authors' exclusive reliance on cross-sectional data, and cited selectivity bias as a major shortcoming of the evaluation. Studies of school outcomes are commonly criticized for selection bias. This occurs due to a lack of random assignment. This self-selection may lead to selectivity bias where evaluators cannot be certain that differences associated with outcomes are due exclusively to the efficacy of Catholic schools over public schools, and not simply to differences in the types of students who enroll in each kind of school. It is possible that some unmeasured or uncontrolled student characteristic is responsible for the distinct findings in public and Catholic schools. To get around this problem that results from a lack of random assignment, evaluations use sophisticated statistical models. They may, however, suffer from omitted variable bias where not all of the variables that affect outcomes are included.

The study was also criticized for making insufficient statistical adjustments to account for differences in student characteristics (as opposed to schools). For example, the analysts' use of the curriculum as a variable for analysis was questioned on the grounds that the academic tracks selected by students could have been a function of the students' initial differences, not the schools' effectiveness. Coleman and his co-authors' claim that Catholic schools embodied the "common school" ideal more than their public school counterparts was also challenged. This suggestion that the similar achievement levels and educational goals of racially and economically diverse students in Catholic schools could be at least partially attributed to the successful practices of these schools (and not pre-existing parental and student characteristics) spawned many re-analyses of the data, as well as allegations that the authors were biased. Moreover, Coleman's use of his findings to suggest that public funds might be used to support vouchers or other financing schemes like tuition tax credits to support private schools (including religious schools) politicized the debate and heightened scrutiny of these findings.

Greeley's 1982 study *Catholic High Schools and Minority Students* used the HS&B base-year data to measure the impact of Catholic high schools on Black and Hispanic students, and confirmed and elaborated upon Coleman and his colleagues' earlier suggestions that Catholic schools were particularly effective for minority students. Greeley's study was the first detailed analysis that focused exclusively on minority students in Catholic schools. It discovered that the most disadvantaged students (as determined by family income levels, parental education levels, and enrollment in non-academic curricular programs) experienced the greatest differential in achievement between public and Catholic schools. The effect was attributed to both the type of student attending Catholic high schools and the schools themselves. In the words of Convey (1989), "Greeley attributed the effectiveness of Catholic schools to the quality of their discipline and their teaching; he also found religious order ownership to be a good predictor of effectiveness" (p. 75). Moreover, Greeley found that students with multiple disadvantages (such as those coming from families with low levels of educational attainment) were particularly well served by Catholic schools. He attributed this success to the school environment and sense of community, which was a finding that Coleman and Hoffer (1987) later analyzed in more detail.

In *Public and Private High Schools: The Impact of Communities* (1987), Coleman and Hoffer used the newly released HS&B data to compare the achievement levels of public and private school students between grades 10 and 12. Their findings confirmed and extended the conclusions of their 1982 report on the efficacy of Catholic schools (particularly for minority students). But this time their analysis drew much less criticism because of their reliance on longitudinal data. In this second study, they found that students in Catholic high schools had greater improvements in their verbal and math skills between 10th and 12th grade than students in public schools. In addition, graduation rates and college enrollment and completion figures were higher for students who attended

Catholic high schools. The authors were also able to compare different types of private schools and could distinguish the impact of the faith community found in Catholic schools.

The 1987 report confirmed the "common school effect," where student achievement was higher for those attending a Catholic school and achievement differences between affluent and poor students or minority and White students were less in Catholic schools. Coleman and Hoffer expanded the scope of their second study to look at the role of the school as a social unit in a social context. They suggested that the religious environment of Catholic schools formed a functional community in which "social norms and sanctions, including those that cross generations, arise out of the social structure itself, and both reinforce and perpetuate that structure" (Coleman & Hoffer, 1987, p. 7). The functional community of Catholic schools fosters the development of social capital or "the empowerment that exists in relationships between individuals" (Convey, 1992, p. 20).

The *National Education Longitudinal Study of 1988* (NELS:88) (National Center for Education Statistics, 1996) collected information about student achievement, enrollment, demographic characteristics, and attitudes from students, parents, and faculty. It provided data on 8th graders and their transition to high school, and in doing so enabled comparisons of public, Catholic, and other private schools. Analyses of the NELS:88 data showed greater achievement for Catholic school students, though the advantage was not as great as that shown in the HS&B data. Nonetheless, Goldhaber (1999) suggests that even if Catholic schools don't "have a larger impact overall, . . . [they] might benefit students in select areas (e.g., inner cities)" (p. 20).

The base-year NELS:88 findings (Hafner, Ingels, Schneider, & Stephenson, 1990; Rock & Pollack, 1990; Snyder, 1989) showed that approximately 25% of 8th graders enrolled in parochial schools were minorities and Catholic schools enrolled 8th graders from diverse socioeconomic backgrounds. The findings of NELS:88 also mirrored those of HS&B in relation to the orderly and communal environment of parochial schools. Students in Catholic schools reported greater satisfaction with their teachers' skills and commitment and the overall safety and order of their schools as compared to students in public schools.

According to Derek Neal's research (1997) using the National Longitudinal Survey of Youth, Catholic schooling in urban areas increases the probability of high school graduation and college attendance, which in turn leads to wage gains in the labor market. Moreover, Neal finds that wage gains due to Catholic school attendance are much more significant for minorities than non-minorities. Neal contends that selection bias has little to do with these outcomes and instead credits Catholic schools with these gains in educational achievement.

Perhaps the best summary review and analysis of the findings from HS&B, NELS:88, and NAEP are provided by Hoffer in Youniss and Convey (2000). He concludes his review and extension of empirical research in the following manner:

Catholic high schools have positive effects on verbal and mathematics achievement, but no discernable effects on science.

Catholic school effects are greater for students from disadvantaged backgrounds, especially with respect to family structure and functioning. The evidence for "common school effects" is consistent but statistically weak for low-SES students.

The main "schooling" mechanism for the Catholic school effects is the greater concentration of academic course taking among Catholic school students. The main "macro" theories of the Catholic sector effects are (1) aggregate-student composition, (2) market competition, (3) institutional character, and (4) functional community. (p. 108)

Finally, the National Household Education Survey (NHES) (National Center for Education Statistics, 1995) is an important source of data for looking at the families of students who attend Catholic (and other private and home) schools. NHES is a nationally representative sample of 9,393 parents of school-age children. One line of inquiry using these data has examined family involvement in different civic activities, differentiating families of public school students from families of Catholic school students. Smith and Sikkink (1999) constructed a civic participation scale from nine of the items in the survey to investigate whether families that choose Catholic schools are more socially isolated and withdrawn from civic participation than families involved in public schools. Contrary to popular beliefs, they found that "Catholic, Protestant, and nonreligious private schooling and home schooling families are consistently more involved in a wide spectrum of civic activities than are families of public schools children" (p. 16).

Other analyses looking at the issue of democratic education from the perspective of the students in Catholic (and other private) schools, conclude that the so-called "private" education of young people does not have the "privatizing" effect of lessening attachment to civic life. On the contrary, that "private" education has the effect of fostering student attachment to democratic principles and institutions (Campbell, 2000; Wolf, Greene, Kleitz, & Thalhammer, 2000).

OTHER RESEARCH ON INNER-CITY SCHOOLS AND MINORITY STUDENTS

The work of Vitullo-Martin and the U.S. Catholic Conference (1979) synthesized existing information on inner-city Catholic schools. It reported that these schools were experiencing a dramatic reduction in overall enrollment while increasingly enrolling non-Catholic minority populations. Vitullo-Martin also discussed how declining parish revenues, decaying buildings, and difficulties associated with adapting parish practices to new ethnic populations in inner-city parochial schools raised questions about the future of these schools. Vitullo-Martin's work challenged the Catholic Church to take a position on the future of inner-city parochial schools, and argued that inner-city parochial schools provided much-needed quality education and played an important role in engaging parents and reinforcing community and family values. He argued that because these schools were often more diverse than public schools, they played an important role in resisting the racial and class segregation of cities brought on by public school district boundaries.

The Catholic League for Religious and Civil Rights released the findings of their major study on inner-city Catholic elementary schools three years after Vitullo-Martin's report. *Inner-City Private Elementary Schools: A Study* (Cibulka, O'Brien, & Zewe, 1982) evaluated 54 predominantly Catholic Title I schools with over 70% minority enrollment, to determine the reasons low-income minority parents chose private schools. Data from approximately 4,000 parents, 300 teachers, and 50 principals were collected from schools located in Chicago, Detroit, Los Angeles, Milwaukee, Newark, New Orleans, Washington, DC, and New York. The authors reported that the schools were not selective and enrolled a large percentage of students from low-income, single-parent families (50% of whom were not Catholic.) Cibulka and his colleagues also found that parents chose these schools for the superior education they offered their children and their responsiveness to student needs. Just as Greeley's work had done for Catholic high schools in 1982, the work of Cibulka documented the success of parochial elementary schools for minority youth student achievement, and credited teacher attitudes and the communal atmosphere of the schools with much of this success.

A more recent analysis of minority group issues in Catholic schools appears in Youniss and Convey (2000). It includes a discussion of family background and school issues found in Catholic schools that serve more than 50% minority students; a portrait of 31 "Cornerstone" high schools that serve over 75% African-American students; and a look at post-1970 Catholic immigrants from countries like Mexico, Vietnam, and Korea that use Catholic schools to educate their children. In the words of Youniss and Convey, this "look . . . is sobering . . . [and] shows how fragile these schools are" (pp. 114–115).

CATHOLIC SCHOOL ORGANIZATION AND SOCIAL CAPITAL

Bryk, Lee, and Holland's 1993 work, *Catholic Schools and the Common Good*, offers an explanation of the ability of Catholic schools to both improve student achievement and create greater social equity in student outcomes, while their public counterparts struggled to achieve either end. The authors seek to explain why "student achievement becomes more socially differentiated over time in public schools, but becomes more homogeneous in Catholic schools" (Bryk, 1994, p. 27).

Catholic Schools and the Common Good (Bryk, Lee, & Holland, 1993) built on the earlier analyses of Coleman and his colleagues and Hill, Foster, and Gendler (1990). Bryk, however, employed a more complex statistical methodology than Coleman, which relied on path analysis and hierarchical linear modeling techniques to analyze the relationship between variables and student achievement. The authors focused primarily on student outcomes in public and private schools, and paid particular attention to the educational and organizational variables that differed between school types and how students' backgrounds and achievement levels varied in relation to aspects of school organization.

The authors employed a three-part approach in which they analyzed the first two waves of HS&B data, studied the internal operations of Catholic schools by collecting field data in a sample of seven exemplary schools nationwide, and conducted a rigorous analysis of the schools' intellectual and social history. As a result of their research, Bryk and his co-authors found that achievement differences between public and Catholic schools disappear when classroom and school variables (such as time spent on homework, disciplinary climate, and number of math classes taken) are controlled for (Bryk, Lee, & Holland, 1993). To explain these achievement differences, the authors identified several features unique to Catholic schools that were likely to help disadvantaged students, including a limited and deliberate curriculum, a strong communal structure, an expanded role for faculty, a decentralized system of governance, and a well-established mission and value set.

CORE CURRICULUM

The academic organization of Catholic high schools is centered on a core curriculum for all students, regardless of background or educational goals, and this standardization makes a difference, particularly among disadvantaged students. The focused and constrained core curriculum of the Catholic high school is a counterpoint to the comprehensive public high school described so memorably in the phrase "shopping mall high school." It is also a bulwark against the fads that frequently sweep through education and ensures that all students are held to high standards of achievement; in doing so it better comes closer to creating a common school approach. According to Bryk (1994), "the constrained academic structure in Catholic high schools minimizes the normal differentiating effects that accompany wide individual choice" (p. 27).

SENSE OF COMMUNITY

Along with demanding the mastery of a common body of knowledge from all students, it is apparent that schools that communicate high levels of care and concern create a genuine basis for engaging parents, teachers, and students. Individuals experience a network of relationships that bind them to the school. While the proverbial carrots and sticks in public education—like teachers' merit pay or withholding drivers' licenses from poor performing students—have some extrinsic role to play in motivating people and enhancing engagement, these must be placed within a broader, less utilitarian, less instrumental context of interior motivation. Inner drive springs from the self-confidence of knowing that there are people—especially authority figures—who care for you and demand the best from you. Bryk, Lee, and Holland found that in schools with a strong communal organization (albeit Catholic or public), classroom disruptions, class cutting, absenteeism, and dropout rates were much lower. In addition, teachers expressed greater job satisfaction (Bryk, 1994, p. 28).

EXPANDED FACULTY ROLE

Bryk and his colleagues found evidence that the extended role teachers play in shaping not just what students learn, but who they become (known as personalism) is correlated with greater student outcomes. As schools must be free to act, teachers must be free to exercise not merely the technical skills and expertise their position requires, but also the sense of calling and obligation that incites greater achievement in their students. Contemporary discussions about professional development that neglect normative or moral dimensions of teaching are not likely to improve or develop the profession.

DECENTRALIZED GOVERNANCE

To develop these strong relationships between students, parents, and teachers, schools must have the autonomy to react to different situations. Effective Catholic schools have a great deal of leeway in educational, fiscal, and management matters. Rejecting a purely bureaucratic conception of the role they must play, Bryk, Lee, and Holland introduce the notion of "subsidiarity" whereby Catholic schools mitigate efficiency concerns with an overarching concern for human dignity (Bryk, 1994, p. 29). In addition, the small size of most Catholic schools facilitates this decentralized governance structure, contributes to community building, and helps foster a more personalized role for teachers.

IMPORTANCE OF THE MISSION AND VALUES OF CATHOLIC SCHOOLS

Finally, a clear and overriding sense of mission that is guided by an educational philosophy shapes the organization of the Catholic high school. This philosophy includes an affirmation of human reason, moral knowledge, and respect for individual dignity, combined with a responsiveness to markets. It also incorporates a shared set of values about what should be taught, and the important role social justice plays in those teachings. These comprehensive ideals encourage students to advance beyond relativism and material self-interest, and search for ways to foster the interior lives of students.

PUBLIC AND PRIVATE VOUCHER PROGRAMS

Two cities (Cleveland and Milwaukee) and one state (Florida) are currently allowing public dollars to be used by low-income families to pay for tuition at private (including religious) schools. Litigation on the constitutionality of using taxpayer money for these vouchers is underway for all three programs. The Florida program began in 1999 and has not yet been evaluated, though at least one major evaluation is being planned. The Cleveland program began in the fall of 1996. Early evaluations are inconclusive because of issues related to poor data. The Milwaukee program began in the fall of 1990 and has been evaluated by several different individuals (Greene, Peterson, & Du, 1999; Rouse, 1998; Witte, 2000). Finally, there are over 40 privately funded voucher programs across the United States.

What is most interesting about the early analyses and evaluations of some of these public and private voucher programs is the use of a randomized field trial methodology that includes both test and control groups (Peterson, 1999a). Early indications from the eight studies that have been done of five different programs suggest that there are academic and social benefits to attending Catholic (and other private) schools (Greene, 2000; Peterson, 1999b).

PRIORITIES FOR FUTURE RESEARCH

There are many topics that provide fertile ground for future research on Catholic schools and their effectiveness. Convey (1992) and others (Hunt, 1998; Hunt & O'Keefe, 1998) provide comprehensive discussions of this topic. For our part, two are worth special mention.

First, to echo Convey and others, the dearth of information available on Catholic elementary schools warrants a research focus on them, with special need for longitudinal analyses. It can be argued that the last comprehensive study of Catholic elementary schools in the United States was Neuwien's *Catholic Schools in Action*, conducted in 1966. In addition, the National Assessment of Educational Progress (NAEP) offers some data that allow for comparisons between Catholic school students and public school students, although analyses are limited by the cross-sectional nature of these data.

Second, we need further research on what Catholic schools tell us about good schools generally. In other words, what insights can Catholic schools give us to reinvigorating our conception and understanding of all schools—including public schools—especially the need for schools to be seen as community institutions? Catholic schools are examples of what contemporary analysts term "civil society." They are voluntary institutions, neither compulsory nor monopolistic. They are anchored in their communities more than schools that are created by system bureaucracies.

Within this context, revitalizing all our schools—whether public or private—falls under the banner of what Kristol (1994) has called fostering a sociology of virtue: "Strengthening the institutions of civil society that attend to the character of the citizenry—this is the sociology of virtue" (p. 21). "Today's sociology of virtue . . . implies a thinking through of the way in which social institutions can be reinvented, restructured, or reformed to promote virtue and to foster sound character" (1994, p. 35). Perhaps the most interesting and important research issue to pursue in this regard is this: How is the task of reinventing all our schools aligned with the task of fostering a sociology of virtue? Maybe the most significant contribution to be made to that research effort is to be found in the history of U.S. Catholic education, an effort that has striven to foster in students an ethical and moral vision for preparing them to enter the worlds of work, family, and citizenship.

REFERENCES

Bryk, A. S. (1994). Like a bridge. *Boston College Magazine, 53 (1)*, 26–31.

Bryk, A. S., Lee, V. E., & Holland, P. B. (1993). *Catholic schools and the common good*. Cambridge, MA: Harvard University Press.

Campbell, D. E. (2000, March). *Making democratic education work: Schools, social capital, and civic education*. Paper presented at the Conference on Charter Schools, Vouchers, and Public Education, Harvard University.

Cibulka, J. G., O'Brien, T. J., & Zewe, D. (1982). *Inner-city private elementary schools: A study*. Milwaukee, WI: Marquette University Press.

Coleman, J., & Hoffer, T. (1987). *Public and private high schools: The impact of communities*. New York: Basic Books.

Coleman, J. S. (1966). *Equality of educational opportunity*. Washington, DC: U.S. Department of Health, Education & Welfare, U.S. Government Printing Office.

Coleman, J. S., Hoffer, T., & Kilgore, S. (1982). *High school achievement: Public, Catholic, & private schools compared*. New York: Basic Books.

Convey, J. J. (1989). Research on Catholic schools. In *New Catholic Encyclopedia* (Vol. XVIII, Supplement 1978–1988, pp. 73–78). Washington, DC: The Catholic University of America.

Convey, J. J. (1992). *Catholic schools make a difference: Twenty-five years of research*. Washington, DC: National Catholic Educational Association.

Convey, J. J. (1994). *Priorities for research on Catholic schools*. Prepared for the Research Symposium: Catholic Schools: A Tradition of Excellence—A Future with Hope, University of Dayton.

Goldhaber, D. (1999). School choice: An examination of the empirical evidence on achievement, parental decision making, and equity. *Educational Researcher, 28 (9)*, 16–25.

Greeley, A. M. (1982). *Catholic high schools and minority students*. New Brunswick, NJ: Transaction Books.

Greeley, A. M. (1998). The so-called failure of Catholic schools. *Phi Delta Kappan, 79 (1)*, 24–25.

Greeley, A. M. (1999). More assertions not backed by data. *Phi Delta Kappan, 79 (6)*, 463.

Greeley, A. M., McCready, W. C., & McCourt, K. (1976). *Catholic schools in a declining church*. Kansas City, MO: Sheed and Ward.

Greeley, A. M., & Rossi, P. H. (1966). *The education of Catholic Americans*. Chicago: Aldine Publishing Co.

Greene, J. P. (2000, March). *A survey of results from voucher programs, where we are and what we know.* Paper presented at the Conference on Charter Schools, Vouchers, and Public Education, Harvard University.

Greene, J. P., Peterson, P. E., & Du, J. (1999). Effectiveness of school choice: The Milwaukee experiment. *Education and Urban Society, 32 (2),* 190–224.

Guerra, M. J. (1998). *CHS 2000: A first look.* Washington, DC: National Catholic Educational Association.

Hafner, A., Ingels, S., Schneider, B., & Stevenson, D. (1990). *A profile of the American eighth grader: NELS:88 students' descriptive summary.* Washington, DC: National Center for Education Statistics.

Hassenger, R. (1967). Essay review: American Catholics and their schools. *The School Review, 75,* 437–460.

Hill, P. T., Foster, G. E., & Gendler, T. (1990). *High schools with character.* Santa Monica, CA: Rand.

Hoffer, T. B. (2000). Catholic school attendance and student achievement: A review and extension of research. In J. Youniss & J. Convey (Eds.), *Catholic schools at the crossroads: Survival and transformation* (pp. 87–112). New York: Teachers College Press.

Hunt, T. C. (Ed.). (1998). *Private schools: Conference proceedings.* Dayton, OH: University of Dayton Press.

Hunt, T. C., & O'Keefe, J. M. (1998). Private schools: Partners in American education: Overview and directions for further research. *Catholic Education: A Journal of Inquiry and Practice, 1 (4),* 464–469.

Kristol, W. (1994, July/August). The politics of liberty, the sociology of virtue. *American Enterprise,* 32–37.

Manno, B. (1999, January). What public education can learn from Catholic schools. *Crisis,* 20–25.

McCluskey, N. G. (1968). *Catholic education faces its future.* Garden City, NY: Doubleday.

McDonald, D. (1999). *United States Catholic elementary and secondary schools 1998–1999: The annual statistical report on schools, enrollment and staffing.* Washington, DC: National Catholic Educational Association.

National Assessment of Educational Progress. (2001). *The nation's report card.* Washington, DC: National Center for Education Statistics. Retrieved January 29, 2001 from the World Wide Web: http://nces.ed.gov/NAEP/site/home.asp.

National Center for Education Statistics. (1995). *National household education survey.* Washington, DC: Author.

National Center for Education Statistics. (1996). *National education longitudinal study of 1988* (NELS:88). Washington, DC: U.S. Department of Education, Office of Educational Research and Improvement.

Neal, D. (1997). The effects of Catholic secondary schooling on educational achievement. *Educational Achievement, 15 (1),* 98–123.

Neuwien, R. (Ed.). (1966). *Catholic schools in action.* Notre Dame, IN: University of Notre Dame Press.

Peterson, P. (1999a, January 22). Rigorous trials and tests should precede adoption of school reforms. *The Chronicle of Higher Education,* pp. B4–B5.

Peterson. P. (1999b, January/February). Vouchers and test scores. *Policy Review,* 10–15.

Riordan, C. (2000). Trends in student demography in Catholic secondary schools, 1972–

1992. In J. Youniss & J. Convey (Eds.), *Catholic schools at the crossroads: Survival and transformation* (pp. 33–54). New York: Teachers College Press.

Rock, D. A., & Pollack, J. M. (1990, April). *Test achievement of NELS:88 eighth grade students.* Paper presented at the Annual Meeting of the American Educational Research Association, Boston, MA.

Rouse, C. (1998, May). Private school vouchers and student achievement: An evaluation of the Milwaukee parental choice program. *Quarterly Journal of Economics*, 555–602.

Smith, C., & Sikkink, D. (1999). Is private schooling privatizing? *First Things, 3 (3)*, 55–59.

Snyder, T. (1989). *The condition of education.* Washington, DC: National Center for Education Statistics.

Vitullo-Martin, T. (1979). *Catholic inner-city schools: The future.* Washington, DC: United States Catholic Conference.

Witte, J. F. (2000). *The market approach to education: An analysis of America's first voucher program.* Princeton, NJ: Princeton University Press.

Wolf, P. J., Greene, J. P., Kleitz, B., & Thalhammer, K. (2000, March). *Private schooling and political tolerance: Evidence from college students in Texas.* Paper presented at the Conference on Charter Schools, Vouchers, and Public Education, Harvard University.

Yeager, R. J., Benson, P. L., Guerra, M. J., & Manno, B. V. (1985). *The Catholic high school: A national portrait.* Washington, DC: National Catholic Educational Association.

Youniss, J., & Convey, J. (2000). *Catholic schools at the crossroads: Survival and transformation.* New York: Teachers College Press.

Youniss, J., Convey, J., & McLellan, J. (2000). *The Catholic character of Catholic schools.* Notre Dame, IN: University of Notre Dame Press.

Author Index

Subject Index

About the Contributors

BARBARA M. DE LUCA received her doctorate in Consumer Economics and Economics at the Ohio State University. She is currently an Associate Professor in the Department of Educational Leadership, but has assumed many positions in her 25 years at the University of Dayton. De Luca has taught a variety of applied economics and finance courses but at this time specializes in teaching graduate courses in school finance. Although her research efforts also vary, her present work focuses on adequacy in school funding.

JAMES M. FRABUTT received his doctorate in Human Development and Family Studies from the University of North Carolina at Greensboro. He has served as Project Director for the Transition to Middle School Study, funded by the William T. Grant Foundation, and is currently a post-doctoral research fellow at the Center for the Study of Social Issues at UNC-Greensboro. His primary research interests center on children's social development and parenting in racial and ethnic minority families. Specifically, Dr. Frabutt has studied the impact of social support on parenting and child outcomes in African-American families, as well as parenting practices, parent–child relationship quality, and children's psychosocial competence in African-American families.

HEATHER GRAHAM is a Program Associate at the Annie E. Casey Foundation. Prior to her position at the Casey Foundation, she served as Director of Corps Programs for Teach for America. She also worked as a junior high school teacher at New York City's Intermediate School 74. She holds an M.S. degree in Public Policy from Princeton University's Woodrow Wilson School of Public and International Affairs, and a B.S. from the University of Wisconsin–Madison.

JESSICA A. GREENE serves as Data Analyst/Project Specialist at the Lynch School of Education at Boston College. As the primary institutional researcher for the Lynch School, she conducts studies regarding the professional preparation of teachers, standardized testing, and the ranking practices of colleges and universities by external agencies, among other areas. Her research interests are largely focused on Catholic education, specifically, secondary level Catholic education, urban Catholic education, and the organizational climate of Catholic schools.

THOMAS C. HUNT currently holds the position of Professor of Foundations in the Department of Teacher Education in the School of Education and Allied Professions at the University of Dayton. His major career interest has been the history of American education, with an emphasis on religion and schooling, especially with Catholic schooling. He has authored/edited 10 books on religion and schooling in the past 20 years. His articles have appeared in many educational and religious education journals. A past president of the Associates for Research on Private Education, Hunt was the editor of the *Private School Monitor* from 1998 to 2000 and has served as co-editor of *Catholic Education: A Journal of Inquiry and Practice* since 1998. He was the recipient of the Thayer S. Warshaw Award in 1986 for his essay entitled "Religion, Moral Education, and Public Schools: A Tale of Tempest."

ELLIS A. JOSEPH served as Dean of the School of Education at the University of Dayton for 23 years. Currently, he is Dean Emeritus and Distinguished Service Professor. He has authored over 75 publications, including two books: *Jacques Maritain on Humanism and Education* and *The Predecisional Process in Educational Administration: A Philosophical Analysis*. He received the A.B., M.A., and Ph.D. degrees from the University of Notre Dame, and was awarded an honorary doctorate in humane letters from the College of Mount Saint Joseph. He has chaired the Ohio Teacher Education and Certification Advisory Commission, has served as president of the Ohio Association of Colleges for Teacher Education, and was a member of the American Association of Colleges for Teacher Education's Task Force on Inquiry. Currently, he chairs the Ohio State Superintendent's Task Force for the Preparation of Personnel for the Handicapped.

BRUNO V. MANNO is a Senior Program Associate with the Annie E. Casey Foundation. He is a former U.S. Assistant Secretary of Education for Policy and Planning and was Chief of Staff in the Office of Educational Research and Improvement in the U.S. Department of Education. Prior to that, he was the Director of Research and In-service for the National Catholic Educational Association. He is the co-author of *Charter Schools in Action: Renewing American Public Education*.

DALE McDONALD is Director of Public Policy and Educational Research at the National Catholic Educational Association, Washington, DC. She has been a high school teacher and administrator, president of the Sisters of the Presentation, and director of the Catholic School Leadership Program at Boston College. She edited *Partners for Justice: Catholic Schools and School Choice*, proceedings of a national symposium she conducted, and is a regular contributor to *Momentum*, writing on public policy issues.

RONALD J. NUZZI is a priest in the Diocese of Youngstown, Ohio, and is an Associate Professor in the Department of Educational Leadership and Higher Education at Saint Louis University. He serves as co-editor of the research journal *Catholic Education: A Journal of Inquiry and Practice*.

JOSEPH M. O'KEEFE is Associate Professor of Educational Administration at Boston College, Chestnut Hill, MA. He has authored a number of chapters and articles and has been the contributing editor of five books, most notably, *The Contemporary Catholic School: Context, Identity, and Diversity* (1996). His interests include urban education, the religious identity of schools, international comparative education, and the preparation of prospective teachers and administrators.

PATRICIA J. POLANSKI is an Assistant Professor in the Department of Counselor Education and Human Services at the University of Dayton. Prior to receiving a Ph.D. in Counseling and Counselor Education from the University of North Carolina at Greensboro, Polanski worked as a clinical counselor with troubled and troubling youth in residential treatment. Her research interests are in the areas of counselor supervision and spirituality and counseling.

THOMAS W. RUETH holds a B.S. in Biology/Chemistry and an M.A. in Clinical Psychology from the University of Dayton. He received a Ph.D. in Clinical Psychology from Loyola University of Chicago. He is currently an Associate Professor and Chair of the Department of Counselor Education and Human Services at the University of Dayton. Prior to becoming a counselor educator, Rueth worked in community mental health, particularly in the area of crisis management.

CHARLES J. RUSSO is a Professor in the Department of Educational Leadership and Fellow in the Center for International Studies at the University of Dayton. The president of the Education Law Association for 1998–1999, he has written and spoken extensively, both nationally and internationally, on a wide array of topics in education law as it relates to both Catholic and public schools.

GINI SHIMABUKURO is an Associate Professor and the Associate Director of the Institute for Catholic Educational Leadership at the University of San Francisco. Shimabukuro published her dissertation for Catholic school educators in the form of *A Call to Reflection: A Teacher's Guide to Catholic Identity for the 21st Century* (1998). She has written numerous articles, and contributed a chapter to *Catholic School Leadership: An Invitation to Lead* (1999).

MARY PETER TRAVISS earned her Ph.D. at Stanford University in 1973, and did graduate work at Harvard University (1971) and Oxford University (1995). She was awarded honorary doctorate degrees from Christian Brothers University, Memphis (1994), and the University of Dayton (2000) for her work to promote research on Catholic schools. Traviss has served Catholic education for several decades as teacher, principal, supervisor, and director of schools for her religious community, and she is currently director of the Institute for Catholic Educational Leadership at the University of San Francisco.

ROBERT B. WILLIAMS is a member of the Psychology Department at New Hampshire Hospital in Concord, and an Adjunct Assistant Professor of Psychiatry in the Clinical Psychology Internship Program of the Dartmouth Medical School. He has taught history and social studies at the secondary level, religion to first graders and children with developmental disabilities, and has evaluated youngsters at all age levels as a psychologist.